Social Policy for
Child and Family Development

A Systems/Dialectical Perspective

SECOND EDITION

Thomas W. Roberts

cognella®
academic publishing

Bassim Hamadeh, CEO and Publisher
Carrie Montoya, Manager, Revisions and Author Care
Kaela Martin, Project Editor
Berenice Quirino, Associate Production Editor
Jess Estrella, Senior Graphic Designer
Alexa Lucido, Licensing Associate
Kim Scott, Interior Designer
Natalie Piccotti, Director of Marketing
Kassie Graves, Vice President of Editorial
Jamie Giganti, Director of Academic Publishing

Cover images: copyright © 2017 Depositphotos/VadimVasenin.
copyright © 2012 iStockphoto LP/philsajonesen.

Printed in the United States of America.

ISBN: 978-1-5165-2116-6 (pbk) / 978-1-5165-2117-3 (br)

www.cognella.com   800-200-3908

ACTIVE LEARNING

Interactive activities are available to complement your reading.

Your instructor may have customized the selection of activities available for your unique course. Please check with your professor to verify whether your class will access this content through the Cognella Active Learning portal (http://active.cognella.com) or through your home learning management system.

Table of Contents

PREFACE. XV

MESSAGE TO STUDENTS XVII

CHAPTER 1   A PROCESS MODEL FOR SOCIAL POLICY FOR CHILD AND FAMILY DEVELOPMENT 1

CHAPTER 2   THE SOCIAL POLICY PROCESS 23

CHAPTER 3   SOCIAL POLICY AND CHILDREN 47

CHAPTER 4   SOCIAL POLICY AND CONTROVERSIAL ISSUES: ALCOHOL, NICOTINE,
            AND DRUG USE DURING PREGNANCY 73

CHAPTER 5   SOCIAL POLICY AND POVERTY 97

CHAPTER 6   SOCIAL POLICY AND EDUCATION 121

CHAPTER 7   SOCIAL POLICY AND FAMILY DEVELOPMENT. 143

CHAPTER 8   SOCIAL POLICY AND CHILD ABUSE AND NEGLECT. 167

CHAPTER 9   SOCIAL POLICY AND DOMESTIC VIOLENCE .193

CHAPTER 10   SOCIAL POLICY AND TECHNOLOGY. 215

CHAPTER 11   SOCIAL POLICY AND ETHNICITY. 241

CHAPTER 12   POSTSCRIPT: THE FUTURE OF SOCIAL POLICY AND CHILD AND FAMILY 267

INDEX. 283

Detailed Table of Contents

PREFACE. XV

MESSAGE TO STUDENTS XVII

CHAPTER 1   A PROCESS MODEL FOR SOCIAL POLICY FOR CHILD AND FAMILY DEVELOPMENT . . . 1
    Learning Objectives 1
    A Process Model 1
    Defining Social Policy. 2
    Process Model for Social Policy. 4
        Systems Theory 4
        Components of Systems Theory. 4
    The Dialectical Perspective 7
        Systems/Dialectical Model of Social Policy 9
        Social Policy and the Dialectics of Politics. 9
    Systems/Dialectical Thinking. 13
        Convergent versus Divergent Thinking 15
        Procedure for Systems/Dialectical Thinking 16
        A Guide for Thinking from a Systems/Dialectical Position 16
    Key Terms 18
    Study Questions to Accomplish the Learning Objectives. 18
    Debate Activity for Students 19
    Additional Reading Resources 19
    References 20

CHAPTER 2   THE SOCIAL POLICY PROCESS 23
    Learning Objectives 23
    The Social Policy Defined 23
    Models for Social Policy Development 26
        Rationalism/Comprehensive Model 27
        Elitism. 28
        The Process Model. 29
        Group Theory 30
        Incrementalism (Incremental Theory) 30

Game Theory. 31
The Risk and Resilience Model 31
The Institutional Model. 32
The Systems Model 32
The Systems/Dialectical Model 33
Applying the Models to an Example. 33
The Policymaking Process. 36
Steps in the Policymaking Process. 37
The Policy 39
The Systems/Dialectical Perspective of Policymaking 40
Key Terms 41
Study Questions to Accomplish the Learning Objectives 42
Debate Activity for Students. 42
Additional Reading Resources 43
References 43

CHAPTER 3   SOCIAL POLICY AND CHILDREN **47**
Learning Objectives 47
Social Policy and Children 47
Family Structure 48
Child Health and Safety 52
Victims of Crime 53
Children's Mental Health 54
Attention Deficit Hyperactivity Disorder (ADHD). 54
Oppositional Defiant Disorder (ODD) and Conduct Disorder. 55
Depression. 55
Anxiety Disorders 57
Alcohol and Substance Use 57
Tourette Syndrome and Tic Disorders. 58
Child Care. 58
Research on Child Care. 59
Child Care and Attachment 60
Other Concerns. 60
Preschool for All 61
A Systems/Dialectical Perspective on Social Policy and Children 63
Key Terms 66
Study Questions to Accomplish the Learning Objectives 66
Debate Activity for Students. 67
Additional Reading Resources 67
References 68

CHAPTER 4   SOCIAL POLICY AND CONTROVERSIAL ISSUES: ALCOHOL, NICOTINE, AND DRUG USE DURING PREGNANCY **73**

Learning Objectives 73

Social Policy and Controversial Issues 73

Rights of the Unborn 74

Exposure to Legal Drugs. 74

Alcohol Exposure. 76

    Fetal Alcohol Syndrome (FAS) 77

    The Pharmacology of Alcohol 77

Exposure to Cocaine and Other Drugs. 79

    Pharmacology 79

    Methamphetamine Exposure 81

Prescription Medication and Other Effects 81

A Systems/Dialectical Perspective of a Child's Right to be Born Free of Damage Versus the Mother's Rights. 83

    Two Opposing Camps. 83

        Criminalizing the Mother's Behavior during Pregnancy. 84

        Constitutional Rights Argument 86

        Reproductive Rights 86

        Sex Discrimination and Equal Protection 87

        Right to Privacy. 87

        Cruel and Unusual Punishment. 87

        Drug Possession 88

        Civil Commitment. 89

        Education and Treatment. 89

    Key Terms 90

    Study Questions to Accomplish the Learning Objectives 91

    Debate Activity for Students. 91

    Additional Reading Resources 92

    References 92

CHAPTER 5   SOCIAL POLICY AND POVERTY. **97**

Learning Objectives 97

Setting the Parameters for Understanding Poverty 97

    What Is Poverty?. 97

The Effects of Poverty on Children 101

    School Readiness. 102

    Behavioral Effects 103

    Attachment 105

    Environmental Factors Related to Poverty and Children. 106

Brief History of the American Anti-Poverty Program 107
    The Market versus the Welfare State 111
A Systems/Dialectical Perspective on Poverty 113
Key Terms 115
Study Questions to Accomplish the Learning Objectives 115
Debate Activity for Students 116
Additional Reading Resources 116
References 116

CHAPTER 6   SOCIAL POLICY AND EDUCATION **121**
Learning Objectives 121
Social Policy and Education 121
The History of American Public Education 122
    No Child Left Behind (NCLB) 124
American Education in Crisis 126
    Some Problems in Education 127
    Common Core 130
Future Directions In Education 133
A Systems/Dialectical Perspective of Education 134
Key Terms 138
Study Questions to Accomplish the Learning Objectives 139
Debate Activity for Students 139
Additional Reading Resources 140
References 140

CHAPTER 7   SOCIAL POLICY AND FAMILY DEVELOPMENT. **143**
Learning Objectives 143
Social Policy and Family Development. 143
Marriage 144
    Defining Marriage and Family 144
    Gay and Lesbian Marriage 145
        The Argument for DOMA *147*
        The Argument against DOMA *147*
Family Social Policy 149
    Parental Rights 149
    Universal Declaration 151
    Parenting Education 152
Family Structure 152
    The Family Is a Diverse Institution 153

Stepfamilies 154
Adoption 156
    Birth Records 159
Unwed Fathers' Rights 159
Cohabitation 159
Key Terms 162
Study Questions to Accomplish the Learning Objectives 162
Debate Activity for Students 163
Additional Reading Resources 163
References 163

CHAPTER 8 SOCIAL POLICY AND CHILD ABUSE AND NEGLECT **167**
Learning Objectives 167
Child Abuse and Neglect 167
Physical Abuse 169
Spanking (Corporal Punishment) 169
Beaten or Hit with Objects Causing Physical Damage 170
Signs of Physical Child Abuse 171
Neglected Children 173
Effects of Neglect on the Child 174
Risk Factors 176
Emotionally Abused Children 177
Child Sexual Abuse 178
Sex Trafficking of Children 179
Effects of Child Sexual Abuse 179
Intrafamilial Sexual Abuse (Incest) 181
Female Sexual Perpetrators 181
Mandatory Reporting of Abuse 182
Perpetrators 182
Sexual Abuse and Recidivism Rates 183
    Sexual Predator Laws 183
    False Allegations 185
    Treatment of Sexual Abuse 186
A Systems/Dialectical Perspective of Child Abuse and Neglect 186
Key Terms 187
Study Questions to Accomplish the Learning Objectives 188
Debate Activity for Students 189
Additional Reading Resources 189
References 189

CHAPTER 9   SOCIAL POLICY AND DOMESTIC VIOLENCE 193

Learning Objectives 193

Social Policy and Domestic Violence 193

The Effects of Domestic Violence on Victims 197

    Effects of Domestic Violence on Children. 199

    Ethnicity and Race and Domestic Violence. 201

    Resilience in Children 202

Social Policy and Domestic Violence 203

A Systems/Dialectical Perspective Of Domestic Violence .209

Key Terms 210

Study Questions to Accomplish the Learning Objectives 210

Debate Activity for Students. 211

References 211

CHAPTER 10   SOCIAL POLICY AND TECHNOLOGY 215

Learning Objectives 215

Social Policy and Technology 215

Television. 216

    Early Brain Development 220

    Sexualization. 222

    Children's Direct Response to Media Stimuli 222

Video Games 223

Social Media and Child and Family Social Policy 224

    Facebook. 226

    Cell Phones 227

    Children and iPods and iPads 228

    Children and Sexting 229

Social Policy and Technology Regulation. 230

    Social Policy and TV. 230

    Social Policy and Social Media Regulation 231

    Media and Social Policy Debate 232

Key Terms 233

Study Questions to Accomplish the Learning Objectives 234

Debate Activity for Students. 234

Additional Reading Resources 235

References 235

CHAPTER 11   SOCIAL POLICY AND ETHNICITY 241

    Learning Objectives 241

    Social Policy and Ethnicity 241

    Changing Demographics resulting from Immigration. 243

        Legal Immigration Policy 243

        Illegal Immigration 244

    The Black American Family 246

    The Asian American Family 248

        Asians and Education 249

    Latino/Hispanic American Family 252

        Latinos/Hispanics and Education 252

        The Quality of Family Life and Divorce 253

        Acculturation 254

    Native American Families 255

        Values 256

        Native Americans and Alcohol Abuse 257

        Life on the Reservation 257

        Social Policy and Native Americans and Pacific Island Natives. 258

    Social Policy and Race and Ethnicity 258

    Key Terms 261

    Study Questions to Accomplish the Learning Objectives 261

    Debate Activity for Students 262

    Additional Reading Resources 262

    References 262

CHAPTER 12   POSTSCRIPT: THE FUTURE OF SOCIAL POLICY AND CHILD AND FAMILY
            DEVELOPMENT 267

    Polarization of Social Issues 268

    A Systems/Dialectical Perspective. 272

    A Final note 277

    Key Terms 280

    References 280

INDEX 283

Preface

For the past several years, I have taught a course at San Diego State University on professional ethics and public policy in child and family development. I used a textbook by Zigler and Hall published in 1999 and now out of print. While the content of this book was appropriate for child and family development social policy topics, the material was outdated. Current textbooks on the market either did not cover relevant topics or focused too much on philosophical issues rather than on specific areas of social policy. Bogenscheider's book, *Family Policy Matters: How Policymaking Affects Families and What Professionals Can Do*, makes a philosophical case for why child and family social policy is important and is an excellent book but does not address specific issues, such as child care, family structure, education, gay marriage, technology, diversity, and other topics that are on the forefront of debate on child and family social issues.

Another current textbook by Jensen and Fraser, *Social Policy for Children and Families: A Risk and Resilience Perspective*, is well written and covers some of the relevant topics in child and family social policy but from the lens of risk and resilience. Since most social policies emerge out of debate of opposing views, there is no leverage from the risk and resilience point of view to challenge any policy. It would assume that a government program aimed at reducing poverty reduces risk and helps families increase resilience. Although the authors emphasize the need for programs to be based on research, they do not distinguish between short- and long-term outcomes. In other words, debating the types of programs, such as whether a program improves self-reliance or perhaps increases dependency on the government and whether this would be good for children and families in the long-term is never questioned in this book. As such, the book obfuscates the debate of what kinds of programs actually work.

Another current textbook on controversial issues in social policy is another good source but again failed to meet a need for addressing specific topics related to children and families. *Controversial Issues in Social Policy* by Karger, Midgley, Kindle, and Brown is an interesting discussion of social policy issues in a debate format. While some topics are relevant for child and family development, such as "Should same sex marriage be legalized?' and "Can child protective services be reformed?" most of the topics do not apply. The strength of the book is recognition that all social policy issues can be debated with valid points made from different sides. Not only can all issues be debated, but since no position is set in stone, policies should always be subject to revisiting relative to changes in individuals and families.

Social Policy for Child and Family Development: A Systems/Dialectical Perspective was conceived to address the inadequacies addressed above. Systems theory and dialectical theory were combined to provide a framework for enumerating the process of the formation of and changes in social policies. Systems theory provides an overarching view that focuses on the whole rather than parts, and dialectical theory provides a process model for how change occurs. The strength of this model rests in viewing change as constantly in motion and, for that matter, so are social policies since they represent social issues that are constantly in flux. Social policies tend to mirror the majority public opinions at the time and are subject to critiquing, reevaluating, and debunking. This book is written in the belief that a good debate does not lessen a social policy but should be the foundation out of which a policy develops.

I wish to thank a number of persons who made this book possible. First, my thanks go to my wife, Karen, who patiently put off some projects until this book was finished. My son, Spencer, and my daughter, Kara, read parts of the text and made valuable comments. Crystal Smith, a student at San Diego State University, provided extensive help in library research.

Finally, I wish to express my thanks to the following university professors who read the manuscript and provided valuable input for the second edition of this textbook: Dr. Eytayo Onifade, Florida State University; Dr. John Orwat, Loyola University, Chicago; Dr. Joseph Wronka, Springfield College, Massachusetts; Dr. Paul Force-Emery Mackie, Minnesota State University, Mankato; and Dr. Sharon N. Obasi, University of Nebraska, Kearney. In addition, I appreciate the staff at Cognella with special thanks to Carrie Montoya, Manager of Revisions, and Kaela Martin, Project Editor, for their high level of professionalism and support in writing this textbook.

This book is dedicated to my mother, Clara Mae Roberts, who helped me understand the importance of seeing more than one point of view.

Message to Students

I wrote *Social Policy for Child and Family Development* to review and reflect on current social policies that affect children and families. The term "social policy" is used in place of "public policy" because it tends to portray a more interactive dimension of policies. The topics covered are relevant to the overall study of child and family development, which you, no doubt, are familiar with from other courses. Typically, the social policy class in most universities is taught near the end of the study program. While you have usually been introduced to the topical areas covered in this book, this textbook allows you to think critically and dialectically about policies that reflect these topics.

A second reason for writing this textbook, especially the way in which it was written, is based on my understanding of the true meaning of a college education. I believe that the purpose of a college education is to teach the tools to critically evaluate different perspectives and make appropriate decisions. Debating various points of view is not only healthy; it can lead to new and more effective ways of thinking. This view is in sharp contrast to the idea that learning the right information and eliminating other information is the purpose of education. It reflects a recent letter to incoming university students signed by 28 professors from renowned universities, including Princeton, Harvard, and Yale, that encourages students to think for themselves. Here is an excerpt from that letter:

> In today's climate, it's all-too-easy to allow your views and outlook to be shaped by dominant opinion on your campus or in the broader academic culture. The danger any student—or faculty member—faces today is falling into the vice of conformism, yielding to groupthink.
>
> At many colleges and universities what John Stuart Mill called "the tyranny of public opinion" does more than merely discourage students from dissenting from prevailing views on moral, political, and other types of questions. It leads them to suppose that dominant views are so obviously correct that only a bigot or a crank could question them.
>
> Since no one wants to be, or be thought of as, a bigot or a crank, the easy, lazy way to proceed is simply by falling into line with campus orthodoxies.
>
> Thinking for yourself means questioning dominant ideas even when others insist on their being treated as unquestionable. It means deciding what one believes not by conforming to fashionable opinions, but by taking the trouble to learn and honestly consider the strongest arguments to be advanced on both or all sides of questions—including arguments for positions that others revile and want to stigmatize and against positions others seek to immunize from critical scrutiny.

In fact, my view of education goes beyond critical thinking, which is such an important skill and allows individuals to identify the best choice among choices. While critical thinking is extremely important, dialectical thinking takes critical thinking a step further, because it posits that no position is completely right, and no position is completely wrong. Instead of finding the best choice among options, dialectical thinking suspends choices and creates a debate whereby new choices emerge from the debate that are different from the original ones. The free debate of ideas allows for new, innovative, and creative thinking to emerge.

While this approach is touted throughout the book, a caveat is necessary. There is no middle ground between some points of view, and no new or innovative options can arise from debating them. I believe that this is true for a limited number of options but nevertheless true. For example, I cannot think of a middle ground between the point of view that would say that it is okay and even desirable for an adult to have sex with young children and the opposite point of view that sex with young children will damage them and is exploitative. All moral imperatives say that it is deplorable and damaging to the child for an adult to have sex with a young child.

The textbook was designed with a number of features to enhance critical and dialectical thinking. To enhance dialectical thinking, each chapter, with the exception of Chapter 12, has a debate activity where a proposition statement can be debated. It is hoped that this activity will broaden your thinking and help determine a new position. In addition, more textbook resources can be found online by accessing Cognella's Active Learning Resources. These resources include flash cards for all key terms; true/false, multiple choice, and essay practice questions; video clips; debate topics; and additional reading resources. The debate activity requires further reading and research beyond the textbook.

The chapters in the book are organized as a progression from the discussion of the systems/dialectical model in Chapter 1 followed by various topics of social policies, including social policies that affect children, the rights of the fetus to be born free of damage versus the rights of the mother, the long-term effects of poverty on families and children, education, family development, domestic violence, technology, and ethnicity. Chapter 12, *Postscript: The Future of Social Policy and Child and Family Development* theoretically explores how we develop different beliefs systems and become very rigid in holding on to them even in the face of their demonstrated inadequacy. In addition, Chapter 12 develops the systems/dialectical perspective as an antidote to polarization that currently hampers the formation and maintenance of social policies.

I hope that this textbook challenges you and causes you to explore your belief system in an objective manner. I encourage you to contact me directly for feedback, dialogue, or debate of the ideas presented in this textbook.

CHAPTER 1

A Process Model for Social Policy for Child and Family Development

LEARNING OBJECTIVES

At the end of this chapter, the student will be able to:

✓ Identify the components of systems theory and dialectical theory. Explain how systems theory and dialectical theory can be combined. Evaluate the usefulness of a systems/ dialectical model for social policy;

✓ List conservative influences on social policies for child and family development and determine the effectiveness of the policies;

✓ List progressive influences on social policies and determine the effectiveness of the policies;

✓ Define convergent thinking and illustrate the strengths and shortcomings;

✓ Define divergent thinking, illustrate the strengths and shortcomings of divergent thinking, and justify how divergent thinking goes beyond convergent thinking; and

✓ Name and examine the steps for systems/dialectical thinking and construct a mock debate using the steps.

A PROCESS MODEL

Social policy for children and families may be difficult to define, but the task in this chapter is to both define it and create parameters around it so that occurrences in daily living can be understood in terms of policy. While a process model was engaged for reviewing relevant literature to guide the discussion of social policy for child and family development, such an endeavor was not the primary purpose of this book. The approach was to look broadly at various social policy writings and represent disparate views that may be overlooked from applying a narrow and limited model. Although there are numerous topics that could be covered regarding social policy and children, the present work limited the topics to social policy and children, families, health, education, child abuse and neglect, domestic violence, ethnicity, and technology. All of these topics are important, but three concepts underlie the others: the parent–child relationship, particularly prenatally until the age of three years; education beginning with preschool; and the economic standing of the family. In order to understand the complexity of social policy in the lives of children and families, this

1

book coupled family systems theory with dialectical development concepts and labeled it systems/dialectical theory.

Most discussion on social policy takes a decidedly political path. The first thought on social policy is usually whether it reflects a liberal or a conservative view. This link with politics is not very enlightening, since neither a conservative nor a liberal perspective has been particularly successful in reducing social ills, especially the poverty level. For example, the Reagan years may have slowed the growth of spending for welfare programs from the Carter years, but it did little to reduce the number of families in poverty (Jencks, 1992). The Obama administration focused on increasing government intervention and income redistribution, but the outcome was an increase of persons on food stamps and welfare (Burke, 2013). Political points of view tend to merge in outcomes, which suggest that strict ideological politics fail to effectively produce ongoing change. It remains to be seen how the election of Donald Trump as president will affect policy development. Six months into his term found him focused on fulfilling his campaign promises, which tended to be toward the conservative side of the Republican Party rather than the moderate side. This chapter will preview the relevant issues regarding social policy for children and families and conclude with a discussion of the systems/dialectical model, a broad process framework that will allow a dialectical discussion of opposing views.

DEFINING SOCIAL POLICY

In the vast literature on **social policy** and **public policy**, these terms are used interchangeably and have the same meaning. In some ways, the term public policy may be a more generic term with broader meaning than the term social policy. The meaning of social policy is a particular course of action initiated to address, correct, or improve the well-being of humans (Epstein, 2010). It is, therefore, a general or abstract term for a specific course of action that will have a huge impact on human well-being. The goal of social policy is to improve human functioning through education, crime prevention, health care, participation in the workforce, and equal opportunity. Social policy can be considered ideologically, that is, from a particular belief system about human well-being, or it can be approached from the standpoint of how persons behave. This book will address both meanings of social policy. For the sake of simplicity, the following definition will be used: social policy is the direct action taken by the government to improve the well-being of its citizens.

This book is concerned with social policy as it affects children and families. Some of the most notable issues regarding children include child care, parent/child relationships, education, poverty, disabilities, child abuse and neglect, and child health, including accidents and injuries. Because children are embedded within families, family issues, such as the quality of the marriage, family disruption in the form of death and divorce, single-parent families including never-married mothers, domestic violence, substance and alcohol addiction, and mental illness, are all interlinked with family functioning. In addition to family influence, the kinship network and the larger community affect the well-being of children and families. Consequently, social policy for children and families is interconnected to a context that has bidirectional influence on individuals and families. This view reflects the work of Urie Bronfenbrenner (1979) and depicts development as a continuing interaction with the environment (see Figure 1.1).

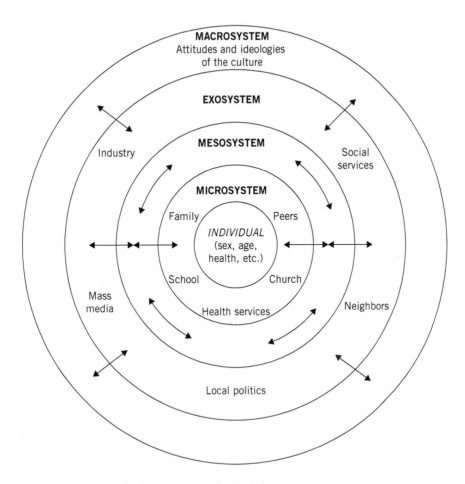

FIGURE 1.1 Bronfenbrenner's ecological theory

Bronfenbrenner's (1979) model views child development as embedded systems in which the child interacts. The **microsystem** includes family, close friends, and school and has the most direct influence. When the components of the microsystem interact, the **mesosystem** is created. For example, when a child starts preschool two mornings a week, resulting in a different routine, the child will be forced to make adjustments because of the link between the family system and the school system. Interactions in the mesosystem include the child's direct participation. An indirect influence on the child is the **exosystem,** which refers to such things as the parents' work experiences. When a parent loses his/her job, there may be many effects on the family as a result. Lastly, the child is influenced by the **macrosystem** or the larger culture and political systems. While the child does not participate actively on this level, he/she will be affected by political forces that help determine values and laws.

One of the main characteristics of a contextual approach, such as the ecological model, is **bidirectional**; the individual and the environment mutually affect each other (Leonard, 2011). Bronfenbrenner's theory evolved in later writings to also focus on the personal aspects of development and what was defined as "proximal processes" (Tudge, Mokrova, Hatfield, & Karnik, 2009). This more evolved model was based on the interaction of the overall process, the personal component, the context, and the time dimension Bronfenbrenner (1995, 1999). Dialectical explanations for development builds on Bonfenbrenner's later writings. Dialectical thinking, based on contradiction, conflict, and opposites, provides an explanation for how developmental change occurs in a particular context (Merriam, Caffarell, & Baumgartner, 2007). For the most part, dialectical thinking emphasizes the process of how one thinks and makes decisions, rather than the actual content of that decision. The model presented in this book adheres to a contextual approach but also provides a process approach grounded in systems and dialectical thinking that allows an understanding of how change occurs.

PROCESS MODEL FOR SOCIAL POLICY

Systems Theory

The thrust of this book is to apply a process model to the study of social policy for child and family development. A process model allows for an unrestricted look at social policies without being forced into a particular theoretical framework. While it is impossible to extricate oneself from theory, it is possible to limit the effects of dogmatic theoretical explanations. This perspective departs from some of the current textbooks in the field that attempt to apply a theoretical framework to the understanding of policies (e.g., Hill, 2012; Jenson & Fraser, 2011). The purpose of this book is to provide a framework for how social policies emerge from disparate ideas.

The process model in this book is called systems/dialectical, which has been applied to parent/child relationships (Roberts, 1994) and supervision in marriage and family therapy (Roberts, Winek, & Mulgrew, 1999). Two perspectives in the child and family development field, general systems theory (Bertalanffy, 1968) and dialectical theory (Basseches, 1984; Riegel, 1976, 1979), were influential in developing this model. Combining general systems theory and dialectical theory allows for a unique way of thinking that focuses on wholeness in both content (**ontology**) and how the content is expressed (**epistemology**).

A systems perspective, applied to family functioning since the 1950s, is considered broad and lacks specificity (Mele, Pels, & Polese, 2010). Consequently, it is an "umbrella theory" and is, therefore, weak overall in understanding concrete behavior. While systems theory may be more general than specific, it can provide principles that explain how parts of the environment create reciprocal loops that produce change. This bidirectional aspect of systems theory and the process of how components in a system influence each other will be discussed below.

Components of Systems Theory

First, systems theory implies **wholeness**, or a unit that is greater than merely the sum of component parts (Bertalanffy, 1968; Goldenberg & Goldenberg, 2008). Each part contributes to the functioning of the whole and cannot be understood as having a separate identity or function. The American society can be diced up into various components, such by gender, race, social class, family structure, and infinite other categories. Yet, having an understanding of how all of these components are part of the same unit or system provides a better way to understand how to address the needs of individual components. In the end, a social policy that pits component parts against each other must take away from one component in order to support or enhance another.

Second, systems theory implies that all systems are governed by **rules,** also known as the **redundancy principle** (Day, 2009; Jackson, 1964). The concept of rules implies that behavior is governed by patterns that repeat in the ongoing interactions of individuals and societies and do not happen accidentally. Applied to social policy, the concept of rules means that policies can become ineffective when they lack flexibility and limit the range of options for addressing social concerns. An effective social policy must include an understanding of **metarules** (Day, 2009), or rules about rules. Only by examining the underlying and overarching rules about rules can effective changes occur in social policy. Changing metarules may have to be a deliberate activity, because once set up, patterns continue even if they are not effective. *The most common error in trying to solve any social problem is to do more of the same or try harder doing the same things.*

Third, **boundaries** refer to barriers that define individuals or larger systems so that individuals or systems can be distinguished from each other (Goldenberg & Goldenberg, 2008). Communications patterns set the boundary for the sharing of information among family members. Rigid boundaries prevent adequate input from the environment, signaling that change is needed. In terms of social policy, boundaries refer to ideologies or belief systems about how to provide the best social well-being to at-risk individuals. Too often social policy issues become ideological arguments in which different sides insist on their own perspectives. The outcome may mean that ineffective or even wasteful policies continue, because they fit a particular ideology, while a more effective policy would be dismissed, because it does not fit the ideology.

Fourth, a basic premise of systems theory is the concept of **homeostasis**, or the tendency of a system to maintain a steady state (Hammond, 2010). A system frequently becomes stressed, which can result in becoming unbalanced, and it takes specific action to reduce the stress by putting into place behaviors to return to normal, or the pre-stressed state. Parts of the system may serve a homeostatic function in keeping the system balanced. Consequently, the part of the system that serves a homeostatic function will be rigidly used over and over, so that the system perpetuates itself. Applied to social policy, it can be evident to the casual observer that maintaining balance may be more desirable and easier than changing rigid and dysfunctional systems. For example, a society can organize around a dysfunctional social policy, because it restores balance but leaves the system dysfunctional. Changing the homeostatic function of the system so that it is organized functionally may require changing policies.

Fifth, systems theory posits that a system and the environment influence each other through **feedback loops**, which allows new input to enter the system (Goldenberg & Goldenberg, 2008). The system and the environment are related in such a way that when one changes, new input enters the other, and reorganization can take place. One feedback system is related to the homeostatic function, and the other is related to change. The interaction of the two acts as a self-corrective mechanism that keeps the system in balance and helps it change. Applied to social policy, feedback loops refer to the ongoing process of evaluating outcomes of social policies and changing them when feedback supports it. Unfortunately, ideological rigidity, poor evaluation procedures, and a limited focus on components of the system, rather than on the whole system, prevent the natural function of feedback loops to introduce change.

Sixth, systems theory maintains that systems are organized from the least to the most complex, resulting in a **hierarchy** within and between systems (Goldenberg & Goldenberg, 2008). A hierarchy applied to social policy refers to the power of the policy to remain in spite of criticism, although there may be some credible questions about its effectiveness. One example of this is Head Start, a program initiated for high-risk children living in poverty to give them an equal start to school. While Head Start has been around since the "War on Poverty" in the 1960s and many researchers have questioned its effectiveness in providing more than a slight bump in performance, it has continued (Mongeau, 2016). One of the major concerns with Head Start is that the early gains of cognitive improvement for starting first grade fade away in subsequent school grades. The fact that Head Start continues despite this uneven effect is a credit to its relative power to influence legislators.

Seventh, the simplest way to address social policy is through the belief in causality (Monat & Gannon, 2015). A single cause for a social problem can be identified, such as poverty causes poor educational outcomes, which is then followed by a policy to alleviate poverty to improve educational outcomes. This position holds that anything can be understood if the causal links are known. Policies put in place that correct the problems tend to be either preventative or treatment-focused. Unfortunately, this piecemeal approach to social policy happens without an overview of how such policies are related or how they reflect a holistic view. Systems theory posits that **nonlinear systems**, systems that are made of human interaction, operate through a **circular causation**, that is, one thing does not cause another (Goldenberg & Goldenberg, 2008). Rather, in nonlinear systems each entity is antecedent to the other. Therefore, causes do not begin or end in the sequence but represent the point at which components in the sequence overlap. A nonlinear view of social policy means that attempts to reduce the complexity of interacting components by making one the cause of the other often leads to minimizing other parts of the sequence. Reducing the complexity in this manner leads to establishing policies that are one-dimensional and, in the long run, ineffective.

Eighth, to understand the meaning of circular causality in more depth, the concept of **equifinality**, or numerous beginning points can lead to one outcome or one beginning point can lead to numerous outcomes (Goldenberg & Goldenberg, 2008). Applied to social policy, it suggests that there is more than one effective way to address problems in society. It also indicates that, because of limited perspectives, governments tend to solve problems in the same way even when outcomes are negative.

Ninth, change, or **morphogenesis** as referred to in systems theory, is an important function of social systems (Zastrow & Krist-Ashman, 2010). While homeostasis tends to keep the system balanced, morphogenesis is a force for change. These two forces, homeostasis and morphogenesis, are constantly at work in social systems. Too much or too little of each will create a dysfunctional system. In social policy, there is always the tension between maintaining the status quo and changing. This tension is maintained by a number of factors, including the type of social policy. Social entitlements tend to change slowly, because persons rely on them and feel an ongoing right to receive them.

The first application of systems theory to government and governmental policies was made by David Easton (1965). Easton believed that governmental policies are allocations according to the particular values of a society. The government is a system that has a distinct role and function and can be separated from its environment. According to Easton, how the government is structured is dependent on the nature of the interaction with the environment, which relies on input from the environment and output to the environment to keep it operational. Consequently, the nature of the relationship between the government, or decision makers, and the people is more important than the particular structure of the government.

The government system operates by receiving two distinct type of input labeled **demands** and **support** (Easton 1965). Demand inputs come from various groups in society that have a need for certain resources, which tend to be scarce and require the government decision makers to ponder a course of action. Mass demonstrations and grassroots movements are internal types of input that attempt to shift scarce resources in the direction of one group over another. On the other hand, support input is when there is mass approval for certain political stances made by the government, as has been seen recently in the populism movement in America (Inglehart & Norris, 2016). A case in point is the election of Donald Trump and the immediate executive orders to accomplish his campaign promises, which he labeled as looking out for the forgotten citizens (Scherer, 2016).

Easton (1965) viewed **outputs** as the action that the government takes in response to the inputs. This response to the environment has two consequences. First, it provides a resolution to the input, and second, it simultaneously paves the way for future input. Changing environmental conditions directly affects the establishment of governmental structures and function. While Easton's position is similar in a number of ways to the model presented in this textbook, he does not clearly focus on the process whereby policies develop and are maintained.

THE DIALECTICAL PERSPECTIVE

The perspective in this book is equally influenced by the concept of dialectics. Dialectical philosophy has a long and influential history in defining ethical and moral decision making. One of the most influential theorists was Georg Hegel (1830/1991), whose philosophy centered on human reflection. The underlying guide for Hegel was that all things are processes, or **phenomena**, of ongoing contradictions between opposite or different poles. These poles are labeled **thesis** and **antithesis,** out of which emerges the **synthesis.** The **synthesis** is not an end point but becomes the new thesis, which has its opposite or antithesis, which, in turn, forms a synthesis and continues the process.

Klaus Riegel (1976; 1979) developed the **dialectical theory** of child development. Since his death in the 1970s, there has been little development of his ideas, but they provide important input for developing this process model. Something is **dialectical** if it constitutes disparate elements. A dialectic occurs naturally in any interaction, because any statement or position (thesis) has its opposite (antithesis); negotiation of these two positions will produce a synthesis. Riegel believed that this process is constantly in flux and never in balance. Any synthesis will immediately become a thesis that will have its opposite or antithesis, which will form a synthesis. Change always occurs in this process of opposites, forming a synthesis.

For Riegel (1979), child development occurs not through stages but through the interaction of four dimensions: the inner/biological, the individual/psychological, the outer/physical, and the social/cultural. Development occurs in the conflict within the individual

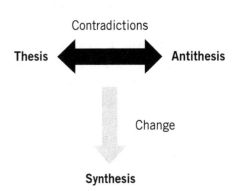

FIGURE 1.2 The Dialectical Process

in one or more of these four dimensions and the resultant syntheses that occur as outcomes from the conflict. The process, or dialectic, is undetermined, and different outcomes can emerge. Like Piaget (1926), Riegel believed that conflicts can result in a synthesis or resolution, but he believed that this process was ongoing, without periods of equilibrium. For Piaget, the dialectic was between the individual and the environment, but for Riegel, the dialectic occurs between or among the four dimensions of the individual. As the child ages, these four dimensions come in conflict when one dimension changes more than another. For example, in puberty, the body has changed, but emotionally, the person may be quite immature. The conflict in these two dimensions may be easily recognized when one has an adult physical body but the emotions of a child.

This model is also influenced by the **relational dialectics** approach of Baxter and Montgomery (1998). Applied mainly to dyadic relationships, the relational dialectic model rightly emphasizes the frequent occurrence of contradictions in human relationships. The meaning of dialectic goes beyond opposing forces to an understanding of the fundamental structural component of systems. Baxter and Montgomery discuss their approach using a number of concepts, such as totality, change, contradiction, praxis, and relational dialectics.

First, **totality** is roughly the same concept as wholeness in systems theory. The use of totality or wholeness for social policy is appropriate, because no social policy is permanent, nor does it represent the total society. Any social policy represents an attempt to address a problem in the present tense, which may be changed, altered, or discarded in the future. A social policy must be considered a component of a system, but not a system (Baxter, 2004).

Second, the concept of **change** means that there is always flux (Baxter & Montgomery, 1998). Social policies regarding education, health, welfare, and the like undergo changes as required by new demands. One of the main problems with social policy and change is that many policies remain in effect long after their usefulness. More often than not, governmental programs reflect the political party in power and continue unabated as long as that party is in power. If the program happens to fail, the other political party is blamed for the failure. On the other hand, some policies are revised or changed, reducing their effectiveness.

Third, **contradiction** broadly refers to the inability of any one thing to completely have all the answers. Implied in any statement or belief is another view that may be just as plausible. This definition goes beyond a simple explanation of contradiction as an either/or confrontation to a belief of multiple ways of addressing the same issue. In social policy, there can be a debate or critique of any policy (Baxter, 2004; Baxter & Montgomery, 1998).

Fourth, the concept of **praxis** means that humans are both active and reactive. It takes the position that unity is best known as diversity, and diversity is best illustrated through unity. To really understand what comprises anything, one must also know what it is not. So, something is simultaneously what it is and what it is not (Baxter & Montgomery, 1998).

In terms of relational dialectics and social policy, one can only understand any point of view by grasping its polar opposite, which means that this view is quite radical in terms of social policy. Some feel that certain polices are the absolute right course to take, and any other point of view could never be right. This unidirectional stance can explain how some policies have lives of their own and continue without regard to their effectiveness.

Systems/Dialectical Model of Social Policy

Riegel's (1979) model of child development is a process model that has profound implications for social policy when combined with a systems orientation. A **systems/dialectical model** is flexible and provides a process model of social change (Roberts, 1994). It postulates that social policy is enacted, maintained, and changed by dynamic conflicts between disparate points. It also postulates that, while these tensions are constantly occurring, it is heavily influenced by the power differential between the two opposites.

Another dialectical theorist that impacted the development of the perspective in this book is Michael Basseches (1984), who investigated adult development starting where Piaget left off. Basseches pointed out that the **formal operations stage** defined by Piaget had limitations in that it did not encompass systematic thinking and, therefore, was largely ineffective in making decisions in an ever-changing and complex world (Candler & Boutilier, 1992). Basseches believes that developmental change occurred through a dramatic transformation of the constitutive elements of the individual and not simply by the adding on of experiences. These changes are constantly occurring and point to the importance of understanding processes rather than content, since there is no permanence of any entity.

Basseches' (1984) writings on development contrast a dialectical model of thinking with positivist and postmodern views. The positivist tradition assumes that there is objective truth that can be discovered through experimentation. Postmodernism implies that there are many truths that are equally valid and embedded in different cultures and traditions. The dialectical perspective emphasizes neither an objective nor relative view of reality, but posits an ongoing process of integration and change. The ongoing process is always one of integration by identifying similar elements and, at the same time, identifying differences and noting differentiation. This ongoing process of change is referred to by Basseches as **transformation**, which is a fundamental change in both form and content. What this means is that that forms are changing, and individual entities, including persons, are not as important as the ongoing process of existing. Consequently, the future is continuing to unravel, leading to new forms and new content.

One of the most important aspects of Basseches' (1984) thinking is the relationship between that which is constitutive to the individual and that which is an add-on. **Constitutive** means the very nature of an entity. Transformative changes realign this constitutive part of the individual and, therefore, do not box one into a label. For example, the past is useful to the future only in informing how to evaluate the events of the past for future action, not in determining a fixed response to experiences. As an individual ages, he/she becomes more adept at dialectical thinking and logic (Baltes & Staudinger, 1993; de Langhe, van Osselaer, & Wierenga, 2011). According to Tetlock (1985), older persons are better able to see both sides of controversial issues, referred to as **integrative complexity.**

Social Policy and the Dialectics of Politics

Nowhere is social policy more explicitly different than in politics. In the United States, two political parties have dominated the landscape of social policy. Generally, the Democratic Party has been more **liberal** or **progressive** in its views, while the Republicans are characterized as more

conservative. Constituents of each party fundamentally express different philosophies concerning social policies. It must be noted, however, that not all persons who label themselves conservatives think alike, and likewise not all persons who label themselves liberal think alike. While this is fully recognized, the stated positions of conservatives and liberals do fall along certain ideological lines, and speaking of them in terms of these ideological differences makes good heuristic sense (Haidt, 2012). For example, liberals generally view the need to provide a safety net for persons in the U.S. who are unable to provide for their basic needs (Alterman, 2008). On the other hand, conservatives generally believe that persons are capable of supporting themselves. While conservatives would not necessarily disagree with a safety net for persons below the poverty line, they are more likely to view aid as temporary, which will improve their ability to be more self-reliant in the future. Conservatives generally believe that reliance on the government for assistance reduces the motivation to be self-reliant and, therefore, creates a long-term dependency on the government that perpetuates poverty (Parker 2003).

Liberals believe that the government should provide a safety net for low-income and high-risk individuals. The government's role is not only to protect the rights of individuals to succeed but also to reduce poverty, provide universal medical care, and keep persons safe. Liberals believe in more equalization of persons that results from the redistribution of wealth, which could result from governmental programs and increasing income tax withholdings from persons making over a certain amount. They want to reduce the gap between the wealthiest and the poorest of American citizens. While they recognize that some gains have been made in higher wages for middle-income families, the income of the top 20% has grown more than 11 times the income of the lowest 20% since 1970 (Reich, 2004).

Liberals believe in greater regulation of corporations and banks because of underlying greed that, when left unregulated, will be driven by only profit, not the welfare of persons and families. The role of government is to provide regulation that will protect the most vulnerable in society. Governmental programs are viewed as improving the economy, since they add spendable funds for consumer items (Alterman, 2008). Job creation is a function of the government, which depends on higher taxation and greater governmental spending.

Conservatives tend to believe that the government should have a more restricted role in the lives of its citizens (Hollis-Brusky, 2015). They believe that the more government regulates various aspects of society, the more will individuals lose freedom and liberty. They believe in lower taxes for everyone and less regulation. Lower taxes for the wealthy benefit society because of charitable contributions and because wealthy Americans create jobs. Conservatives also point out that the top 10% of wage earners pay 78% of taxes (Levin, 2009). The major role of the government according to conservatives is to provide a strong defense and to follow the mandates of the U.S. Constitution (Parker, 2003).

A number of recent national surveys concluded that differences in the beliefs of liberals and conservatives are deeper than the gender gap (Pew Research Center, 2010). A recent study investigating the ideological belief systems of liberals and conservatives developed a scale to measure **social dominance orientation (SDO)** (Pratto, Sidanius, & Levin, 2006). They concluded that conservatives scored higher on this scale, which makes them less benevolent and less willing to support programs that emphasize economic aid. Researchers Jon Haidt and Jesse Graham (2007) come to different conclusions, pointing out that conservatives are most interested in the welfare of persons, as noted in their strong support for the family. Consequently, conservatives tend to take firm stands on such issues as abortion, the rights of the unborn, and a definition of marriage as between a man and a woman that may be misinterpreted as rigid or extreme positions by liberals. Furthermore, Haidt and Graham found that, in terms of morality, liberals tend to place at least half of their efforts on issues related to social justice, while conservatives place only about 20% of their concerns on social justice. Of six basic moral values, including loyalty, compassion, liberty, fairness, piety, and respect for others, Haidt and Graham found that liberals emphasize compassion while conservatives have a good balance of all six. Overall, they found that conservatives were more balanced in their moral concerns than were liberals. As a result, Haidt and Graham concluded that conservatives are sometimes not recognized for the moral values they hold, because they are less expressive of them.

Other researchers have taken a route to identify both the strengths and weaknesses of liberal and conservative views so that neither is demonized by taking a superior stance over the other (Gairdner, 2015). By identifying both strengths and weakness, a more balanced position can be attained that provides more clarity in why public opinions can shift back and forth between a liberal or a conservative position. For example, in one election, the liberal position may get more of the vote, while in other elections, the conservative position wins.

On child and family social policy issues, it is not surprising that liberals and conservatives not only differ but believe that their own position is right while the other position is wrong (Gairdner, 2015). For example, both liberals and conservatives believe that their respective positions support the family better than the opposing position. Liberals believe that families differ in construction, but not in their value and importance (Alterman, 2008). They tend to view family composition in terms of equal rights and equality and that gay and lesbian families need the same opportunity to marry as heterosexuals. Liberals also believe that the role of government is to provide financial support to families below a certain income level. On the other hand, conservatives believe that they best serve the needs of families by reinforcing the traditional institution of the family and heterosexual marriage (Parker, 2003). They put more effort into helping families reach a position in which they can support themselves without relying on government assistance.

Conservatives believe that current changes in society that affect the family reduce the family's role in society (Gairdner 2015). Overall, such changes as divorce and having children out of wedlock have negative effects on children and do not lead to optimal development. Noting that children of divorce are 10% to 20% more likely to have social, emotional, or psychological problems than children in intact families (Coltrane & Adams, 2003) gives conservatives more salience in supporting the traditional family structure. Conservatives believe that fathers are important family members and that children need fathers in their lives. Since changes affecting the traditional family are viewed as negative, conservatives want to reduce the divorce rate and reverse trends that weaken the family structure.

Conservatives point to numerous research studies that illustrate the importance of the intact family for good outcomes with children. For example, while controlling for confounding variables, researchers found that intact homes reduce the likelihood that teens will use illegal drugs (McArdle, 2002). Other researchers found that children of divorced families are more likely to use cocaine in the 12 months prior to the research than children of intact families, which was true regardless of a number of factors, including race, religion, and education (Cubbins & Klepinger, 2007). Furthermore, teens raised in intact families exhibit fewer behavioral problems, such as fighting, drinking, or sexual promiscuity, than cohorts in stepfamilies or single-parent families (Rodgers & Rose, 2002).

Other research on the father's importance in the family comparing children reared in biologically intact families with those raised in stepfamilies and families with a biological mother and non-biological partner found that children of intact biological parents scored higher on standardized tests and had fewer behavioral problems (Joffert, 2006). A close relationship with the biological father is related to the overall well-being of adolescents (Falci, 2006), their aggression and anti-social behavior was reduced (Carlson, 2006), they were less likely to be incarcerated later in life (Harper & McLanahan, 2004), and they had higher levels of education (Flouri, 2004). Researchers have also found that religious involvement of fathers correlates with involvement in their young children, and if the religious involvement declines during the first year, involvement with the child also declines (Petts, 2007).

Liberals take a different view about changes in the family over the past several decades (Horwitz, 2015). They believe that the structure and the role of the family are changing, but not necessarily in a negative way. They point out that there never has been a golden past in which the family existed in wonderful harmony. Family disruption today is not that dissimilar from disruptions in the past, only the causes of the disruptions have changed from death of a spouse to divorce. Liberals do not view abortion, single-parent families, and children born out of wedlock as a disintegration of the family. According to Howitz, these changes have not occurred fast enough to satisfy some persons who believe that further revisions in the family are needed to accomplish greater growth and equality.

Liberals believe that many of the negative findings regarding the effects of divorce on children and living in a single-parent family are related to the methods of research and the samples generally chosen. For example, much of the research is correlational, although it has generally been interpreted as causal (Rathus, 2014). In addition, while much of the research is on a White sample, minorities tend to make up approximately one-third of the population. Even with these limitations in research, some findings are worth noting. Some children report a relief of stress after divorce (Kurdek & Siesky, 1980), while others report that the best outcome was their parents not fighting any more (Stewart, Copeland, Chester, Malley, & Barrenbaum 1997). Furthermore, researchers have found that more than 70% of children raised in single-family homes graduated from high school, and at least half will go on to higher education at either the community-college level or a four-year school (Sigle-Rushton & McLanahan, 2004).

The liberal view suggests that research regarding the negative effects of single-parent families should be taken with a caveat regarding methodology (Barajas, 2011). More qualitative methods are needed, and the sample should represent the diversity of families. Moreover, few longitudinal studies have been conducted that follow children into adulthood. Longitudinal studies would also be especially helpful to further determine the effects of living in a single-parent family in terms of gender. Research generally finds that boys are more affected than girls, but little is known how this difference is played out over the lifespan (Barajas, 2011).

Liberals and conservatives also differ on their views of women. Conservatives think that they are supportive of women by addressing the inherent biological differences in men and women but, at the same time, are supportive of women who choose careers (Parker, 2003). Liberals believe that women should have the same opportunities as men and generally see women who choose to stay at home as being disrespected by society at large. Reproductive rights of women are verbally affirmed by liberals, which include the right to abortion. Conservatives, on the other hand, believe in the rights of the unborn child and that abortion should not be used as a method of contraception.

The role of education has been a hotly contested social policy issue since the 1960s. Liberals have invested in an expanded role, which attempts to supplement the social and psychological development of children (Zigler & Hall, 1999). The rationale behind this expanded role is that poor children do not have their basic developmental needs met by their families of origin. Curricula over the past several decades reflect this expanded role in what conservatives refer to as nonacademic subjects. Conservatives believe that education has become restricted to a liberal ideology that excludes other points of view. For example, conservatives lobby to have alternate views of creation added to school curricula alongside evolution (Forsythe, 2011). Other coursework on topics such as global warming and anti-capitalism has also spurred criticism and complaints from conservatives.

Conservatives believe that school choice promotes better educational outcomes, because there is more competition between schools for students. Schools that lack quality will find that students opt for better education at another school. Conservatives believe in supporting homeschooling, because it gives some parents the option of opting out of a poor public school education. In addition, stronger regulation of charter schools and expanding the share of the market given to charter schools would give more options for students. Expanding other options includes online courses, which appeals to conservatives (Marshall, 2011).

Liberals view marketplace-type options for education as inappropriate and, instead, believe that schools need better teacher training, more consistent curricula, and a greater understanding of how culture and family background contribute to school outcomes. Liberals also believe that neither school testing nor school choice is a good answer for improving educational outcomes (Ravich, 2011). The most obvious outcome for school choice, according to liberals, is alienation of teachers and students alike.

All of the issues related to child and family development social policy represent dialectical opposites. For example, child care is a major topic that can be viewed from the standpoint of the contact with a primary caregiver or taking place in a child care facility. The debate over mothers caring for their infants or using supplemental child care, so the mother can return to work, forms a dialectic and can be argued from either point of view. Parenting education interventions tend to create a dialect on the questions of types of interactions with children, such as to spank or not to spank. Interventions for domestic violence and child abuse also can be dialectical. Family issues, such as abortion and same-sex marriage, tend to also be rigid dialectical positions. One of the most salient policy issues affecting children and families is poverty, which is addressed with opposing viewpoints.

SYSTEMS/DIALECTICAL THINKING

At this point in the discussion on various child and family issues above, it would follow script to decide who has the best ideas for addressing the well-being of families: liberals or conservatives? Does the liberal view have better results than the conservative view? Does the conservative view

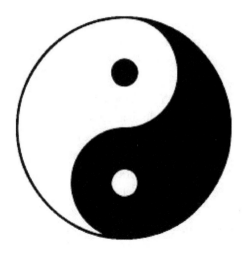

FIGURE 1.3 The yin and the yang of tao

provide a better path to lift more persons out of poverty and help them receive a quality education? While it is important to ask these questions, this way of thinking logically has partly resulted in the stalemate in coming to solutions, however, and a new way of critical thinking is required. **Critical thinking** has been defined by scholars in a number of ways, but the underlying premise is a search for the truth (Steutel & Spiecker, 2002). Critical thinking allows persons to engage in self-correcting behaviors. Critical thinking is considered a process whereby existing knowledge enters into dialogue with new input, and the foundation of what one knows is changed (Reynolds, 2011). **Systems/dialectical thinking** is a type of critical thinking related to change in which new information that may be opposite of old information is allowed to challenge and, through a diligent process of exploration, one may come to an alternate position that has characteristics of both the old and new. Systems/dialectical thinking originates from confrontation, argumentation, or debate that is not oppositional or mutually exclusive. This debating process, however, is not just understanding an opposing view but allowing for a synthesis whereby an entirely new perspective emerges. Opposing positions must be considered changing and relative.

One way of understanding systems/dialectical thinking is through the Taoist concept of the Yin and the Yang (see Figure 1.2). The yin and yang are bound together and are inseparably connected. All existence is represented by the relationship of unity of entities rather than their separateness. The yin and yang represent the unity of opposites and the interpenetration of each other. In dialectical thinking and decision-making, one moves back and forth between contrary positions. The major lesson to learn from dialectical thinking is that no one position is the answer; excluding the opposite point of view will only eventually lead to it, and holding on to a position will at some future point turn into its opposite. Consequently, all human values that are held dear must be held dialectically rather than in a mutually exclusive manner.

The ability to make decisions based on analyzing and interpreting complex information is the basic characteristic that separates humans from other animals (Priest, 2008). This characteristic is also considered a foundation of education. A systems/dialectical model is a different kind of reasoning than logical reasoning, which is based on the premise "A is A and nothing but A." Reasoning from a systems/dialectical perspective begins with the premise "A is not simply A." Consequently, systems/dialectical thinkers see change as normal and constantly occurring, while logical thinkers refrain from changing unless they can be proven wrong. Systems/dialectical thinkers see things as they are and what they may become simultaneously. At the heart of systems/dialectical thinking is paradox, because in applying these principles of dialectics ,what might seem to be common sense could be folly or vice versa. Applied to opposing positions in child and family development social policy, a systems/dialectical perspective suggests that any social position that takes a purely ideological stance becomes illusory and, when taken to its extreme, turns into its opposite.

Convergent versus Divergent Thinking

Convergent thinking is the term used to describe finding a logical and well-thought-out solution to a problem (Hajesfandiari, Mehrdad, & Karemi, 2014). Convergent thinking illustrates the desire to find a solution and generally means that one believes that only one solution will work. It is an objective approach that minimizes other solutions. In fact, other solutions not only would not be considered once the correct path was chosen but would have no values to even critique the chosen path. According to Hajesfandiari et al., **divergent thinking**, on the other hand, seeks the ultimate solution, but acknowledges that many viable solutions exist simultaneously. Finding solutions to social problems requires more attention to divergent thinking because of continuous change in social relationships and because some positions would tend to dominate. One of the main problems in social policy is attempting to solve a problem with a specified solution that is too limited and ineffective.

Divergent thinking is characterized by flexibility in thinking and producing new ideas (Hajesfandiari et al., 2014). A misconception of divergent thinking is that different ideas are evaluated, and the most plausible is chosen. If this were the case, divergent thinking would be subsumed under convergent thinking. Divergent thinking allows one to see beyond the immediate and shift course accordingly (Gomez, 2007). Divergent thinking uses a number of techniques, such as brainstorming, but is much more than brainstorming. In divergent thinking, even the problem can be formulated from different perspectives.

Rappaport (1981) discussed in depth how divergent and convergent thinking are reflected in social policy in a very intriguing article. For example, in critiquing the role of policymaking for the mental health field from early to the middle of the 20th century, Rappaport points out that the guiding impetus was to alleviate the problems of the mentally ill without any focus on individual rights. Whether it was treating persons in the hospital or the community, the

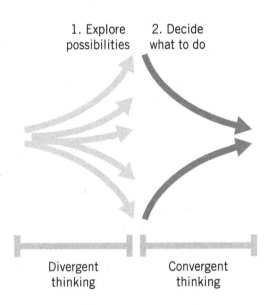

FIGURE 1.4 Convergent vs. Divergent Thinking

result was the same—packaged programs were supposedly created to meet the needs of persons but, in fact, were one-sided convergent attempts to solve social problems. On the other hand, when the focus swung in the 1960s to the rights of individuals, the shift became one sided as the importance of rights overwhelmed the actual needs of individuals.

According to Rappaport (1981), what is needed to address social policy issues, not only of the mentally ill but also other problems, is dialectical thinking. While he believes prevention is useful, when it becomes a one-sided affair (as it will unless checked by dialectical and divergent thinking), it will lead to stagnant outcomes. According to Rappaport, a more dialectical approach is to empower people to reach their potential. Empowerment requires that policymakers take a closer look at how people solve their own problems and how to integrate that into ways of offering assistance. Empowerment would break the model of dependency that persons in need have and take them out of the child role in society. Furthermore, empowerment allows for a variety of solutions, rather than the centralized sole solution so often advocated.

Procedure for Systems/Dialectical Thinking

In summation, systems/dialectical thinking differs from logical reasoning in several aspects. The main difference is that logical thinking seeks to find an answer to the conflict or different opinions by adopting the best option. Systems/dialectical thinking, on the other hand, focuses more on the process of making the decision, emphasizing the unity of both positions, and finding a solution that would be different from the opposing positions. Systems/dialectical thinking goes beyond the polarizing polemic of ideological positions that do not form consensus. The position taken in this book is that social policies are fluid and can be transformed, questioned, or critically evaluated. In discussions on various social policies, a position will be introduced, and an alternate or opposing view will be presented. In this way, when a policy does not work, it can be challenged from the logic and fervidity of another perspective. Systems/dialectical theory is based on the premise of divergent rather than convergent reasoning.

A systems/dialectical perspective addresses both the content of a social policy and how the content developed. For example, the various dimensions of the context for social policy include persons and all aspects of their environment. The context includes the individual, family, social network, community, persons with similar beliefs, persons with different beliefs, ethnic groups, socio-economic status, educational system, government, and culture, to name a few. For brevity's sake, these dimensions could be grouped similarly to Bronfenbrenner (1979) and include the individual, the immediate social network of relatives and close friends, environmental factors, such as work and neighborhood, government and work environments, and culture. Periodically different facets of this overarching system confront other aspects of the system, and this confrontation produces a need for change. Sometimes traumatic events and crises among various subtypes necessitate a need to change. Policies grow out of this dynamic to meet specific needs that have arisen. For example, the economic level of the family challenges individual and family development and gives rise to policies to alleviate alienation and despair that proliferate from economic inadequacy.

A Guide for Thinking from a Systems/Dialectical Position

First, an in-depth understanding of each opposite position(s) must be made. For example, in attempting to find a solution to poverty, both the conservative and liberal views must be understood impartially and without prejudice. The thesis and the antithesis must be addressed by suspending one's own beliefs and objectively examining the evidence for each position. In terms of the systems/dialectical model, this view demands observing the whole or totality.

Ancillary to this first step in understanding each position is promoting underrepresented persons in expressing their positions. Gaining an in-depth understanding of the concern at hand involves being heard and listening to all positions. Some segments of society may not be represented because they do not speak up and because they are not listened to when they do speak. Bringing all factions to the table to make their positions known is essential to ensure that an emerging social policy allows for justice for all.

Second, one must understand the ethical implications of taking a position on social policy issues. When the welfare of persons is involved, one is making an ethical decision (Feeney & Freeman, 2005). A basic question for applying ethics to the process of systems/dialectical reasoning is Emanuel Kant's (1968) categorical imperative, or making a decision on the basis of how others might resolve the same dilemma. Systems/dialectical reasoning considers how any decision might affect others; therefore, decisions are never unidirectional. For example, in understanding poverty, the ethical question is how interventions are actually helpful in improving the lives of people in poverty. The ethical question is not how it is solved in the short-term, but how, in the long-term, persons can escape poverty.

Step 1   Understand each position impartially and without prejudice. This may require doing research on opposing views and being aware of and promoting underrepresented views.

Step 2   Make bilateral and not unilateral decisions and consider the ethical implications of such decisions.

Step 3   Identify any common elements.

Step 4   When common ground cannot be found, work to create a new position based on long-term outcomes.

FIGURE 1.5 Steps for Thinking from a Systems/Dialectical Perspective

The third step is the identification of common elements, if any, in the opposing views. Where are there overlaps, or even consensus, in the opposing positions? For example, one area of consensus in understanding poverty is that both sides are interested in improving the welfare of individuals. They also agree that persons in poverty need a safety net and that some governmental intervention is needed. They agree that improving the ability of persons in poverty to work and to live in affordable housing is important. They agree that education is a major factor in poverty and that single-parenthood is a prevalent characteristic of families in poverty. These areas of consensus are not sufficient to resolve the social policy of poverty, but they do lay the groundwork for collaboration and programs that could bridge the span of conservative and liberal thinking. It could be noted that two governmental programs to improve the welfare of persons in poverty had support from liberals and conservatives, namely Temporary Assistance for Needy Families (TANF) and No Child Left Behind, a major accountability system to improve education.

Fourth, for components of the opposing positions in which a consensus cannot be attained, it is necessary to evaluate the competing viewpoints so that a synthesis or new position can be postulated. This type of critical thinking requires persons to give up their need to win or be right and allow evidence to emerge that will drive the move toward synthesis. It also requires persons to move beyond short-term thinking, impulsive decisions, and emotional persuasions. Dialectical thinking presupposes that some decisions are better than others, because they have better utility for those affected by it.

While this book will address social policy affecting children and families dialectically, it will not attempt to provide a synthesis for opposing views. Rather, it is hoped that it can be used to promote critical and dialectical thinking about the issues presented that will allow persons to make more informed decisions. The basis of education is to give the tools to think and critically evaluate outcomes. The purpose of this book is to meet that challenge in understanding child and family social policies.

KEY TERMS

Public policy	Hierarchy	Praxis
Social policy	Nonlinear systems	Systems/dialectical model
Microsystem	Circular causation	Formal operations stage
Mesosystem	Equifinality	Transformation
Exosystem	Morphogenesis	Constitutive
Macrosystem	Phenomena	Integrative complexity
Bidirectional	Thesis	Liberal or Progressive
Ontology	Antithesis	Conservative
Epistemology	Synthesis	Social dominance orientation
Wholeness	Dialectical theory	Critical thinking
Rules or redundancy principle	Dialectical	Systems/dialectical thinking
Meta-rule	Relational dialectics	Convergent thinking
Boundaries	Totality	Divergent thinking
Homeostasis	Change	Demands
Feedback loops	Contradiction	Support
Outputs		

STUDY QUESTIONS TO ACCOMPLISH THE LEARNING OBJECTIVES

1. Discuss components of systems theory and how they apply to social policy.

2. Discuss the dialectical theory of Klaus Riegel. Explain how dialectical theory is related to social policy.

3. Define and explain the concept of relational dialectics.

4. Analyze how systems/dialectical thinking goes beyond the formal operations stage of Piaget?

5. Discuss basic differences in liberal and conservative beliefs about social policy for children and families? Predict how policies might differ on education, healthcare, and childcare from the liberal and conservative points of view.

6. What are social policy issues affecting children and families?

7. According to Basseches, logical thinking and dialectical thinking differ. Why does Basseches consider dialectical thinking more advanced than logical thinking?

8. Describe what is meant by cause and effect in nonlinear systems. Discuss how cause and effect in nonlinear systems are related to social policies.

9. What is systems/dialectical theory? How does it differ from an ecological theory?

10. Define, explain, and illustrate the differences in critical, convergent, and divergent thinking.

DEBATE ACTIVITY FOR STUDENTS

Consider the following proposition: The purpose of social policy is to determine the right way to address a social issue.

- Review scholarly literature on this topic. Do a library and Internet search to find relevant material. Investigate some of the additional readings.

- Develop three arguments for the proposition.

- Develop three arguments against the proposition.

- How do the arguments relate to other systems, such as the community or culture?

- Is there common ground?

- What are the long-term consequences of taking action?

- What new or common-ground solutions should be offered? If no common ground, what new position could emerge from a dialogue between the two positions?

- How is the new position superior to the original positions?

ADDITIONAL READING RESOURCES

Riegel, K. F. (1970). Dialectic Operations: The Final Period of Cognitive Operations, Retrieved from http://files.eric.ed.gov/fulltext/ED085072.pdf

Sameroff, A. (2010). A unified theory of development: A dialectic integration of nature and nurture. *Child Development*, 81(1), 6–22.

Paquette, D., & Ryan, J. (2000). Bronfenbrenner's Ecological Systems Theory. Retrieved from http://www.floridahealth.gov/AlternateSites/CMS-Kids/providers/early_steps/training/documents/bronfenbrenners_ecological.pdf

Roberts, T. W. (1994). *A Systems perspective of parenting: The child, the family, and the social network.* Pacific Grove, CA: Brooks-Cole.

Dialogical and Dialectical Thinking. Retrieved from https://www.criticalthinking.org/data/pages/31/75b0624ef03956ca540026f3bd0884b85136312571895.pdf

Davies, M., & Barnett, R. (Eds.). (2015). The Palgrave handbook of critical thinking in higher education. New York, NY: Palgrave Macmillan.

REFERENCES

Alterman, E. (2008). *Why we are liberals*. New York, NY: Penguin.

Baltes, P. B., & Staudinger, U. M. (1993). The search for a psychology of wisdom. *Current Directions in Psychological Science, 2*, 75–80.

Barajas, M. (2011). Academic achievement of children in single-parent families: A critical review. *The Hilltop Review, 5*(1), 13–21.

Basseches, M. (1980). Dialectical schemata: A framework for the empirical study of the development of dialectical thinking. *Human Development, 23*, 400–421.

Basseches, M. (1984). *Dialectical thinking and adult development*. Norwood, NJ: Ablex.

Baxter, L. A. (2004). Relationships as dialogues. *Personal Relationships, 11*, 1–22.

Baxter, L. A., & Montgomery, B. M. (1998). *Dialectical approaches to studying personal relationships*. Mahwah, NJ: Erlbaum.

Bertalanffy, L. (1968). *General systems theory: Foundation, development, applications*. New York, NY: Braziller.

Bronfenbrenner, U. (1979). *The ecology of human development*. Cambridge, MA: Harvard University Press.

Bonfenbrenner, U. (1995). Developmental ecology through space and time: A future perspective. In P. Moen, GH. Elder, Jr., & K. Luscher (Eds.) *Examining lives in context: Perspectives on the ecology of human development* (pp. 619-647). Washington, DC: American Psychological Association.

Bronfenbrenner, U. (1999). Environments in development perspectives: Theoretical and operational models. In S.L. Friedman, & T.D. Wachs (Eds.), *Measuring environments across the life span: Emerging methods and concepts* (pp. 3-28). Washington, DC: American Psychological Association.

Burke, P. (January, 2013). First term: Food stamps recipients increase 11,133 per day under Obama. Retrieved from CNSnews.com/news/article/first-term-food-stamp-reciepeints-increased11133-day-under-Obama

Carlson, M. J. (2006). Family structure, father involvement, and adolescent behavioral outcomes, *Journal of Marriage and the Family, 68*(1), 137–154.

Chandler, M. J., & Boutilier, R. G. (1992). The development of dynamic system reasoning. *Human Development, 35*(3), 121–137.

Coltrane, S., & Adams, M. (2003). The social construction of the divorce problem: Morality, child victims and the politics. *Family Relations, 52*(4), 363–372.

Cubbins, L. A., & Klepinger, D. H. (2007). Childhood, family, ethnicity, and drug use over the life course. *Journal of Marriage and the Family, 69*(3), 810–830.

Day, R. D. (2009). *Introduction to family processes*. New York, NY: Routledge.

de Langhe, B., van Osselaer, S. M. J., & Wierenga, B. (2011). The effects of process and outcome accountability on judgement process and performance. *Organizational Behavior and Human Decision Processes, 115*, 238–252.

Easton, D. (1965). *A framework for political analysis*. Englewood Cliffs, NJ: Prentice Hall.

Epstein, W. H. (2010). *Democracy without decency*: Good citizenship and the war on poverty. University Park, PA: Pennsylvania State University Press.

Falci, C. (2006). Family structure, closeness to residential and nonresidential parents, and psychological distress in early and middle adolescence. *The Sociological Quarterly, 47*(1), 123–146.

Feeney, S., & Freeman, N. K. (2005). *Ethics and the early childhood educator: Using the NAEYC Code*. Washington, D.C.: NAEYC.

Flouri, E. (2004). Early father's and mother's involvement and child's later educational outcomes. *British Journal of Educational Psychology 74*(2), 141–153.

Forsyth, J. (2011). Texas Education Board sticks to teaching evolution. Retrieved from www.reuters.com/articles/2011/07/22/us-creationism-texas-idUSTRE76L54S20110722

Gairdner, W.D. (2015). *The great debate: Why liberals and conservatives will never, ever agree*. New York, NY: Encounter.

Goldenberg, H., & Goldenberg, I. (2008). *Family therapy: An overview*. (7th ed.). Belmont, CA: Thomson.

Gomez, J. G. (2007). What do we know about creativity? *The Journal of Effective Teaching, 7*(1), 31–43.

Haidt, J. (2013). *The righteous mind: Why good people are divided by politics and religion*. New York, NY: Vintage.

Haidt, J., & Graham, J. (2007). When morality opposes justice: Conservatives have moral intuitions that liberals may not recognize. *Social Justice Research, 20*(1), 98–166.

Hajesfandiari, B., Mehrdad, A. G., & Karimi, L. (2014). Comparing the effects of convergent and divergent thinking methods on using articles by Iranian EFL learners, *International Journal of Education, 1*(1), 313–327.

Hammond, D. (2010). *The science of synthesis: Exploring the social implications of general systems theory*. Boulder, CO: University Press of Colorado.

Harper, C. C., & McLanahan, S. S. (2004). Father absence and youth incarceration, *Journal of Research on Adolescence 14*(4), 369–397.

Hegel, G. W. F. (1830/1991). *The encyclopedia logic*. (T. F. Geraets, Trans.). Indianapolis, IN: Hackett.

Hill, S. (2012). *Families: A social class perspective*. Thousand Oaks, CA: Sage.

Hollis-Brusky, A. (2015). *Ideals with consequences: The federalist society and conservative counterrevolution*. New York, NY: Oxford University Press.

Horwitz, S. (2015). *Hayek's modern family: Classical liberalism and the evolution of social institutions*. New York, NY: Palgrave Macmillan.

Inglehart, R. F., & Norris, P. (2016). Trump, Brexit and the rise of populism: Economic have-nots and cultural backlash. Working Paper Series, August, 2016 of The John F. Kennedy School of Government, Harvard University. Retrieved July 17, 2017, https://research.hks.harvard.edu/publications/workingpapers/Index.aspx

Jackson, D. (1964). *Myth of madness: New facts for old fallacies*. New York: Macmillan.

Jencks, C. (1992). *Rethinking social policy: Race, poverty and the underclass*. Cambridge, MA: Harvard University Press.

Jensen, J. M., & Fraser, M. W. (2011). *Social policy for children and families: A risk and resilience perspective*. Thousand Oaks, CA: Sage.

Joffert, S. L. (2006). Residential father family type and child well-being: Investment versus selection, *Demography, 43*(1), 53–77.

Joint Center for Housing Studies at Harvard University (2004). *The state of the nation's housing*. Cambridge, MA: Joint Center for Housing Studies at Harvard University.

Kant, I. (1968). *Critique of pure reason*. (N. K. Smith, Trans.). London, UK: Macmillan; New York, NY: St. Martin's Press.

Kurdek, L., & Siesky, A., Jr. (1980). Children's perceptions of their parent's divorce. *Journal of Divorce, 3*, 339–378.

Leonard, J. (2011). Using Bronfenbrenner's ecological theory to understand community partnership: A historical case study of urban high school. *Urban Education,* Retrieved from http://journals.sagepub.com/doi/abs/10.1177/0042085911400337

Levin, M. R. (2009). *Liberty and Tyranny*. New York, NY: Simon and Shuster.

Marshall, J. A. (2011). *Freeing schools from Washington's education overreach*. In the Heritage Foundation *WebMemo No. 3214*. Washington, DC: The Heritage Foundation.

McArdle, P. (2002). European adolescent substance use: The roles of family structure, function, and gender. *Addiction, 97*(4), 329–326.

Mele, C., Pels, J., & Polese, F. (2010). A brief review of systems theories and their managerial applications. *Service Science, 2*(1/2), 126–135.

Merriam, S. B., Caffarell, R. S., & Baumgartner, L. M. (2007). *Learning in Adulthood: A Comprehensive Guide*. San Francisco, CA: Jossey-Bass.

Monat, J.P., & Gannon, T.F. (2015). What is systems thinking? A review of selected literature plus recommendations. *American Journal of Systems Science, 4*(1), 11–26.

Mongeau, L. (2016). The never-ending struggle to improve Head Start. *The Atlantic*, August 9, 2016, Retrieved from https://www.theatlantic.com/education/archive/2016/08/is-head-start-a-failure/494942/

Parker, S. (2003). *Uncle Tom's plantation: How big government enslaves America's poor and what can be done about it*. Nashville, TN: Thomas Nelson.

Pew Research Center for the People and the Press. (2010). *Independents oppose party in power … Again: More conservative, more critical of national conditions*. Retrieved from http://people-press.org/658/

Petts, R. J. (2007). Religious participation, religious affiliation, and engagement with children among fathers experiencing the birth of a new child. *Journal of Family Issues, 28*(9), 1139–1161.

Piaget, J. (1926). *The language and thought of the child*. New York, NY: Harcourt Brace.

Pratto, F., Sidanius, J., & Levin, S. (2006). Social dominance theory and the dynamic of intergroup relations: Taking stock and looking forward. *European Review of Social Psychology, 17*, 271, 320.

Priest, G. (2008). *An introduction to non-classical logic: From if to is*, (2nd ed.). New York, NY: Cambridge University Press.

Rappaport, J. (1981). In praise of paradox: A social policy of empowerment over prevention. *American Journal of Community Psychology, 9*(1), 1–25.

Rathus, S.A. (2014). *Childhood and adolescence: Voyages in development*, (6th ed.). Boston, MA: Cengage.

Ravitch, D. (2011). *The life and death of the great American school system: How testing and choice is undermining education*. New York, NY: Basic Books.

Reich, R. B. (2004). *Reason*. New York, NT: Vintage.

Reynolds, M. (2011). Critical thinking and systems thinking: Toward a critical literacy of systems thinking in practice. In C.P. Horvath and J.M. Forte, (Eds.) *Critical thinking* (pp. 37–68). New York, NY: Nova.

Riegel, K. F. (1976). The dialectics of human development. *American Psychologist, 31*, 689–700.

Riegel, K. F. (1979). *Foundations of developmental psychology.* New York, NY: Academic Press.

Roberts, T. W. (1994). *A systems perspective of parenting: The child, the family and the social network.* Pacific Grove, CA: Brooks-Cole.

Roberts, T. W., Winek, J., & Mulgrew, J. (1999). A systems/dialectical model of supervision: A symbolic process. *Contemporary Family Therapy, 21*, 291–302.

Rodgers, K. B., & Rose, H. A. (2002). Risk and resiliency factors among adolescents who experience marital transitions. *Journal of Marriage and the Family, 64*(4), 1024–1037.

Sigle-Rushton, W., & McLanahan, S. (2004). Father absence and child well-being: A critical review. In D. Moynihan, T. Smeeding, and L. Rainwater (Eds.), *The future of the family* (pp. 116–155). New York, NY: Russell Sage Foundation.

Steutel, J., & Spiecker, B. (2002). Liberalism and critical thinking: On the relation between a political ideal and an aim of education. In R. Marples (Ed.), *The aims of education* (pp. 61–73). New York, NY: Routledge.

Stewart, A. J., Copeland, A. P., Chester, N. L., Malley, J. E., & Barrenbaum, N. B. (1997). *Separating together: How divorce transforms families.* New York, NY: Guilford.

Tetlock, P. (1985). Integrative complexity of American and Soviet foreign policy rhetoric: A time-series analysis. *Journal of Personality & Social Psychology, 49*, 1565–1585.

Tudge, R.H., Mokrova, I., Hatfield, B.E., & Karnik, R.B. (2009). Uses and misuses of Bronfenbrenner's bioecological theory of human development. *Journal of Family Theory and Review*, 1. 198-210.

Zastrow, C., & Krist-Ashman, K. K. (2010). *Understanding human behavior and the social environment.* Belmont, CA: Brooks/Cole.

Zigler, E. F., & Hall, N. W. (1999). *Child development and social policy: Theory and applications.* Boston, MA: McGraw-Hill.

CREDITS

CHAPTER TWO

The Social Policy Process

LEARNING OBJECTIVES

At the end of this chapter the student will be able to:

✓ Identify the four types of social policy and compare and contrast the policies that would emanate from each one;

✓ Recognize the different models of social policy, compare and contrast how policies would be formed from each model, and justify which model he or she believes is the most effective;

✓ List the elements of the policymaking process and evaluate how policies related to child and family development reflect this process;

✓ Describe how social policies for children and families differ from other social policies; and

✓ Explain how a systems/dialectical model provides a unique way to understand policymaking.

THE SOCIAL POLICY DEFINED

Just about any human activity that can be thought about or engaged in emanates from some type of social policy. In fact, there is no escaping the hand of policies on everything from personal relationships to business deals. It certainly behooves humans to know as much about social policy as possible. Social policies can reflect a range of values and beliefs, from Tea Party conservatives to far left social progressives. While everyone is influenced by policies, not everyone is involved in the formation of them. At any one time, no social policy will have the support of everyone. There are always distractions and those who feel the policy is wrong and even detrimental to people and institutions. For example, many conservatives believe that the welfare system is one of the main factors in the decline of marriage, particularly among groups that are most likely to participate in welfare (Teitler, Reichman, Nepomnyaschy, & Garfinkel, 2009). A characteristic of social policies is that they are created for specific purposes and to solve specific problems. As a result of this purpose, they require monitoring, process evaluation, and revision and/or termination.

Social policies typically take some time to develop and, therefore, have a history. Rarely do they just appear on the scene, but they result from discussion, negotiation, and compromise (Clancy, Glied, & Lurie, 2012). Since social policies have gone through this process of development, they tend to have long lives and are difficult to significantly change. In addition, social policies arise out of some civic demand, which means that a constituency will already support and promote the policy. By and large, others will be swayed to support the efforts of those most vocal about the issue.

Lawmakers and other government officials also hear the concerns of citizens and craft legislation that creates policies. Court rulings create policies, which generally are the concerns that drive significant public issues. At times, policies can be supported or not supported by the government. For example, the Obama administration decided not to defend the Defense of Marriage Act (DOMA), which, although the administration did not repeal it, made it a non-entity (Delahunty, 2011). Likewise, the Obama administration did not enforce the immigration law, which amounted to an open border with Mexico (Delahunty & Yoo, 2013). Many laws on the books go unnoticed and unenforced, such as criminal laws relating to marijuana (Grabarsky, 2013).

This chapter will focus on the process of how social policy affecting child and family development is created and developed. Noting that there are different stakeholders in the process of social policy development, the chapter will discuss models for understanding policy, such as advocacy and grass-roots endeavors, governmental legislation, and court rulings. Future directions for social policy and how systems/dialectical thinking can influence this development will provide a concluding reflection.

The number of social policies continues to increase with the annual addition of new laws, regulatory agency rules and procedures, and court decisions (Umberson & Montez, 2010). These regulations, such as changes with the Internal Revenue Service (IRS), education, and housing industry, all affect the quality and happiness of everyday life. In recent years, more attention has been given to regulations stemming from environmental issues, such as climate control and sustainable forms of energy.

According to Anderson (2003), social policy is considered **substantive**, which refers to *what* the government is doing to enhance the welfare of citizens, and **procedural**, or *how* the government will accomplish getting things done. Laws or court rulings must be carried out by specific agencies that follow rules and procedures. Both substantive and procedural social policies are intertwined and interdependent. For example, what is being done and how something is being done may be mutually dependent.

Some policies may be considered **distributive**, **regulatory**, **self-regulatory**, or **redistributive** in nature (Anderson, 2003). A policy is distributive if it is related to the allocation of services, funds, or other tangible assets to a target group of persons. Congress has a pet name, pork projects, for much of the distribution from the federal government for state and community projects. In recent years, much financial support to businesses and municipalities has been to promote green energy companies. Some of these projects have been severely criticized, especially when supported by the tax dollars of companies that went bankrupt, such as the 2011 bankruptcy case of Solyndra, a manufacturer of cylindrical panels based in Fremont, California (Caprotti, 2016).

Regulative policies refer to rules and guidelines set in place to accomplish certain outcomes, including telephone use, electricity, water, and the buying and selling of property (Gattuso & Katz, 2016). Perhaps the most criticized in recent years are building restrictions; in some cases, it takes months and even years of red tape to obtain a building permit. Consumer protection policies fall in the category of regulative policies. They regulate everything from what one can put on the table to how much emission can come from the tailpipe of one's car.

Self-regulative policies tend to shore up and advance the interests of a particular group (Anderson, 2003). One example of self-regulatory policy is professional licensing. The profession is more or less in charge of developing and implementing the policy through a board of peers. Professions create a code of professional conduct as a guide to maintain consistent professional behavior across all membership. The procedure for membership into the profession may change with the passage of time and new or different environmental or cultural demands.

Redistributive policies knowingly put into action ways to shift wealth and resources from some individuals or groups to other individuals and groups (Anderson, 2003). In recent years, the Obama administration has initiated a number of policies that critics label redistributive (Hodge, 2014). For example, the IRS has created more regulations to collect more money from wealthy citizens with annual incomes over $250,000 (Theodoulou & Cahn, 2012). Critics claim that this move will hurt small businesses, which produce a large share of the jobs in the U.S. Another effort at redistribution was the passage of Obamacare, which was built on higher health insurance premiums for the young adult cohort to pay for the older cohort of citizens who have greater need for health care (Saks, 2012). Furthermore, critics, to some degree, believe that the educational plan, Common Core, is also redistributive, because schools that meet standards will lose resources while schools that do not meet standards will gain resources (Halterman, 2013). One of the most ambitious redistribution programs was the War on Poverty (Brady & Bostic, 2015). Critics point out that the efforts in most of the programs to empower poor people have had the opposite effect and have, instead, destroyed the family by making single-parent mothers dependent on the government, reduced self-reliance, and institutionalized poverty. On the other hand, not all redistributive policies help the poor. Depending on the historical time frame, some policies have helped the affluent while hurting those at the lower rung of society. For example, segregation in the South gave White southerners privileges that African Americans lacked, which reduced their participation in social and political affairs.

Social policies can also be characterized as providing tangible resources that have a distinctive material advantage over policies that give no material advantage but appeal to the inherent ideals of the general public (Mackie, 2009). Policies that provide support for poverty-level families provide tangible material resources, while policies that appeal to patriotism or nationalism could be considered symbolic or intangible. Some policies, such as environmental, may limit or obfuscate individual rights. In this sense, some polices for the greater good may impact personal decisions and freedoms.

TABLE 2.1 Types of policies

TYPE OF POLICY	DESCRIPTION
Distributive	Allocation of funds to a target group; e.g., Solyndra
Regulatory	Rules and guidelines to accomplish certain goals; e.g., Real estate
Self-Regulatory	Policies set up by a group to advance its interests; e.g., MFT professional ethics
Redistributive	Policies to shift resources from one group to another; e.g., Obamacare

Social policies may also be geared for public or private participation (Faricy, 2011)). In recent years, the concept of privatization has become prominent among some lawmakers. Some believe that programs operated by the government would be more cost-effective and efficient if run by private companies. Furthermore, some argue that the economic capitalistic system in the U.S. is not compatible with a system with immense governmental functions, such as the U.S. Postal Service, which loses millions of dollars each year (Netnewscheck, 2013).

A social policy is established from deliberate efforts to solve a social problem in which the welfare of people is at stake (Anderson, 2003). Some of the players are individuals who have particular concerns or private foundations that attempt to influence social policy and lawmakers. Individuals generally form advocacy groups that attempt to pressure lawmakers into supporting their positions (Veglia, Pahwa, & Demers, 2017). Advocacy groups generally have little professional training on how to influence lawmakers but rely on passion and numbers to get across their message. The Heritage Foundation and the Brookings Institute are two private groups that represent different perspectives on public policy. Each engages in research, writes blogs, and creates reports that attempt to influence lawmakers regarding legislation and the public regarding being advocates for certain viewpoints. Other groups that attempt to influence the direction of public policy include faith-based organizations, such as the Christian Coalition of America, the U.S. Conference of Catholic Bishops, and the National Association of Evangelicals. Lobbyists are paid professionals who are hired by corporations or other groups to influence lawmakers regarding pieces of legislation related to policy development. In addition, a Political Action Group (PAC) is formed to help get certain persons elected that will benefit the creation of specific policies.

MODELS FOR SOCIAL POLICY DEVELOPMENT

Social policy is complex and involves many different facets. It is dynamic and changing and is, thus, referred to as a process. It may involve compromise and negotiation, revisions, and in some cases, outright debunking. While social policy requires the act of a large and influential stakeholder, such as the government, it also involves individuals or the private sphere (Hojnacki, Kimball, Baumgartner, Berry, & Leech, 2012). Generally, public and private spheres come together at critical times when policies are initiated but may become divergent due to changing beliefs or experiences (Knill & Tosun, 2008). Some models of the process of public policy development include Rationalism/Comprehensive Model, Elitism, Systems Theory, Group Theory, Process Model, Systems/Dialectical Model, Game Theory, Risk and Resilience, Institutional Model, and Incrementalism (Incremental Theory).

TABLE 2.2 Theoretical models of social policy

THEORY	DESCRIPTION	WEAKNESS
Rationalism/Comprehensive Model	Based on maximizing the greatest good for the greatest number	Hard to abandon the policy even if it does not work
Elitism	Small group has the knowledge and expertise to shape policy	Depends completely on the knowledge and ethics of the elite group
Process Model	A coherent succession of development	Pays too much attention to events
Group Theory	Coalition of persons that advocate for specific policies	Too focused on self-interest
Incrementalism (Incremental Theory)	Changes occur from small and unplanned	Does not grasp the significance of intense events

THEORY	DESCRIPTION	WEAKNESS
Game Theory	Strategic interaction between individuals	Tends to be mechanistic and deterministic
Risk and Resilience Model	Based on reducing risks and increasing protective factors	Tends to focus on short-term outcomes
Institutional Model	The "what" of policy making Includes important functions such as education and health care	Disjointed government agencies are inconsistent
Systems Theory	How disparate parts act in coordination with the whole	Does not describe the process of the interaction
Systems/Dialectical Model	Contradictions, crises, and policy failure interact	Does not address the status quo, except as absence of differences

Rationalism/Comprehensive Model

Rationalism has a long history dating back to and beyond Thomas Hobbs (1651) (Schofield, 2006), who postulated that political systems functioned on the basis of making choices framed on attractions and distractions, later devolving into rewards and costs. Adam Smith (1776) (1977) reinforced this view through the association of choice with the well-being of people. Further development of these ideas was instrumental in evolving models such as **Utilitarianism** and **Preference Choice Theory**. Utilitarian theory states that choices are made on the basis of their usefulness to a person and to others (Schofield, 2006). The best moral decisions are based on maximizing the greater good for humankind. Decisions must be judged from the future standpoint of the consequences of those acts. Utilitarianism is clearly an important aspect of public policy given that outcomes of policies, e.g., the greatest good for the greatness numbers, should be an integral part of all policies (Schofield, 2006).

Preference Choice Theory is based on the view that individuals have preferences, which affect the decisions they make (Page & Shapiro, 2010). Consequently, decisions are often the result of what people want, which must be considered before a course of action can be determined. Preferences change from one generation to another and find their way into new policy formations. The changes in policy based on preferences are not serendipitous but are based on new consensus. These changes are the result of new understandings of social, economic, and political realities (Page & Shapiro, 2010). While public policy that the majority of the people would not want may be influenced by the public, it could be argued that policy is sometimes forced on the public by legislators and courts. At times, the public is forced to accept court opinions or laws passed by Congress that a referendum by the people would not support.

This model is akin to some principles of **Social Exchange Theory**, namely that the process of policy development must have rewards that outweigh the costs, or the resulting policy is useless (Page &Shapiro, 2010). This approach would demand that alternative positions are known and evaluated in terms of possible gains and costs. The final decision must be one that satisfies the weighing of options and selection of the most appropriate course of action (Page & Shapiro, 2010).

Rationalism is only as good as the decision-making process and may reflect flawed thinking to achieve expected outcomes. An inherent weakness in this approach is that policymakers are cautious to abandon a given policy that creates tremendous hope, even if it does not perform up to standard. Since this chosen approach was deemed the most rational and cost-effective, it would be unfeasible or even irrational to shift, even if there is evidence that it is ineffective.

Some writers on rationalism have profound concerns about the relative ignorance of the general public on political and social issues. Surveys indicate that people know much more about popular celebrities than they do about political leaders or social policy issues (Page & Shapiro, 2010). Instead of being fully informed on social policy, people tend to have fragmented information. Because of this shallow knowledge of social policy, people can be swayed by pervasive arguments or, in some cases, sheer propaganda. While, on the surface, individuals appear to have unstable and volatile beliefs, researchers have found that there tends to be a consistent preference in an individual's beliefs over time (Cipiriano & Gruca, 2015). Collectively, the pooled preferences of the public tend to maintain a stable set of beliefs and actually change slowly, if at all, at least in terms of the pendulum swing. The collective stance is always more solid and stable than the individual view and represents a rational point of view.

Elitism

Elitism is the view that a small group of a governing body has the knowledge and expertise to shape policy and that the public in general lacks both the knowledge and inclinations to do so (Knill & Tosun, 2012). In this perspective, policy has a decided hierarchy from the elite group down to the people, or a top-down approach. There is little room for dissent, since the elite group controls the process. The citizens lack clout to influence the process unless they become an extension of the elite. The resulting policies reflect the desires and wishes of the elite and do not reflect the needs of the people. The weakness of this approach is obvious: the public has little protection or redress and depends entirely on the honor of the elite. The public is largely voiceless and passive and fails to advocate for alternative measures that might be more effective. According to Knill and Tosun (2012), changes in policy from the elite perspective would be slow and represent only changes of values among the elite. The overall range of alternative positions is limited in that most of the elite would believe the same fundamental premises. Ideas that greatly varied from the mainstream would have no audience.

This approach would control the agenda for public policy and, therefore, the process (Knill & Tosun, 2012). It would suggest that the elite, generally those in power, will limit the agenda and prevent competing agendas to be voiced. Maintaining the status quo is a policy decision, although it may not be evident (Peters, 2012). Issues may arise to overwhelm the systems, however, depending on the degree to which persons feel disenfranchised and can mobilize support.

A less sinister view of Elitism and public policy was noted by Peter Woll (1974). Although leaders may emerge from a small number of privileged persons, such as presidents who graduate from Harvard or Yale, they may also hold the same values as the masses and see their duty as meeting the public's needs (Smith & Larimer, 2017). In this sense, the elite serves the people, and the people give the feedback and, in point of fact, participate democratically in the process. For example, Presidents of the U.S. tend to graduate from prestigious universities and have much more wealth than the average person. Many elite leaders take up the cause of the poor or disenfranchised. Some might argue that privileged persons have the rational understanding and the connections to truly take on such responsibilities.

The Process Model

The **Process Model** of public policy stresses the necessity of a coherent succession of actions in the development of policies (Sabatier & Weible, 2014). The Process Model is broader and more inclusive than most models and applicable to all belief systems. The model affirms that decisions are outcomes, but they are never a finished product. Rather than producing unchangeable outcomes, there is cognition that human systems do not neatly comply with rigid formulas of interaction. Reassessment of policy formation because of new input, negative evaluation of the effectiveness, or fresh information plays a huge role in maintaining a policy. The Process Model pays less attention to players and outcomes and more attention to events.

This model is perhaps more helpful than some models, because it defines the steps or stages in the development of a policy (Sabatier & Weible, 2014). Starting with the first stage of problem recognition, the Process Model points out that the problem must first be recognized. The recognition may come from a grassroots contingency, a legislator, or in response to a traumatic public event that affects a large swath of the population. The second stage involves estimating various factors related to the event or events involved in moving the concern to an agenda. For child and family issues, an economic status, namely determining how much implementing a policy will cost, generally precedes the effort put into it. If the costs are too great and the perceived benefits too low, little support is garnered for that program (Zigler & Hall, 1999). Many questions involve programs for preschoolers, and after-school programs are scrutinized under the umbrella of costs. Future benefits may sometimes outweigh present concerns, as in the case of programs that benefit school readiness. It may take years for the benefit to be evident, but when high-end preschool educational programs produce participants who have higher high school graduation rates, better paying jobs, and less reliance on welfare, the benefits are recognized, and costs are justified. The third step is that the concern has risen to the level that it can be placed on an agenda. The fourth step is for ongoing evaluation of the issue, and possible ways of addressing it are determined. This step involves determining a course of action from consensus or negotiation. The fifth step is making concrete strides to implement the policy. Ongoing evaluation of the policy's success is the last step.

To become a policy, there must be a groundswell of public outcry that appears and demands that some action be taken (Sabatier & Weible, 2014). An example of this is how the child abuse law evolved (Zigler & Hall, 1999). A nine-year-old girl was severely beaten by her foster parents in New York City. The child sustained broken bones and other severe injuries that required hospitalization. Because there was no law to prosecute the foster parents, they were not punished for this egregious act. The media latched on to this event and well-known and influential persons, such as Henry Berg, who the year before was instrumental in getting a law passed for cruelty to animals, created enough pressure to pass a child protection law. Some issues may be prevented from rising to the agenda status because of political ideation, as was the case in the pro-segregation era in the South when legislators consistently blocked desegregation efforts; it took a Supreme Court decision to finally end segregation.

Group Theory

According to **Group Theory** and public policy, various forces act in ways to drive policy makers in certain directions (Sabatier & Weible, 2014). The pressure exerted by these various forces requires flexibility, negotiation, and compromise. This theory can also be called **Equilibrium Theory**, because it attempts to hold things in balance, which is typically in short order, because change is constant. Groups of various types, including labor unions, vie for control against competing groups. Policy emerges from the interactions of these various groups and might shift in balance when related to broader public support. Groups are made up of people who have similar interests and beliefs. The group is able to accomplish what an individual would not have the clout to accomplish. The groups give voice to issues and create interest from lawmakers because of the potential concerns of a large constituency. While a group gives more attention to a concern than an individual, all groups do not have equal access to particular lawmakers. For example, the National Rifle Association would not have the same influence on a lawmaker who does not believe in gun control than on a lawmaker who believes in gun control (Baumgartner & Leech, 1998).

Grassroots efforts to influence social policy have been successful in a number of ways. For example, a mother of a daughter killed by a drunk driver was able to marshal support for legislation to keep drunk drivers off the highway through the creation of Mothers Against Drunk Driving (MADD). Likewise, Megan's Law (n.d.) and Jessica's Law (n.d.) were both created to influence social policy on sexual predators by parents of abducted and murdered children. On the other hand, some groups have been created in response to particular social policies, such as the National Welfare Rights Organization (Anderson, 2003).

One of the major shortcomings of the group approach is that some interests may prevail while others may not have clear voice. Sometimes disenfranchised or underrepresented individuals bond together to champion issues that are overlooked. Lawmakers may make use of Group Theory to create interest in particular issues, such as gun control. In addition, not all public policies emanate from group involvement. Many social policy issues are created from scholarly writings and research, think tanks, and revisionary efforts on the part of lawmakers (Baumgartner & Leech, 1998).

Incrementalism (Incremental Theory)

Incremental Theory posits that changes to social policy occur from small and unplanned changes (Smith & Larimer, 2014). This model is in contrast to the belief that changes occur because of planned wide-ranging sudden events. Incremental changes may happen over a longer period of time and represent adjustments from the original policy. In time, these small incremental changes may add up to a significant change. Since many things do not entail a need for planning, unplanned incremental changes represent a more natural approach to policy formation. Incremental Theory has been referred to as **"muddling through"** (Lindblom, 1959) because little time or effort needs to be placed on planning or structure. In addition, incremental changes are less likely to draw opposition and, therefore, can be used in place of ideological differences in order to gradually accomplish what a more detailed, planned, and radical change could not accomplish (Jones & Baumgartner, 2005).

This model is based on the work of Charles Lindblom (1959), who postulated that there are limited alternatives to a public policy that differs only slightly from the status quo. The government budget process was particularly geared toward an incremental approach (Jones & Baumgartner, 2005). Changes in the budget tend to drift rather than result in wholesale change. The changes that occur in policy over time are more random than organized. They are based on continuity over time and usually do not significantly upset the status quo. A formula is given by Padgett (1980), which states that current policy is yesterday's policy in addition to a random element. Padgett demonstrated that if the random elements were then added together, a normal distribution would result. The normal distribution would not be an expected outcome but would suggest that it would be the only appropriate outcome, or the model would be considered flawed (Jones & Baumgartner, 2005).

Game Theory

Game Theory was the brainchild of Neumann and Morgenstern (1953) and has been further developed over the ensuing decades. Game Theory focuses on the interaction of humans as being the foundation of social policy (McCain, 2009). Game Theory is multidimensional and includes aspects of various perspectives, such as economics, mathematics, business, law, political science, computer science, social policy, and philosophy. In the literature, there are two types of Game Theory, **cooperative** and **non-cooperative**. In a non-cooperative game, participants operate in privacy and mistrust of each other's motives. Communication between opposing parties is minimal to nonexistent depending on a number of extenuating circumstances. On the other hand, cooperative games allow participants to assist the efforts of others by forming partnerships and pooling mutual resources. Communication between entities is essential in problem solving in a cooperative structure. Games that combine both cooperative and non-cooperative elements are called **hybrid games** and commonly begin as groups joining together but playing the game out in competitive ways.

Game Theory applies mathematical scripts to understanding the intricacies of decision making (McCain, 2009). To be considered a game, the parties involved must be identified, appropriate information must be available, and there must be rewards for the results. Strategies for the game create a stable equilibrium of effort that denies advantage to either party for deviating from the strategy (Rasmusen, 2007). When players play the game to maximize their benefits, and the strategy of each player is known by the other, and no changes can be made to the strategy, it is referred to as the **Nash Equilibrium** (Nash, 1950). Each player is viewed as making his/her decisions based on what the other person has chosen.

The Risk and Resilience Model

The risk and resiliency model for social policies for children and families has been touted for several decades and generally reflects advances in child development research (Jensen & Fraser, 2015). Consequently, the development of social policy for children should be based on the expanding knowledge of vulnerabilities that reduce developmental trajectories of children. Adolescent violence, drug use, sexual promiscuity, poverty, and school failure are persistent problems that affect the developmental trajectory of adolescents. None of these risk factors alone account for the totality of the problem. Rather taken as a whole, there is a cumulative effect of various risk factors that affect the developmental trajectory of children.

These risk factors form the basis for policy interventions that would help children develop resiliency and, thus, improve their future developmental trajectory (Jensen & Fraser, 2015). This model was also enhanced by the observation that not all children exposed to risk factors developed problems. Some children have protective factors that tend to insulate them from the negative effects of the risk factors. These protective factors are viewed as individual characteristics or environmental factors that prevent the negative influence of risk factors on children and adolescents. Social policy should focus on reducing risk factors and increasing protective elements that allow for resiliency (Jensen & Fraser, 2015).

The Institutional Model

The **Institutional Model** is founded on the belief that public institutions create public policy (Birkland, 2011). A major function of government is to produce public policy. Since all citizens are subject to the same policies, the type of government is extremely important for understanding outcomes of policy. While much has gone into discerning the structure of government, little has gone into understanding how institutions work. According to Hanekom (1987), the liaison between the composition of government and public policy must be analyzed. Primary governmental structure is linked to such functions as education, welfare, housing, and the court system. How these governmental systems function may vary from time to time depending on overall societal values.

Since governments occur on different levels, for example, national, state, and local, conflicts and discrepancies may occur among these various levels. Policies are not always for the benefit of all citizens and may benefit some more than others (Birkland, 2011). The court systems also may, at times, make rulings that are overturned by another court. Some states have imitated some polices that are not made on the national level. For example, some states have advocated for an English-speaking only policy in the U.S., while the national government has not moved in this direction.

The Systems Model

The **Systems Model** was the work of David Easton (1968) and Chester Barnard (1965) and is based on the concept that disparate parts act in coordination with the greater whole. The system is comprised of various entities made up of **subsystems,** which create a bidirectional effect. In order to maintain equilibrium, adjustments are made in a continuous manner. There is a dynamic interaction between systems and subsystems and the environment in contrast to models, such as Elitism, that posit little or no feedback from the environment. In contrast to models that posit that there is a right way and a wrong way to change, the equifinality concept of the Systems Model emphasizes that the end point may be reached from various starting points. Another advantage of the Systems Model is that it allows for a broader perspective than a single point of view and, consequently, means that future considerations may be taken into account. As global considerations become more evident in social policy and increase a system's complexity, systems theory permits an expansive view that considers past, present, and future. It is clearly a hedge against tunnel-vision approaches that fail to connect all the interactive dots.

The Systems Model, as described by Easton (1968) and Barnard (1965), receives input from the stakeholders (the environment), which enters into the "black box" where decision making on policies is made, which then forms policies as outcomes. These outcomes become feedback to the environment, which may act to stimulate additional feedback and continue the process.

The Systems/Dialectical Model

While Easton (1968) and Barnard (1965) developed similar concepts to the systems/dialectical approach taken in this book, they do not describe the process whereby the input from the environment is assessed to create the policy as output. The systems/dialectical approach utilizes the dialectical scheme to explain how the decision-making process works to form the policy as outcome. The systems/dialectical model has been described above, and only a few comments will be made here. The combining of systems and dialectical theories helps explain the complexity, as well as the process by which social policies come into existence and are maintained. It also can help explain why policies are so slow at changing. The analogy of a human is helpful in understanding this process. The dialectical process espoused by Riegel (1976) identified various dimensions of the developing human that interact in a confrontational style, which produce a different outcome. The outcome is discontinuous with the past in the sense that it cannot be repeated.

APPLYING THE MODELS TO AN EXAMPLE

While all of the models are effective for some public policy issues, the position taken in this book is that combining systems theory and dialectical theory provides a potent model, broad in scope but effective in outcome, which can address the formidable issues in social policy related to children and families. Many social policies affecting children and families are paradoxical and dialectical. Individuals or groups can be pitted against each other so that helping one may inadvertently affect the other negatively. For example, one of the most obtuse problems facing policymakers for children and families is how to reduce child poverty versus how to reduce dependence on welfare. Welfare participation could be pared down so that families would no longer be dependent on the government, but doing so would only increase poverty. Likewise, more efforts could go into reducing child poverty by increasing welfare support, only to create more dependency on government (Corbett, 1993, as cited in Bogenschneider, 2011).

A systems perspective would help in understanding such a paradox as the above example and would provide a path for addressing all of the issue. The systems view would go beyond a simple view of parts of the dilemma and would see how the parts, such as the needs of the child, and the needs of the family, interact in a paradoxical way. The solution would be in applying a broad perspective that would allow for reduced child poverty while, at the same time, reducing the family's dependency on the government. Other approaches would address this from more of a piecemeal approach that would tend to pit reducing child poverty and getting families off government assistance against each other. While a systems approach is appropriate and useful, without the dialectical combination the process would lack a description of how changes take place.

Rationalism may appear to be a good theory, since the greatest good for the most people is considered to be sacrosanct; however, in actuality, it appears that most persons are governed by beliefs systems or ideologies rather than reasoning based on the best interest for all. Generally, reasoning on the basis of what is in one's self interest is a rather small focus and irreconcilable with a societal focus (Page & Shapiro, 2010). In addition, if preferences guide the choices made, there would be limited capacity for an unbiased assessment. Applied to the example above, the decision would be based on individual values of whether to reduce child poverty or to eliminate dependency on welfare. With Rationalism, it would be difficult to see both outcomes and devise a plan that would allow both to succeed.

Elitism might give a definite, clear, and forceful policy in the above example, but the policy would be established for the best interest of the governing elite (Knill & Tocun, 2012). The prevailing ideology of the elite would dictate how the dilemma would be resolved so that either reducing child poverty or reducing the number of families dependent on the government would prevail. The bottom line would clearly rest on what would benefit the government more. If having a large percentage of the population dependent on the government was the goal, increasing government subsidies to families would take precedence, which would tend to increase dependence on the government. This perspective holds that the general public is uninformed and lacks knowledge of what is in its self-interest. As long as the decisions of public policy support the policies of the elite, no ethical or moral principles would guide the process.

The Process Model is very compatible with the Systems/Dialectical Model and describes the stages that occur sequentially when a policy is enacted (Sabatier & Weible, 2014). Both are process models, although the process varies. The recognition stage would differ somewhat, because the systems/dialectical model focuses more on competing viewpoints, or confrontation as the starting point, which may not create a groundswell of concern. While the systems/dialectical model would change as a result of new information, feedback, or evaluation, it would not progress in such a staged manner as the Process Model. In a Systems/Dialectical Model, change is constant and in flux so that the process of change drives the outcome. Like the Process Model, the Systems/Dialectical Model is flexible and allows for change but defies the establishment of reified policies that may have public support and would cause widespread outrage if changed, even though the policy was ineffective. The Process Model, however, may be more likely to resolve the conflict given in the example by determining the best solution of options, while a systems/dialectical approach would more likely find a solution that incorporates both polar opposites of the debate. For example, the Process Model is more likely to conclude that poor children need resources, so providing more support from the government is the only way to address this issue. The tension between polar opposites, and the concept of the unity of opposites would play little role in how the Process Model would resolve this issue.

Group Theory helps explain how some issues rise to the top of the list to form public policy while other issues are pushed to the back burner. It clearly articulates how coalitions and political and civic groups contribute to the formation of social policies (Sabatier & Weible, 2014). One of the major factors is how issues are recognized as being important for social policy, and this model emphasizes this aspect of the process. However, it does not address the process that groups use to champion a particular issue. Why are groups concerned about this issue? What kind of reasoning went into this concern? Are the concerns those of the general public at large? What role does the media play in promoting or dampening the public knowledge of the issue? The answers to these questions are not readily known or discussed by proponents of the group model. In the example discussed above, it may be likely that a group with much political clout and financial backing may campaign for reducing child poverty without considering the outcome such as that families may be more dependent on the government from increased subsidies. If the group approach was the only means of affecting social policies, the groups with the most support, best funding, and greater media coverage would dominate social policy development and maintenance.

Incrementalism posits that change is slow and a limited number of alternate moves are available to tweak the policy but not drastically change it (Smith & Larimer, 2014). At first glance, this model seems to explain much social policy but fails to address some very divisive issues that lead to policies that were drastically different and changed the playing field. A quick reflection brings up a number of radical changes that deviated immensely from the status quo. For example, segregation in the South was not accomplished by incremental changes but resulted from a Supreme Court decision. In California, the legal marriage of same-sex couples was denied by a state referendum of voters in which 55% of the population voted against the measure but was later overturned by the courts (State Vote, n.d.). Many policies would, therefore, not fit into the incremental model and were created by a radical or drastic departure from the status quo. Not only do they vary widely from the status quo, but in many cases, they might not have the majority support from the public. The Affordable Health Care Act was passed by Congress at a time when it lacked more than 50% support and, as persons learned more about it, the support continued to fall (Oberlander, 2010).

Game Theory has an interesting perspective on public policy based on the strategy of participants. When opposing groups vie for support, it is evident that certain moves are made by each faction (McCain, 2009). It is also evident that each opposing faction wants the outcome to favor its own faction. While some opposing forces are competitive and others are cooperative, Game Theory provides little clarification as to why cooperation or competitive games occur. With Game Theory, the outcome can be assumed by how the game is played; that is, the series of moves involved determines the outcome. There is a lack of understanding of the unity of opposites or how positions may be combined to form different outcomes from either of the original positions. Game Theory would deemphasize the influence of spontaneous events and serendipity in altering outcomes. Consequently, it would tend to analyze the example given above as a game of strategy in which the outcome would be predicable.

The Risk and Resiliency Model would concede that not all risks have negative effects, nor is it possible or even desirable to control all of them, because they alone do not cause dysfunction in children (Safe Schools, Healthy Students, 2004). Social policy from a risk and resilience perspective would emphasize interventions to reduce risks and increase protective factors. This model, perhaps more than other models, would lack a clear understanding of the relation between reducing dependence on government programs and lifting families out of poverty. Those supporting this model might argue that reducing poverty would both decrease risk and increase protective factors, which would decrease dependency of government, but how that could be accomplished is not clear, since most attempts to reduce poverty by adding government programs has only increased reliance on government (Spalding, 2012).

According to the Institutionalism (Institutional Model), governmental function is the primary shaper of social policy (Birkland, 2011). This argument is strong given the number of laws, executive orders, court rulings, and regulations imposed by governmental agencies. Government plays a pivotal role, but the process of how policies are made is not enlightened by the Institutional Model. While the process model may be the "how" of policymaking, the Institutional Model is the "what" of policymaking. In this sense, the Institutional Model is the vehicle, but it is not sure who is driving the car. As a means of understanding the policy process, the Institutional Model offers little help. In the example, this approach would simply acknowledge that any solution offered would involve the government and that this involvement would be the cause of change. From this perspective, even when individuals raise concerns regarding the safety of children and the need to protect them from harm, such as in sexual abuse, it is the government that advocates for the children in order to really get something done.

The Systems/Dialectical Model would address the dilemma in the example by first understanding how the parts contribute to the whole. It would need to address family dependence on the government as an equal priority to that of reducing child poverty. The idea that less dependency on the government will, in the long run, stimulate more incentive on the part of the family would be another possible avenue for policy. No easy, quick, or partial solution would be attempted, but it would be acknowledged that solutions can and do occur from different starting points. No starting point would be eliminated, because it seemed strange or out of touch. Paradoxical solutions and those that may seem on the surface as unreasonable would be allowed as possible policy positions.

A Systems/Dialectical Model would not overemphasize either solution in polar opposite positions, but it would recognize that if a policy has been in place for a long time without improvement, it might be time to shift the scales and do something differently (Bogenschneider, 2011). In the arena of free dialogue, opposites come into contention with each other frequently, and this confrontation produces changes in the policy. Elitists have the greatest problem with the belief that it is good for opposing ideas to confront each other in the public sphere. From a systems/dialectical perspective, the confrontation of ideas is a natural process that requires the initiation of new directions.

Perhaps the most difficult aspect of Systems/Dialectical Model is finding solutions out of opposing views. Most policymakers have been trained to pursue one point of view, thus creating polarization in which neither side gives in and tries to defeat the other (Conner & Jordan, 2009). Sitting down with others with opposite views and attempting to carve out a path that each can buy into is a difficult task. For example, one of the ongoing parent-child debates centers around aiding with career development on the one hand and more parental time with their children on the other. Those who want to support parental careers, including mothers with young children, tend to be on one side of this argument, and those who propose more time with children tend to be on the other side. While advocates for both positions tend to dig in and hold on to their perceptive views, neither seems to realize that both goals could be achieved if there were more dialogue between the two points of view (Bogenschneider, 2011). The type of problems that families face in contemporary America requires diligence in a wide-ranging perspective that includes opposite points of view.

A benefit of a systems/dialectical perspective of policymaking is that it offers an alternative to polarization in which both sides believe that they are right and are unwilling to negotiate a compromise. Most of the American public, however, are centrists and want political parties to find common ground on issues rather than refuse to acknowledge the legitimacy of the opposing view (Newport, 2011).

THE POLICYMAKING PROCESS

In general, social policies do not magically appear, although some policies result from single events that garner the attention of the public and media (Sabatier & Weible, 2014). Often policies come from a snowballing effect of recurrent social and political problems. For example, drunk driving was known to be a serious problem and caused major damage to property and loss of life each year. However, it took a single event to mobilize a group of parents to press for stricter laws to remove these drivers from the road. Candy Lightner, the founder of MADD (n.d.), along with several others mothers who had lost children due to drunk drivers wanted to reduce drunk driving and affect social policy to restrict these drivers from operating vehicles. Another successful parental policymaking effort was from the parents of seven-year-old Megan Kanka who was abducted and killed by a sexual predator who served a sentence of less than one year for the crime. Megan's parents were instrumental in developing Megan's Law, which was passed in the New Jersey Legislature as the New Jersey Sexual Offender and Registration Act of 1994 (Megan's Law Now, n.d.). This law required that sexual predators register as sexual offenders and, if circumstances warranted it, that the community would be notified of their presence after release.

Not only must events occur that are traumatic or hideous, but they must also create widespread concern from citizens in order to lead to policymaking. The examples above are descriptive of this process. Consequently, for events to rise to the level of policy, they must impact a large number of people and have the attention of a passionate advocacy group (Sabatier & Weible, 2014).

In addition to a large group of advocates who champion a particular cause, there must also be pressure placed on persons who are able to bring about the desired results (Smith & Larimer, 2017). In the examples above, pressure was brought on legislators who crafted laws to protect future victims of such crimes. Without a compelling problem that resonates with a large advocacy group and the capacity to bring about the desired change, policymaking would be handcuffed (Zigler & Hall, 1999).

Steps in the Policymaking Process

The first step in policymaking is when the trouble is initially discovered; this is referred to as the **initiation phase** (Lunenburg, 2010). This discovery may take some time. Often, a problem can incrementally increase without reaching a critical point of discovery until an event catches the public's attention; then, the media become the mouthpiece. The public is generally made aware of a pressing problem when newspapers, radio, and TV news programs broadcast information about it. Recently, a concern emerged about children in the U.S. being overweight or obese. While there have always been overweight school children, a number of factors coalesced to bring this problem into public awareness. This kind of "tipping" phenomenon helps to explain how a problem seems to suddenly appear. In other words, the weight of school children has been increasing for some time, but this increase went largely unnoticed until a certain percentage of children were obese. In some states, this number had reached 40% of school children before it was noticed. Also, advocacy groups can bring these hidden issues—ones that may never increase sufficiently in number to suddenly get attention—to the public and legislators. For example, in 2013, California Governor Brown signed into law a bill regarding equity for transgender school children in grades K–12 (Bidwell, 2013). This law provides for a student of any biological sex to define him/herself as the opposite sex and to be able to experience all of the privileges of that sex, such as using a given bathroom or playing on a given sports team. While sheer numbers of transgender persons are small, the recent focus on gay marriage may have set the tone for other issues relating to gender.

TABLE 2.3 How policy develops

PROCESS	EXAMPLES
An Event that Snowballs	Creation Of MADD, Megan's Law, Jessica's Law

STEPS	
a. Initiation	Who are affected?
b. Implementation	What are solutions?
c. Evaluation	Did it work?

After a problem has been identified, the next step is referred to as the **implementation phase**, an assessment of how many people have the problem and possible actions to take (Lunenburg, 2010). Along with pondering actions and solutions, the question could also be raised as to what might happen if nothing is done. Regarding the concern over childhood obesity, the conclusion in this stage was that something had to be done, or children would not outlive their parents. A dire medical outcome for obese children confronted those who investigated obesity. The fear that one-third of obese children would grow up with reduced life expectancy due to higher risks for diabetes, heart disease, and reduced satisfaction and well-being gripped experts and policymakers. The option of doing nothing appealed to no one. The implementation phase leads to the third step—**proposing ideas**. Reducing sugar content in soda drinks, labeling all food products, removing fast-food options at schools, educating parents and children about healthy eating, and providing more supervision of children's eating habits were all possible solutions. Some of these solutions have been debated. Some have said that to reduce the size of a soda drink—as was initially implemented and then rescinded in New York City—smacks of government control of every aspect of one's life (Chumley, 2013). Some argue that it is an intrusion into privacy to make laws that forbid personal choice. Some also find common ground with the advocates for stricter control by supporting labeling of ingredients of food products much in the same way cigarettes are labeled and known health effects are acknowledged; however, the choice to engage in smoking or eating high-fat foods, they argue, should be left up to individuals.

The next stage in the process is to **evaluate** how the solution is working (Lunenburg, 2010). In some ways, this is like asking if someone is attractive and then getting different answers, since "beauty is in the eye of the beholder." Every policy will have detractors and holdouts for solutions that were not attempted. The objective assessment of real outcomes is hard to trust. Those supporting the policy will reframe negative outcomes in ways to convince others of their effectiveness, and those opposed will find faults where none exist. It would be great if ideological differences played a small place here, but unfortunately those differences continue to drive the process.

A criticism of stage models of policy development is that they fail to capture the intricacies of policymaking, which usually is not a linear sequence. Stages in policymaking are frequently undetected, and many circumstances preempt a smooth policy process. Since all of the interactions around policymaking occur simultaneously, a linear process fails to capture this complexity. If policy is driven by a dialectical process, and various persons from different points of view carved out the initial solutions, all stakeholders would have some claim to the outcome. Reconvening this group to assess the effectiveness and offer new solutions or continue the status quo would be a more objective basis for evaluation than having the party in power make attempts to salvage its program simply because it does not want to acknowledge that it does not work.

TABLE 2.4 The legislative policymaking process: How a Senate bill becomes a law

BILL STATUS	LEGISLATIVE OFFICES INVOLVED
Drafted bill introduced	Senate chamber
Bill read twice	Senate chamber
Enters Senate Journal, given a number, marked up for printing, printed	Senate chamber and bill's clerks' office
Printed bill made available electronically	Printing office
Goes to appropriate committee	Printing office
Bill placed on legislative calendar	Senate chamber
Unanimous consent request, and if granted, legislative clerk reports the title	Senate chamber
Bill is debated and amended	Senate chamber
Clerk calls for third reading	Senate chamber
Call for vote	Senator; Senate chamber
Voted on by roll call	Senators; Senate chamber
If passed bill in final copy is prepared	Enrolling clerk
Bill signed	Secretary of Senate
Bill delivered to House of Representatives	House chamber
Bill passed by House and sent back to Senate if not amended	House chamber
Enrolled bill is signed	President Pro Tempore of Senate and Speaker of House
Bill delivered to White House	Secretary of Senate
Bill is signed by President or vetoed	White House

Adapted from U.S. Senate Publication (https://www.senate.gov/reference/resources/pdf/legprocessflowchart.pdf)

The Policy

While the above steps are only approximations because of the complexity and lack of prediction for all policy development, the process of policy development for child and family development takes a strikingly similar path. That path includes a concern about the cost and economic impact of the program. Policies are inevitably targeted toward certain groups, such as those with incomes below the poverty line (Heckman & Masterov, 2004). These programs do not benefit all persons, and recent governmental efforts aim to redistribute resources. The argument for redistribution is that if those with more resources are doing well and others are failing, redistributing resources from those doing well to those doing poorly is justified (Feinman, 2005). In other words, the resources go largely to waste if persons already have adequate well-being. This practice could also mean that if redistribution of resources is not possible, curtailing resources to those doing well is also a viable option (Feinman, 2005). A case in point is a recent decision by the principal of an elementary school in New York City who eliminated the program for gifted children because of a lack of cultural diversity in the program (Chasmar, 2014). Those who argue against shifting resources say that improving the well-being of all is desirable and that there should be no ceiling above which resources are limited or eliminated.

Perhaps one of the most distinctive characteristics of policymaking for children and families is the overall model of treatment versus prevention (Bradshaw, 2006). Certainly treatment is desirable and mainly dominated the views of experts for much of the history of social policy. This model of treatment had a slow death, because new interventions to address social problems, such as high school dropout rates and the health of children, were the great pastime of experts in the field. With the rise of industrialization and the need to have an educated workforce and other events, the focus began to shift toward being more proactive regarding the well-being of persons. With the end of World War II and some refocusing on the plight of citizens, it became clear that some families struggled while other families thrived. This inequality in the status of persons based on social class became a growing concern. For persons to achieve their full potential, it became necessary to establish prevention strategies, rather than waiting to intervene after they needed help (Bradshaw, 2006). According to Bradshaw, the rise of the civil rights initiatives and, later, the feminist movement gave voice to the need to change models to be proactive and prevention-oriented. This change in focus is noted particularly in the War on Poverty. One of the guiding lights of the War on Poverty is the belief that it is much more cost-effective to provide quality child care and employment opportunities for those below the poverty level than to provide comprehensive mental and physical health to adults who lack basic education and skills. Furthermore, adults who lack these basic life skills have long ago given up and lost the motivation to help themselves. The cost involved in supporting female-headed single-parent families and giving the mother and child a leg up early on reduces the need to provide more costly programs later.

The Systems/Dialectical Perspective of Policymaking

The nature of child and family social policy is unique because it deals with interdependent parts and non-recursive interaction patterns. To fully understand the policymaking process affecting children and families, an approach that understands the underlying systems dynamics is important. A systems/dialectical perspective first defines the issue, which creates a boundary that separates it from other issues and delimits the process. Continuous feedback from stakeholders provides an ongoing way to assess and direct the policymaking content. This feedback should represent all segments of society, including underrepresented groups. The process of systems/dialectical policymaking is very similar to developing a theory about a social issue that provides knowledge and information; it

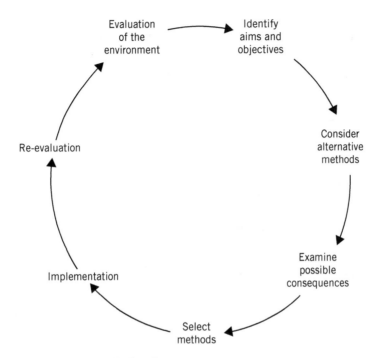

FIGURE 2.1 The Policy Process

combines lived experiences with academic research to provide an avenue to make it possible to explore the totality of the issue at hand. This process is more than simply examining the parts; it requires a holistic analysis. The problem at hand must be understood from this holistic point of view, which is assumed to have developed from the interaction of many factors. In nonlinear systems, a small change can produce a large outcome because of the redundant interaction. Over time, these small changes are magnified, due in part to the unpredictable characteristics in non-recursive systems. Changes occur. because the interactional processes create contradictions and crises, which must be rectified. The system becomes destabilized in the struggle of opposing forces but is able to reach a level of stability again at a compromised outcome.

KEY TERMS

Substantive	Social Exchange Theory	Hybrid games
Procedural	Elitism	Nash Equilibrium
Distributive	Process Model	Institutional Model
Regulatory	Group Theory	Systems Theory
Self-regulatory	Equilibrium Theory	Subsystem
Redistributive	Instrumentalism	Initiation phase
Pork projects	Muddling through	Implementation phase
Rationalism/Comprehensive	Game Theory	Preparing ideas
Utilitarian	Cooperative	Evaluate
Preference Choice Theory	Non-cooperative	Incrementalism (Incremental Theory)

STUDY QUESTIONS TO ACCOMPLISH THE LEARNING OBJECTIVES

1. Define regulatory, self-regulatory, and distributive social policies. Explain the differences in regulatory, self-regulatory, and distributive social policies.

2. Social policy can be characterized as providing both tangible and intangible resources. How would you define them? What are the differences in these resources? Is one more desirable?

3. Define Rationalism as a method of social policy. Compare and contrast the strengths and weaknesses of Rationalism to other models.

4. Since the Process Model and the systems/dialectical perspective are similar, discuss how they differ. Is one more effective? Justify your position.

5. List the benefits in using Game Theory. Evaluate if Game Theory can be incorporated into other theories.

6. Define Instrumentalism and how it differs from other models. Explain how Instrumentalism posits that policy changes occur in a random manner based on continuity over time.

7. Name the basic tenets of Easton's Systems Theory. Define the "black box," and evaluate how it operates from the systems' perspective.

8. Compare and contrast how the different models would address a social policy issue, such as the desire to both reduce dependence on government and reduce child poverty.

9. Which model(s) provide(s) the best outcome in social policy? Defend your answer.

10. Discuss the steps in the policymaking process. Determine if there is a weakness in understanding all the nuances of policymaking from applying the steps.

DEBATE ACTIVITY FOR STUDENTS

Consider the following proposition: Incrementalism is the most realistic theory when considering how social policies actually occur in real life.

- Review refereed literature on this topic. Do a library and Internet search to find relevant material. Investigate some of the additional readings.

- Develop three arguments for the proposition.

- Develop three arguments against the proposition.

- How do the arguments relate to other systems, such as the community, or culture?

- Is there common ground?

- What are the long-term consequences of taking action?

- What new or common-ground solutions should be offered? If no common ground, what new position could emerge from a dialogue between the two positions?

- How is the new position superior to the original positions?

ADDITIONAL READING RESOURCES

Birkland, T.A. (2011). *An introduction to the policy process: Theories, concepts and models of policymaking* (3rd ed.). New York, NY: Routledge.

Brady, D., & Bostic, A. (2015). Paradoxes of social policy: Welfare transfers, relative poverty, and redistribution preferences. *American Sociological Review, 80*(2), 268–298.

Sabatier, P.A., & Weible, M. (2014). *Theories of the policy process.* Boulder, CO: Westview.

Knill, C., & Tosun, J. (2012). *Public policy: A new introduction.* United Kingdom: Palgrave.

REFERENCES

Anderson, J. E. (2003). *Public Policymaking.* Boston, MA: Houghton Mifflin.

Bradshaw, T. K. (2006). Theories of poverty and anti-poverty programs in community development. Rural poverty Research Center—Working Paper Series. Retrieved from http//www.rupri.org/forms/wp06-05.pdf/

Barnard, C. (1968). *The functions of the executives.* Cambridge, MA: Harvard University Press.

Baumgartner, F. R., & Leech, B. L. (1998). *Basic interest: The importance of groups in politics and political science.* Princeton, NJ: Princeton University Press.

Bogenschneider, K. (2011). *Family policy matters: How policymaking affects families and what professionals can do* (2nd ed.). New York, NY: Routledge.

Bidwell, A. (2013). California governor signs landmark bill for transgender students. *U.S. News and World Report Online.* Retrieved from http//www.usnews.com/news./articles/2013/08/13/California-governor-signs-landmark-bill-trnagender-students/

Birkland, T.A. (2011). *An introduction to the policy process: Theories, concepts and models of policy making* (3rd ed.). New York, NY: Routledge.

Brady, D., & Bostic, A. (2015). Paradoxes of social policy: Welfare transfers, relative poverty, and redistribution preferences. *American Sociological Review, 80*(2), 268–298.

Caprotti, F. (2016). Protecting innovative niches in the green company's investigating the rise and fall of Solyndra, 2005–2011. *Geo Journal,* May 19, 2016. Retrieved from http://link.springer.com/article/107.1007/s10708-016-9722-2

Chasmar, J. (2014). NYC school cuts gifted program over lack of diversity: Report. *The Washington Times,* January 30, 2014. Retrieved from http://www.washingtontimes.com/news/2014/jan/30/nyc-school-cuts-popular-gifted-program-over-lack-d/

Chumley, C. K. (2013). NYC Mayor Bloomberg's soda ban bolstered by study on obesity. *Washington Times Online.* Retrieved from http//www.washingtontimes.com/news/2013/jun/mayor-bloomberg-soda-ban-bolstered-study-obese/

Cipiriano, M., Gruca, T. S. (2015). The power of priors: How confirmation bias impacts market prices. *The Journal of Prediction Markets,* November, 2015. DOI:10.5750/jpm.v8i3.974

Clancy, C. M., Glied, S. A., & Lurie, N. (2012). From research to health impact. *Health Services Research, 47*(1/2), 337–343.

Conner, R., & Jordan, P. J. (2009). Never being able to say you're sorry: Barriers to apology by leaders in group conflicts. *Law and Contemporary Problems, 72*(2), 233–260.

Delahunty, R. J. (2011). The Obama administration's decisions to enforce, but not defend, DOMA. *Northwestern Law Review, 106,* 69–76.

Delahunty, R. J.,& Yoo, J. C. (2013). Dream on: The Obama administration's non-enforcement of immigration laws, the DREAM act and the Take Care Clause. *Texas Law Review, 91,* 781–857.

Easton, D. (1965). *A framework for political analysis.* Englewood Cliffs, NJ: Prentice Hall.

Faricy, C. (2011). The politics of social policies in America: The causes and effects of indirect versus direct social spending. *The Journal of Politics, 73*(1), 74–83.

Feinman. R. D. (2005). Wealth Distribution. Retrieved from http//www.robertsfeinman.com/society/wealth_distribution

Gattuso, J., & Katz, D. (2016). Red tape rising 2016: Obama regs top $100 billion annually. *Government Regulations Report*. Retrieved from www.heritage.org/government-regulation

Grabarsky, T. (2013). Conflicting federal and state Medical marijuana policies: A threat to cooperative federalism. *West Virginia Law Review, 116*, 2–31.

Halterman, K. (2013). "Common core" ... coming to a school near you ... Educate yourself now. Saturday Morning Line. Retrieved from http//www. Smillibertyroad.com/common-core-coming-to-a-school-near-you-educate-yourself-now/

Hanekom, S. (1987). *Public policy: Framework and instrument for action*. Braanfontein, Johannesburg: Macmillan.

Heckman, J. J., & Masterov, D. V. (2009). The productivity argument for investing in young children. Working Paper 5, Invest in Kids Working Group, Committee for Economic Development. Retrieved from http//www.readynation.org/doc/ivk/report_ivk_heckman_2004pdf/

Hodge, S. (2014). Official statistics on inequality, the top 1% and redistribution. Tax foundation. Retrieved from http//www.taxfoundation.org/article/official-statistics-inequality-top-1and-redistribution

Hojnacki, M., Kimball, D. C., Baumgartner, F. R., Berry, J. M., & Leech, B. L. (2012). Studying organizational advocacy and influence: Reexamining interest group research. *Annual Review of Political Science, 15*(9), 1–21.

Jensen, J. M., & Fraser, M. W. (2015). A risk and resiliency framework for reducing for child, Youth and family policy. Retrieved from https://ncfy.acf.hhs.gov/sites/default/files/docs/21065-A_Risk_and_Resilience.pdf

Jessica's Law Now. (n.d.). Retrieved from http//www.jessicaslawnow.wordpress.com/about-jessicas-law/

Jones, B. D., & Baumgartner, R. F. (2005). A model of choice for public policy. *Journal of Public Administration, Research, and Theory, 15*(3), 325–351.

Knill, C., & Tosun, J. (2012). *Public policy: A new introduction*. United Kingdom: Palgrave.

Knill, C., & Tosun, J. (2008). Policy making. In D. Caramani (Ed.), *Comparative politics* (pp. 495–519). Oxford, UK: Oxford University Press.

Lindblom, C. (1959). The science of "muddling through," *Public Administration Review 19*(2), 79–88.

Lunenburg, F. C. (2010). The decision making process. *National Forum of Educational Administration and Supervision Journal, 27*(4), 1–12.

Mackie, C. (2009). *Intangible assets: Measuring and enhancing their contribution to corporate value and economic growth.* Washington, DC: The National Academic Press.

MADD. (n.d.). Mothers Against Drunk Driving. Retrieved from http//www.madd.org/

McCain, R. A. (2009). *Game theory and public policy*. Northampton, MA: Edward Elgar.

Megan's Law Now. (n.d.). State of California, Department of Justice, Office of Attorney General. Retrieved from http//www.meganslaw.ca.gov/

Nash, J. F. (1950). Equilibrium points in n-person games. *Proceedings of the National Academy of Science 36*(1), 48–49.

Netnewscheck (2013). USPS decides not to cut Saturday mail. Retrieved from http//www.netnewscheck.com/articles/25513/usps-decides-not-to-cut-Saturday-mail/

Neumann, J., & Morgenstern, O. (1953). *Theory of games and economics behavior*. Princeton, NJ: University of Princeton Press.

Newport, F. (2011). Americans strongly desire that political parties work together. *Gallop politics* January 19, 2011. Retrieved from http://www.gallup.com/poll/145679/americans-strongly-desire-political-leaders-work-together.aspx

Oberlander, J. (2010). Long time coming: Why health reform finally passed. *Health Affairs, 29*(6), 1112–1116. doi: 101377/hlthaff.2010.0447

Padgett, J. F. (1980). Managing garbage can hierarchies. *Administrative Science Quarterly 25*(4), 583–604.

Page, B. I., & Shapiro, R. Y. (2010). *Fifty years of trends in Americans' policy preferences*. Chicago, IL: University of Chicago Press.

Peters, B. G. (2012). *American public policy: Promises and performance*. Los Angeles, CA: Sage.

Rasmusen, E. (2007). *Games and Information: An introduction to game theory*. Carlton, Australia: Blackwell.

Riegel, K. (1976). *Psychology of history and development*. New York, NY: Plenum.

Sabatier, P. A., & Weible, C. M. (2014). *Theories of the policy process*. Boulder, CO: Westview.

Safe Schools, Healthy Students. (2004). Risk and Resilience 101, National Center Brief. Retrieved from http://www.promoteprevent.org/sites/www.promoteprevent.org/files/resources/Risk%20and%20Resilience.pdf

Saks, M. (2012). What do polls really tell us about the public's view of the affordable care act? Health Affairs Blog. Retrieved from http//www/healthaffairs.org/blog/2012/09/21/what-do-polls-really-tell-us-about-the-public-view-of-the-affordable-care-act/

Schofield, P. (2006). *Utility and democracy: The political thought of Jeremy Bentham*. Oxford, UK: Oxford University Press.

Smith, A. (1776/1977). *An inquiry into the nature and causes of the wealth of nations*. Chicago, IL: University of Chicago Press.

Smith, K.B., & Larimer, C.W. (2017). *The public policy theory primer* (3rd ed.). Boulder, CO: Westview.

Spalding, M. (2012). Why the U.S. has a culture of dependency. CNN. Retrieved from http://www.cnn.com/2012/09/21/opinion/spalding-welfare-state-dependency/index.html

State Vote. (n.d.). Same-sex marriage and domestic partnership on ballot. National Conference of State Legislatures (NCSL). Retrieved from http://www.ncsl.org/research/elections-and-campaigns/same-sex-marriage-on-the-ballots/

Teitler, J., Reichman, N., Nepomnyaschy, L., & Garfinkel, I. (2009). Effects of welfare participation on marriage. *Journal of Marriage and the Family, 71*(4), 878–891.

Theodoulou, S. Z., & Cahn, M. A. (2012). *Public policy: The essential reading*. Englewood Cliffs, NJ: Prentice Hall.

Umberson, D., & Montez, J.M. (2010). Social relationships and health: A flashpoint for health policy. *Journal of Health and Social Behavior, 51*(suppl), s54–s66.

Woll, P. (1974). *Public policy*. Cambridge, MA: Winthrop.

Zigler, E., & Hall, N. (1999). *Child development and social policy*. New York, NY: McGraw-Hill.

CREDITS

Social Policy and Children

SOCIAL POLICY AND CHILDREN

Since 1996, the Federal Interagency Forum on Child and Family Statistics released an annual summary of the current well-being of children based on the following categories: "Family and Social Environment, Economic Circumstances, Health Care, Physical Environment and Safety, Behavior, Education, and Health" (Wallman, 2012, para. 4). These areas of well-being are reviewed, because they display a profile of all aspects of children's lives. The annual report for 2017 reveals that the well-being of many children is still an area of concern, but some positive news was reflected in education with an increase in standardized scores, and more high school graduates are attending college with the percentage at 69% in 2015. In regard to poverty, the American family had been in economic decline for the decades 2001–2011, but since 2011, there has been a decrease of children in poverty from 22% to 20% in 2015. In terms of health, children's blood lead content declined from 26% in 1988–1994 to 1% in 2011–2015. More children are covered with health insurance dropping from 14% in 1993 to 5% in 2015 (Childstats.gov, 2017). The National Child Well-Being Index (CWI) 2015 Report released annually by the Foundation for Child Development (FCD) compared recent years to a base year of 1975 concluded that the well-being of children has oscillated between being higher and lower than the base year but, in 2013, was slightly higher (Land, 2014).

Demographics alone create a picture of concern for American children. The overall number of children in the U.S. has increased, but the number of children compared to adults has decreased. The growth in the number of children is largely due to the growth of the Hispanic population. Children, as is the overall population, are much more diverse today than in the past. For example, in 1990, the White non-Hispanic share of the total child population was about 70%; in 2016, that share had dropped to about 51% (Childstats.gov, 2017). The future projection is that the White non-Hispanic percent of the total child population will continue to drop until 2050 to about 39%. These changing demographics will necessitate changes in social policy affecting children.

FAMILY STRUCTURE

The family structure and social environment that children are reared in can have a major impact on the short- and long-term effects on their well-being. The **home environment,** which includes the type and quality of parenting, the presence of both parents in the home, the immigration status of parents, and the language spoken in the home, are all factors in the well-being of children (Graham, Gosling, & Travis, 2015; Kennedy & Bumpass, 2008). These factors are important, because they are directly related to the amount and quality of resources available to the family.

One of the major risk factors in families for poor children's well-being is the **female-headed single-parent family**. This family structure has been increasing for the past several decades, and the number of children born to unwed mothers compared to married mothers has almost doubled since the 1980s (Kennedy & Bumpass, 2008). According the National Center for Health Statistics (2011), as many as 40% of children are currently born out of wedlock. Approximately 60% of the out of wedlock births are to mothers in their 20s, and only about 20% are to teenage mothers, which has dropped in recent years.

While births to unwed mothers have increased overall, unmarried women with a college degree have the lowest incidences (Camarota, 2015). On the other hand, women with little education past high school have the highest rates of unwed pregnancies and, concomitantly, the highest rates of poverty. In fact, according to Camarota's report, women in poverty who have children out of wedlock have poverty rates that are approximately five times the poverty rate of women with college degrees.

Marriage rates have decreased significantly since 1960 when approximately 94% of adult persons married compared to 59% were married in 2010. The marriage rate for women in 2010 was 32.1 per 1,000 women and has remained stable since 2010 with a rate of 32.4 per 1,000 women in 2015. What this means is that the percentage of children born to two-parent families also took a nosedive during this same period (Figure 3.2). Because marriage rates declined and the number of children born to unwed mothers increased, many more children are at risk for living in poverty with reduced resources. In 2010, the out-of-wedlock births to single mothers was at 40.8% and has remained relatively the same through 2015 with a rate of 40.4 (Camarota, 2017). Consequently, there is more reliance on government to play the role that two-parent families provided in the past, which can be easily documented by a quick glance at Figure 3.2. The decrease in children born to two parents in marriage escalated after the Johnson Administration's War on Poverty initiative in the 1960s. Researchers have found that children born out of wedlock have greater social/emotional problems and lower cognitive scores (Bzostek & Beck, 2008: Collins, Rankin, & David, 2016). Children who live with both biological parents who share in child care and economic resources for the family would be expected to have better outcomes than children living in a single-parent family (Cherlin, 2004).

From the above discussion, it could be concluded that the structure of single-parent families leads to the decreased well-being of children. However, the systems/dialectical approach would necessitate that an opposing view be evaluated. An opposing view might begin by asking a simple question: Is there a difference in being raised in an unmarried single-parent family and being raised in a family experiencing trauma related to family instability? In other words, does family structure at birth account for the higher risk factors in these families or do significant events post-birth account for them? If the unit of analysis is family changes over time rather than the structure of the family the child is born into, does a different picture emerge for child outcomes? If stability is found as a factor, the structure of the intact family may be less significant than stability of the family and, therefore, the underlying factors for the differences noted (Waldfogel, Brooks-Gunn, & Craigie, 2010).

Structure and **stability** have a close relationship in that changes in structure are often the prelude for changes in stability (Magnuson & Berger, 2009). Some studies addressing the factors of single-parent status and stability have found that children in single-parent families have poorer well-being than children in intact families irrespective of stability (Carlson & Corcoran, 2001). In addition, being unmarried at the time of the birth of children has been related to greater instability and less well-being in children than being a single-parent family following divorce (Craigie, Brooks-Gunn, & Waldfogel, 2012); Fomby and Cherlin, 2007). Recent research demonstrates that stability is a strong factor, but even when distinguishing between stable and unstable single-parent homes, the well-being of children in intact two-parent families was better.

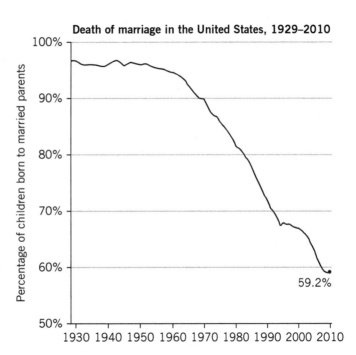

FIGURE 3.1 Percentage of children born to married couples.
Source: U.S. Government, U.S. Census Bureau, and National Center for Health Statistics.

Moreover, the well-being of children born to single-parent mothers, stable or unstable, is worse than that of children born in intact families (Waldfogel, Brooks-Gunn, & Craigie, 2010).

One concern in the stability of female single-parent families is the involvement of the biological father (Craigie, Brooks-Dunn, & Waldfogel, 2012). In many single-parent families, the father no longer has a relationship with the mother. Non-resident fathers may have a greater role in outcomes with children than generally thought, because they reduce some of the stress experienced by the mother, which helps to improve her parenting behaviors. On the other hand, non-resident fathers who have no relationship with the mother, or who have a negative relationship, may increase the stress of the mother and decrease her parenting quality. Fathers who live with the single mothers have key roles in the well-being of their children (Waldfogel, Brooks-Gunn, & Craigie, 2010).

A compelling argument for the differences in intact versus single-parent families is that single-parent families have limited resources, a sizable number of which are below the poverty level (Craigie, Brooks-Dunn, & Waldfogel, 2012: McLanahan, Knab, & Meadows, 2009). The argument from this position would be that the financial limitations of these families, in addition to increasing stress, reduce their ability to openly participate in society due to their poverty status. If the systems/dialectical perspective is applied to this argument, an opposite point of view is illustrated by a recent report of the Congressional Research Service (U.S. Committee on the Budget, 2012). The total spending per household below the poverty line is $168 a day compared to $137 a day for the average household income for those above the poverty line in the U.S. Another way of looking at this is to convert various benefits to cash payments, which would be equivalent to approximately $30.60 an hour for a 40-hour work week. The average household income of families above the poverty line is approximately $25 an hour. Federal taxes drop that to between $21 and $23, and state and local taxes drop it even further. Since welfare benefits are not taxed, households below the poverty line have greater financial resources than the average income households (see Figure 3.3). Some could argue that economic disadvantage may not be the prevailing culprit in why single-parent families have more problems than intact families. Other factors, such as the quality of the parent-child relationship, parenting skills, and other intangible resources caused by a lack of education may account for these problems.

Kessler (2013) disagrees with the conclusion that the U.S. spends $168 dollars a day on families on welfare, and that this figure, computed for a year, is roughly $60,000, or $10,000 more than the average household income. According to Kessler, about half of the spending goes to Medicaid, but the elderly take up most of that. In addition, he claims that many persons above the poverty line receive some of the funds that would make up the $168 dollars a day, and this is not included in the calculations. Since many persons slightly above the poverty level receive benefits, the means-tested approach does not give an accurate picture. Kessler believes that a more accurate picture might be to use the divider of the lower-third income, which would give a more realistic figure of about $36,000 dollars a year.

In addition to financial resources, family members invest personally through emotional support and time spent with children. Single-parent families generally have less of these resources than other families (Craigie, Brooks-Dunn, & Waldfogel, 2012). Typically single-parent mothers who work lack time and energy for family responsibilities. Consequently, even routines may be lacking, as most activities are accomplished in a hit-or-miss fashion (Sigle-Rushton & McLanahan, 2002). While cohabiting couples have two persons present in the home, the roles they play tend to diverge from the intact two-parent households. The cohabiting fathers and "**social fathers**," live-in boyfriends of the mothers, are generally less emotionally supportive and spend little time in parenting (Goldberg, Tan, & Thorsen, 2009).

In single-parent homes in which the father is non-residential, there is typically limited contact. What may start as frequent involvement tends to decrease with time (Carlson & McLanahan, 2009). According to Carlson and McLanahan, research generally concludes that the father's and social father's involvement is an important variable in well-being outcomes for children. Overall, children have less behavioral and emotional problems and display greater social and cognitive development when the father is involved with them whether residential, non-residential, or social. It is estimated that a **non-cohabiting unmarried mother** will be unlikely to ever have a cohabiting partner for her child(ren).

Some efforts have been made to increase marriage and improve relationship skills among non-married and/or cohabiting couples. The question remains as to whether improving relationship quality will also increase relationship stability. The **Building Strong Families Project** (Wood, McConnell, Moore, Clarkwest, & Hsueh, 2010; Wood, Moore, Clarkwest, & Killewald, 2014) resulted in some positive relationship skills among African American couples, although stability in marriage was not one of the findings. To date, there has been little study of relationship-enhancing programs that have often been used for married couples applied to non-married or cohabiting couples (Reinhold, 2010). These programs need to be altered to fit the needs of **fragile families,** because many of these families are poor and lack sufficient education. Seen in its totality, non-married cohabiting families are both a cause and an outcome of family instability (Cowan, Cowan, & Knox, 2010). Non-married cohabiting families frequently lead to families comprised of single mothers and their children in which the father is less involved resulting in the mother seeking another partner, which causes greater stress and instability (Guzzo, 2014).

Research indicates that persons who cohabit tend to have higher risks for relationship instability and disruption, especially for non-Hispanic White women (Reinhold, 2010). It is believed by some researchers that the risk factors for cohabiting couples may decrease as cohabiting becomes more normative in the future (Reinhold, 2010). A recent assessment research study on this question conducted by Reinhold shows that the link between cohabitation and marital instability does not exist for recent marriages. He postulates that since cohabiting has become more common and accepted by the general society and is now possibly a cultural norm, the self-selection of high-risk persons who cohabit has decreased. Consequently, the link between cohabiting and instability has decreased.

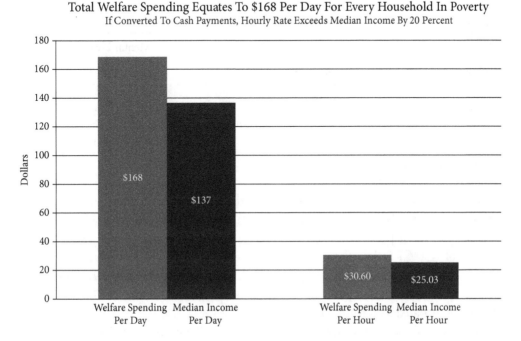

FIGURE 3.2 Welfare spending equals $168 per day for families in poverty

CHILD HEALTH AND SAFETY

Another major dimension of child well-being is child health and safety, which includes infectious diseases, environmental pollutants, adequate housing, and victimization of crimes (Federal Interagency Forum on Child and Family Studies, 2012). Environmental pollutions, such as air quality, are related to childhood conditions, including **aggravated asthma** (U.S. EPA, 2008). A recent report reveals that 67% of children around the world breathe air that consists of pollutants below air quality standards (Federal Interagency Forum on Child and Family Statistics, 2012).

Perhaps one of the most serious air quality pollutants for children is **secondhand smoke** (Milanzi et al., 2017). The concentration of carbon monoxide (CO) from secondhand smoke indoors can easily exceed an acceptable level of outdoor concentration. **Sidestream smoke**, air that is saturated with tobacco smoke, and secondhand smoke, breathing air that is exhaled from a smoker, are linked to decreased lung growth in children, which may affect long-term health problems into adulthood. While both forms of smoke are damaging, sidestream smoke tends to have more toxins than secondhand smoke. These toxins are mixed into secondhand smoke and depend on a number of variables, such as the distance the smoke travels and the absorption rate into materials, such as curtains, carpets, and furniture. Studies have shown that this can lead to premature death in children, such as **sudden infant death syndrome (SIDS)**, respiratory syndromes, and even ear infections (U.S. Department of Health and Human Services, 2013). While exposure is still an ongoing health problem for children, there has been a reduction in exposure, with the exception of those in some demographic categories.

TABLE 3.1 The building family skills model

INDIVIDUAL SUPPORT FROM FAMILY COORDINATORS	GROUP SESSIONS AND RELATIONSHIP SKILLS	ASSESSMENT AND REFERRAL TO SUPPORT SERVICES
Encouragement for Participant	Communication Management	Education
Reinforcement of Skills	Intimacy and Trust	Mental Health
Ongoing Emotional Support	Considering Marriage	Child Care
	Transition to Parenthood	Housing
	Parent-Infant Relationship	Legal Services Employment

(Adapted from Cowan, Cowan,& Knox, 2010)

Another health concern for the well-being of children is exposure to lead, which causes an elevation of **blood lead level (BLL)** (Rubio-Andrade, Valdez-Perezgasga, Alonzo, Rosado, Cebrian, & Garcia-Vargas, 2017). At present, the generally accepted BLL for children is set by the Center for Disease Control (CDC) at less than 10 ug/d; however, no level is definitive in establishing the risk for harm or set as a standard for identifying children for intervention. The greatest source of exposure to lead is in lead-based paint found in older homes built before 1978. After 1978, builders of new homes eliminated lead from paint.

Research has established a number of adverse health problems associated with high lead levels in children (Bellinger, 2008). One of the major areas of research is in the effects of lead on learning, intelligence quotient (IQ), and cognitive functioning. Research across various domains has concluded that a high BLL is associated with lower IQ, both in performance and verbal scores. In a recent study, children with an average BLL of 1.9 were compared to a sample of children with BLLs that averaged greater than 10; researchers found that children with the higher BLLs scored lower on the **Wide Range Achievement Test (WRAT)** and the **WISC-R** (Lanphear, Dietrich, Auinger, & Cox, 2000). Researchers have also found that other neurological disorders occur with exposure to lead, such as attention deficit hyperactivity disorder (ADHD) and behavioral disorders (Bellinger, 2008). Even low levels of exposure to lead appear to have detrimental effects on neurological functioning.

Because 98% of all U.S. children have levels lower than 10 BLL, some researchers have addressed the effects on this group of children. A recent study of 534 children from ages 6–10 in Boston, Massachusetts, and Farmington, Maine, comprised the New England Children's Amalgam Trial (NECAT) (Surkan et al., 2007). Controlling for intervening variables, such as race, socioeconomic status (SES), and parent's IQ, the study found that children with BLLs of 5–10 had significantly lower scores on IQ tests than children with BLLs of 1–2. In addition, children with the higher BLLs scored significantly lower on reading and math than children with lower BLLs. Furthermore, the study found that the **Wechsler Individual Achievement Test (WIAT)** showed marked differences due to lead exposure.

Children's health is also affected by environment and housing (Solari & Mare, 2012). For example, approximately 45% of children live in housing that is cramped or where the cost of the housing creates undue stress. Approximately 37% of families with dependent children have significant housing issues (Breysse et al., 2004). Children who live in crowded households fare poorer in regards to academic, social, and psychological adjustment.

VICTIMS OF CRIME

The rate at which children are victims of crimes has dropped over the past several decades to a low of seven per 1,000 in 2010 (Bureau of Justice Statistics, 2010). This statistic is especially encouraging for males ages 12 to 17 where the crime victimization rate in 2010 was nine per 1,000 compared to 15 per 1,000 in 2009. A national telephone survey of 4,549 children ages zero to 17 by Finkelhor, Turner, Ormrod, and Hamby (2009), however, paints a bleak picture of childhood crime victimization. For example, approximately 60% of the sample were either victimized or viewed victimization of another person. In addition, almost 10% had been injured from a direct experience and about 11% witnessed five or more victimizations. They concluded that the full portrait of victimization of children is not recognized, and there exists a need for further investigation and identification of children who have directly or indirectly been exposed to victimization.

Some recent research adds important new information of **childhood victimization**. According to a recent article, one of the main problems in victimization of children is that **primary care practitioners (PCP)** do not document or follow-up on victimization, thus not only minimizing the effects but also limiting treatment options (Sigel & Harpin, 2013). Another study conducted by the Office of Juvenile Justice and Delinquency Prevention (OJJDP) found that 15% of children ages zero to six who were not identified as being victimized through the state protective services programs and almost 50% of parents showed clinical signs of distress. The authors concluded that information from these families is valuable for fully understanding victimization of children and should be made more available to policymakers. Finally, a national survey of a sample of children under two years of age revealed that about 31% had experienced direct or indirect victimization (Turner, Finkelhor, Ormrod, & Hamby, 2010). The highest rate for direct assault of infants was from older siblings (15.4%) and about 10% had witnessed victimization during the past year. The researchers called for more focused attention on infant victimization and greater intervention strategies. A study by Finkelhor, Turner, Shattuck, and Hamby in 2015 found that for children under the age of 18, two-thirds had experienced some form of violence against them in the past year.

CHILDREN'S MENTAL HEALTH

Mental health disorders among children is an underdeveloped phenomenon that has been largely ignored until in recent years (Collins et al., 2011). These disorders include some common diagnoses, such as autism, Attention-Deficit/Hyperactivity Disorder (ADHD), behavior disorders and mood disorders, to name a few. **Childhood schizophrenia** and other psychotic disorders are less common and have been largely undiagnosed until recently. Children with mental disorders typically have problems learning and responding appropriately to various emotional input. The key to treating childhood mental illness is early detection and treatment (National Research Council and Institute of Medicine, 2009). Without early detection and treatment, many of the conditions will continue throughout the lifespan. The cost of treating these disorders over the lifespan are enormous when not detected early, or treatment is delayed until adulthood. Current estimates are that 20% of children carry a mental disorder diagnosis in the U.S., and close to 250 billion dollars a year is spent on treatment (National Research Council and Institute of Medicine, 2009).

The CDC (2013) recently released a report on the mental illness of U.S. children describing the type and occurrences of disorders and bringing public attention to the problem, which has been missing in the past. The report found that ADHD comprises the greatest number of cases of depression, conduct disorders, and anxiety disorders, following in that order. Autism tends to affect younger children in greater numbers while other diagnoses tend to increase with age. Furthermore, the report stated that boys are more likely than girls to be diagnosed with most of the disorders, including behavior problems, ADHD, suicide, and autism, while girls have higher frequencies of alcohol use and depressive disorders.

Recent studies indicate that insurance usage for childhood mental disorders has increased in recent years (Health Care Cost Institute, 2012). There is not only an increase of hospitalizations but also of prescription drug usage, especially among teenagers. In 2010, a report stated that the most common diagnosis for hospitalization was mood disorder, and since the late 1990s, hospitalization rates for children have increased 80% (Pfuntner, Weir, & Stocks, 2013).

Attention Deficit Hyperactivity Disorder (ADHD)

Researchers have found that **ADHD** and **Oppositional Defiant Disorder (ODD)** tend to be linked together (Visser et al., 2013). In ADHD, functioning is impaired because of lack of attention, hyperactivity and impulsivity, or a combination. Typically, academic, social, and psychological problems are associated with this disorder. Other behavioral anomalies associated with ADHD include alcohol or substance use and abuse and accidents (American Psychiatric Association, 2000). The current estimate for the number of children from ages three to 17 who have, at some point in time, had a diagnosis of ADHD is approximately eight % (Visser et al., 2013). Data collection for this diagnosis is interesting, because the highest number of cases are for children with health insurance and children not below the poverty line. The highest incidences were White non-Hispanic and the lowest were Hispanic and Asian. In addition, the South has higher incidences, while the Western states had the lowest number of cases. Generally, education of parents was not a factor in the diagnosis.

Oppositional Defiant Disorder (ODD) and Conduct Disorder

Children with ODD are characterized with behavior disorders, are non-compliant with parental requests, and engage in behaviors that are oppositional to parents, teachers, and others in authority. They react in anger to requests for compliance and may be physically confrontational with others (Biederman et al., 2008). These aggressive behaviors must have occurred for more than 12 months to meet the criteria for a diagnosis in the DSM-IV. There is a high probability that this disorder will continue into adulthood in the form of antisocial personality disorder or a mood disorder and be a lifespan condition.

While this disorder affects both boys and girls, boys are about twice as likely to be diagnosed as girls. The number of cases tends to increase with age, affecting 4.7% of adolescents ages 12–17 (Merikangas, He, Brody, Fisher, Bourdon, & Koretz, 2010a). More cases are reported for parents with low education, but health insurance coverage is not a factor. There is no difference in the number of cases by regions in the U.S., but Black children are diagnosed more often than any other racial or ethnic group.

Depression

Depression is a common childhood mental condition that affects social, academic, and adjustment in daily living (Merikangas et al., 2010b). While in the past depression was not believed to affect young children, it is now known that depression can affect children as young as two years of age. Depression is sometimes undiagnosed in children, because parents and others assume that changes in moods or behaviors are just part of the maturation process. Common symptoms include loss of interest in daily activities and feelings of sadness and hopelessness. For younger children, symptoms may be masked and include angry acting-out episodes that are mislabeled as misbehaving. Current estimates are that almost 4% of children from ages three to 17 have received a diagnosis of depression. Children in low-income homes with poorly educated parents are more likely to receive this diagnosis. According to Merikangas et al. (2010b), it is more likely to be diagnosed in adolescence, and girls are more likely than boys to be depressed in their teenage years. Curiously, preadolescent boys tend to be more depressed than preadolescent girls.

Researchers have investigated whether infants can have clinical depression or if their symptoms mainly reflect momentary changes in mood. Most of the developmental research concludes that infants are emotionally reactive to the primary caregiver, and this reaction is noticed as early as three months (Luby, Belden, Pautsch, Si, & Spitznagel, 2009). Luby and associates linked emotions of guilt and shame, generally thought to be complex emotions related to depression in older children and adults, to young children. Since most parents, teachers, and other adults interacting with children may fail to recognize symptoms of depression in young children, there is a need for education and information regarding these specific symptoms.

Suicide is generally linked with depression for adolescents and is the second most common cause of death for the age group 12–17 (Luby et al., 2009). Other risk factors include a history of mental and emotional illness, substance abuse, and reluctance to seek help. The most common methods of suicide are the use of guns, hanging oneself, or asphyxiation. Suicide ranks highest among non-Hispanic Whites and Hispanics, and lowest among Black children. The overall risk is four per 1,000 with teenage girls more likely than teenage boys.

Treatment for depression in children has not taken a clear path (Luby et al., 2009). Applying treatment models used primarily for older adolescents and investigating new innovative models are recommended as plausible avenues for treatment. Generally, some treatments for older adolescents would not be the best approach for young children. For example, the medication fluoxetine, which is effective for adolescents, produces different effects on the brains of young children and is not recommended as an effective treatment. Medications for young children are recommended only in severe cases because little is known about how they affect the developing brain. In addition, all medications have side-effects that can have long-term consequences, which have not been adequately analyzed for children. A recent new therapy that focuses on interaction with the parents and aims to improve emotional development and regulation in children appears to have success in outcome studies (Zisser & Eyberg, in press as cited in Luby et al., 2009). The purpose of the therapy is to improve emotional experiences and enhance the expression of positive emotions.

TABLE 3.2 Children and Mental Disorders

DIAGNOSTIC CATEGORY	GENDER AND AGE	SYMPTOMS AND TREATMENT
Attention Deficit Hyperactivity Disorder (ADHD)	8% of children, more boys than girls	Lack of attention, hyperactivity and impulsivity Medication—Ritalin
Oppositional Defiant Disorder (ODD)	Boys 2X more affected than girls 4.7% of adolescents ages 12–17	Non-compliant and oppositional to parents, teachers and others in authority Family therapy and Behavioral modification
Depression	4% of children from ages 3–17	Loss of interest in daily activities and feelings of sadness and hopelessness. Symptoms masked in younger ages Fluoxetine helps adolescents,
Anxiety	3-5% of children. Affects White non-Hispanic males living in poverty in greater numbers	Traumatic experiences or phobias Play therapy, Cognitive behavior therapy

DIAGNOSTIC CATEGORY	GENDER AND AGE	SYMPTOMS AND TREATMENT
Alcohol and Substance Abuse	1.7 million adolescents 12–17 years of age have a substance abuse problem Rates higher for girls than boys and for White non-Hispanic adolescents	Poor school performance, sexual promiscuity, social maladjustment, and mental and emotional problems Family therapy
Tourette Syndrome and Tic Disorders	20% of children estimated to have some form of tic disorder	Uncontrollable jerky movements or unrelated vocal expressions Cognitive behavioral therapy

Anxiety Disorders

The information on the prevalence of **anxiety disorders** comes from surveys of parents. In mild forms, anxiety may affect the child only slightly, but anxiety as the result of trauma may negatively affect the child's daily functioning. Estimates are that between 3–5% of children have diagnoses of anxiety, which may also include phobias (Merikangaset et al., 2010a). Male non-Hispanic children living in low-income families were more likely to suffer from anxiety disorders than other children.

Anxiety in children is a normal part of development, since children are beset with many fears and phobias as they develop (Merikangas, 2010a). Young children less than two years of age experience separation anxiety, and children a little older can experience anxiety over images and sounds that scare them. Since many fears and anxieties are part of development and do not persist, there is a difference between them and more severe or pathological anxieties. Younger children lack the ability to explicitly communicate their fears, which can further limit correct distinction in the type and severity of the fear or anxiety they are experiencing. Proper diagnosis requires thorough knowledge of child development and of the current situation affecting the child (Beesdo, Knappe, & Pine, 2009). Parents' reaction to the child's anxiety may also be an underlying issue in the etiology of this disorder. A number of treatment modalities have been used with anxiety disorders in children, including play therapy and cognitive behavioral therapy.

Alcohol and Substance Use

Children's use of alcohol and other drugs pose financial, social, and emotional problems for families (Kessler et al., 2012). Among adolescents, the use of marijuana and other illegal drugs is related to poor school performance, sexual promiscuity, social maladjustment, and mental and emotional problems. Research generally finds a link between early drug use and later use throughout the lifespan (Substance Abuse and Mental Health Services Administration, 2012). Recent surveys of adolescents indicate that approximately 1.7 million adolescents 12–17 years of age have a substance abuse problem (Kessler et al., 2012), but this figure represents a decreasing trend in substance use. Rates for alcohol use were higher for girls than boys and for White non-Hispanic adolescents than for other ethnic groups. In addition, adolescents without health insurance were more likely to have alcohol-related problems.

Of concern among researchers is the age of first marijuana and alcohol drug use (U.S. Department of Health and Human Services, 2011). Early use is related to both continued use into adulthood and use throughout the lifespan, but also to the use of hard drugs, such as cocaine and heroin. For example, in 2010, children who initiated drug use younger than age 14 had a much higher rate of drug dependence than those who started using drugs after age 18 (U.S. Department of Health and Human Services, 2011). Children 12 years of age and younger are more likely to use inhalants than alcohol or marijuana.

Tourette Syndrome and Tic Disorders

Tourette syndrome and tic disorders in children can be expressed through movement or vocally, such as through uncontrollable jerky movements or unrelated vocal expressions (Bitsko et al., 2012). Tourette syndrome always includes tic disorder, but not vice versa. In children, the onset is usually between the ages of three and 10. As noted in Bitsko et al. (2012), researchers have found that as many as 20% of children may have some form of a tic disorder during childhood. The cause is unknown, but researchers believe a genetic anomaly during early development is the best explanation. Researchers have linked Tourette syndrome to ADHD, ODD, or obsessive/compulsive disorder, which may be the main cause of academic and social problems. Some typical tics include blinking the eyes and meaningless repetitive hand and arm movements. While the tic behavior can be very annoying to parents and others, the child is not able to consciously control it. Because of the lack of control over the tic, treatment modalities are limited. Behavioral techniques for reducing habitual behavior and medication have been the most effective treatments.

In sum, the prevalence of all categories of childhood mental illness has been increasing in recent years (Collins et al., 2011). It is unclear what has caused the increase, but general awareness and identification of childhood mental illness has also increased over the same period and is likely related. A recent report shows that from 1987 to 2007 there was a 35 times increase in the number of Supplemental Security Income (SSI) recipients for a mental disability, which far outdistanced typical disabilities, such as Down Syndrome (Deaton, 2007). It is estimated that the annual cost of mental illness in children is approximately 245 million dollars.

CHILD CARE

Child care in the past was largely the responsibility of the family and primarily fell to the mother (Raley, Bianchi, & Wang, 2012). Since the end of World War II, however, a trend began that has resulted in drastic changes for stay-at-home mothers. After WWII, women tended to stay in the work force, rather than return to the home. With the rise in feminist writings in the 1960s and the increase in women attending and graduating from college, the need for alternate child care became a huge concern. Child care in current usage has come to mean non-parental care because of the large number of mothers with small children who work. In addition, the number of children born to single mothers has greatly increased the need for non-parental child care because of the lack of a support system for child care. Research has focused on how child care is related to outcomes in children, particularly as it relates to insurance against early emotional and psychological risks (Crosnoe, Prickett, Smith, & Cavanagh, 2014).

Child care is important, because it represents a complex arrangement between the child, family, and extra-familial resources for the optimal development of children (Crosnoe et al., 2014). Settings for child care include center-based care, in-home child care by a nanny or au pair, a family child care home in which only a few children are cared for, and child care provided by a relative. In-home arrangements are the most popular for children under the age of one, but about 12% of mothers use child care centers. Infants younger than one year of age are also more likely to be cared for by family child care homes.

Research on Child Care

Early research in the 1960s and 1970s took place in universities with mainly middle-class families or in government-supported programs, such as Head Start (Lamb, 1998). The focus in this early research was to determine if non-parental child care was damaging to the child's development. By the 1980s, researchers began to focus on **quality of care,** which included two components: **structure**, or measures related to the physical environment of the care, and **process**, which referred to the interactions between the child care providers and the child (Hungerford, Brownell, & Campbell, 2001). Researchers found that quality of child care was interlinked with variables external to the child care setting, namely the parent-child relationship and the home environment. In general, research in child care has been inconsistent, and simple main-effects conclusions do not address the complexity of co-variables for outcomes. Some of these co-variables include **child characteristics**; such as temperament and intelligence; **family characteristics**, such as composition, income, and whether the mother works; and **community and environmental** factors.

The most extensive research on the effects of child care on child development were performed in a study conducted by the National Institute of Child Health and Human Development (NICHD) Early Child Care Research Network (ECCRN). The study was longitudinal, cost more than $150,000,000, and began in 1991 with a sample of one-month-old infants (Belsky et al. and the NICHD Early Child Care Research Network, 2007). Studying 1,300 children at 10 sites, data were collected at four intervals: ages zero to three and when children were in first grade, sixth grade, and ninth grade (NICHD-ECCRN, 2003). The study raised some concerns about the overall quantity of time that a child spends in child care. The study found that the more time an infant spent in non-parental child care, the greater the likelihood for disobedience and behavioral problems at older ages. What makes this study compelling is that confounding variables, such as child and family characteristics, and child care variables, were controlled.

The purpose of the NICHD-ECCRN study was to pay attention to the multiple variables affecting child care from an ecological perspective. Findings were expected to shed light on how the complex web of influences interacted as the child developed. Findings from the study point to the importance and pivotal factor of quality of care over demographic variables such as family background. Quality of care was defined as the degree to which caregivers responded to the child's needs, were emotionally available, and used stimulating words and expressions as measured by direct observation. Recent studies have shown that quality of child care and amount of time that children spend in large groups are moderating factors in aggressive child behaviors (McCartney et al., 2010).

The NICHD findings lend further support to other research over the past 30 years that children benefit from high-quality child care when compared to low-quality care. On the other hand, the NICHD research further supports a steady stream of findings over the past three decades that child care early in life is associated with later aggressive and noncompliant behavior (Belsky, 1988). Subsequent researchers noted that Belsky's findings of a risk to attachment for infants in child care for more than 20 hours a week used the stranger test in a way that it was not meant to be used. Other criticism of Belsky's study was that family background variables were not controlled and, therefore, tainted the results. Notwithstanding the level of criticism against Belsky's research, other findings also support his conclusions that aggression is linked with the amount of time in child care (e.g. Cote, Borge, Geottroy, Rutter, & Trembley, 2008).

Findings from the NICHD-ECCYD (2003), which was designed specifically to address weaknesses in earlier research, affirmed Belsky's (1986, 1988) earlier findings that child care in center-based settings is associated with aggressive and externalizing behavior, even when family background and intervening variables are controlled. Although these findings may appear small, Belsky (2009) believes that they should not be dismissed; small effects are cumulative and, over time, have huge effects. Furthermore, children exposed to poor quality child care can affect other children by making them more aggressive and noncompliant (Dmitrieva, Steinberg, & Belsky, 2007). This conclusion that aggressive children influence other children to be aggressive is a neglected area of study.

Child Care and Attachment

One of the concerns about child care, as noted above, was the effects of child care on secure attachment. Following Belsky's (1986) original research and the criticism noted above, other researchers also found a difference in secure attachment with children and child care (Lamb, 1998). Some researchers argued that the difference in secure attachment between children in child care and those not in child care are explained by the avoidant behavior of mothers of children in child care (Egeland & Hiester, 1995). Consequently, the maternal avoidant behavior of children in child care is related to their greater independence. While this conclusion is an interesting assumption, research has not supported this argument. Other researchers have found that the rate of insecure attachment to mothers of children in child care does not significantly differ from the rate in a middle-class sample (Barton & Williams, 1993). This finding concluded that while there are differences in attachment, there is no overall significant difference in children in child care and those taken care of by mothers. The differences that are found may reflect family variables, since families that use child care select this option freely, as well as families that do not select child care. Since there is no randomization of assignments to child care or family care, the differences in attachment may be accounted for by family variables (Hungerford et al., 2001).

Other Concerns

Other concerns that researchers have addressed in relation to the effects of child care are the age of entry into child care, peer relationships, and cognitive development (Bates et al., 1994). The reason for concern over the entry age is the assumption that what occurs early has a profound effect on what occurs later. If children are distressed as infants, their later development will be affected. The idea is that there might be sleeper effects that would appear later. When confounding variables have been controlled, research on the age at entry shows that early entry into child care does have a negative effect on children's development, but the amount of variance accounted for was quite small (Bates et al., 1994).

Some researchers found that there is an association with child care and poor peer relationships (Bates et al., 1994). Some recent researchers found that children in child care exhibited more negative behavior toward their peers than children who were cared for at home (Dmitrieva et al., 2007). The researchers concluded that poor behavior among peers is contagious in that small negative effects can be multiplied. In an interesting study recently on peer relationships and quality of child care, Kim (2012) found that center-based child care is highly segregated and that quality is related to child outcomes. White non-Hispanic and Hispanic center-based care has the highest quality while other ethnic groups have the lowest quality. As a consequence, peer relationships reflect the overall quality of the child care. Researchers have found that approximately 10% of children experience poor relationships with peers in child care (see Boivin, 2005). While toddlers play with peers around objects, children three to five years old develop social interaction engaging in pretend play. These interactions form the basis for later mutual social play and interaction. Generally, by age four, preschoolers will identify some peers who are friends and some who are not friends. Children who are aggressive are not necessarily without friends and can even be popular; children tend to respond positively to other children who are assertive versus children who are shy or withdrawn. Children's problems with peers have received little attention in the literature, but no doubt, the environment and quality of the child care and the responsiveness of the caregivers are major factors.

PRESCHOOL FOR ALL

Researchers on child care and cognitive and language development were especially concerned with the quality of care from caregivers. Perhaps the best research conducted on IQ and preschoolers was the Abcedarian study (Ramey & Ramey, 1998). The research found that infants in low-income families who received high-quality child care scored higher on IQ measures that extended into grade school than a control group. As they moved through the grade school years, they were more likely to be successful in school when compared to the control group. More recent research underscores the relationship between enhanced quality teaching and better language development and cognitive development (Cote et al., 2012).

While there are consistent positive findings regarding high-quality child care programs and language and cognitive development in children, there is little known about the intensity of exposure as a variable for increased outcomes. This consideration is germane for the question of whether all children should participate in preschool for all. The other question is whether preschool should be targeted for specific populations that have been found to benefit from high-quality programs like the Abcedarian Project and the Perry Project. An **achievement gap** of about two months in scores on language cognitive development exists between White and Black children; Hispanic children are about three months behind at the start of kindergarten (Reardon, 2003). This same level of two months exists for preschool children when comparing different SES groups, but tends to widen as they matriculate through the school years.

The success of the above-mentioned projects raises the question that such programs might help reduce the gap between racial and economic groups. Center-based programs (with the exception of Head Start, which has mixed results) provide the best hope for improvement in children's cognitive development. Although children from poor backgrounds appear to benefit the most, researchers have also found that center-based programs produce better outcomes for middle-class children who attended prekindergarten (Freyer & Levitt, 2004). Research indicates that the earlier the intervention, that is, the earlier entering a preschool program, the better outcomes for poor children, but some researchers have found that this may not be the same for more affluent children above the poverty line (Duncan & Magnuson, 2013). For example, when a child in poverty enters preschool in infancy, the outcome is better language and cognitive development, but when a middle-class child enters preschool as an infant, the outcome may be detrimental.

In sum, from the research on child care, irrefutable outcomes emerge: disadvantaged children have better outcomes for language and cognitive development than more affluent children, small differences have been noted in attachment from long exposure to child care, and social and behavioral problems have been associated with center-based child care. Loeb, Bridges, Bassok, Fuller, and Rumberger (2005) found that the best age for a child to begin a preschool program was between two and three years of age. Children who began earlier than two had even lower average reading and cognitive scores than children who started at an older age. Loeb and associates also found that social and behavioral problems were much more pronounced for children who began child care at less than one year of age. Furthermore, low-income children tend to benefit in language and cognitive development the more time they spend in child care without additional increases in negative behavior, while more affluent children show no greater increase in language and cognitive development but do exhibit more negative social and behavioral problems. In addition, they found that the most optimal average length of time in child care for all children should be a half-day program. However, disadvantaged children benefit more from a full-day program, although no program will close the achievement gap.

To address the achievement gap in schools, the Obama administration proposed a sweeping plan for **preschool for all** that promised to improve language and cognitive skills and reduce the achievement gap (Weissberg, 2013). However, evaluation from other countries that had implemented preschool for all showed mainly negative effects. Baker, Gruber, and Milligan (2008) found that the preschool for all initiative in Quebec produced poor social, behavioral, and health outcomes in children, harsher parenting, lower parental health, and poorer parent/child relationships. This research suggests that the full impact of preschool programs must be addressed and not merely children's language and cognitive development.

Within the U.S., some states have provided preschool for all for at least a decade. The state of Georgia is one state that has a preschool program; it spends approximately $4,300 per child per year. Another state, Oklahoma, spends $7,700 per student on its preschool program. Both states use the **National Assessment of Educational Progress (NAEP)** reading test given to fourth grade students to evaluate their current level of reading. If there are long-term benefits from preschool for all, it would be expected that scores on the NAEP would show a decided improvement across time. Unfortunately, neither of these states showed the expected consistent improvement (National

Assessment of Education Progress, 2013). Georgia's scores on the NAEP were two points below the national average when the preschool program was instituted in 1993; it paralleled national scores until 2011 when it finally barely exceeded national scores by one point (Burke & Sheffield, 2013). In Oklahoma, the reading scores on the NAEP in fourth grade are even more dismal than in Georgia. For example, when the preschool program began in 1998, the average score on the reading test for Oklahoma students was 220, while the national average of all fourth graders was 215. By 2011, the numbers were reversed: the average Oklahoma student score was 215, and the national average was 220 (Burke & Sheffield, 2013).

The Obama administration's proposal for a national expanded program of preschool for all would have increased funding for Head Start subsidizes to middle- and upper middle-class students to attend but provided no new advantages for poor children. The argument against the proposal stated that three-fourths of American children are already in child care, and there was no demand from the public for more assistance (Barnett, Carolan, Fitzgerald, & Squires, 2011). Furthermore, research on Head Start, since its inception in the 1960s, has not been stellar. A recent report on the effectiveness of Head Start found that it has little effect on social-emotional growth, child health, parent/child relationships, and cognitive development (U.S. Department of Health and Human Services, Administration for Children and Families, 2010).

During the 2016 presidential campaign, both Hillary Clinton and Donald Trump presented plans on improving child care (Save the Children Action Network, n.d.). Clinton's plan called for putting a cap on the yearly cost of child care not to exceed 10% of income, increase the opportunities for child care for college students with dependent children, offer full-day Early Start and Head Start programs, and provide universal preschool programs for children less than four years of age. Trump's plan provided a write-off on income taxes for child care, or if below the income for withholding income tax, the deduction could instead be taken for Social Security and Medicare, allowing parents who care for their children at home to deduct the average cost of child care from their taxes. According to Save the Children Network, both of these plans have been criticized for the staggering costs of implementation, and in Trump's case, a disincentive to work. However, the first year of Trump's term as president found no legislation on child care.

Another concern about a national preschool for all voiced by private providers and other policymakers is the belief that a massive public preschool program would eliminate private child care (Burke & Sheffield, 2013). New regulations and reducing parental choices would lessen the number of private care providers who would have to compete against free government-operated child care. According to Burke and Sheffield, some experts in the field believe that the market model is a better model, because parents have more options to choose from, and children are not all forced into the same environment.

A SYSTEMS/DIALECTICAL PERSPECTIVE ON SOCIAL POLICY AND CHILDREN

Social policy for children can be summarized as: children need protection, support, and nurturance to be able to grow and development normally and be productive contributors to the society as adults (Midgley & Livermore, 2012). The responsibility for providing this environment for the child is mainly viewed as the purview of the family. When the family fails at this responsibility, it becomes the role of governments and nonprofit organizations to fill in the blanks left by poor family functioning. However, most established policies benefit not only dysfunctional families but also the wide range of all families in such areas as health and safety, use of alcohol and drugs, and child care.

A systems/dialectical perspective of social policies for children means that one must view concerns that include the ecological context of the child, namely one must look at the whole and not merely the parts. If one takes a reductionist view and narrowly focuses on the child and not the child's context, long-term outcomes could be detrimental to the child. For example, child poverty in single-parent families might be eliminated by increasing payments to welfare mothers; however, increasing the funds for single mothers might further increase dependence on the government and lower self-sufficiency in single-parent families (Bogenschneider, 2011). The accepted view is that for welfare to be efficient, it must help families improve their ability to provide for the needs of family members without reliance or dependency on the government. Programs that increase dependency on the government are detrimental to children in the long term.

A close look at policies to reduce poverty, particularly for single-parent families, has been to provide government subsidies. As mentioned above, the cash value of all programs, from Women, Infants, and Children (WIC) subsidies to cash payments, adds up to a higher income than that of the average working family. An opposing view to this policy would contend that children are not benefited optimally in the long-term; there are higher rates of juvenile delinquency, drug use and addiction, early sexual experiences, and lower academic achievement, among a host of other negative consequences, when compared with intact families. This opposing view would emphasize the importance of marriage in providing for the well-being of children (Jayakody & Cabrera, 2002). According to Huston and Melz (2004), marriages are created by partners in an economic context that is, to some degree, unique to each couple. They view the need to strengthen marriage by addressing these social, economic, and psychological factors implicit in the creation of marriage.

The focus on marriage is based on research evidence that the majority of women who have a child outside of marriage are romantically involved with the child's father and that this relationship continues for some time after the birth of the child. For this group of romantically unmarried couples, researchers believe that child poverty rates would be decreased by 17% if the couple married (Rector, 2012). If the couple does not marry, it is estimated that the poverty rate for these single-parent women would be 55%.

While researchers promoting marriage acknowledge that marriage for single-parent mothers would not eliminate poverty, it would be a step in the right direction (Rector, 2012). The argument is that policies to reduce poverty have been one-sided, and the number of people receiving benefits continue to rise. Moving toward the other end of the dialectic would broaden the discussion to include ideas that are generally discarded. For example, a pregnant mother in an unmarried relationship might benefit more in marriage; both partners may be more committed to sharing economically by taking on complimentary responsibilities. Persons with this point of view might further argue that the need for future planning might encourage one or both partners to further his or her education. A further benefit might be the increased potential for income and improved focus on work. In addition, increased support from an extended family network and a more balanced division of labor may bring further benefits to married couples over single and cohabiting persons.

Research has found that married fathers work more and have higher incomes than their unmarried counterparts (Waite & Gallagher, 2000).

The other side of this argument would point out that married couples are also in poverty, accounting for about 43% of those below the poverty line today (Harris-Perry, 2011). This perspective would also argue that one of the major factors in divorce is poverty; thus, poverty in married families is one of the *causes* of single-parent families (Harris-Perry, 2011). This position also argues that gender equity must be addressed. Thus, marriage for the sake of marriage may endanger women by placing them in relationships that would be detrimental to their growth and development. Since low income, low education, and poverty combine to put women at risk in romantic relationships, protecting women by not creating a false sense of security in marriage is desired.

A systems/dialectical perspective of social policy on child health would also provide for a unique analysis. For example, in most interventions to prevent or treat childhood diseases the sacrosanct idea is that the earlier the intervention, the better (Gotzche, Young, & Crace, 2015). The idea is prevalent for conditions ranging from accidents to mental health, and to question it makes one a heretic. A systems/dialectical perspective would promote a challenge to this idea, such as in prescribing medication to children in the belief that it will treat or prevent chronic illnesses in adulthood. Mental illness in children is being diagnosed at very early ages, and young children are being treated with early interventions with the hope that they will prevent later more chronic conditions. In some cases, adult-strength psychotropic medications are being given to children even though these medications have not been tested on children (Gotzche, Young, & Crace, 2015). In addition, it is not known how the brains of children will react to adult-strength medications, since the brain continues to develop until about age 25. Grotzche argues that instead of helping, early intervention may, in fact, be detrimental. For example, most people diagnosed with depression, including children, spontaneously go into remission. Furthermore, even medications for ADHD are largely ineffective, and it would be better to drop all medication except for a few children whose conditions warrant the risks.

Young and Crace, who co-authored the paper with Grotzche, have opposite views to Grotzche (Grotzche et al., 2015). The joint paper reflects a debate the three participated in and presented arguments on both sides of the issue. Young and Crace argue that Grotzche is wrong, because the world is beset with many mental problems that increase each year, and children are more vulnerable to life-long emotional problems today. Furthermore, they acknowledge that risks exist for any treatment of mental illness, but the benefits to risks ratio is necessary to make an informed decision about the treatment procedure. Another related concern is the number of children diagnosed with ADHD and autism. The diagnoses have increased without a concomitant understanding of why the increase. In the case of ADHD, medication is usually the first treatment option. Some recent research supports Grotzche's (Grotzche et al., 2015) claims that medication for children's emotional or behavioral problems does more harm than good. For example, a recent longitudinal study on the long-term treatment effects of ADHD found no improvement, and medication over this timeframe had negative effects on brain development (Molina et al., 2009). On the other hand, some research supports that drug treatment is as effective as other forms of treatment of these conditions and is, therefore, a viable option (Leucht, Hierl, Kissling, Dold, & Davis, 2012).

In summation, a systems/dialectical perspective helps to understand the complexity of policies related to family structure and well-being of children. It suggests that both short- and long-term outcomes help determine which policy to pursue, and policies affecting children should always reflect the latest research and be open to analyses and critique. It is also expected that any policy will need to change when a crisis and confrontation occur.

KEY TERMS

Home environment
Female-headed single-
   parent families
Structure
Stability
Social fathers
Non-cohabiting
   unmarried mothers
The building strong
   families project
Child characteristics
Family characteristics
Community environment
Fragile families
Aggravated Asthma

Secondhand smoke
Sidestream smoke
Sudden infant death
   syndrome (SIDS)
Blood lead level (BLL)
Wide Range Achievement
   Test (WRAT)
Wechsler Individual
   Achievement Test (WIAT)
Achievement gap
Preschool for all
Wechsler Intelligence Scale for
   Children-Revised (WISC-R)
Childhood victimization
Primary care practitioners (PCP)
Childhood schizophrenia

Attention Deficit Hyperactivity
   Disorder (ADHD)
Oppositional Defiant
   Disorder (ODD)
Depression
Anxiety disorders
Tourette syndrome
   and tic disorders
Quality of care
Structure
Process
National Assessment of
   Educational Progress (NAEP)
Social policy for children

STUDY QUESTIONS TO ACCOMPLISH THE LEARNING OBJECTIVES

1. What are issues created by the change in child demographics? Discuss how the demographics of children illustrate children at risk for poor well-being.

2. What does family structure and family stability refer to? How does family structure affect the well-being of children? How are structure and stability related? What are the implications of family structure and stability for social policy?

3. Discuss economic factors in single-parent families. Explain how the economic status of single-parent families below the poverty level may not be the main factor in why these families experience lower well-being in their children.

4. Child health is a major concern for social policy. How do secondary and sidestream smoke and other environmental pollutants negatively affect children?

5. Noting that the highest rate of direct assault of infants was from an older sibling, what issues are raised for policymakers?

6. Research currently estimates that 20% of children have been diagnosed with a mental disorder. Describe these disorders, and explore policy alternatives.

7. Does child care outside the home and specifically in a child care facility present risks for children? What precautions should be taken to protect children and ensure their well-being?

8. What does preschool for all (universal child care) mean? Should states adopt a preschool for all? Give arguments for adopting preschool for all and against it. Should some children be exempt from preschool for all?

9. What does the achievement gap mean? What are some ways to address it with preschool programs?

10. How does a systems/dialectical approach address social policy for children? Evaluate examples of applying the system/dialectical approach to social policies for children.

DEBATE ACTIVITY FOR STUDENTS

Consider the following proposition: Excessive non-parental child care for children can have long-term effects on attachment to the mother.

- Review scholarly literature on this topic paying close attention the research of Jay Belsky and those who criticized his findings. Do a library and Internet search to find relevant material. Investigate some of the additional readings.

- Develop three arguments for the proposition.

- Develop three arguments against the proposition.

- How do the arguments relate to other systems, such as the community or culture?

- Is there common ground?

- What are the long-term consequences of taking action?

- What new or common-ground solutions should be offered? If no common ground, what new position could emerge from a dialogue between the two positions?

- How is the new position superior to the original positions?

ADDITIONAL READING RESOURCES

Belsky, J. (2009) Early child care and infant-mother security, *Encyclopedia of Early Childhood Development*. Retrieved from www.child-encyclopedia.com/attachment/according-experts/early-day-care-and-infant-mother-attachment-security

Bradley R. H., & Varnell, D. L. (2007). Child care and the well-being of children, *Archives of Pediatrics and Adolescent Medicine, 161*, 669–676. doi: 10.1001/archpedi.161.7.669

Lang, H. (2005). The trouble with day care, *Psychology Today*. Retrieved from https://www.psychologytoday.com/articles/200505/the-trouble-day-care

Sun, Y., & Li, Y. (2011). Effects of family structure types and stability on children's academic performance trajectories, *Journal of Marriage and the Family, 73,* 541–556.

REFERENCES

American Psychiatric Association. (2000). *Diagnostic and statistical manual of mental disorders*. (4th ed. text revision). Washington, D.C.

Baker, M., Gruber, J., & Milligan, K. (2008). Universal child care, maternal labor supply, and family well-being. *Journal of Political Economy, 116*(4), 709–745.

Barnett, W. S., Carolan, M. E., Fitzgerald, J., & Squires, J. H. (2011). *The State of Preschool 2011*. National Institute for Early Education Research. Retrieved from http://nieer.org/sites/nieer/files/2011yearbook.pdf

Barton, M., & Williams, M. (1993). Infant day care. In C.H. Zeanah (Ed.), *Handbook of infant mental health* (pp. 445–461). New York, NY: Guilford.

Bates, J. E., Marvinney, D., Kelly, T., Dodge, K. A., Bennett, D. S., & Pettit, G. S. (1994). Child care history and kindergarten adjustment. *Developmental Psychology, 30,* 690–700.

Beesdo, K., Knappe, S., & Pine, D.S. (2009). Anxiety and anxiety disorders in children and adolescents: Developmental issues and implications for DSM-V. *Psychiatric Clinics of North America, 32*(3), 483–524.

Bellinger, D. C. (2008). Low level lead exposure and children's neurological development. *Current Opinion in Pediatrics, 20*(2), 172—177.

Belsky, J. (1986). Infant day care: A cause for concern? *Zero to Three, 6,* 1—7.

Belsky, J. (1988). The "effects" of infant day care reconsidered. *Early Childhood Research Quarterly, 3,* 235–272.

Belsky, J., Vandell, D. Burchinal, M., Clarke-Stewart, K. A., McCartney, K., Owen, M. & the Eunice Kennedy Shriver National Institute of Child Health and Human Development Early Child Care Research Network. (2007). Are there long-term effects of early child care? *Child Development, 78,* 681–701.

Belsky, J. (2009). Effects of child care on child development: Give parents real choices. Retrieved from http://www.mpsv.cz/files/clanky/6640/9_Jay_Belsky_EN.pdf

Biederman J., Petty C. R., Dolan C., Hughes, S., Mick, E., Monuteaux, M.C., ... Faraone, S.V.(2008). The long-term longitudinal course of oppositional defiant disorder and conduct disorder in ADHD boys: Findings from a controlled 10-year prospective longitudinal follow-up study. *Psychological Medicine, 38,* 1027–36.

Bitsko, R. H., Danielson, M., King, M., Visser, S. N., Scahill, L., & Perou R. (2012).Health care needs of children with Tourette syndrome. *Journal of Child Neurology, 28*(12), 1628–1636.

Bogenschneider, K. (2011). *Family policy matters: How policymaking affects families and what professionals can do about it* (2nd ed.). New York, NY: Routledge.

Boivin, M. (2005). The origin of peer relationship difficulties in early childhood and their impact on children's psychosocial adjustment and development. *Encyclopedia on Early Childhood Development*, Center of Excellence for Early Childhood Experience.

Breysse, P., Farr, N., Galke, W., Lanphear, B., Morley, R., & Bergofsky, L. (2004). The relationship between housing and health: Children at risk. *Environmental Health Perspectives, 112*(15), 1583–1588.

Bureau of Justice Statistics. (2010). National Crime Victimization Survey and Federal Bureau of Investigation, Uniform Crime Reporting Supplementary Homicide Reports, Washington, D.C.

Burke, L., & Shefield, R. (2013). Universal preschool's empty promise. The Heritage Foundation. Retrieved from http://www.heritage.org/education/report/universal-preschools-empty-promises

Bzostek, S., & Beck, A. (2008). Family structure and child health outcomes in fragile families. Center for Research on Child Well-being Working Paper WP08-11-FF.

Camarota, S.A. (2017). Births to unwed mothers by nativity and education. Center for Immigration Studies. Retrieved from https://cis.org/Camarota/Births-Unmarried-Mothers-Nativity-and-Education

Carlson, M. J., & Corcoran, M. E. (2001). Family structure and children's behavioral and cognitive outcomes. *Journal of Marriage and Family, 63,* 779–792.

Carlson M., & McLanahan, S. (2009). Fathers in fragile families. In M. E. Lamb (Ed.), *The role of the father in child development*. (5th ed). New York, NY: Wiley and Sons.

Centers for Disease Control and Prevention. (2013). *Mental health surveillance among children—United States 2005–2011, 62*, 1–35.

Cherlin, A. J. (2004). The deinstitutionalization of American marriage. *Journal of Marriage and Family, 66*, 848–861.

Childstats.gov. (2017). America's child: Key indicators of well-being, 2017.

Collins, P. Y., Patel, V., Joestl, S. S., March, D., Insel, T. R., & Daar, A. S. (2011). Grand challenges in global mental health. *Nature, 475*(7354), 7–10. doi: 10.1038/475027a

Collins, J. W., Rankin, K. M., & David, R. J. (2016). Prenatal lifelong sociological and low birth weight rates: Relative to African American women's birth outcome disadvantage. *Maternal and Child Health Journal, 20*(8), 1759–1766.

Cote, S. M., Borge, A. I., Geoffroy, M., Rutter, M., & Tremblay, R. E. (2008). Nonmaternal care in infancy and emotional/behavioral difficulties at four years old: Moderation by family risk characteristics. *Developmental Psychology, 44*, 153–168.

Cote, S. M., Mongeau, C., Japel, C., Xu, Q., Seguin, J. R., & Tremblay, R. E. (2012). Child care quality and cognitive development: Trajectories leading to better preacademic skills. *Child Development, 84*(2), 752–766.

Cowan, C. A., Cowan, C. P., & Knox, V. (2010). Marriage and fatherhood programs. *Future Child, 20*(2), 205–230.

Craigie, T.-A.L., Brooks-Dunn, J., & Waldfogel, J. (2012). Family structure, family stability, and outcomes of five-year-old children. *Families, Relationships, and Societies: An International Journal of Research and Debate 1*(1), 43–61.

Crosnoe, R., Prickett, K. C., Smith, C., & Cavanagh, S. (2014) Changes in young children's family structures and child care arrangements. *Demography, 5*(2), 459–483

Deaton, A. (2007). Consequences of childhood mental disorders. *National Bureau of Economic Research (NBER): Bulletin on Aging and Health, 20*, 1–6.

Dmitrieva, J., Steinberg, L., & Belsky, J. (2007). Child Care History, Classroom Composition and Children's Functioning in Kindergarten. *Psychological Science, 18*, 1032–1039.

Duncan, G. J., & Magnuson, K. (2013). Investing in preschool programs. *Journal of Economic Perspective, 27*(2), 109–132.

Egeland, B., & Hiester, M. (1995). The long-term consequences of infant day-care and mother–infant attachment. *Child Development, 66*(2), 474–485.

Federal Interagency Forum on Child and Family Statistics. (2012). *America's Children in Brief: Key National Indicators of Well-Being.* Washington, D.C.

Finkelhor, D., Turner, H. L., Shattuck, A., & Hamby, S. L. (2015). Prevalence of childhood exposure to violence, crime, and abuse: Results of the national survey of children's exposure to violence. *JAMA Pediatrics, 169*(8), 746–754.

Finkelhor, D., Turner, H., Ormrod, R., & Hamby, S. L (2009). Violence, abuse, and crime exposure in a national sample of children and youth. *Pediatrics, 124*(5), 1411–1423.

Fomby, P., & Cherlin. A. J. (2007). Family instability and child well-being. *American Sociological Review, 72*, 181–204.

Freyer, R., & Levitt, S. (2004). Understanding the black-white test score gap in the first two years of school. *The Review of Economics and Statistics, 86*, 447–464.

Goldberg, W. A., Tan, E. T., Thorsen, K. L. (2009). Trends in academic attention to fathers, 1930–2006. *Fathering, 7*(2), 159–179.

Gotzche, P., Young, A., & Crace, J. (2015). Does long-term use of psychiatric drugs cause more harm than good? *British Medical Journal, BMJ, 2015, 350.* H2435. doi: 10.1136/bmj.h2435

Graham, L. T., Gosling, S. D., & Travis, C. K. (2015). Psychology of home environments: A call for research on residential spaces. *Perspectives on Psychological Science, 10*(3), 346–356.

Guzzo, K. B. (2014). Trends in cohabitation outcomes: Compositional changes and engagement among never-married young adults. *Journal of Marriage and the Family, 76*(4), 826–842.

Harris-Perry, M. (2011). *Sister Citizen: Shame, Stereotypes, and Black Women in America.* New Haven, CT: Yale University Press.

Health Care Cost Institute. (2012). *Children's health care spending report 2007–2010.* Washington, D.C.: Health Care Cost Institute.

Hungerford, A., Brownell, C. A., & Campbell, S. B. (2001). A child in infancy: A transitional perspective. In C.H. Zeanah, Jr. (Ed.), *Handbook of infant mental health* (2nd ed.) (pp. 519–532). New York, NY: Guilford.

Huston, T. L., & Melz, H. (2004). The case for (promoting) marriage: The devil is in the details. *Journal of Marriage and the Family, 66*(4), 943–958.

Jayalody, R., & Cabrera, N. (2002). What are the choices of low-income families? Cohabitation, marriage and remaining single. In A. Booth and A. C. Crounter (Eds.), *Just living together: Implication for cohabitation on families* (pp. 85–95). Mahwah, NJ: Erlbaum.

Kennedy, S., & Bumpass, L. (2008). Cohabitation and child living arrangements: New estimates from the United States. *Demographic Research 19*, 663–692.

Kessler, G. (2013, February 13). A misleading chart on welfare spending. *Washington Post Online.* Retrieved from http://www.washingtonpost.com/blogs/fact-checker/post/a-misleading-chart-on-welfare-spending/2013/02/20/1b40bcde-7ba4-11e2-82e8-61a46c2cde3d_blog.html

Kessler, R. C., Avenevoli, S., Costello, E. J., Georgiades, K., Green, J.G., Gruber, … Merikangas, K.R., (2012). Prevalence, persistence, and socio-demographic correlates of DSM-IV disorders in the National Co-morbidity Survey Replication Adolescent Supplement. *Archives of General Psychiatry, 69,* 372–80.

Kim, J. (2012). Segregated from the start: Peer context in center-based child care. *Children and Schools, 34*(2), 71–82.

Lamb, M. E. (1998). Non-parental child care: Context, quality, correlates, consequences. In W. Damon (Series Ed.) and I. E. Sigel and K. A. Renniger (Vol. Ed.), *Handbook of Child Psychology,* Vol. 4, *Child Psychology and Practice* (5th ed.) (pp. 73–133). New York, NY: Wiley.

Land, K. C. (2014). Child and youth well-being index report, 2014. Duke Center for Child and Family Policy, Durham, NC. Retrieved from https://childandfamilypolicy.duke.edu/wp-content/uploads/2014/12/Child-Well-Being-Report.pdf

Lanphear, B. P., Dietrich, K. N., Auinger, P., & Cox, C. (2000). Cognitive deficits associated with blood lead concentrations <10 ug/dL in U.S. children and adolescents. *Public Health Report, 115,* 521–529.

Leucht, S., Hierl, S., Kissling, W., Dold, M., & Davis, J.M. (2012). Putting the efficacy of psychiatric and general medicine medication into perspective: A review of meta-analyses. *British Journal of Psychiatry, 200,* 97–106.

Loeb, S., Bridges, M., Bassock, D., Fuller, B., & Rumberger, R.W. (2007). How much is too much? The influence of preschool centers on children's social and cognitive development. *Economics of Education Review, 26,* 52–66.

Luby J., Belden A., Pautsch J., Si X., & Spitznagel E. (2009). The clinical significance of preschool depression: Impairment in functioning and clinical markers of the disorder. *Journal of Affective Disorders, 112,* 111–119.

MacKenzie, M. J., Liu, D., & Sameroff, A. J. (2010). Moving beyond the child care debate toward implications for social and political agendas. *Children and Youth Services Review, 35,* 3–6.

Magnuson, K., & Berger, L. M. (2009). Family structure states and transitions: associations with children's well-being during middle childhood. *Journal of Marriage and Family, 71,* 575–591.

McCartney, K., Burchinal, M., Clarke-Stewart, A., Bub, K. L., Owen, M. T., & Belsky, J. (2010). Testing a series of causal propositions relating time in child care to children's externalizing behavior. *Developmental Psychology, 46*(1), 1–17.

McLanahan, S., Knab, J., & Meadows, S. (2009). Economic Trajectories in Non-Traditional Families with Children. Working Paper 09–10–FF. Center for Research on Child Well-Being. Princeton: September 2009.

Merikangas, K. R., He, J. P., Brody, D., Fisher, P. W., Bourdon, K., & Koretz D. S. (2010a). Prevalence and treatment of mental disorders among U.S. children in the 2001–2004 NHANES. *Pediatrics, 125,* 75–81.

Merikangas, K.R., He, J.P., Burstein M., Swanson, S.A., Avenevoli, S., Cui, … Swendsen, J. (2010b). Lifetime prevalence of mental disorders in U.S. adolescents: Results from the National Co-morbidity Survey Replication—Adolescent Supplement (NCS-A). *Journal of American Academy of Child Adolescent Psychiatry, 49,* 980–989.

Midgley, J., & Livermore, M. (2012) (Eds.). *The handbook of social policy.* Thousand Oaks, CA: Sage.

Milanzi, E. B., Brunekreef, B., Koppelman, G. H., Wijga, A. H., van Rossem, L., Vonk, J.M., … Gehring, U. (2017). Lifetime secondhand smoke exposure and childhood and adolescent asthma: Findings from the PIAMA cohort. *Environmental Health, 16,* 14. doi:org/10.1186/s12940-017-0223-7

Molina, B. S., Hinshaw, S. P, Swanson, J. M., Arnold, L. E., Vitiello, B., Jensen, P. S., … Houck, P.S. (2009). The MTA in 8 years: Prospective follow-up of children treated for combine type ADHD in Multisite study. *Journal of the American Academy of Child and Adolescent Psychiatry, 48*(5), 484–500.

National Assessment of Education Progress. (2013). *Reading framework for 2013.* Washington D.C.: U.S. Department of Education.

National Research Council and Institute of Medicine. (2009). *Preventing mental, emotional, and behavioral disorders among young people: Progress and possibilities.* Washington, D.C.: The National Academic Press.

NICHD-ECCRN (Eunice Kennedy Shriver National Institute of Child Health and Human Development is one of the National Institutes of Health Study of Early Child Care and Youth Development) (2003). Does amount of time spent in child care predict socioemotional adjustment during the transition to kindergarten? *Child Development, 74*(4), 976–1005.

Pfuntner, A., Wier, L. M., & Stocks, C. (2013). Most frequent conditions in U.S. hospitals 2010. Rockville, MD: Agency for Healthcare Research and Quality. *Healthcare Cost and Utilization Project (CUP) Statistical Brief #148.* Retrieved from https://www.hcup-us.ahrq.gov/reports/statbriefs/sb148.pdf

Raley, S., Bianchi, S.M., & Wang, W. (2012). When do fathers care? Mothers' economic contribution and fathers' involvement in child care. *American Journal of Sociology, 117*(5), 1422–1459. doi: 10.1086/663354

Ramey, C. T., & Ramey, S. L. (1998). Early intervention and early experience. *American Psychologist, 53,* 109–120.

Reardon, S. (2003). Sources of educational inequality: The growth of racial/ethnic and socioeconomic test score gaps in kindergarten and first grade. State College, PA: Penn State University (Manuscript).

Rector, R. (2012). Marriage: America's greatest weapon against child poverty. *Special report #117 on Poverty and inequality*. The Heritage Foundation. Retrieved from http://www.heritage.org/research/reports/2012/09/marriage-americas-greatest-weapon-against-child-poverty.

Reinhold, S. (2010). Assessing the link between premarital cohabitation and marital instability. *Demography, 47*(3), 719–733.

Rubio-Andrade, M., Valdez-Perezgasga, F., Alonzo, J., Rosado, J.L, Cebrian, M.E., Garcia-Vargas, G.G. (2017). Follow-up study on lead exposure in children living in smelter community in northern Mexico. *Environmental Health, 10*, 66, 2017. doi.org/10.1186/1476-069x-10-66

Save the Children Action Network. (n.d.). Where do the presidential candidates stand on investing in Kids? Retrieved from https://www.savethechildrenactionnetwork.org/where-do-candidates-stand/

Sigel, E. J., Harpin, S. B. (2013). Primary care practitioners' detections of youth violence involvement. *Clinical Pediatrics, 52*, 411–417.

Sigle-Rushton, W., & McLanahan, S. (2002). The living arrangements of new mothers. *Demography, 39*(3), 415–433.

Solari, C.D., & Mare, R.D. (2012). Housing crowding effects on children's well-being. *Social Science Research, 41*(2), 464–476.

Substance Abuse and Mental Health Services Administration. (2012). Results from the 2011 National Survey on Drug Use and Health: Mental Health Findings and Detailed Tables, Rockville, MD: Substance Abuse and Mental Health Services Administration. Retrieved from http://www.samhsa.gov/data/NSDUH/2k11MH_FindingsandDetTables/Index.aspx

Surkan, P. J., Zhang, A., Trachtenberg, F., Daniel, D. B., McKinlay, S., and Bellinger, D.C. (2007). Neuropsychological function in children with blood lead levels <10 ug/dL. *NeuroToxicology, 28*(6), 1170–1177.

Turner, H. A., Finkelhor, D., Ormrod, R., & Hamby, S. L. (2010). Infant victimization in a national representative sample. *Pediatrics, 126*(1), 44–52.

U.S. Committee on the Budget (2012). Total welfare spending equals to $168 a day for every household in poverty. Retrieved from http://www.budget.senate.gov/republican/public/index.cfm/2012/12/total-welfare-spending-equates-to-168-per-day-for-every-household-in-poverty

U.S. EPA. (2008). *Integrated Science Assessment (ISA) for Sulfur Oxides—Health Criteria (Final Report)*. Washington, D.C. U.S. Environmental Protection Agency.

U.S. Department of Health and Human Services (2013). *The Health Consequences of Involuntary Exposure to Tobacco Smoke: A Report of the Surgeon General*. Washington, D.C.

U.S. Department of Health and Human Services, Administration for Children and Families. (2010). Head Start Research: Head Start Impact Study Final Report, January 2010. Retrieved from http://www.acf.hhs.gov/sites/default/files/opre/hs_impact_study_final.pdf

U.S. Department of Health and Human Services. (2011). Results from the 2010 National Survey on Drug Use and Health: Summary of National Findings. Rockville, MD: Substance Abuse and Mental Health Services Administration Center for Behavioral Health Statistics and Quality.

Visser, S. N., Danielson, M. L., Bitsko, R. H., Holbrook, J. R., Kogan, M. D., Ghandour, R. M., … Blumberg, S. J. (2013). Trends in the parent report of health care providers—diagnosed and medicated Attention Deficit/Hyperactivity Disorder: United States, 2005–2011. *Journal of the American Academy of Child and Adolescent Psychiatry, 53*(3), 34–46.

Waite, L., & Gallagher, M. (2000). *The case for marriage.* New York, NY: Doubleday.

Waldfogel, J., Brooks-Gunn, J., & Craigie, T. L. (2010). Fragile families and child well-being. *Future Child, 20*(2), 87–112.

Wallman, K. K. (2012). American children in brief: Key national indicators of well-being, 2012. Federal Interagency Forum on Child and Family Statistics. Retrieved from https://www.childstats.gov/pdf/ac2016/ac_16.pdf.

Weissberg, R. (2013). The limits of charter schools. The Mencken Club. Retrieved from http://hlmenckenclub.org/2011-conference-audio/2013/5/7/robert-weissberg-the-limits-of-charter-schools

Wood, R. G., McConnell, S., Moore, Q., Clarkwest, A., & Hsueh, J. (2010). *The building strong families project: Strengthening unmarried parents' relationships: The early impact of building strong families.* The Office of Planning, Research, and Evaluation, Administration for Children and Families. Princeton, NJ: Mathematica Policy Research.

Wood, R.G., Moore, Q., Clarkwest, A., & Killewald, A. (2014). The long-term effects of building strong families: A program for unmarried parents. *Journal of Marriage and the Family, 76*, 446–463.

CREDITS

CHAPTER FOUR

Social Policy and Controversial Issues: Alcohol, Nicotine, and Drug Use During Pregnancy

LEARNING OBJECTIVES

At the end of the chapter the student will be able to:

✓ Identify drugs ingested by the mother that affect the fetus. Determine if drugs ingested by the mother that harm the fetus should require legal or criminal intervention on the part of authorities;

✓ Identify neurotransmitters that are active during pregnancy. Compare and contrast how the functions of neurotransmitters during pregnancy differ from their functions after birth;

✓ Recall the specific effects of substances, such as nicotine, cocaine, alcohol, and crystal meth on the fetus. Analyze the danger of these substances imposed on the fetus;

✓ List the effects of legal drugs, such as antidepressants and antipsychotic medications on the fetus, take a position of whether these drugs would be used for pregnant women, and justify your position;

✓ Recall the debate of the rights of the fetus to be born free of damage vs. the rights of the mother and determine which argument is supported by facts and justify your conclusions; and

✓ List treatments and legal interventions for mothers who are addicted to drugs and evaluate the effectiveness of these treatment and intervention programs.

SOCIAL POLICY AND CONTROVERSIAL ISSUES

In thinking about social policies for children and families, it becomes apparent that many issues have various points of view and consensus cannot be easily reached. In some cases, consensus cannot be reached at all. Some of these issues cause deep emotional responses that tend to preclude not only resolution but even public discourse. This chapter takes the view that the very issues that the public shies away from must be brought to the surface to create open dialogues and allow competing views to be heard; in the long run, a new position may emerge that is more effective in influencing social policy. Some of these issues include abortion, fetal rights, gay and lesbian marriage, legalization of marijuana, gun control, illegal immigration, and legalization of prostitution. This chapter will limit the discussion of these topics to alcohol, nicotine addiction, and drug use and addiction. Covered in this chapter will be exposing the fetus to alcohol, nicotine, and legal and illegal drugs when the mother has decided to give birth.

RIGHTS OF THE UNBORN

An understanding of social policy for children must take into consideration the welfare of children, which broadly considers topics such as poverty, relationship to parents, abuse, health care, nutrition, and numerous other topics. Rarely does the subject of fetal rights find itself front and center in a discussion on social policy for children. In large part, addressing fetal rights is like the elephant in the room. The ignored question is: At what point does the "child" meet the qualifications for being protected under social policy provisions? Generally, this protection through social policies is made after the birth, not before; therefore, prenatal concerns receive only cursory attention. However settled this issue may seem to be, surveys and research reflect that attitudes and beliefs about fetal rights and abortion defy consensus and generally have equally strong advocates on both sides of the issue (Wilkinson, Skene, De Crespigny, & Savulescu, 2016).

The concerns for the rights of the unborn fall into a number of categories, such as fetal alcohol spectrum disorder, neglectful attention to the fetus, poor nutrition, ingestion of illegal substances, the use of fetal tissue in stem cell research, and abortion. While all of these topics are related, they fall into two major categories: issues related to abortion or ending the pregnancy and a decision on the part of the mother to carry the fetus to term. Moral or ethical concerns on the part of the mother differ significantly depending on her decision to abort or carry the fetus to term. Issues related to her decision to give birth will be discussed next (Wilkinson et al., 2016).

EXPOSURE TO LEGAL DRUGS

The risk factor is related to specific **teratogens** in the form of prescribed medications that affect the fetus in all three trimesters. Harm can be done during the first trimester, because the zygote is not attached to the womb for the first two weeks (Hinman, 2016). During the embryonic period, or the next five weeks, organs develop in the embryo, and exposure to teratogens can result in serious morphological anomalies. **Central nervous system** damage occurs during this stage in the form of **neural tube malformation**. The fetal period begins after the eighth week of conception; it is during this period that teratogens can affect neural migration and cause physiological deficits.

Of primary concern for neonatal development is exposure to legal or illegal drugs. During the past several decades researchers have discovered the role that neurotransmitters play in the prenatal period (Behar, Shaffner, Scott, Greene, & Barker, 2000). Limited specialized nerve cells called **neurons** act as receptors and transmitters of neural information. The **dendrites** provide information from neighboring neurons that travels to the **soma**, or main cell body of the neuron. The information processed in the soma then moves to the **axon**, which has a bulb-like appendage, **terminal button**, that transmits the information to neurons, body organs, muscles, and glands. Aiding in the sending of messages are chemical **neurotransmitters**, secreted by the pituitary and adrenal glands, which provide a way for neurons to communicate across the synapses. The most common neurotransmitters include acetylcholine, **norepinephrine**, dopamine, y-amirobutyric acid (GABA), glutamate, serotonin, and endorphin (Behar et al., 2000). Each neurotransmitter has a specialized function. For example, dopamine and acetylcholine facilitate learning, low levels of norepinephrine and high levels of acetylcholine are related to depression, endorphins affect glucose metabolism, and GABA retards anxiety.

Early in development, particularly prenatally, these neurotransmitters carry out different functions than in later development, as discussed above. While in later development, these neurotransmitters are located on neural synapses and aid the linking of neurons; in early development, they precede synoptic development (Whitaker-Azmitia, 2001). For example, researchers have discovered that dopamine has the pre-synaptic development function of enhancing dendrite growth (Ohtani, Goto, Waeber, & Bhide, 2003), and serotonin is involved in cell proliferation (Bonin, Torii, Wang, Rakic, & Levitt, 2007). In addition, GABA stimulates the creation of neurons. Unfortunately, the presence of legal or illegal drugs affects the proper functions of these neurotransmitters and alters the developing brain. For example, it is widely known that nicotine has a detrimental effect on neural development in the fetus throughout the gestational period (Thompson, Levitt, & Stanwood, 2009b). The neurotransmitters involved in nicotine exposure include acetylcholine and result in a smaller hippocampus, a region of the brain related to memory, and lower cognitive capacity (Snow & Keiver, 2007).

The effect of nicotine exposure on the acetylcholine receptors (nAChRs) act to both stimulate and depress reception and, therefore, affect brain replication and differentiation during the critical maturation period, which ultimately can alter synaptic activity (Slotkin et al., 2005). Not only does nicotine affect the fetal developing brain, but because of close alignment with **catecholaminergic systems,** it can cause deficiencies in learning that appear in childhood and adolescence. This link is further noted in the predisposition to **hypoxia,** a condition resulting from reduced oxygen to the brain, which is related to infant mortality, most notably in sudden infant death syndrome (SIDS).

Critical periods during the development process are especially vulnerable to neurotransmitter receptors linked to signaling cascades (Thompson, Levitt, & Stanwood, 2009a). Numerous outcomes are possible for the same neurotransmitter and receptor depending on the context. As in Figure 4.1, the outcome can vary from cell replication, cell differentiation, cell growth or death, or it can program the cell for future responses to stimulation (Slotkin, 1998). Exposure to nicotine prenatally appears to lead to cell loss, irreversible **apotheoses**, and death of cells.

While risks to the fetus are known to most pregnant women, approximately 15–20% continue to smoke during pregnancy (Bergman et al., 2003). Because nicotine is highly addictive, even women who sincerely want to quit smoking have difficulty giving it up (Ebert & Fahy, 2007). The negative effects of withdrawal such as irritability and restlessness mitigate against cessation. The use of **Nicotine Replacement Therapy (NRT)** has similar effects as smoking, but some researchers believe that, overall, it is not as harmful, primarily because the dose of nicotine is less than the average woman receives from smoking (Glynn et al., 2009). While taking NRT may be less damaging to the fetus than smoking, it does not equate with cessation of smoking during pregnancy. Slotkin and colleagues (2005) believe that non-pharmaceutical treatment is advantageous over NRT, because the danger in cigarette smoke is nicotine, which is present in NRT at the rate of approximately 10 cigarettes.

As stated above, nicotine exposure prenatally affects the developing neural pathways of the fetal brain and has long-term effects, including, among others, impairment in learning, attention deficit hyperactivity disorder (ADHD), and a host of behavioral disorders (Dwyer, McQuown, & Leslie, 2009). Research studies imply that prenatal exposure to nicotine and not intrauterine growth restrictions account for long-term psychological and health effects on children (Syme et al., 2009). Animal models have been used to determine that prenatal exposure to nicotine alters the acetylcholine receptors (nAChR), ligand-gated ion channels, which have a direct effect on the hypothalamus, which controls one's appetite. Ultimately, obesity, type 2 diabetes, and even hypertension may be the result of hypothermic function formed prenatally (Huang & Winzer-Serhan, 2007). Animal studies shed light on how nicotine exposure affects the development of obesity and type 2 diabetes. Type 2 diabetes results from the inability of the pancreas to produce enough insulin for glucose balance (Bergmann et al., 2006). A major reason for this inability may be the result of fewer beta cells or impaired glucose conduction, both of which are affected by nicotine exposure (Bruin, Gerstein, & Holloway, 2007).

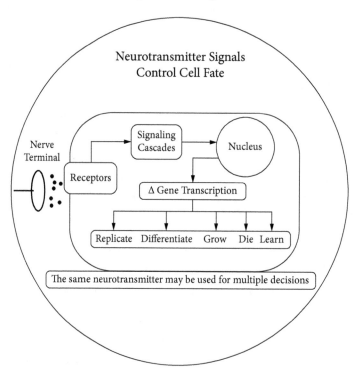

FIGURE 4.1 Linkages of neurotransmitters and cell development

ALCOHOL EXPOSURE

Alcohol use, and to a lesser degree, abuse, are fairly common during pregnancy and affect the fetus throughout gestation (Maier & West, 2004). While most women do not drink during pregnancy, some women do consume various amounts of alcohol. Since approximately 50% of all pregnancies are unplanned, many women consume alcohol before they know they are pregnant. In addition, about 12% of all women do not use birth control effectively, which further increases the likelihood that a woman might be pregnant and engage in risky behavior, such as drinking alcohol.

Approximately 12% of women engage in binge drinking or excessive periodic alcohol intake. Binge drinking is related to high **blood alcohol concentration (BAC),** which can also produce withdrawal symptoms in the fetus (Maier & West, 2004). Binge drinking has not been found to be related to a higher probability of **Autism Spectrum Disorder (ASD)** (Eliasen et al., 2010).

Fetal Alcohol Syndrome (FAS)

Fetal Alcohol Syndrome (FAS) was first diagnosed in 1973 and has been considered a major social and health issue for the fetus since that time (Jones & Smith, 1973). The prenatal and postnatal effects on the developing child have been labeled variously as fetal alcohol effects, alcohol-related birth defects (ARBD), alcohol-related neurodevelopment disorder (ARND), and fetal alcohol spectrum disorders (FASDs), which broadly include all of the short- and long-term effects that alcohol has on the developing fetus (Hepper, Dronan, & Lynch, 2012). In current literature, FAS is considered an aspect of FASDs when brain damage is present. It is estimated that in the United States the likelihood of FAS is 3.1 per 1,000 people (U.S. Department of Health and Human Services, 2001).

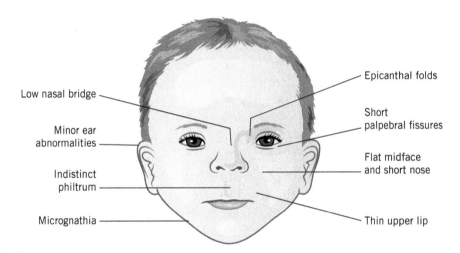

FIGURE 4.2 Facial patterns of FAS.

Researchers have found that adolescents with FAS share a number of abnormalities (See Figure 4.2). For example, physical characteristics include being shorter than average though weighing about the same as other adolescents (Streissguth et al., 1991; Vaux & Chambers, 2016). In addition, other characteristics include low academic functioning ranging from second to fourth grade competencies, poor judgment, and deficiencies in social adjustment. Others studies have shown that children with FAS have a high proclivity for problems with the law, academic problems, and social maladjustment in which confinement in a mental or substance abuse facility is needed (Streissguth et al., 2004).

The Pharmacology of Alcohol

Alcohol blocks N-Methyl-D aspartate (MNDA), acting as a depressant, and increases GABA, resulting in a decrease in cortical functioning (Huang, DiCristo, & Ango, 2007). Because this happens during the period of synapse development, literally millions of synapses are deleted. FAS is a widely acknowledged condition resulting from fetal alcohol exposure in high concentrations during pregnancy. A wide range of disorders are related to fetal alcohol syndrome; they include abnormal facial features (Bada et al., 2005), intellectual and motor deficiencies, microcephaly behavioral disorders (Vaux & Chambers, 2016), including ADHD (Williams & Ross, 2007), cleft palate, heart defects, and problems in seeing and hearing (American Academy of Pediatrics, 2000). A recent animal study demonstrated that retinal neural cells, particularly the dendrite receptor fields, were significantly smaller than for controls (Deng et al., 2012).

Frequent exposure to alcohol throughout pregnancy has the most negative effects on the fetus and is more likely to be the cause of FAS, although any amount of alcohol can cause it (Redila et al., 2006). Serious effects of alcohol on the fetus include brain and spinal damage, hippocampal shrinkage, and slowing of neural migration (Vaux & Chambers, 2016). Using animal models, recent research focuses on the concept of neural plasticity, which results from neural wiring. Alcohol ingestion creates a disruption in this process of neural wiring, which is related to later cognitive and memory deficiencies (Medina, 2011). The part of the brain most affected by prenatal exposure to alcohol is the cerebral cortex, causing an increase in apoptosis and permanent realigning of cortical neurons (Granato, Palmer, De Giorgio, Tavian, & Larkum, 2012). Consequently, the electrophysiological function of the cortical neurons is altered. Altering the cortical neurons from "downregulation of dendrite electogenesis in L5 pryamidal neurons" (p. 381) is a direct effect of alcohol ingestion. Further, it is known that "impairment of dendritic calcium signaling is responsible for the observed alterations" (p. 381). As a result, cortical processing that relies on pyramid processing would be affected.

The alterations in the cortical network affect the brain structure. The first trimester seems especially vulnerable, because the alcohol acts to block cell migration, resulting in structural abnormalities. Alcohol use or abuse in other periods in gestation can affect other processes, such as hippocampal damage that occurs during the third trimester. Damage to the **hippocampus** results in deficits in memory, cognitive development, and emotional expression and visual and hearing impairment.

These alterations and anomalies have been studied from both animal and human autopsies. Autopsies of infants who died from FAS have revealed a plethora of negative outcomes, which usually include **hydrocephalus** (water on the brain), **microcephaly** (small cranium), missing olfactory bulbs, migration errors, decreased size of the corpus callosum, and abnormalities in the brain stem and the cerebellum.

Not all effects of alcohol are caused from structural damage to the brain; they can be the result of damage to the central nervous system and the peripheral nervous system (Vaux & Chambers, 2016). However, these neurological abnormalities may also be diagnosed as FAS if a number of factors apply and they cannot be attributed to other conditions. These symptoms may include epilepsy, reduction in the use of fine motor skills, eye-hand coordination, hearing, and gait. When these symptoms do not exist in the context of other conditions, their causes would most likely be attributed to alcohol ingestion by the mother during pregnancy.

Central nervous system damage resulting from FAS may be diagnosed from observations of the child in daily living. For example, when a child has deficiencies in memory, math, abstract thinking, social interaction and communication, and overall academic performance, a diagnosis of FAS may be made (Vaux & Chambers, 2016). While most of the deficiencies related to FAS occur in childhood, some appear later in adolescence and adulthood, such as alcohol and substance abuse problems, incarceration, sexual promiscuity, disruptions in education from dropping out of school or suspensions, and various types of mental or emotional problems, including depression and ADHD.

In summation, FAS can be diagnosed from different levels of analysis. There must be prenatal exposure to alcohol, characteristic facial features (see Figure 4.3), deficiencies of the central nervous system, and the presence of stuntedness (short height) or thinness (low weight) (Vaux & Chambers, 2016). While the diagnostic categories are defensible, there is no consensus among researchers about the amount of alcohol exposure. Heavy drinking is usually considered to be more than five ounces of alcohol a day.

EXPOSURE TO COCAINE AND OTHER DRUGS

It has been estimated that approximately 1.6 million persons in the United States use cocaine (Substance Abuse and Mental Health Services Administration, 2009). The first concern about cocaine usage by pregnant mothers arose in the 1980s with the fear that cocaine exposure led to long-term debilitating outcomes. Most of the studies during this time used small samples and were methodically deficient. What complicates research is that cocaine usage coincides with other variables that impede a strict causal alignment with various outcomes (Ackerman, Riggins, & Black, 2010). For example, mothers who use cocaine may also use an assortment of other substances, including nicotine from smoking. They may live in poor environments, receive little medical care, and have stressful relationships. Even with these confounding variables, recent research has found an association between prenatal cocaine use and effects on the fetus, which will be discussed below (Behnke & Smith, 2013).

Studies show that cocaine not only crosses the placenta and directly enters the bloodstream of the fetus but accumulates in the amniotic fluid, which can be easily absorbed through the skin during the first and second trimesters (Doweiko, 2008). Like nicotine and alcohol, the most influence on the fetus occurs in the first trimester. A major effect of maternal cocaine use is restriction of blood flow and increase of blood pressure. This can result in serious complications for the fetus, such as stokes, which may later be associated with neurological problems. Further, the restricted blood flow may mean that the fetus does not receive proper nutrients from the mother. Restricted blood flow in the fetus from prenatal maternal cocaine use may lead to fetal strokes or other heart conditions, such as a hole in the heart or other structural heart defects or dysfunctions.

Pharmacology

Fetal exposure to cocaine is related to altering the structure and functioning of the brain. Chemically, cocaine alters the reuptake of norepinephrine and **epinephrine**, two neurotransmitters related to stimulation of the sympathetic nervous system (Aronson, 2008). Researchers have also found that cocaine delays the reuptake of serotonin in the presynaptic neuron, thus prolonging the feeling of euphoria (Feng, 2005). New research discovered that the **placenta** produces serotonin; it does not come from the mother as previously thought (Velasquez, Goedin, & Bonnin, 2013). The role of the placenta has largely been ignored in the research of early development. However, it is widely known that cocaine interferes with the placenta and contributes to placenta detachment, spontaneous abortion, and low birth weight (Feng, 2005). Other complications from maternal use of cocaine affecting the environment of the placenta include vitamin deficiencies (Doweiko, 2008). According to Bonnin and colleagues (2011), the placenta plays a major role in signaling the brain through its production of serotonin, which influences the production of brain cells through the process of **syncytiotrophoblast**. What this means is that if the placenta is restricted from producing serotonin by the mother's ingestion of cocaine, it also interferes with brain cell production.

It is estimated that approximately 200,000 pregnant women use cocaine, which result in various types and degrees of damage and risk factors for the developing fetus (Lee et al., 2008). Recent research using laboratory rats demonstrated that maternal use of cocaine interferes with the development of a protein, cyclin A, which is related directly with cell division (Lee et al., 2008). After exposure, the rats were treated with cimetidine, a drug used to reduce the metabolism of cocaine. Researchers found that cimetidine neutralized the effects of cocaine in inhibiting brain cell development.

Studies on the long-term effects of fetal exposure to cocaine have been somewhat mixed. Lester and Lagasse (2010) found that fetal exposure to cocaine affects the development of language and attention disorder. Others have found that, at six months after birth, exposed infants will have noticeable differences in posture as compared to unexposed infants (Chiriboga, Kuhn, & Wasserman 2007). Studies on intrauterine cocaine exposure and developmental delays and mental performance have been mixed. Some studies have found little effect on intelligence quotient (IQ) scores (Frank, Augustyn, Knight, Pell, & Zuckerman, 2001). Others have found that, while there is no direct effect on IQ, indirect effects were mediated by the environment in the home (Chasnoff, Anson, Hatcher, Stenson, Iaukea, & Randolph, 1998). A more recent study of 231 children ages four, six, and nine years of age, ninety-one exposed prenatally to cocaine and 140 not exposed, were given the Stanford-Benet IV IQ test (Bennett, Bendersky, & Lewis, 2008). The study found that gender played a role in that boys exposed to cocaine prenatally scored lower on the IQ measure than girls or unexposed boys. Enriched home environment and the mother's IQ were moderating factors. It can be concluded that the effects of prenatal exposure to cocaine on the fetus vary depending on a number of variables, including the home environment.

Some evidence exists for the link between prenatal maternal cocaine use and latter attention and behavioral disorders in children; this is because the prefrontal cortex and other cortical areas are highly influenced by dopamine receptors, which are altered from cocaine exposure (Thompsonet et al., 2009b). School-aged children exposed to cocaine prenatally are more likely than other children to be referred to special needs programs (Levine et al., 2008). In addition to problems with attention, these children are more likely to have difficulty with emotional regulation than children not prenatally exposed (Stanwood & Levitt, 2008).

A recent study has also shed light on the genetic altering from prenatal cocaine exposure that can be passed to offspring (Vassoler, White, Schmidt, Sadri-Vakili, & Pierce, 2012). This study with laboratory rats found that resistance to future addiction can be passed to sons but not to daughters from fathers who were addicted to cocaine. Upon examination of the brains of the addicted rats, a protein that inhibits the effects of cocaine, **brain-deprived neurotrophic factor (BDNF)**, was found in the prefrontal cortex. While the researchers did not understand the exact mechanism for their findings, this research suggests that sex hormones, testosterone, and estrogen may play a role in the development of the BDNF protein.

Methamphetamine Exposure

Recent research links a host of complications when pregnant women use methamphetamine, which can be smoked, snorted, injected, or swallowed (Richards, 2016). Methamphetamine, referred to as meth or crystal meth, acts on the brain by flooding it with **dopamine**, a neurotransmitter that produces a feeling of pleasure. Crystal meth, usually smoked in a pipe similarly to marijuana, is one of the most common drugs abused by pregnant mothers. A recent study by Solt and associates (2010) found that of the 274 subjects in their study who used meth, approximately one-half had premature births and 29% had C-sections, compared to 23% for controls. Other complications included 20% of the meth users experiencing excessive high-blood pressure compared to 10% for the control group and a significantly higher **placenta abruption**, separation from the wall of uterus before delivery. The researchers also noted that only 12% of the meth users were married.

Research findings suggest that the effects on the fetus from maternal meth use mirror that of cocaine (Smith et al., 2008). Meth tends to restrict blood flow to the fetus, resulting in both premature births and low birth-weight babies, generally below five pounds. Low birth weight heightens the possibility of long-term post-delivery growth restriction. **Growth restriction** is related to the development of type 2 diabetes, high blood pressure, obesity, and cardiac problems. In addition, psychosocial and behavioral disorders, such as attention deficits, and cognitive or learning problems, are common in children exposed prenatally. A recent study of children exposed prenatally to meth at follow-up at ages three and five found that emotional regulation and anxiety disorders were the most common behavior problems of both groups (LaGasse et al., 2012). However, for the five-year-old group, attention deficit hyperactivity disorder was a common diagnosis. Another recent study found that, due to the restricted blood flow, **fetal anemia** is a common outcome; it means that nutritional concerns should be addressed immediately after birth for fetuses exposed to meth (Goldberg et al., 2010).

PRESCRIPTION MEDICATION AND OTHER EFFECTS

Prescription medication can be damaging to the fetuses of pregnant women, who typically would be prescribed by physicians before knowing they are pregnant (Ross, Graham, Money, & Stanwood, 2015). One of the most serious consequences to the fetus is the mother's use of prescribed antidepressants, which are characterized as **serotonin reuptake inhibitors** and affect cardiac functions in the fetus (Kallen & Otterbald-Olausson, 2006). As has been pointed out previously, serotonin production and receptors are involved in brain development through dendrite and axon formations, particularly in the first trimester. Animal studies reveal that exposure to antidepressants during the third trimester may affect learning and emotional regulation, particularly the regulation of anxiety (Bonnin et al., 2007). While these effects on learning and anxiety have not yet been demonstrated with fetuses, researchers believe that there may be sleeper effects that might affect children, in tandem with a host of other factors. Researchers conclude that antidepressants during pregnancy must be used with caution, weighing the risks against the benefits, especially for women who would be emotionally dysfunctional without the medication.

Researchers have found that antipsychotic medications, which affect dopamine receptors, carry more risk than antidepressants. The extent of the effects on fetus exposure is unknown with most antipsychotics medications, and there are no definitive guidelines for prescribing them. Researchers demonstrate the need for concern about pregnant women's mental health given that approximately 500,000 pregnant women exhibit psychiatric symptoms during and after pregnancy. As many as 70% of pregnant woman experience depression during pregnancy, and a significant number develop postpartum depression. Animal studies show long-term neurobehavioral anomalies from prenatal exposure, although the findings are somewhat inconsistent; overall it is not known how applicable they are to fetuses (Andrade et al., 2008).

Some studies have focused on post-delivery outcomes, specifically on the **Apgar score** (Rahi, Baneshi, Mirkamandar, Maghsoudi, & Rastegari, 2011). The Apgar score is a scale that measures the alertness of the neonate in terms of grimacing, activity, breathing, skin color, and tone immediately after birth from one to a maximum of 10 points. A low Apgar score corresponds to developmental delays. Psychotropic drugs given during the third trimester can result in withdrawal symptoms and a low Apgar score. Studies show that low Apgar scores, generally below seven, are associated with mental retardation (Bercovici, 2005).

Anxiety inhibiting drugs, or benzodiazepines (BZD), are prescribed to approximately two % of women during pregnancy to reduce the effects of general anxiety disorders or anxiety experienced during delivery (Oberlander, Warburton, Misri, Riggs, Aghajanian, & Hertzman, (2008). BZD works to inhibit GAMA A receptors. A number of disorders have been associated with BZD, including cleft palette, facial dysmorphorism, and various degrees of mental retardation. Researchers have also found that fine and gross motor skills were delayed and lower scores were recorded on the general quotient (GQ) at 18-month follow-ups from BZD prenatal exposure (Oberlander et al., 2008).

While some effects of antipsychotic and antidepressant drugs are known, it is conclusive from research that not all effects are clearly delineated (Thompson, Levitt, & Stanwood, 2009b). For example, it is known that these drugs cross the placenta and enter the fetus, but the extent of the short- and long-term effects are unknown. Furthermore, researchers have demonstrated that these drugs affect neurotransmitters in the brain. For example, maternal exposure to psychotropic drugs can change the levels of serotonin and dopamine. Animal studies have shown that these changes can have long-lasting effects (Thompson et al., 2009b).

Although the use of antidepressants and antipsychotic medications may have long-lasting effects on fetuses, mentally distressed mothers who do not take them may create even more risks for their fetuses (Lattimore, Donn, Kaciroti, Kemper, Neal, & Vasquez, 2005). Mothers in a state of deep depression are more prone to suicide than other mothers, and mothers experiencing acute mental or emotional episodes may endanger their fetuses or newborns in enumerable ways. The use of psychotropic drugs should be closely monitored and dispensed according to their **half-life**: drugs with longer half-lives are less likely to cause withdrawal effects. In addition, drugs with active metabolite classifications prolong the effects in the brain and reduce withdrawal symptoms (Lattimore et al., 2005).

A SYSTEMS/DIALECTICAL PERSPECTIVE OF A CHILD'S RIGHT TO BE BORN FREE OF DAMAGE VERSUS THE MOTHER'S RIGHTS

Since the early 1980s, there has been increasing concern over the rights of the unborn. This concern was first fueled by public awareness of what was colloquially termed "**crack babies,**" infants born to inner-city mothers who received little prenatal care and gave birth to crack cocaine–addicted neonates (Lyttle, 2006). Not only did these women use cocaine, but some seemed to do so with impunity, in addition to drinking alcohol. While the damaging effects of drinking alcohol have been well documented in research literature, alcohol use in pregnancy failed to sound the alarm with the same intensity as that of pregnant mothers who sometimes blatantly use illegal drugs. The question arises as to whose rights or what rights are involved. This section will address the question of rights from a systems/dialectical perspective.

When the question of whose rights should prevail, the mothers' or the fetus', it is usually in the context of discussing abortion. The contents of this chapter, however, raise the question of fetal versus mothers' rights based on the mother's decision to carry the fetus to term and not to have an abortion. The overriding question is whether a mother who chooses to carry a fetus to term has a moral, ethical, and even legal responsibility to not engage in behaviors that harm the fetus. This discussion is dialectic; one side believes that the fetus has a right to be born free of damage and that a pregnant woman can be held legally liable for behavior that might impede a healthy intrauterine environment. The other side believes that giving rights to the fetus would deprive a woman of her fundamental rights and would create a confused and restricted environment in which a woman could be punished for almost any innocuous behavior (Reitman, 2002).

Two Opposing Camps

The concern over maternal behavior during pregnancy over the past several decades has been bolstered by findings in neuroscience that neural networks are laid much sooner than formally believed; interruptions (Dirix, Nijhuis, Jongsma, & Hornstra, 2009) in the development of the brain caused by maternal behavior should be in the legislative interest of the state. Some lifelong problems of people could be eliminated if women did not engage in some risky behaviors during pregnancy. And, the cost to the state for treatment, not to mention the unnecessary suffering of children, could drastically improve the quality of human life (Coady, 1997). The major concern of those who advocate fetal rights is that pregnant women should engage in behaviors that lead to the best outcomes in their children. Based on irrefutable research evidence of prenatal brain development, advocates for fetal rights argue that the prenatal period is as important for long-term health as the first three years of life post birth (Dirix et al., 2009). This point of view effectively sidesteps the belief that rights suddenly appear at viability or after birth and sees all of life as moving from one developmental stage to another.

On the other hand, an opposing view posits that the fetus is part of the mother's body and, therefore, not an entity in its own right. This view would also argue that giving the fetus rights on the same standing as that of the mother undermines her individual rights (Paltrow, 1999). This position would also say that it is inappropriate to attempt to turn the mother's body into nothing more than a conduit for the child. Specific arguments from the opposing sides will be explored in greater detail below. Generally, the arguments center on the following points: 1) criminalizing the mother's behavior during pregnancy; 2) the question of constitutional rights, which includes the right to privacy; 3) alcohol and drug addiction as diseases rather than choices that women make; 4) race and gender discrimination; and 5) addressing the issues through education and prevention.

Criminalizing the Mother's Behavior during Pregnancy

Since the 1980s, there has been much attention paid to prenatal smoking and drug use by mothers and the resultant damage to the fetus (Xiao, Huang, Yang, & Zhang, 2011). Generally, the concern was that fetuses exposed to drugs and alcohol would receive irreparable harm in cognitive, emotional, behavioral, and social development. It was believed this damage would cause lifelong impairments in functioning and require costly treatment (Xiao et al., 2011). As a result of these concerns, many states began to prosecute women who seemed to have little regard for the health of their fetuses (Kampschmidt, 2015). Most often, the charges, ranging from drug possession to child abuse, were levied against women who abused drugs, particularly cocaine. Prosecution, which generally led to prison time, was a way to both reduce prenatal use of drugs and alcohol and protect the fetus from further damage. While no states had explicit laws that applied to fetal abuse, prosecutors claimed that the mother's action of injecting alcohol or drugs amounted to an assault on the fetus.

The fetal rights movement is intent on protecting the rights of the unborn and builds on the statement in *Roe v. Wade* (1973) that a viable fetus deserves protection under the law, but at the same time, it ignores the premise that the fetus is a separate person from the mother. The rights of the fetus advocates were further bolstered by the Supreme Court decision in *Planned Parenthood of Southeastern Pennsylvania v. Casey* (1992), which allowed states to address prenatal environment unless doing so would levy an undue burden on the mother. This ruling made each state the determining factor in what constitutes a viable fetus, therefore meeting the criteria to be protected under the law. Consequently, most states have some statutes that allow for mothers to be charged for criminal misconduct, homicide, or neglect, depending on the mother's actions during pregnancy.

The above rulings had the consequence of doing away with the longstanding beliefs and practices that the fetus had no rights and only after birth was the fetus considered a "person" (Linder, 2005). Not all states have adopted this new interpretation of the fetus' rights before birth, but those that do allow for prosecution of the mother for a range of behaviors that endanger the fetus, homicide being one of them. A few states have moved to protect the rights of the fetus regardless of the rights of the mother.

Drug and alcohol use and abuse by pregnant mothers have provided the basis for many of the cases brought against the mother during pregnancy (Kampschmidt, 2015). The widespread use of cocaine by pregnant women became newsworthy in the 1980s with frequent stories in the media about mothers giving birth to babies addicted to crack cocaine (Paltrow, 1999). According to advocates for the rights of mothers, much of the fear and hysteria about drug babies was exaggerated. These advocates claim that early scientific research on the effects of prenatal cocaine exposure was methodologically weak and generalized the findings (Paltrow, 1999). Many of the early studies were case studies with small samples and did not control for other substances, such as nicotine and alcohol exposure. Since pregnant women who used cocaine also used alcohol and smoked cigarettes, the results were ambiguous at best.

Advocates for the rights of the fetus believe that the effects of cocaine exposure on the fetus are real, however, and some of the effects can be very damaging. As pointed out above, the restriction of blood flow caused by prenatal exposure to cocaine can have devastating damage on the fetus and result in death (Gilloteaux & Ekwedike, 2010). Prenatal exposure to cocaine, which causes "focal ischemic damage in the Purkinje myofibers" (p. 90) in the heart, can result in fatal arrhythmias and cardiac arrest. Advocates for the rights of the fetus in this continuing debate believe that pregnant mothers who exposed their fetuses to cocaine should be arrested for fetal abuse. The reasoning was that the mother chooses to endanger her fetus without proper regard for the long-term effects on the academic, social, physical, and emotional development of the child after birth. Many advocates for this position believe that these women blatantly disregarded the advice of doctors or law enforcement officers and, therefore, need to be stopped. Charges varied depending on the state and statute under which the charges are filed.

Advocates for fetal rights also note that some women were not amenable to treatment and continue to expose their fetuses without regard for later consequences (Kassada, Marcon, & Waidman, 2015). Since most women want to have a healthy baby and behave in ways that promote healthy delivery, advocates for fetal rights make no attempts to interfere or be intrusive in women's childbearing privacy. They focus instead on the mother's blatant disregard for the health of the fetus and her refusal to voluntarily submit to treatment, which has resulted in forcing compliance by arresting and charging her with child abuse. While a mainstay in the medical and legal communities has been that a person has a legal right to refuse treatment, this policy has been called into question for pregnant mothers who willfully endanger their fetuses.

Advocates for the mother's rights argue that the criminalization of the mother's prenatal behavior will lead to many women not receiving treatment, because they will be afraid of being discovered as a drug addict (Lyttle, 2006). Consequently, the argument states that they will engage in even more harmful behavior, because they will be more secretive and receive less support from others, which will affect their mental health by increasing the likelihood of depression and other mood-related disorders. The advocates for the fetus view this argument as creating a straw man based on emotions. Further, they would claim that some drug-addicted mothers openly abuse drugs and show no evidence of being swayed to curtail drug use unless they are forced by prosecution or the threat of it (Fatemeh & Marzieh, 2016).

While cases of fetal child abuse have been brought against pregnant mothers in a majority of states, most state supreme courts have overruled these prosecutions (Lyttle, 2006). For example, one noted landmark court case exception was the 1996 ruling in *Whitner v. South Carolina* (1997). This decision, made by the Supreme Court of South Carolina, allowed for pregnant mothers who abused substances, especially illegal drugs, to be charged with child abuse under existing child abuse laws. An underlying issue in this decision was the vulnerable state of the fetus, which was determined to be completely dependent on the mother. This ruling clearly identified that the fetus has a right to be protected under the law in the same way that a child is protected from harm. In this case, the mother was addicted to drugs and continued to use illegal drugs throughout her pregnancy and, consequently, gave birth to an infant addicted to crack cocaine. The mother was initially charged with criminal child neglect and received a prison sentence of eight years but was released after serving less than two years through the intervention of the American Civil Liberties Union (ACLU). A **Post-Conviction Relief** was then ordered from a state court, which essentially reversed the conviction. This state court ruling was followed, however, by a reinstatement of the conviction of criminal child neglect by the South Carolina Supreme Court.

This ruling is very important, because the decision was based on medical evidence, not only on the effects of the drugs but also with knowledge about the developing fetus. The South Carolina Supreme Court ruled that, due to the direct damage inflicted on the fetus and the long-term effects of exposure to cocaine prenatally being as harmful as damage that could occur after birth, the fetus has a right to be protected similarly to other children. This ruling did not suddenly appear on the horizon but developed from a number of earlier cases that paved the way, such as in the case of *Bonbrest v. Kotz* (1946), which allowed for the fetus to receive compensation for injury. However, a drawback with this ruling was that the protection for the fetus began with viability, which has typically been interpreted to mean being able to live outside the human body. In terms of criminal liability law, *Commonwealth v. Cass* (1984) ruled that the fetus killed by a car accident was declared a person in the sense of vehicular homicide laws.

Another important case that affected the decision in *Whitner* was *State v. Horne* (1984) in which a husband was tried for involuntary manslaughter in the death of the fetus after stabbing his nine-month pregnant wife in the abdomen. The ruling underscores that a viable fetus can legally be considered a person regarding laws pertaining to homicide. While other states have allowed criminal cases for acts against the fetus, none have joined South Carolina in granting the fetus the status of person within the meaning of the state statutes. There is no doubt that numerous challenges of state laws must be undertaken to change statutes that do not include the fetus as a person and that further court cases will actively decide the direction of fetal rights.

Constitutional Rights Argument

On the other side of the fetal rights issue is the argument that mother's rights are undermined. This argument holds that many women become pregnant before being aware of it and may have already harmed the fetus; thus, the damage is already done. This view claims that the early period is extremely important because of migration of cells and the development of organs (Shonkoff & Phillips, 2000). Pregnant mothers may drink alcohol, smoke cigarettes, and use legal and illegal drugs, damaging the fetus unintentionally. In other words, from this perspective, it is impossible to remove the prenatal risk of damage to the fetus. Fetal rights advocates would argue that development takes not only nine months but continues after birth, and that holding the mother responsible for damage during all three trimesters of the prenatal period is needed. Furthermore, fetal rights advocates might argue that the specific trimester of development is irrelevant to the question of the damage received. They would also argue that damage received by the fetus is no less damaging merely because it occurred before viability.

Reproductive Rights

Advocates for mothers rights believe that granting rights to the fetus will undermine the mothers' reproductive rights guaranteed in *Roe v. Wade* (1973). This belief is based on the rights of the mother for reproductive choice that could be weakened if the fetus has acknowledged rights (Paltrow, 1999). Furthermore, the Fourteenth Amendment to the Constitution allows for abortion rights under the **Due Process Clause**. According to advocates for women's rights, the Due Process Clause is violated when charged with fetal abuse because of no notice from the government about prenatal conduct through the passage of specific laws. Advocates for fetal rights would contend that a woman would have to be aware that her behavior, by specifically engaging in substance abuse and smoking, directly affects the fetal environment and the fetus (Jost, 2002). Further, states have not acted in a vacuum in bringing charges against pregnant women for decades; this knowledge is certainly public.

Sex Discrimination and Equal Protection

A similar argument used by advocates for women's rights is **equal protection under the law** (Paltrow, 1999). To prosecute women for child abuse of a fetus, they argue, would, in effect, discriminate against women. They argue that since only women are punished for damage to the fetus, the Equal Protection Clause is violated. For example, there is some inconclusive research that implies that the fetus can be harmed by the father's sperm (see Paltrow, 1999). No male has ever been charged for possible harm he may have inflicted through his sperm. Advocates for fetal rights would refer to *Geduldig v. Aiello* (1974), which states that even if only women can become pregnant, there is no basis for claiming that laws regarding pregnancy are gender discriminatory. The application of this ruling is that the government would only have to show that a woman is in a position to protect the fetus, thus the criterion is met for the state to have an interest in scrutinizing her behavior.

Noting that the majority of women charged with harming their fetuses have been poor and Black, advocates for women's rights claim that prosecuting pregnant women for child abuse crosses the line of racial discrimination. For example, one research study found that while a similar or equal number of White and Black women used drugs, about 10 times more Black mothers are charged than White mothers (Roberts, 1991). Advocates for fetal rights would point to the Supreme Court ruling that defines racial discrimination under the Equal Protection Clause; it cannot be based simply on difference in numbers. In others word, to be considered racial discrimination under the Equal Protection Clause, there must also be the intent of the state to discriminate through established and longstanding practices (Jost, 2002).

Right to Privacy

Advocates for women's rights also use the constitutional argument that prosecuting women denies them the **right to privacy** (Reitman, 2002). The argument avows that women prosecuted by the state lose their fundamental guaranteed rights to privacy simply because they are pregnant. The women's status as addicted persons, therefore, is immaterial, and the state should not be permitted to charge women with crimes during pregnancy. On the other hand, advocates for fetal rights argue that a person's rights to privacy, including pregnant women, is not 100% guaranteed because of the state's granted interest in protecting persons or potential persons against harm (Jost, 2002).

Cruel and Unusual Punishment

Advocates for women's rights believe that prosecuting pregnant alcohol- or drug-addicted mothers is **cruel and unusual punishment** as stated in the Eighth Amendment (U.S. Const. Amend. VIII) (Reitman, 2002). The purpose of the Eighth Amendment was to ensure equality, that is, specific groups of persons, including minorities, should not be singled out for punishment that is not levied against the majority group. The bedrock of this amendment is to protect the dignity of persons. This position claims that these mothers are not criminals and do not need punishment. Rather, they have a disease of addiction, which began before pregnancy, and there is no overt intention of harming the fetus. Advocates for mothers' rights argue that prosecuting pregnant mothers is cruel and unusual punishment, because the punishment does not fit the crime. A major court decision in addressing this issue was in *Robinson v. California* (1962) in which the court ruled that the state's right to regulate behavior cannot be secondary to that of human dignity.

Advocates for the rights of the fetus would point to court cases in which a defendant is adjudicated responsible for behavior committed while on drugs or alcohol (Jost, 2002). One such case was *Powell v. Texas* (1968). In this case the decision of the court was that prosecuting an alcoholic for acts committed while drunk did not punish the alcoholic for being addicted to alcohol, but for committing a reprehensible act while drunk. Advocates for the rights of the fetus interpret rulings such as this one to support the contention that pregnant women who endanger the lives of the fetus are not being punished because they have a disease, but because their behavior while pregnant endangers the fetus. Advocates for the mother's rights would counter this argument by arguing that the addicted mother is not choosing to use alcohol or drugs. As a result she should not be punished for behavior that she cannot help; to punish her is cruel and unusual punishment (Reitman, 2002).

Drug Possession

Additional arguments for mothers' rights rest on the definition of being in possession of an illegal drug as usual grounds for prosecution. In the case of a pregnant mother, it cannot be argued that she is in possession of a drug since, once injected, it is out of her control and no longer something she possesses (see *State v. Thronsen*, 1991). This argument rests on the court's interpretation that a person should not be prosecuted for his/her status of being an addict. The advocates for the rights of a fetus would argue that the courts have essentially missed the major point of the use of drugs. For example, the drug might need to be recharacterized as a weapon in the same way a person may use a gun, a knife, or even a vehicle to harm a person, while the mother used a substance to harm the fetus.

Advocates for the mother believe that treatment for the alcohol or drug addiction is the appropriate response to prenatal damage. They point to numerous convictions that have been overturned on appeal (Lyttle, 2006). Some court decisions affirm this position. For example, South Carolina passed a law that required hospitals to drug test pregnant women. On appeal, this law was overturned in *Ferguson v. City of Charleston* (2001), with the court ruling that reporting the results of the drug test to the police amounted to unreasonable search and violated the mother's constitutional rights. Furthermore, advocates for the mother's rights argue that excessive legal regulation of the mother's behavior during pregnancy is an intrusive act that will not stop there. They reason that if such laws as drug testing widely exist, pregnant women may, at some future point, be subjected to penalties for extremely minor illegal activities. Advocates for the mother believe that if there is consistency with regulating the mother's behavior, it would not stop with illegal drugs. Consequently, pregnant mothers would have no rights to privacy, due process, or equality under the law (Reitman, 2002).

Advocates for the rights of the fetus might counter the above arguments noting that illegal drugs are a violation of the law and, therefore, illegal (Jost, 2002). This argument would also say that smoking and drinking alcohol are not illegal. In the Due Process Clause, the courts have clearly allowed for intervention and regulation for specific behaviors, such as for illegal behavior. In fact, fetal rights advocates would argue that criminalizing illegal behavior would not in any way violate the woman's rights. Engaging in illegal behavior is a clear violation of the law, and there is no legal right for any person to engage in illegal behavior. Fetal rights advocates believe that criminalizing illegal drug use is necessary to reduce the damage to the fetus.

While the above argument of fetal rights at viability would coexist alongside *Roe v. Wade,* it is not the full answer for advocates for fetal rights who are concerned about behavior before viability, particularly when the mother made the decision not to abort the fetus. Based on evolving neuroscience research of the prenatal environment, the damage may have already been done before viability. Furthermore, advocates for the rights of the fetus would argue that many of the problems that must be addressed after birth could be avoided if certain behaviors were not allowed during the prenatal period. They reason that if there was as much emphasis on the prenatal period as there is on ages zero to five, many children would have a drastically different developmental trajectory throughout the lifespan.

Civil Commitment

A related issue to criminalization is the **civil commitment**, or forced treatment of pregnant mothers addicted to alcohol or drugs. One state that instituted a civil commitment law was Wisconsin (Linder, 2005). Advocates for mothers' rights acknowledge that civil commitment might reduce damage to the fetus by mothers who persist in ingesting drugs or alcohol, but it also has negative consequences (Reitman, 2002). For example, these mothers are not more likely to be cooperative, or even follow through with health care providers. Because the Wisconsin law only provides for taking pregnant habitual drug-abusing women into custody, the underlying causes and reasons for alcohol and drug abuse are not addressed. From this perspective, it would also mean that the damage was not prevented by civil commitment and the need for treatment and long-term medical care after birth is relatively unchanged. This argument can also be bolstered by addressing the negative effects on the family when the mother is removed by civil commitment. The advocates for the mother would argue that civil commitment creates more instability within the family. Many families may suffer economic stress because of removing the pregnant mother from the home. It can be assumed that advocates for the fetus would argue that the argument of financial strain is a moot point, since the majority of the women who have been prosecuted are not contributing to the family and are actually reducing the family's financial standing by engaging in drug and alcohol abuse.

Education and Treatment

Advocates for mothers' rights argue for a two-pronged approach: start with education and include treatment (Paltrow, 1999). Education about the dangers of alcohol and drug consumption should begin at an early age. Most research supports the view that education is most effective for preventing drug and alcohol abuse at the preschool level (Zigler & Hall, 1999). Education should continue through high school with particular emphasis on the effects of alcohol and drugs on fetal development. In general, the media and advertising should have to pay more attention to the deleterious effects of nicotine and alcohol on the fetus.

Advocates for the mother would say that far too little has been done in terms of treatment (Reitman, 2002). Treatment should be comprehensive since others are affected by this behavior and should not create instability in the family unit by applying generic legal statutes, such as removing the mother from the home. Taking the mother out of the home would have negative consequences for the family. Treating the mother's alcohol or drug addiction in the context of the family would be most helpful. In addition, treatment that provides residential and child care services would be optimal.

Advocates for the fetus would agree that education and treatment are not only essential for reducing the harmful effects of alcohol and drugs on the fetus but that education alone is not effective. Studies on sex education (Wright et al., 2002) and medical conditions, such as asthma (Blessing-Moore, 1996), affirm that persons benefit from having more knowledge, but knowing more does not translate into changing behavior. Fetal advocates point out that there is much knowledge of the harmful effects of drugs even when not pregnant, but this knowledge has little effect on users. They would also point out that the treatment that is available for pregnant alcohol and drug abusers exists but is typically not used by these mothers, thus, the mandate that to reduce the damage more stringent methods must be used.

In sum, a systems/dialectical perspective on whose rights, the rights of the fetus to be born free of damage or the rights of the mother to privacy in child birth, do not lead to one outcome but rather point to ongoing dialogue where these disparate views can be expressed. In constructing this debate, it becomes clear that different paths could be taken if both sides really understood their own positions and equally understood the opponent's views. Views that are based on a particular closed belief system add little to the process of debate. Debates require not only an openness to diverse points of view, but as Haidt (2013) so eloquently pointed out, it requires reflection on one's own views and how these views developed. Reared in a different context, the truths that are so often relied on would be different from what one takes for granted. In reality, our views represent a particular upbringing and depending on that, one could have just as easily taken a different view. Truth is always elusive and never quite attainable, but depends on divergent outcomes where one is capable of reflecting on all perspectives, including one's own.

KEY TERMS

Teratogens
Central nervous system
Neural tube malformation
Neurons
Dendrites
Soma
Axon
Placenta
Syntiotrophoblast
Brain-derived neurotrophic factors (BDNP)
Dopamine
Placenta abruption
Growth restriction

Terminal buttons
Neurotransmitters
Catecholominergic system
Hypoxia
Apotheosis
Nicotine replacement therapy (NRT)
Blood alcohol concentration (BAC)
Fetal anemia
Serotonin reuptake inhibitors
Apgar score
Half-life
Crack babies
Post-Conviction Relief

Autism spectrum disorder
Fetal Alcohol Syndrome (FAS)
Hippocampus
Hydrocephalus
Microcephaly
Norepinephrine
Epinephrine
Due process clause
Equal protection under the law
Right to privacy
Cruel and unusual punishment
Civil commitment

STUDY QUESTIONS TO ACCOMPLISH THE LEARNING OBJECTIVES

1. List and explain how the fetus' central nervous system and neurotransmitters are affected by exposure to legal and illegal drugs.

2. Identify neurotransmitters and their roles during the prenatal period. Analyze how the function of neurotransmitters differ in the prenatal period compared to after birth.

3. Discuss the effects of nicotine exposure during the prenatal period. Should more effort be made to reduce exposure?

4. Explain the pharmacology of alcohol abuse. Discuss the effects of FAS on the fetus.

5. List the effects of cocaine on the fetus. Evaluate if the effects of cocaine have been exaggerated. Explain the evidence that exists for damage to the placenta.

6. While nicotine, alcohol, cocaine, and crystal meth all have negative effects on the fetus, which do you think offers the greatest risk? Justify your answer.

7. Identify legal drugs, antidepressants, and antipsychotics that are the most damaging. Justify your answer.

8. Give arguments for the rights of the mother and for the rights of the fetus. Identify any points of common ground for policymakers. Create a new position on rights of the mother and rights of the fetus.

9. Determine if viability is the appropriate time to focus on damage to the fetus. Give arguments for both sides of the issue, and justify which argument is the strongest.

10. Determine if women should be prosecuted for damaging the fetus when education and treatment fail to stop her behavior. Give arguments for both sides; state a position that is common ground. Create a new position that can be accepted by both sides.

DEBATE ACTIVITY FOR STUDENTS

Consider the following proposition: Stimulants are over-prescribed for school-age children.

- Review refereed literature on this topic. Do a library and Internet search to find relevant material. Investigate some of the additional readings. Develop three arguments for the proposition.

- Develop three arguments against the proposition.

- How do the arguments relate to other systems, such as the community or culture?

- Is there common ground?

- What are the long-term consequences of taking action?

- What new or common-ground solutions should be offered? If no common ground, what new position could emerge from a dialogue between the two positions?

- How is the new position superior to the original positions?

ADDITIONAL READING RESOURCES

Alcorn, R. (2000). *Pro-life answers to pro-choice arguments.* Colorado Springs, CO: Multnomah.

D'Agostino, R. (2014). The drugging of the American boy. *Esquire.* Retrieved from http://www.esquire.com/news-politics/a32858/drugging-of-the-american-boy-0414/

Horn, M. (2008). Mothers vs. babies: Constitutional and policy problems with prosecutions for prenatal maternal substance abuse. *William and Mary Journal of Women and the Law, 14*(3), 635–657.

Lester, B. M., Adrezzi, L., & Appiah, L. (2004). Substance use during pregnancy: Time policy to catch up with research, *Harm Reduction Journal, 1*, 5. doi: 10.1186/1477-7517-1-5

McKoy, J.M. (2003). Can the courts protect a fetus from maternal harm? *Virtual Mentor, 5*(5). Retrieved from http://journalofethics.ama-assn.org/2003/05/hlaw1-0305.html

Wilkinson, D., Skene, L., de Crespigny, L., & Salvuescu, J. (2016). Protecting future children from in-utero harm. *Bioethics, 30*(6), 425–432.

REFERENCES

Ackerman, J., Riggins, T., & Black, M. (2010). A review of the effects of prenatal cocaine exposure among school-aged children. *Pediatrics, 125*(3), 554–565.

American Academy of Pediatrics. (2000). Fetal alcohol syndrome and alcohol-related neurodevelopment disorders. *Pediatrics, 106*(2), 358–361.

Andrade, S.E., et al., (2008). Use of antidepressant medication during pregnancy: A multisite study. *American Journal of Obstetrics and Gynecology, 198*(2), 194.

Aronson, J. K. (2008). *Cocaine: Meyler's side effects of psychiatric drugs.* Amsterdam, Netherlands: Elsevier Science.

Bada, H. S., Das, A., Bauer, C. R., Shankaran, S., Lester, B. M., Gard, C. C., … Higgins, R. (2005). Low birth weight and preterm births: Etiologic fraction attributable to prenatal drug exposure. *Journal of Perinatology, 25*(10), 631–637.

Behar, T. N., Shaffner, A. E., Scott, C. A., Greene, C. L., & Barker, J. L. (2000). GABA receptor antagonists modulates postmitotic cell migration in slice culture of embryonic rat cortex. *Cerebral Cortex, 10,* 899–909.

Behnke, M., & Smith, V.C. (2013). Prenatal substance abuse: Short-and long-terms effects on the exposed fetus. *Pediatrics, 131*(3), 1009–1024.

Bennett, D. S., Bendersky, M., & Lewis, M. (2008). Children's cognitive ability from four to nine years old as a function of prenatal cocaine exposure, environmental risk, and maternal verbal intelligence. *Developmental Psychology, 44*(4), 919–928.

Bercovici, E. (2005). Prenatal and perinatal effects of psychotropic medication on neurocognitive development in the fetus. *Journal of Developmental Disability, 11*(2), 1–20.

Bergmann, K. E., Bergmann, R. L., Von, K. R., Bohm, O., Richter, R., Dudenhausen, J. W., & Whan, U. (2003). Early determinants of childhood overweight and adiposity in birth cohort: Role of breast-feeding. *International Journal of Obesity and Related Metabolic Disorders, 27,* 162–72.

Blessing-Moore, J. (1996). Does asthma education change behavior? *CHEST, 109*(1), 9–11.

Bonbrest v. Kotz, 65 F.Supp. 138 (1946).

Bonnin A., Goeden N., Chen, K., Wilson, M. L., King, J., Shih, J.C., Levitt, P. (2011). A transient placental source of serotonin for the fetal forebrain. *Nature, 472,* 347–350.

Bonnin, A., Torii, M., Wang, L., Rakic, P., & Levitt, P. (2007). Serotonin modulates the response of embryonic thalamo-cortical axons to netrin-1. *Nature Neuroscience, 10,* 588–597.

Bruin, J. E., Gerstein, H. C., & Holloway, A. C. (2007). The effect of rosiglitazone on peripheral insulin signaling and glucose utilization pathways following fetal and neonatal exposure to nicotine in rats. A paper presented at the 67th Annual American Diabetes Association Scientific Sessions. June 22-26, 20017, Chicago Illinois.

Chasnoff, I. J., Anson, A. Hatcher, R., Stenson, H., Iaukea, K., & Randolph, L. A. (1998). Prenatal exposure to cocaine and other drugs: Outcome at four to six years. *Annals of the New York Academy of Sciences, 846*, 314–328.

Chiriboga, C. A., Kuhn, L., & Wasserman, G. A. (2007) Prenatal cocaine exposures and dose-related cocaine effects on infant tone and behavior. *Neurotoxicology and Teratology, 29*, 323–330.

Coady, R. M. (1997). Extending child abuse protection to the viable fetus: Whitner v. State of South Carolina. *St. John's Law Review, 71*(3), 666–690.

Commonwealth v. Cass, 467 N.E.2d 1324 (1984).

Deng, J.-X., Liu, X., Zang, J.-F., Huang, H.-E., Xi, Y., Zheng, H., … Deng, J-B. (2012). The effects of prenatal alcohol exposure on the developmental retina of mice. *Alcohol and Alcoholism, 47*(4), 380–385.

Dirix, C. E. H., Nijhuis, J. G., Jongsma, H. W., & Hornstra, G. (2009). Aspects of fetal learning and memory. *Child Development, 80*(4), 1251–1258.

Doweiko, H. E. (2008). *Concepts of chemical dependency.* Belmont, CA: Wadsworth.

Dwyer, J. B., McQuown, S. C., & Leslie, F. M. (2009). The dynamic effects of nicotine on the developing brain, *Pharmacology and Therapeutics, 122*, 125–139.

Ebert, L. M., & Fahy, K. (2007). Why do women continue to smoke during pregnancy? *Women Birth, 20*, 161–168.

Eliasen, M., Tolstrup, J. S., Andersen, A-M., Gronbaek, M., Olsen, J., & Strandberg-Larsen, K. (2010). Prenatal alcohol exposure and autistic spectrum disorders—a population-based prospective study of 80, 552 children and their mothers. *International Journal of Epidemiology, 39*, 1074–1081.

Fatemeh, G., & Marzieh, A. (2016). The rights of the fetus: Ensoulment as the cut-off point on abortion. *Health Science Journal, 10*(1:15), 1–5.

Feng, Q. (2005). Postnatal consequences of prenatal cocaine exposure and myocardial apoptosis: Does cocaine in utero imperil the adult heart? *British Journal of Pharmacology, 144*(7), 887.

Ferguson, v. City of Charleston (2001).

Frank, D. A., Augustyn, M., Knight, W. G., Pell, T., & Zuckerman, B. (2001). Growth, development, and behavior in early childhood following prenatal cocaine exposure: A systemic review. *Journal of the American Medical Association, 285*(12), 1613–1625.

Geduldig v. Aiello, 417 U.S. 484 (1974).

Gilloteaux, J., & Ekwedike, N. (2010). Cocaine causes atrial Purkinje fiber damage. *Ultrastructural Pathology, 34*(2), 90–98.

Glynn, D. A., Cryan, J. F., Kent, P., Flynn, R. A., & Kennedy, M. P. (2009). Update on smoking cessation therapies. *Advanced Therapy, 26*, 369–382.

Goldberg, L. R., Heiss, C. J., White, L., Kaf, W. A., Becker, A., Schindler, J. B., … Oswalt, J. (2010). Methamphetamine exposure, iron deficiency, and implications for cognitive-communicative function: A case study. *Communications Disorder Quarterly, 31*, 183–192.

Granato, A., Palmer, L. M., De Giorgio, A., Tavian, D., & Larkum, M. E. (2012). Early exposure to alcohol leads to permanent impairment. *The Journal of Neuroscience, 32*(4), 1377– 1382.

Haidt, J. (2013). *The righteous mind: Why good people are divided by politics and religion.* New York, NY: Vintage.

Hepper, G. P., Dornan, J. C., & Lynch, C. (2012). Fetal Brain Function in Response to Maternal Alcohol Consumption: Early Evidence of Damage. *Alcoholism: Clinical and Experimental Research.* doi: 10.1111/j.1530-0277.2012.01832.x1382.

Hinman, L. M. (2016). *Contemporary moral issues: Diversity and consensus* (4th ed.). New York, NY: Routledge.

Huang, Z. J., DiCristo, G., & Ango, F. (2007). Development of GABA innervations in the cerebellar cortices. *Nature Review of Neuroscience, 8*, 673–686.

Huang, L. Z., & Wizner-Serhan, U. H. (2007). Nicotine regulates mRNA expression of feeding peptides in the arcuate nucleus in neonatal rat pups. *Developmental Neurobiology, 67*, 363–377.

Jones, K. L., & Smith, D. W. (1973) Recognition of the fetal alcohol syndrome in early infancy. *Lancet, 302*(7836), 999–1001.

Kallen, B. A., & Otterblad-Olausson, P. (2006). Antidepressant drug use in early pregnancy and infant cardiovascular deficit. *Reproductive Toxicology, 21*, 221–222.

Kampschmidt, E. D. (2015). Prosecuting women for drug use during pregnancy: The criminal justice system should step out and the affordable health care act should step up. *Health Matrix, 25*, 487–513.

Kassada, D. S., Marcon, S. S., & Waidman. M. A. P.(2015). Perceptions and practices of pregnant women attended in primary care using illicit drugs. *Escola Anna Nery, 18*(3), 428-434.

LaGasse, L. L., Derauf, C., Smith, L. M., Newman, E., Shah, R., Neal, C., ...Lester, B.M. (2012). Prenatal methamphetamine exposure and childhood behavior problems at 3 and 5 years of age. *Pediatrics, 129*(4), 681–688.

Lattimore, K. A., Donn , S. M., Kaciroti , K., Kemper, A. R., Neal Jr., C. R., & Vazquez, D. M. (2005). Selective serotonin reuptake inhibitor (SSRI) use during pregnancy and effects on the fetus and newborn: A meta-analysis. *Journal of Perinatology, 25*, 595–604.

Lee, C,-T., Chen, J., Hayashi, T., Tsai, S,-Y., Sanchez, J.F., Errico, S.L., ...Freed, W.J. 2008). A mechanism responsible for the inhibition of neural progenitor cell proliferation by cocaine. *PLOS Medicine, 5*(6), e117 doi:10.1371/journal.pmed.0050117.

Lester, B. M., & Lagasse, L. L. (2010). Children and addicted women. *Journal of Addiction Disorder, 29*(2), 259–276.

Levine, T. P., Das, A., Liu, J., & Higgins, R. (2008). Effects of prenatal cocaine exposure on special education in school-aged children. *Pediatrics, 122*, 83–91.

Linder, E. N. (2005). Punishing prenatal alcohol abuse: The problems inherent in utilizing civil commitment to address addiction. *University of Illinois Law Review, 3*, 873–902.

Lyttle, T. (2006). Stop the injustice: A protest against the unconstitutional punishment of pregnant drug-addicted women. *Legislation and Public Policy, 9*, 781–815.

Maier, S. E., & West, J. R. (2004). Patterns of Alcohol-related birth defects. National Institute on Alcohol and Abuse and Alcoholism.

Medina, A. E. (2011). Fetal alcohol spectrum disorders and abnormal neuronal plasticity. *Neuroscientist, 17*(3), 274–287.

Oberlander, T. F., Warburton, W., Misri, S., Riggs, W., Aghajanian, J., & Hertzman, C. (2008). Major congenital malformations following prenatal exposure to serotonin reuptake inhibitors and benzodiazepines using population-based health data. *Developmental and Reproductive Toxicology, 83*, 68–76.

Ohtani, N., Goto, T., Waeber, C., & Bhide, P. G. (2003). Dopamine modulates cell cycle in the lateral ganglionic eminence. *Journal of Neuroscience, 23*, 2840–2850.

Paltrow, L. M. (1999). Punishment and prejudice: Judging drug-using pregnant women. In J.E. Hanigsberg and S. Ruddick (Eds.), *Mother troubles: Rethinking contemporary maternal dilemmas* (pp. 59–80). Boston, MA: Beacon .

Planned Parenthood of Southeastern Pennsylvania v. Casey, 505 U.S. 833 (1992).

Powell v. Texas, 392 U.S. 514 (1964).

Rahi, E., Baneshi, M.R., Mirkamandar, E., Maghsoudi, S.H., & Rastegari, A. (2011). A comparison between APGAR scores and birth weight in infants of addicted and non-addicted mothers. *Addiction and Health, 3*(1–2), 61–66.

Redila, V. A., Olson, A. K., Swann, S. E., Mohades, G., Webber, A. J., Weinstein, J., & Christie, B. R. (2006). Hippocampal cell proliferation is reduced following prenatal ethanol exposure but can be rescued with voluntary exercise. *Hippocampus,* 16, 305–11.

Reitman, D. R. (2002). The collision between the rights of women, the rights of the fetus, and the rights of the state: A critical analysis of the criminal prosecution of drug-addicted pregnant women. *St. John's Journal of Legal Comment, 267*, 293–294.

Roberts, D. (1991). Punishing drug addicts who have babies: Women of color, equality, and right to privacy. *Harvard Law Review, 104*(7), 1419–1422.

Robinson v. California, 370 U.S. 660 666–67 (1962).

Roe v. Wade, 410 U.S. 113 158 (1973).

Ross, E. J., Graham, D. L., Money, K. M., & Stanwood, G. D. (2015). Developmental consequences of fetal exposure to drugs: What we know and what we must still learn. *Neuropsychopharmachology 40*(1), 61–87. doi: 10.1038/npp.2014.147

Shonkoff, J. P., & Phillips, D. (Eds.). *From neurons to neighborhoods: The science of early child development.* Washington, D.C.: National Academies Press.

Slotkin, T. A. (1998). Fetal nicotine or cocaine exposure: Which one is worse? *Journal of Pharmacology, 285*, 931–945.

Slotkin, T. A., Seidler, F. J., Qiao, D., Aldridge, J. E., Tate, C. A., Cousins, M. M., ... Spindel, E. R. (2005). Effects of prenatal nicotine exposure on primate brain development and attempted amelioration with supplemental choline or vitamin C: Neurotransmitter receptors, cell signaling and cell development, biomarkers in fetal brain regions of Rhesus monkeys. *Neuropsychopharmacolgy, 30*(1), 129–144. Retrieved from http://www.ncbi.nlm.nih.gov/pubmed/15316571?dopt=Abstract

Smith, L. M., LaGasse, L. M., Derauf, C., et al. (2008). Prenatal methamphetamine use and neonatal neurobehavioral outcome. *Neurotoxicology and Teratology, 30*(1) 20–28.

Snow, M. E., & Keiver, K. (2007). Prenatal ethanol exposure disrupts the histological stages of fetal bone development. *Bone, 41*, 181–187.

Stanwood, G. D., & Levitt, P. (2003). Repeat i.v. cocaine exposure produces long-lasting behavioral sensitization in pregnant adults, but behavioral tolerance in the offspring. *Neuroscience, 122*, 579–583.

State v. Horne, 319 SE 2d 703 (1984).

State v. Thronsen, 809 P.2nd 941 (1991).

Streissguth, A., Aase, J. M., Clarren, S. K., Randels, S. P., Ladue, R. A., & Smith, D. F. (1991). Fetal alcohol syndrome in adolescents and adults. *Journal of the American Medical Association, 265*(15), 161–165.

Streissguth, A. P., Bookstein, F. L., Barr, H. M., Sampson, P. D., O'Malley, K., & Young, J. K. (2004). Risk factors for adverse life outcomes in fetal alcohol syndrome and fetal alcohol effects. *Journal of Developmental & Behavioral Pediatrics, 25*(4), 228–238.

Substance Abuse and Mental Health Services Administration. (2009). *Results from the 2008 National Survey on Drug Use and Health: National Findings* (Office of Applied Studies, NSDUH Series H-36, HHS Publication No. SMA 09-4434). Rockville, MD.

Syme, C., Abrahamowicz, M., Mahboubi, A., Leonard, G. T., Perron, M., Richer, L., & Pausova, Z. (2009). Prenatal exposure to maternal cigarette smoking and accumulation of intra-abdominal fat during adolescence. *Obesity, 18*(5), 1021–1025.

Thompson, B. L., Levitt, P., Stanwood, G. D. (2009a). Prenatal exposure to drugs: Effects on brain development and implications for policy and education. *Nature Reviews Neuroscience, 10*(4), 303–312.

Thompson, B. L., Levitt, P., & Stanwood, G. D. (2009b). Prenatal cocaine exposure specifically alters spontaneous alteration behavior. *Behavioral Brain Research, 164*(1), 107–116.

U.S. Const. amend. VIII.

U.S. Department of Health and Human Services (2001). Alcohol alert. *National Institute on Abuse and Alcoholism (NIAAA), No 50.*

Vassoler, F. M., White, S. L., Schmidt, H. D., Sadri-Vakili, G., & Pierce, R.C. (2012). Epigenetic inheritance of a cocaine resistance phenotype, *Nature Neuroscience.* doi:10.1038/nn.3280

Vaux, K. K., & Chamber, C. (2016). Fetal alcohol syndrome. *Medscape, 2016.* Retrieved from http://emedicine.medscape.com/article/974016-overview

Velasquez, J. C., Goedin, N., & Bonnin, A. (2013). Placenta serotonin: Implications for the developmental effects SSRIs and maternal depression. *Frontiers in Cellular Neuroscience, 7*, 47. doi: 10.3389/fncel.2013.00047

Whitaker-Azmitia, P. M. (2001). Serotonin and brain development: Role in human developmental diseases. *Brain Research Bulletin, 56*, 479–485.

Whitner v. South Carolina, 492 S.E.2d 777 778-79 (S.C. 1997).

Wilkinson, D., Skene, L., De Crespigny, L., & Savulescu, J. (2016). Protecting future children from in-utero harm. *Bioethics, 30*(6), 425–432. doi: 10.1111/bioe.12238

Williams, J. H., & Ross, L. (2007). Consequences of prenatal toxin exposure for mental health in children and adolescents. *European Child and Adolescent Psychiatry, 16*(4), 243–253.

Wright, D., Raab, G. M., Henderson, M., Abraham, C., Buston, G., Hart, G., & Scott, S. (2002). Limits of teacher delivered sex education: Interim behavioral outcomes from randomized trial. *British Medical Journal, 324*, 1430.

Xiao, D., Huang, X., Yang, S., & Zhang, L. (2011). Direct effects of nicotine on contractility of the uterine artery in pregnancy. *Journal of Pharmacology of Experimental Therapy, 322*(1), 10–185.

Zigler, E., & Hall, N. (1999). *Child development and social policy.* New York, NY: McGraw-Hill.

CREDITS

- Fig. 4.1: Adapted From: http://jpet.aspetjournals.org/content/285/3/931.full.pdf.

Social Policy and Poverty

SETTING THE PARAMETERS FOR UNDERSTANDING POVERTY

What Is Poverty?

Poverty is usually defined as families who fall below a certain income level, which was based on the cost of food times three (Duncan, Magnuson, Kalil, & Ziol-Guest, 2011). Families in poverty generally lack material possessions when compared to affluent families. For some family researchers, this definition is too narrow and fails to encompass the broader consequences of poverty, namely the lack of social status and participation in community (Engle & Black, 2008). Researchers have demonstrated that raising the income level alone does not alleviate the conditions associated with poverty and, instead, found that addressing the multidimensional components are necessary (Akindola, 2009). Generally, there are three ways of defining poverty: the income basis used by the federal government, the supplemental poverty measure, and the amount of money that families spend (Edsall, 2013). Each one of these approaches not only defines poverty differently but creates different categories of people and suggests different intervention strategies.

The federal government defines poverty based on a formula for computing family income and assessing poverty thresholds (United States Department of Commerce, 2011). In this approach, all forms of pre-tax income are counted from all family members, but non-family members, such as housemates or live-in partners, do not count. Next, the poverty threshold, which does not vary geographically, is assigned to each family member and determined according to the size of family and age of each member. The threshold is calculated to be where the family would spend more than one-third of its income on food, and poverty is determined if the family income falls below this threshold. Poverty level is not computed for children under 15 not living with their family, persons in the military, or college students living in a dormitory (United States Department of Commerce, 2011).

Much criticism has been offered for the traditional method in computing poverty rates (Edsall, 2013). In the mid-1990s the National Academy of Sciences (NAS) set up the Panel on Poverty and Family Assistance to investigate alternative approaches. In its report, the panel recommended a change that would address the economic and social disparities in contemporary society. The panel's report included a number of problems with the traditional method that needed altering (See Table 5.1).

A second way of computing poverty is the Supplemental Poverty Measure, which was devised to gauge government spending in eradicating poverty (Short, 2011). This measure includes taking into account tax and transfer money, such as food stamps, for the support of poor families (Short, 2011). The purpose of this measure is to provide information on economic need for groups on a national or subgroup level. This approach is also based on income and, like the traditional model, views poverty as increasing.

The third method is calculating expenditures and answering the question of what families consume (Edsall, 2012). The consumption approach views the family's economic status over the long term and not merely based on yearly income. It looks at the ownership of homes, cars, and other consumable items that families acquire throughout their lifespans. From this perspective, one assumes that the lack of material possessions is more economically harmful to families than simply the amount of income. It also posits that many sources of income are not included in official income reporting.

TABLE 5.1 The NAS report Identifying weaknesses to the current poverty measure

---

- The traditional income-based measure does not reflect the effects of governmental policies that alter the resources available to families.

- The traditional income-based policy does not take into account expenses that reduce disposable income, such as the cost of holding a job.

- The traditional method does not take into account the variation in medical cost.

- The current poverty thresholds are anomalous and do not take into account important changes in family situations.

- The current poverty thresholds do not adjust for geographic differences in the cost of living across the nation. There exist numerous differences in cost of living and in basic goods and services across the nation, yet there is one standard for all.

Defining poverty is important, because these different methods produce different poverty statistics (Edsall, 2013). For example, if the traditional view is used, the highest poverty groups are children under 18; if the supplemental approach, which takes into account the **Earned Income Tax Credit**, food stamps, housing and other in-kind income, is used as the basis for defining poverty, the highest poverty group is for persons over 65 years of age (See Table 5.1).

The consumption approach concludes that there is a decrease in the overall level of poverty (Edsall, 2013). This approach points out that the amount of money spent on consumable goods remains steady across affluent, middle-class, and lower-class families. Consequently, persons noted as being poor have more and are doing better than generally acknowledged. The proposition states that what families spend on consumable products has steadily increased because of declining costs for these items, even in the face of declining income. This view—more than the other two—would say that current programs for at-risk individuals are working. Therefore, any increase in income is matched by a concomitant increase in spending across various groups. This approach would say that the gap between high-income and low-income persons in terms of income proportional to spending has been stable.

An opposite way of viewing the consumption approach, however, points out the disparity in income and spending over the past several years (Edsall, 2013). For example, in examining the ratio of income to spending, average household income decreased in 2011 by 1.5%, but the rate of spending for the upper fifth increased by 7% (See Figure 5.1). Proponents of this side of the argument believe that the poverty rates of the elderly are overestimated, because they tend to use savings and other means of funds that are not readily identified by statistical data. In fact, some

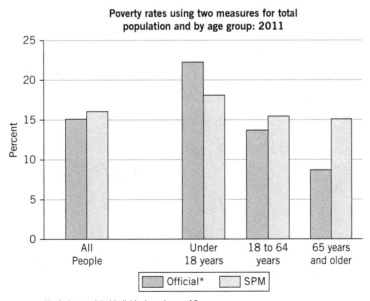

*Includes unrelated individuals under age 15.

FIGURE 5.1 Poverty rates.
*Includes unrelated individuals under age 15.
Source: U.S. Census Bureau, Current Population Survey, 2012 Annual Social and Economic Supplement.

estimate that the poverty rates among the elderly have dropped by as much as 83%, leading to the idea that resources should be divested from the elderly and reassigned to children. The counter to this argument is that many elderly have to pay out-of-pocket health and medical expenses that are ignored in the statistics (Edsall, 2013) (See Figure 5.2, and Figure 5.3). The claim has also been made that the Consumer Expenditure Survey, which is the basis for much of the data on income and consumer spending, has a computing error that has given the false impression that income and spending tend to be in balance (Attanasio, Hurst, & Pistaferro, 2012). Also, a major factor in defining poverty is how escaping poverty is defined. Conservatives are more likely to ascribe individual effort to escaping poverty, while liberals believe that a host of social support is needed to combat the factors that inhibit families from escaping poverty.

Although families can be stuck in poverty and never escape, for many, poverty is a fluid state through which families pass through and return. Typically, poverty tends to perpetuate itself for those born into it while others fall into poverty due to adverse economic times. This can be illustrated by the current economic conditions in the U.S. Today, approximately 30 million Americans are living just above the poverty level, increasing by approximately 10% since 2008 (Luhby, 2012). Near-poverty families tend to be White with low-paying full-time employment and include more elderly than are in poverty. They hover precariously above poverty, generally without employer benefits, and any small financial crisis, such as an unexpected bill, could drop them into poverty.

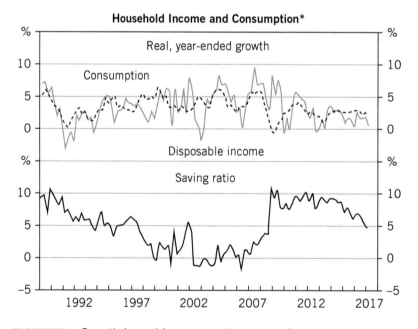

FIGURE 5.2 Growth in real income and consumption

* Household sector includes unincorporated enterprises; disposable income is after tax and interest payments; income level smoothed with a two-quarter moving average between March quarter 2000 and March quarter 2002; saving ratio is net of depreciation

Sources: ABS; RBA

THE EFFECTS OF POVERTY ON CHILDREN

Data indicate that the overall poverty rate for children has increased in the past decade (Fangul, 2014). Most affected by this increase are minorities. According to 2007 census data, Black and Hispanic children are more likely to be in poverty than White children, with 35.4% and 28.6%, respectively (U.S. Census Bureau, 2007). The number of single-parent families is highly correlated with high poverty rates. The U.S. ranks among the highest level of child poverty for rich nations (Fanjul, 2014).

Poverty is related to a host of personal, social, cultural, and economic factors, including family instability, violence, poor housing, poor living conditions, lack of social support, less parental supervision, chaotic communities, and poor child care options (Duncan et al., 2011). Perhaps the most devastating effects are on the brain, especially among the autonomic, immune, and cardiovascular systems. While the bidirectional aspect of stress on these systems can be beneficial in the short term, it is related to long-term deregulation of these interactional systems (McEwen & Gianaros, 2010).

Recent discoveries in neuroscience have made the debate of nature versus environment passé. Instead, development is looked at as an ongoing interaction of biology and ecology. Research demonstrates that fetal exposure to maternal stress can result in a postnatal response to stress. The conclusion is that the environmental context modulates the expression of the genotype. Experiences play the role of promoting certain responses and limiting other responses. Consequently, researchers are attempting to understand this process so that prevention or treatment can be effective (Shonkoff et al., 2012). Researchers point out that stress activates the "hypothalamic-pituitary axis and the sympathetic-adrenomedullary system" (p. 239). This activation stimulates other concomitant

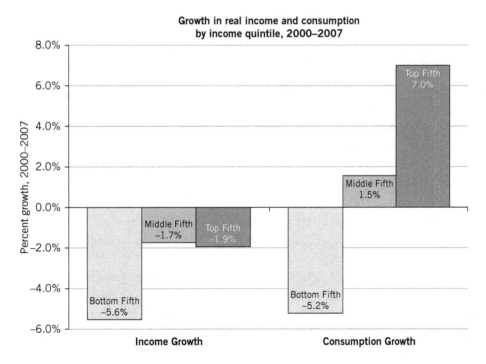

FIGURE 5.3 Marriage rates and poverty
Source: Current Expenditure Survey, CPS ASEC.

events, such as the inflammatory response and the parasympathetic nervous system. If this response is frequent and continuous, emotional and physical dysfunction can occur. The process of balancing these above processes and returning to normal is referred to as allostatic load.

In summation, research in neuroscience concludes that early experiences are wired physiologically in the body, which limits the ability to balance stress and return to normal, resulting in compromised development (Schore, 2009). This kind of toxic stress over the lifespan affects cognitive development, health, and emotional stability.

The effects of poverty on children can be devastating, reducing the quality of life throughout the lifespan (Duncan et al., 2011). Much of the negative effects can be traced to poor educational outcomes and poor health coverage. Cognitive development deficits show up as early as two years of age and continue into adulthood. As noted in the chapter on drug use by the mother, poverty, as a consequence of the family income, may have the least effect on children's academic and social development. Other factors, such as the mother's behavior during pregnancy, may account for long-term effects on children rather than the income level of the family.

School Readiness

Children in poverty score lower on standardized tests. A recent study matched low- and middle-income children on a number of variables and assessed their scores on intelligence tests (Farah et al., 2006). The researchers specifically wanted to find associations between the tests and brain functioning. The findings included differences in the "left perisylvian/language and medial temporal/memory systems" (p. 166), which directly impact learning and the use of language. A recent review of studies that used various methods, including brain scan imaging, revealed that children in poverty consistently have lower performance in language and logical processing and their brains are different as noted in brain imaging research, even when no difference is found in performance (Hackman, Farah, & Meany, 2010).

Recent studies on child heath have confirmed a link between early life experiences and later life illness (Shonkoff, Boyce, & McEwen, 2009). One path this connection takes is by laying down developmental interruptions early in life, which can cause illness many years later. Children in poverty experience more of these developmental blocks. Another pathway for later life illness emanates from an accumulation of detrimental experiences over time that are expressed later in illness (Shonkoffet et al., 2009). Researchers in cognitive development of children assert that the context or environmental atmosphere in the early years account for the disparities noted in children in academic performance. Researchers have found that about 20% of the variance in intelligence quotient (IQ) scores in children is explained by poverty or SES status (Gottfried, Gottfried, Bathurst, Guerin, & Parramore, 2003).

Many children are not ready for school, especially those born into poverty. Children in poverty not only begin school behind other children but tend to fall even farther behind in later grades (Bailey & Danziger, 2013). For example, the gains that impoverished children make in preschool programs like Head Start tend to fade in grade school, and the gap widens. Children who are not ready for the first grade will not be as successful as they move through the educational systems and are more likely to not graduate from high school or go to college. The prospects for self-sufficiency in adulthood decrease for children who suffer academic failure.

Researchers in cognitive development of the brain have demonstrated that the brain develops in a prescribed fashion (Shonkoff, 2009). Initially, the brain develops at an expedited pace of approximately 700 neural connections per second, which is followed by a pruning process. Vision, hearing, and other sensory connections develop next. As brain connections build on one another, language and cognitive circuits develop; pruning occurs to allow greater efficiency (Shonkoff, 2009).

Researchers have found that the **home learning environment** accounts for much of the differences in children's early IQ scores (Nisbett et al., 2012). In assessing the home learning environment through a scale called the **Home Observation for Measurement of the Environment (HOME)**, researchers found that the home learning environment is closely associated with acquiring early reading skills (Molfese, Modglin, & Molfese, 2003). The HOME scale, consisting of 45 items, measures the amount of intellectual stimulation and support the child receives from parents. It consists of six subscales: 1) education or responsiveness of the primary caregiver; 2) avoidance of restriction and punishment; 3) organization of the temporal and physical environment; 4) provision of appropriate play materials; 5) parental environment with the child; and 6) opportunities for variety in daily stimulation. The scale has been used for over 30 years and was most recently updated in 2001 (Totsika & Sylva, 2004); it includes both observational and interview items. The HOME scale has been widely used in research and consists of two classifications of variables: proximal, referring to direct effects on the child, and distal, variables such as the mother's IQ, which indirectly affect the child (see Totsika & Sylva, 2004). The underlying theoretical basis for the measure is ecological theory, and the primary ecosystem is the microsystem of child and primary caregiver. The scale evaluates three basic constructs: the developmental needs of the child, the environment of the child, and parenting effectiveness. While this measure was the most predictive of IQ scores before the age of three, it does not predict changes of IQ over time. Rather, research tends to favor the strong influence of environmental variables to explain the changes in IQ over time.

The frequent use of the HOME measure over the past 30 years by researchers has established a number of irrefutable findings. The HOME measure is significantly correlated with other cognitive measures, and this correlation improves with age (Molfese et al., 2003). For example, the correlation is stronger for children over three years of age than those younger.

Behavioral Effects

Researchers have found that a poor postnatal environment can affect the functioning of the **hypothalalmic-pituitary-adrenal (HPA)** axis resulting in mood and anxiety disorders (Fernald & Gunnar 2009). Two genes, CRHR1 and FKBP5, appear to be involved when the environment for the developing child is abusive. The HPA interaction with the amygdala or limbic brain systems is involved in emotional learning and response to emotional stimuli. When the child experiences trauma in early development, this brain complex is activated, which leads to problems in regulating and maintaining a steady emotional state.

The impact of the family is enormous in understanding how poverty can have direct or indirect influence on children (Mulligan et al., 2013). Direct effects occur, because families have greater interaction with young children than do non-family members. Because children learn from both imitation and observation of their parents, parents who have limited relationship skills do not provide effective models to imitate. What children may witness when parents lack basic relationship skills are parents who have poor impulse control, an external locus of control and blame others for their own shortcomings. Consequently, children grow up with an external locus of control and feel like victims.

Parents who lack relationship skills tend to parent more harshly than parents who have high competency in relationship skills (Lereya, Sumara, & Wolke, 2013). For example, low SES is related to more punitive parenting and less supportive and nurturing behavior. Lower-SES parents have less knowledge of child development, including knowledge of developmental readiness. Lacking this basic knowledge, they are more likely to punish children for age-appropriate behavior. The toddler who says "no" to parental directions or has a temper tantrum when a parent puts away a toy may be punished for behavior that is normal and expected. When children do not learn appropriate self-regulation skills from such parenting, they have more difficulty in establishing trust and forming a deep and abiding bond with parents.

Parenting methods of lower-SES parents tend to use direct interventions, such as spanking or other means of taking control of children (Weinberg, 2001). **Direct punitive methods** tend to stop the behavior but require more force in the future to get the same results. What is missing from lower-SES parents' repertoire is parenting interventions that build the relationship and see the parent/child relationship as bidirectional. Moreover, **indirect methods**, which build relationship skills as opposed to control methods, are less often used by low-SES parents. Indirect methods, such as storytelling or paradoxical interventions, referred to as second-order parenting (Roberts, 1994), are rarely used.

Engle and Black (2008) discuss how families in poverty can also have moderating and mediating effects on outcomes with children. For example, a moderating effect is when parents lack good relationship skills and cannot insulate their children from the devastating effects of poverty. These parents do not spend as much time in activities, such as reading or other cognitive-enhancing activities (Bradley, Whiteside, & Mundfrom, 1994, as cited in Engle & Black, 2008). In addition, the parents' attitude might be a moderating effect in that, even in poverty, parents who have mature and positive attitudes may contribute to children's well-being.

The mediating model is expressed through dysfunctional family relationships (Engle & Black, 2008). For example, the accumulation of stress in the family can lead to chronic stress, which reduces effectives in completing tasks and in relationship development. The presence of chronic stress reduces the ability to deal with normal everyday events and activities.

The lack of emotional regulation coincides with the corticotrophin-releasing hormone (CRH Complex), which activates the secretion of the adrenocorticotropic hormone (ACTH) from the pituitary gland, followed by the secretion of cortisol from the adrenal glands. Researchers have shown a link between the activation of the CRH complex and SES. Children raised in poverty are, therefore, more vulnerable to poor responses to stress, which affect cognitive and emotional development (Cohen, Doyle, & Baum, 2006). In addition, maternal depression has been linked as a moderating variable for the development of this HPA/CRH axis. Depressed mothers of lower SES provide inconsistent attention and care for the fetus, and this causes a failure to meet the age-appropriate development. They provide fewer toys for children to play with, use limited language in communication, and provide less exposure to extra-familial stimulating outings (Bradley, Corwyn, Burchinal, McAdoo, & Garcia-Coll, 2001). Parents of lower SES do not read as often to their children or engage in other verbal activities, such as storytelling. Because of the increased stress level, the overall quality of the emotional relationship is less supportive (Belsky & Jaffee, 2006).

Attachment

Research has definitively linked specific parenting interactions, namely sensitive and responsive caregiving, with secure attachment in children (Nanu & Nijloveanu, 2015). On the other hand, insensitive and unresponsive or inconsistent interactions are highly linked with the development of insecure or disorganized attachment. Initially, researchers identified three styles of attachment: secure, insecure-resistant, and insecure-avoidant (Main, 1990). These early researchers noted that secure children do not seem affected by distance from the mother, while children with insecure-resistant attachment are both distressed by distance from the mother and display angry resistive behavior in close proximity to her. These insecure-resistant children must use other strategies to cope with stress. Children with insecure avoidant style attachment will show little reduction of stress in the presence of the mother (Main, 1990).

More recently, researchers have found that children from the three categories of attachment may respond to stress through disorganized and anxious behavior, which may represent a significant change from their usual attachment style behavior (Hesse & Main, 2006). There are also children who display disorganized attachment without any overt link to other attachment behavioral styles. Some researchers assume that the disorganized attachment style develops from the child's extreme fear of the attachment figure (Hesse & Main, 2006). Children with disorganized style attachment are in a "Catch-22;" namely, they need and desire the caregivers' presence and support but are simultaneously repelled because of their fear of the caregivers. The quality of the parent/child relationship is severely compromised by the harsh, inconsistent, and unresponsive behavior of the parent. Consequently, these children are never able to resolve their fears and conflicts.

Researchers have demonstrated that rough or insensitive parenting is the most likely cause of disorganized attachment in children (Hesse & Main, 2006). Maltreating parents are not able to protect their children from intense fear. Some researchers have suggested at least three pathways associated with the disorganized style (van IJzendoorn & Bakermans-Kranenburg, 2009). First, sexually or physically abusive parents create a dilemma that children cannot resolve. Second, chaotic family or institutional environments in which children do not receive appropriate attention from caregivers and are left to their own devices are prone to develop disorganized attachment styles. Third, when children witness domestic violence, they may experience fear that cannot be relieved through contact with the parent.

Attachment has been investigated through the use of the HOME scale. Researchers found that securely-attached 36-month-old children were more likely to have mothers who scored high on sensitivity and responsiveness on the HOME scale, and insecure avoidance children were more likely to have mothers with low scores (NICHD Early Childcare Research Network, 2001, as cited in Totsika & Sylva, 2004). Other researchers have found comparable evidence that poverty is closely related to higher rates of insecurity or disorganized/disoriented attachment in impoverished families of children 12 and 18 months of age (Shaw & Vondra, 1995). Additionally, children with insecure or disorganized attachment who are high risk for social dysfunction caused by poverty will have later behavioral problems (Lyons-Ruth, 2008). These findings are based on two underlying characteristics, insensitive caregiving and high-risk social environments, such as poverty.

Mansfield and Novick (2012) attempted to answer the question of why there is a link between poverty and poor health in children. In their study in North Carolina, they wanted to find out why children in poverty tend to have more health-related issues than other children. In analyzing data from all counties in North Carolina, they found a high correlation between mortality rates and poverty and a low correlation between mortality rates and counties with high incomes. The total environmental and social context of the children contribute to the increased mortality and diseases.

Over the past several decades, researchers have generally concluded that one of the greatest effects on the developing child is maternal depression (Maughn, Cicchetti, Toth, & Rogosch, 2007). Because maternal depression tends to be linked with poverty, reducing depression among young mothers has been a focal point for intervention. The greatest danger associated with maternal depression on the developing child is in social-emotional development. Researchers have struggled to understand the mechanism of just how maternal depression affects children (Maughn et al., 2007).

One area of research to better understand how depressed mothers affect various developmental domains is cognitive appraisal. Researchers, controlling for verbal ability, gave five-year-old children whose mothers had been diagnosed with major depression during the first 20 months after the birth false belief tasks, or beliefs that one has that may contrast with reality (Rohrer, Cicchetti, Rogosch, Toth, & Maughan, 2011). Results indicated that, when compared to a control group, children of depressed mothers were significantly less likely to understand false beliefs.

Researchers in the area of maternal depression believe that maternal depression initiates a process of developmental risk in the children that involves negative outcomes in a number of developmental domains (Toth, Cicchetti, Rogosch, & Sturge-Apple, 2009). Development is viewed as a series of interlocking stage tasks that become more distinguished across time in which subsequent stages incorporate earlier ones. Consequently, dysfunction in one domain sets in motion dysfunction in other domains. Researchers have concluded, however, that there is variability in both the mother's experience of depression and the concomitant effect on the child (Toth et al., 2009).

One of the most important developmental domains is the emergence of a sense of self during toddlerhood (Toth et al., 2009). Viewing themselves as a distinct entity means that toddlers can understand how they affect specific events around them. According to Toth et al., researchers have found that the degree of maternal depression was associated with the level of insecure attachment at both 20 months and three years, which predicts negative self and prenatal representations at age four. In addition, "the findings demonstrate that the degree of attachment insecurity at age three mediated the relation between early maternal depression and emerging negative representational models of parents by age four" (p. 204).

Environmental Factors Related to Poverty and Children

A major factor affecting children in poverty is being more susceptible to diseases than children not in poverty. Moonie, Sterling, Figgs, and Castro (2006) found that children from impoverished backgrounds, such as inner-city children, miss more days from school and have more severe episodes of asthma than other children. Studies have also demonstrated that high risk factors for diseases included not only the family income level but education, living conditions, community, and support across the entire social class spectrum (Chen, Martin, & Mathews, 2006). As socioeconomic status increases across spectrums such as higher income, education, and living conditions, the incidences and severity of childhood diseases decrease (Chen et al., 2006). While many children of lower SES do not have health insurance, this increased risk for health problems is not affected by having or not having health insurance (Bauman, Silver, & Stein, 2006).

The incidences of asthma are more severe and occur more often in children of poverty. A recent research study using Hispanic and Black children of poverty eight to seventeen years of age found that maternal smoking *in utero* was correlated with greater incidences and management of symptoms (Oh et al., 2012). In addition, children with asthma have higher rates of depression and anxiety (Gillaspy et al., 2002, as cited in Molzon, Hullmann, Eddington, & Mullins, 2011), and their quality of life is lower. Not only are there differences in severity and incidences of asthma related to SES, but disparities also exist in interventions and treatment. Crowder and Broome (2012) suggest that to address this cultural disparity in treatment interventions, a cultural model is needed to guide the intervention. The lack of a cultural sensitivity to treatment modalities is a significant contributor to poor outcomes in treatment. In a recent study designed to determine the effects of depression on self-management treatment of asthma, which is a popular intervention approach, researchers found that depression alters the effect of the intervention and self-management treatment with urban teens (Guglani, Havstadt, Johnson, Ownby, & Joseph, 2012).

Exposure to lead is another environmental hazard that affects poverty-level children more than other children (Evans, 2006). Persons in poverty are more likely to live in old homes with lead-based paint and lead plumbing. Studies have demonstrated that lead affects cognitive development and other central nervous system disorders. The Wechsler Preschool and Primary Scale of Intelligence–Revised was administered to 154 children, six months to six years of age (Jusko, Henderson, Lanphear, Slechta, Parsons, & Canfield, (2008). Jusko et al. adjusted for a number of confounding variables, including the IQ of the mother and the home environment. The researchers concluded that IQ scores for children with high lead blood concentrations scored 4.9 points lower than children with average lead concentrations.

BRIEF HISTORY OF THE AMERICAN ANTI-POVERTY PROGRAM

An underlying principle of social well-being is that some families are not able to provide the support and stability for family members to thrive and prosper. The economic future for American families has been looking bleaker each year (Rugaber, 2012). The hardest hit workers in the job market are the blue-collar industrial high-wage earners. Without higher education credentials, these workers are squeezed out of the labor force and will be at high risk for social welfare programs. The number of participants in the workforce for blue-collar workers is the lowest in 31 years (Rugaber, 2012). Today the unemployment rate in the U.S. is approximately 8% and has been for over three years. There are 43 million Americans out of work, resulting in increasing numbers of people relying on government anti-poverty programs, such as food stamps. It has been noted that, currently, the country is experiencing the highest reliance on food stamps since 1948, which means that an increasing amount of the U.S. federal budget each year goes to support for families.

The beginning of the welfare system resulted from the Great Depression, and attempts to reduce its impact on families culminated in the **War on Poverty** in the 1960s; many of its programs are still in use today (Bailey & Danziger, 2013). The Aid to Dependent Children component, the Social Security Act of 1935 provided financial support for families (Karger & Stoesz, 2006). Over the years, the government made revisions and gradually increased expenditures. For example, in 1937, subsidized housing for low-income families was instituted with participation by over two million families (Danziger, 2010). There is evidence that these programs reduced poverty rates, although, over time, the rate remained consistent but began increasing again in the last decade (Karger & Stoesz, 2006).

Other noted additions to the anti-poverty programs included Women, Infants, and Children (WIC) in 1972, which focused on nutritional support for low-income women (Danziger, 2010). Supplemental Social Security Income (SSI) began in 1974 and provided income assistance to qualified persons over 65 years of age who had limited income and suffered from a disability. According to Danziger, the same year, Section 8 provided vouchers for qualified low-income persons to rent privately owned homes whose owners participated in the program. The following year, 1975, saw the beginning of the Earned Income Tax Credit (EITC), which allowed for a refundable credit for income for families below a certain income limit, especially those with children. The allowable credit for couples filing jointly with three or more children is approximately $48,000, or more than two times above the established poverty index. In 1993, Hope VI attempted to decentralize poverty in public housing by creating alternate sites of public housing. This program attempted to reduce the concentration of public housing in inner cities and move it to middle-class suburban neighborhoods.

The government also provides support for housing for families with children with a disability through SSI and supports youth and adult employment through numerous programs (Bailey & Danziger, 2103). Under the guidelines of the Personal Responsibility and Work Opportunity Reconciliation Act (PRWORA), SSI was harder to obtain for needy families meeting the criteria with a child less than 18 years of age. The average payment was approximately $597 in 2010 (Social Security Administration, 2010). The government provides support for housing through the Department of Housing and Urban Development (HUD) with Section 8, cash vouchers, and public housing. These programs are helpful but limited in the actual number of families that can be served. The government also supports job training and work programs for families in poverty. The Job Training Partnership Act (JTPA) gave way to the Workforce Investment Act (WIA) of 1998, which focused on job placement, rather than training.

PRWORA, one of the most significant pieces of legislation on welfare, was passed in 1996. This program was devised to require states to implement mandatory work guidelines and requirements for participation (Lens, 2002). The program Aid to Families with Dependent Children (AFDC) became Temporary Aid for Needy Families (TANF). Participation in TANF was contingent on participants meeting established criteria, which varied from state to state, and resulted in lack of consistency and non-homogeneous programs. Overall, the outcome of welfare reform was a decrease in reliance on cash payments, although the number of participants in other programs increased (Lens, 2002).

Numerous studies have been conducted on the success of welfare reform and participants and their children (Chase-Landsdale et al., 2003). Generally speaking, there is little evidence that reform has improved or worsened the lives of persons who participate, although there are passionate arguments on both sides (Chase-Landsdale et al., 2003). Studies show that the outcome for children whose parent(s) participate in welfare programs are not directly affected, but tends to be mediated through the stress level of the parent (Johnston, Kalil, & Dunifor, 2010). Poverty rates dropped initially and continued to be approximately 12% until 2008 when the rate began increasing to about 15% in 2013 (Bradley, 2012).

The growing welfare support for families has been referred to as the "**welfare state**," or when an economically developed government provides assistance for poor and needy families in a wide range of services (Karger, Midgley, Kindle, & Brown, 2007). In the U.S., the welfare state has been growing since the 1960s and is generally believed to be currently at unsustainable levels (See Figure 5.4 and Figure 5.5). Liberals generally favor—and conservatives generally disparage—the term welfare state. Conservatives believe that reliance on welfare reduces self-reliance and motivation to work (Gorski, 2008). Furthermore, conservatives believe that the incentive for charities and faith-based missions to help the needy will drastically decrease in a welfare state coupled with high taxes on the wealthy (Olasky, 2010).

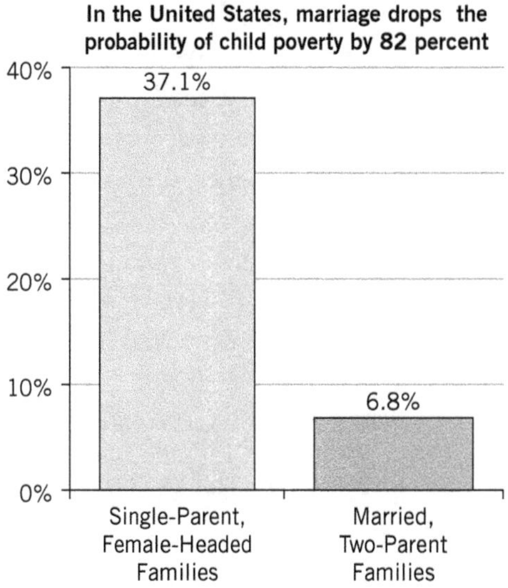

Programs to combat poverty have swung back and forth depending on which ideology, liberal or conservative, is in power, with little or no effect on the poverty rates. While the Obama administration touted redistribution of wealth as a way to combat poverty, poverty rates and poor economic conditions have actually increased. One of the most vexing results of the economic condition under the Obama administration was that more families with children were poor, which will compound the social effects over extended generations. According to census data in 2012, there are 46 million Americans, or 15% of families, in poverty (Income, Poverty, & Health Insurance Data, 2012). Furthermore, median family income decreased from 2011 rates in 2013, and future projections suggest further decrease.

Donald Trump ran for president with the economy as a major campaign focus. His plan called for an annual growth of 4%, increased domestic manufacturing, and reducing regulations that stall growth in housing and other industries (Amadeo, 2017). While Trump is only one year into his term, the economic forecast looks favorable, and the annual rate of growth appears to be stronger, although not expected to reach 4 %. Unemployment has decreased and the stock market continues to climb.

One of the main issues in understanding poverty is how poverty is defined (Greenberg, 2009). Being destitute or not having shelter or enough to eat represent only a small number of persons in poverty. The poverty rate is determined by multiplying the U.S. Department of Agriculture (USDA) food plan devised in the 1960s by three, since families in the 1960s spent about one-third of their budget on food. The definition of poverty does not include "in kind" help, such as food stamps, known as Supplemental Nutrition Assistance Program (SNAP) after 2008, or earned income tax credit. On the one side, poverty is fought by increasing these kinds of governmental programs; on the other side, poverty is decreased by producing more self-sustaining jobs (U.S. Department of Commerce, 2012).

Blank and Greenberg (2010) make a case for a redefinition of poverty with two main components: it should clearly identify the amount of money that families need to meet their essential needs and should also, in addition to income, address other forms of deprivation, such as health care and affordable housing. Using different criteria than cost of food, Blank and Greenberg believe that

FIGURE 5.4 Welfare support for families 1950–2010

the current income approach categories for determining poverty are too low and do not meet the basic needs of persons. For example, if the average family income was used, the poverty threshold would be increased by more than 100%. If criteria other than the food cost were the basis, it might be that in some parts of the U.S., there would be little change, but in other parts, where the cost of housing is higher, the poverty threshold would be far too low. Linking poverty with median income would mean that, as the economy increases, all people would benefit, especially those in poverty. The supporters of the liberal side of the argument believe that using average income as the key for determining poverty rates is more sensitive to all members of society. Moreover, it is a method for sharing the wealth and improving the quality of life for those in poverty.

TABLE 5.2 The 2017 poverty thresholds for the U.S. census

NUMBER OF PERSONS IN FAMILY	INCOME THRESHOLD
1	$12,060
2	$16,240
3	$20,420
4	$24,600
5	$28,780
6	32,960
7	$37,140
8	$41,320

Copyright in the Public Domain.

Liberals would point out that 24.7% of Blacks live in poverty, while 6.9% of White families live in poverty (Cawthorne, 2008). Furthermore, in reviewing census data, Cawthorne concluded that women are more likely than men to be in poverty (13% versus 9.6%). In comparing men and women across racial lines, women in all racial or ethnic groups had higher rates of poverty than men. Among White non-Hispanics, the rates were 11.6% for women and 9.4% for men; for Hispanics, 23.6% for women and 19.6% for men; and for Blacks, 26.5% for women and 22.3% for men.

Conservatives, on the other hand, take a different view using some of the same census data. For example, they point out that, in describing poverty, the drop in marriage rates over the past decades is an important neglected factor (Rector, 2012). According to census data, before the War on Poverty, only 6.3 % of children were born out of wedlock, and in 2008, it was 40.6%. In addition, conservatives point out that, since 1963, the government has spent 16.7 trillion dollars on antipoverty programs (U.S. Department of Commerce, 2012), much of which was for the support of single-parents mothers; they conclude that there is little evidence to support that these programs reduce poverty. The rate of children born out of wedlock is a major factor in child poverty. For example, 36.5% of female-headed households are in poverty, compared to 6.4% of two-parent families. Seventy-one percent of poor families are headed by a single parent, and the majority of those have never been married. Education plays a major role in poverty, since slightly more than two-thirds of persons in poverty are high school dropouts. The more education a woman has, the less likely she will have a child out-of-wedlock: 8.3% for college-educated women compared to 91.7% for high school dropouts (Rector, 2012).

When broken down by race and ethnicity, there is obvious disparity. For example, according to Rector (2012), before the War on Poverty in 1963, 24.2% of Black births were outside of marriage, and by 2008, this number had increased to 72.3 %. For White non-Hispanic women, the figure was about 3% in 1963 and 28.6% in 2008, and for Hispanics the rate rose from approximately 36% in 1988 to 52.5% in 2008. In 2006, the rate for married White families in poverty was 3.1%, but increased to 21% for non-married families. Married Black families in 2006 had a poverty rate of 6.9%, but the rate was 33.5% for unmarried families (Rector, 2012).

The conservative position supports reducing penalties for marriage in welfare programs. It also supports increased educational promotion of marriage in communities with high levels of poverty. This position advocates for federally funded programs for relationship building and marriage education (Rector, 2012).

The liberal side takes a skeptical stance of the importance of marriage in reducing poverty in poor families. Edin (2000) pointed out that many low-income women are reluctant to marry low-income men because of vulnerability for instability. Other research on marriage education for women in poverty results in many of these women feeling that they have to acquiesce to male dominance (Houston & Melz, 2004). While liberals acknowledge that some benefits may accrue from marriage, they believe that these gains are small (Acs, 2007).

The Market versus the Welfare State

The debate over which form of economic systems better serves people is ongoing, and no simple answer suffices. On the one hand, the argument is that a **free market** is the answer in the long run from a historical perspective, while on the other hand, some propose that the free market may directly cause and maintain poverty (Stossel, 2014).

The debate over how to reduce poverty takes many forms. As noted earlier, persons in poverty work less than persons above the poverty level (Rector, 2012). This fact alone has been fundamental to many government programs and is clearly implicated in the original formulation of TANF. Increasing work hours is highly correlated with increasing the educational level of persons. It also includes living in a safe and supportive community and not isolated in pockets of high concentrations of poor persons. Although both sides of this argument would agree with the above brief description, how to achieve these outcomes is not a given. For example, many persons are locked into low-income jobs and are not able to advance to higher-paying jobs.

Advocates to raise the minimum wage point out that no one at the minimum-wage level can support a family and make enough income to live above the poverty level. They point out that persons at the lower end of the economic status fall further behind, while those at the top keep increasing in wealth (Reich, 2011). They argue that it is a matter of fairness in which all persons can participate in economic well-being. Of the many jobs that exist at minimum wage, most require only minimal education and tend to be over represented in restaurants, particularly fast-food restaurants, grocery stores, and other retail jobs.

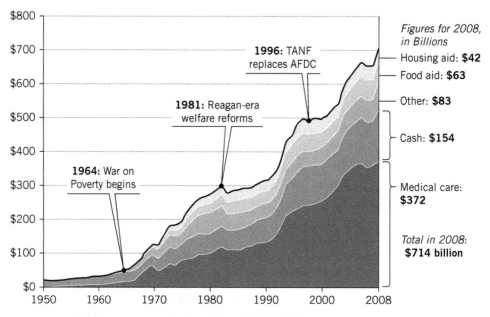

FIGURE 5.5 Welfare support for families 1950–2010

Advocates to raise the minimum wage are met head-on with advocates for maintaining it or only making small cost-of-living adjustments. One of the first arguments against raising the minimum wage is that minimum wage jobs are not meant to create a high standard of living (Huppke, 2014). They point out that minimum wage earners are teenagers or persons in their first jobs who are not supporting a family. Many are high school or college students who are supporting themselves while finishing school. Critics of increasing minimum wage say that most people have had minimum-wage jobs when they were younger. While the first job of most people is minimum wage, they tend to move up the ladder to higher-paying jobs. Advocates for this position claim that minimum-wage jobs introduce people into the workforce and provide a valuable lesson about the workplace. This argument is quickly countered from the other side by the question, "What about those people who do not have upward mobility?"

Advocates against raising the minimum wage find many other reasons to be against it (Huppke, 2014). The idea of raising the minimum wage from $7.25 to over $14 is believed to be excessive and damaging to the economy. Advocates of not raising the minimum wage state that employers cannot stay in business by doubling wages of those at entry levels, because it would also mean that persons at all levels would need income adjustment. They would ask the question, "What about persons making $10 an hour now?" If minimum wage is increased to $14, what would be an equitable increase for those employed persons now making less than minimum wage? If persons make $16 an hour and the minimum wage is increased to $14 an hour, how much equitable adjustment should they receive?

According to Dube, Lester, and Reich (2010), advocates against increasing the minimum wage do not understand basic economic principles. They also believe that most of the opposition comes from commentators and political figures and not from small business employers. In comparing states that had an increase of 10% in the minimum wage to states that did not, Reich and Lester concluded that there were no negative effects.

Other concerns by advocates against increasing the minimum wage include effects on business owners and the overall economy (Huppke, 2014). The argument goes that employers would either be forced out of business or would have to drastically reduce the number of jobs. They argue that another consequence would be that many jobs could be cut back in hours to part-time, which would further reduce the amount of work hours. They also believe that the federal government is the wrong body to set a minimum wage. They point out that about 19 states already have a minimum wage of more than $7.25.

Critics of raising the minimum wage do not believe that it will impact the poverty rate (Huppke, 2014). It would have no effect on students or persons who just want additional income, and effects would be minuscule. For persons with limited education and skills, raising the minimum wage would still not lift persons out of poverty. It is likely that it could have a very damaging effect on reducing motivation to improve one's lot by his/her own efforts. Critics ask this question: Would people be more content at working at a fast-food restaurant and be less motivated to improve their education level for a higher paying job?

Critics of the minimum wage increase would further argue that improving job potential through education and training would be money better spent (Huppke, 2014). Furthermore, education and job training would open up future prospects for the group of lower achievers rather than setting another ceiling that will limit their upward mobility. Training and education would not only improve their competition in the labor market but would further increase their sense of well-being resulting from higher self-esteem and self-worth. The argument is that these intangible gains would far outweigh the gains made by increasing the minimum wage.

Advocates for the minimum wage, however, counter that poverty rates will be unaffected by an increase. Dube (2014), in a careful analysis of minimum wage increase across a number of decades, postulated that a slight increase of only 75 cents (from $7.25 to $8) would decrease the poverty rate by 2.4%. Furthermore, raising the minimum wage to $10 would reduce poverty by 4.6 million people or about 10%. Such a reduction in poverty is hugely touted, because it would require no additional governmental expenditures or resources.

A SYSTEMS/DIALECTICAL PERSPECTIVE ON POVERTY

In reflecting on the above child and family issues, especially poverty, it seems clear that either/or thinking does not present the best answers to complex problems. Choosing between options only leads to weak and largely uninformed policies. Each decision is only a process in a large series of decisions. Dialectical thinking requires one to present ideas that are logically consistent, clear, and based on the ability to discriminate between multitudes of alternative evidence.

A systems/dialectical perspective, first of all, would be distinguished from other perspectives in a number of significant ways. For example, one way of conceptualizing poverty is focusing on the individual (Andy, 2012). This perspective views persons in poverty as either lacking in character or pathological in behavior. It would say that persons create their own conditions, and some people do not have the traits, abilities, or character to achieve and, therefore, are not able to be self-sufficient. Their condition emanates from personal characteristics, such as lacking the ability to compete with others, or having personality traits that both cause and perpetuate poverty.

Another theory that contrasts with a systems/dialectical perspective is contextual, which assigns the cause of poverty to cultural or societal factors and the solution is creating a welfare state (See Figure 5.6) (Andy, 2012). The cultural perspective certainly informs a systems orientation but more as a heuristic principle than a cause of poverty. The cultural perspective means that cultural or ethnic groups of people are prone to be in poverty for reasons inherent in the culture and not because of individual liabilities. For example, The Moynihan Report (1963) was a study of the plight of the Black family and based poverty on the remnants of slavery, which was a unique experience of Blacks in the U.S. This perspective stated that slavery was such a devastating experience that the breakdown of the Black family became institutionalized and passed on through intergenerational transmission.

As stated elsewhere, systems/dialectical theory does not embrace solutions to social problems that resolve them in favor of one end of the polarity. Rather, it takes a both/and approach to solving dilemmas verses an either/or position. In common vernacular, it means a win/win solution is the goal. In addition, a systems/dialectical approach takes both the view that providing a safety net is important and, at the same time, is cognizant of how that safety net could adversely affect recipients of benefits. For example, if persons who are on the boundary of the poverty level but are eligible for benefits increase their income and are no longer eligible for benefits, they are disadvantaged by higher income; this is referred to as "**cliff effects**." In other words, increasing income becomes problematic and even not desirable. A systems/dialectical assessment of this dilemma would seek to find a solution that both benefits them and provides incentive to increase their income.

To a large degree, reducing poverty has taken two opposite poles. One extreme is a growth model that shows that increasing growth in the economy will not only improve the status of those at the top but also those at the bottom of the economic ladder. The other extreme is to target persons in poverty with programs that attempt to lift them out of poverty. Policymakers have acted as if these two positions were somehow mutually exclusive or incompatible. A systems/didactical perspective posits that both positions are mutually supportive. In fact, lifting persons out of poverty depends on economic growth, and growth of the economy depends on lifting people out of poverty.

In order for persons to fully participate in economic growth, they must have access to the tools that allow them to participate. It has become clear in the past several decades that well-being from conception to the first three years of a person's life is extremely important for future development. Identifying high-risk individuals for poverty as early in the life cycle as possible and providing programs of support and conditional cash transfers that do not inhibit their motivation to improve would be a common-ground position in reducing poverty. Policies that improve individual, family, and community well-being would grant low-income persons the tools to participate in a growing economy.

The Welfare State

PROS		CONS
• Provides much needed assistance • Helps children • Helps reduce crime rates • Helps improve skills base • Health care is vital	VS	• System is abused • We lose our sense of community • Hard-working citizens resent having to pay more tax • Results in pattern of dependence • Kills initiative

FIGURE 5.6 Pros and Cons of Welfare State

KEY TERMS

Poverty

School readiness

Pruning process

Home living
  environment

Hypothalamic-
  pituitary-adrenal
  (HPA) axis

External locus
  of control

Direct punitive
  methods

Indirect methods

Dysfunctional family
  relationships

Chronic stress

Emotional regulation

Secure attachment

Insecure disorganized
  attachment

Disorganized and
  anxious behaviors

Maternal depression

Welfare state

Great Depression

War on Poverty

AID to dependent children

Social Security Act

Women, infant, children
  (WIC)

Supplemental Social
  Security Income (SSI)

Section 8

Earned Income Tax
  Credit (EITC)

Hope VI

Personal Responsibility and Work
  Opportunity Reconciliation
  Act (PRWORA)

Department of Housing and
  Urban Development (HUD)

The Job Training Partnership
  Act (JTPA)

Workforce Investment
  Act of 1998 (WIA)

Temporary Aid for Needy
  Families (TANF)

Supplemental Nutrition
  Assistance Program

Free market

Minimum wage

Cliff effects

STUDY QUESTIONS TO ACCOMPLISH THE LEARNING OBJECTIVES

1. Define and discuss the definition of poverty. Explain why defining poverty is important to finding solutions.

2. Explain how the family environment is key to the developing child and how poverty affects this interaction.

3. Identify parenting techniques of low SES parents. Discuss parenting techniques of low SES on poverty families. How do these techniques affect the child?

4. What are attachment styles between the child and parents? Discuss how attachment styles are affected by poverty?

5. Discuss how environmental factors, such as health, affect children in poverty?

6. Outline specific programs of the welfare system. Describe the history of the American welfare system.

7. Critically analyze the effectiveness of the governmental program to combat poverty.

8. What is Blank and Greenberg's definition of poverty? Would Blank and Greenberg's redefinition of poverty open new ways of thinking about how to reduce poverty?

9. Discuss how liberals and conservatives view poverty. Is there a common ground?

10. What is the minimum wage, and how is it related to poverty? What are arguments for and against raising the minimum wage?

DEBATE ACTIVITY FOR STUDENTS

Consider the following statement: Welfare reform was successful in reducing poverty.

- Review refereed articles, books, online sources on research conducted on welfare reform. Do a library and Internet search to find relevant material. Investigate some of the additional readings.

- Develop three arguments for the proposition. Develop three arguments against the proposition.

- How do the arguments relate to other systems, such as the community or culture?

- Is there common ground?

- What are the long-term consequences of taking action?

- What new or common-ground solutions should be offered? If no common ground, what new position could emerge from a dialogue between the two positions?

- How is the new position superior to the original positions?

ADDITIONAL READING RESOURCES

Akindola, R. B. (2009). Towards a definition of poverty: Poor people's perspectives and implications for poverty reduction. *Journal of Developing Societies, 25*(2), 121–150.

Bradley, K. (2012). *Confronting the unsustainable growth of welfare entitlements: Principles of reform and the next steps. The Heritage Foundation,* June 24, 2012.

Bailey, M. J., & Danziger, S. (2013). Legacies of the war on poverty. In M. J. Bailey and S. Danzinger, *Legacies of the war on poverty,* (pp. 1-36). New York, NY: Russell Sage Foundation.

Duncan, G. J., Morris, P. A., & Rodrigues, C. (2011). Does money really matter? Estimating impacts of family income on young children's achievement with data from random-assignment experiments. *Developmental Psychology, 47*(5), 1263–1279. doi: 10.1037/a0oo23875

Duncan, G.T., Brooks-Dunn, J. (2000). Family poverty, welfare reform, and child development. *Child Development, 71*(1), 188–196.

Soss, J., Schram, S. F. (2017). Policy reform as feedback on poverty. *American Political Science Review, 101*(1), 111–127.

REFERENCES

Acs, G. (2007). Can we promote child well-being by promoting marriage? *Journal of Marriage and the Family, 69,* 1326–1344.

Akindola, R. B. (2009). Towards a definition of poverty: Poor people's perspectives and implications for poverty reduction. *Journal of Developing Societies, 25*(2), 121–150.

Amadeo, K. (2017). U.S. economic outlook: For 2017 and beyond. The Balance, June, 2017. Retrieved from https://www.thebalance.com/us-economic-outlook-3305669.

Andy, E. (2012). Critical analysis of poverty theories. Retrieved from http://www.academia.edu/1116707/Critical_Analysis_of_Poverty_Theories

Attanasio, O., Harst, E., & Pistaferri, L. (2012). The evolution of income, consumption, and leisure inequity in the U.S. 1980–2010. NBER Working Paper # 17982.

Attanasio, O., Hurst, E., Pistaferri, L. (2010). The evolution of income, consumption, and leisure inequity in the U.S. 1980–2010. NBER Working Paper No. 17982.

Bailey, M. J., & Danziger, S. (2013). Legacies of the war on poverty. In M. J. Bailey and S. Danzinger, *Legacies of the war on poverty* (pp. 1–36). New York, NY: Russell Sage Foundation.

Bauman, L. J., Silver, E. J., & Stein, R. E. K. (2006). Cumulative social disadvantage and child health. *Pediatrics, 117*(4), 1321–1328.

Belsky, J., & Jaffee, S. (2006). Multiple determinants of parents. In D. Cocchetti and D. Cohen (Eds.), *Developmental psychopathology: Risk disorder, and adaptation* (2nd ed., Vol. 3, pp. 38–83). New York, NY: Wiley.

Blank, R., & Greenberg, M. H. (2010). *Improving the measure of poverty.* The Brookings Institute. Retrieved from http://www.brookings.edu/events/2008/12/09-poverty#ref-id=0fafb99af2dc8c19be64e68cc6470268745402a4

Bradley, K. (2012). *Confronting the unsustainable growth of welfare entitlements: Principles of reform and the next steps.* The Heritage Foundation, June 24, 2012.

Bradley R. H., Corwyn, R. F., Burchinal, M., McAdoo, H. P., & Garcia-Coll, C, (2001). The home environments of children in the United states. Part 2: Relations with behavioral development through age 13. *Child Development, 72,* 1868–1886.

Bradley, R. H., Whiteside, L., Mundfrom, D. J., Casey, P. H., Kellerher, K. J., & Pope, S. K. (1994). Early indications of their resilience and their relation to experiences in the home environment of low weight, premature children living in poverty, *Child Development, 65,* 346–360.

Cawthorne, A. (2008). The straight facts on women and poverty. Center for American Progress. Retrieved from http://archive.truthout.org/article/women_101008/print

Chase-Landsdale, P. L., Moffitt, R., Lohman, B., Cherlin, A., Coley, R., Pittman, L.D., …Votruba-Drzal, E . (2003). Mothers' transition from welfare to work and the well-being of preschoolers and adolescents, *Science, 299,* 1548.

Chen, E., Hanson, M. D., Paterson, L. Q., Griffin, M. J., Walker, H. A., & Miller, G. E. (2006). Socioeconomic status and inflammatory processes of childhood asthma: The role of psychological stress. *The Journal of Allergy and Clinical Immunology, 117*(5), 1014–1020.

Chen, E., Martin, A. D., & Matthews, K. A. (2006). Socioeconomic status and health: Do gradients differ with childhood and adolescence? *Social Science and Medicine, 62*(9), 2161–2170.

Cohen, S., Doyle, W. J., & Baum, A. (2006). Socioeconomic status is associated with stress hormones. *Psychosomatic Medicine 68*(3), 414–420.

Crowder, S. J., & Broome, M. E. (2012). A framework to evaluate the cultural appropriateness of intervention research. *Western Journal of Nursing Research, 34*(8), 1002–1022.

Danziger, S. K. (2010). The decline of cash welfare and implications for social policy and poverty. *Annual Review of Sociology, 36,* 523–545.

Dube, A. (2014). The poverty of minimum wage "Facts". Retrieved from areindube.com/2014/01/22/the-poverty-of-minimum-wage-facts/

Dube, A., Lester, T. W., Reich, M. (2010). Minimum wage effects across state borders: Estimates using contiguous counties. *The Review of Economic Statistics, 92*(5), 945–964.

Duncan, G. J., Magnuson, K., Kalil, A., & Ziol-Guest, K. (2011). The importance of early childhood poverty, *Social Indicators Research, 108*(1), 87–98.

Edin, K. (2000). What do low-income single mothers say about marriage? *Social Problems, 47,* 112–133.

Edsall, T. B. (March 13, 2013). Who is poor? *The New York Times: The opinion pages.* Retrieved from http://opinionator.blogs.nytimes.com/2013/03/13/who-is-poor/

Engle, P. L., & Black, M. M. (2008). The effect of poverty on child development and educational outcomes. *Annals of New York Academy of Science, 1136,* 243–256.

Evans, G. W. (2006). Child development and the physical environment. *Annual Review of Psychology, 57,* 423–451.

Fanjul, G. (2014). Child of the recession: The impact of economic crisis on child well-being in rich countries. UNICEF, Office of Research-Innocenti. Retrieved from www.unicef-irc.org/publications/733

Farah, M. J., Shera, D. M., Savage, J. H., Betancourt, L., Giannetta, J. M., Brodsky, N. L., … Hurt, H. (2006). Childhood poverty: Specific associations with neurocognitive development. *Brain Research, 110*(1), 166–174.

Fernald, L., & Gunnar, M. R. (2009). Effects of poverty-alleviation Salivary cortisol in very low-income children. *Social Science Medicine 68*(12), 2180–2189.

Gorski, P. (2008). The myth of the culture of poverty. *Educational Leadership, 65,* 32–36.

Gottfried, A. W., Gottfried, A. E., Bathurst, K., Guerin, D. W., & Parramore, M. (2003). Socioeconomic status in children's development and family environment: Infancy through adolescence. In M. Bornstein & R. Bradley (Eds.), *Socioeconomic status, parenting, and child development.* Mahway, NJ: Lawrence Erlbaum.

Guglani, L., Havstadt, S. L., Johnson, C. C., Ownby, D. H., & Joseph, C. L. M. (2012). Effects of depressive symptoms on asthma interventions in urban youth. *Annals of Asthma, Allergy and Immunology, 109*(4), 237–242.

Greenberg, M. (2009). It's time for a better poverty measure. The Center for American Progress. Retrieved from https://www.americanprogress.org/issues/poverty/reports/2009/08/25/6582/its-time-for-a-better-poverty-measure/

Hackman, D. A., Farah, M. J., & Meany, M. J. (2010). Socioeconomic status and the brain: Mechanistic insights from human and animal research. *Nature Reviews Neuroscience, 11*, 651–659.

Hesse, E., & Main, M. (2006). Frightened, threatening, and dissociative parental behavior in low-risk samples: Description, discussion, and interpretations. *Development and Psychopathology, 18*, 309–343.

Huppke, R. (2014). In minimum wage debate, both sides make valid points. *BizTIMES*. Retrieved from http://www.thonline.com/biztimes/articles/article_e4a1f226-aeae-11e3-a5d6-001a4bcf6878.html

Huston, T. L., & Melz, H. (2004). The case for marriage: The devil is in the details. *Journal of Marriage and the Family, 66*, 943–958.

Income, Poverty, and Health Insurance Data. (2010). Current population reports issued September 2013. U.S. Department of Commerce.

Johnson, R. C., Kalil, A., & Dunifon, R. (2010*). Leaving welfare for work: How welfare reform has affected the well-being of children*. Kalmazoo, MI: W.E. Upjohn Institute for Employment Research.

Jusko, T. A., Henderson, C. R., Lanphear, B. P., Croy-Slechta, D. A., Parsons, P. J., & Canfield, R. A. (2008). Blood lead concentration μg-dL and child intelligence at 6 years of age. *Environmental Health Perspective, 116*(2), 243–248.

Karger, H., Midgley, J., Kindle, P., & Brown, C. (2007). *Controversial issues in social policy.* Boston, MA: Allyn and Bacon.

Karger, H., & Stoesz, D. (2006). *American social welfare policy: A pluralist approach.* (5th ed.). Boston, MA: Allyn Bacon.

Lens, V. (2002). TANF: What went wrong and what needs to be done next. *Social Work, 47*(3), 279–290.

Lereya, S., Sumara, M., & Wolke, D. (2013). Parenting behavior and the risk of becoming a victim and a bully/victim: A meta-analysis study. *Child Abuse and Neglect, 37*(12), 1091–1108.

Luhby, T. (2012). Worsening wealth inequity by race. CNNMoney. Retrieved from Money.cnn.com/2012/06/21/news/economy/wealth-gap-race/

Lyons-Ruth, K. (2008). Contributions of the mother-infant relationship to dissociative, borderline, and conduct symptoms in young adulthood. *Infant Mental Health Journal, 2008, 29*(3), 203–218.

Lyons-Ruth, K. (2008). Contributions of the mother-infant relationship to dissociative, borderline, and conduct symptoms in young adulthood. *Infant Mental Health Journal, 29*(3), 203–218.

Main, M. (1990). Cross-cultural studies of attachment organization: Recent studies, changing methodologies and the concept of conditional strategies. Human Development, 33, 48–61.

Mansfield, C., & Novick, L. F. (2012). Poverty and health: Focus on North Carolina. *North Carolina Medical Journal, 73*(5), 366–373.

Maughan, A., Cicchetti, D., Toth, S. L., & Rogosch, F. A. (2007). Early-occurring maternal depression and maternal negativity in predicting young children's emotion regulation and socioemotional difficulties. *Journal of Abnormal Child Psychology, 35*, 685–703.

McEwen, B. S., & Gianaros, P. J. (2010). Central role of the brain in stress and adaptation: Links to socioeconomic status, health, and disease. *Annals of the New York Academy of Science, 1186*, 190–222.

Molfese, V. J., Modglin, A., & Molfese, D. L. (2003). The role of environment in the development of reading skills: A longitudinal study of preschool and school-age measures. *Journal of Learning Disability, 36*, 159–167.

Molzon, E. S., Hullmann, S. E., Eddington, A. R., & Mullins, L. L. (2011). Depression, anxiety, and health related quality of life in adolescents and young adults with allergies and asthma. *Journal of Asthma and Allergy Educator, 2*(6), 288–294.

Moonie, S. A., Sterling, D. A., Figgs, L., & Castro, M. (2006). Asthma status and severity affects missed school days. *Journal of School Heath, 76*(1), 18–24.

Moynihan, D. P. (1965). The Negro family: The case for national action. Washington, D.C., Office of Policy and Research, U.S. Department of Labor.

Mulligan, A., Anney, R., Butler, L., O'Regan, M., Richardson, T., Tulewitcz, E. M., … Gill, M. (2013). Home environment: Association hyperactivity/impulsivity in children in children with ADHD and their non-ADHD siblings *Child: Care, Health, Development, 39*(2), 102–112.

Nanu, E. D., & Nijloveanu, D. M. (2015). Attachment and parenting styles. *Procedia – Social and Behavioral Sciences, 203*, 199–201.

Nesbitt, R. E, Aronson, J., Blair, C., Dickens, W., Flynn, J., Halpern, D. F., & Turkheimer, E. (2012). Intelligence: New findings and theoretical developments. *American Psychologist, 67*(2), 130–159.

Oh, S. S., Tcheurekjian, H., Roth, L. A., Nguyen, E. A., Sen, S., Galanter, J.M., … Burchard, E.G. (2012). The effects of secondhand smoke among Black and Latino children. *The Journal of Allergy and Clinical Immunology, 129*(6), 1478–1483.

Olasky, M. (2010). A way out. *World Magazine.* Retrieved from http://www.worldmag.com/2011/12/a_way_out

Rector, R. (2012). Marriage: American's greatest weapon against poverty. *The Heritage Foundation.* Retrieved from http://www.heritage.org/research/reports/2012/09/marriage-americas-greatest-weapon-against-child-poverty

Reich, R. B. (2011). *Aftershock: The next economy and America's future.* New York, NY: Vintage.

Roberts, T. W. (1994). *A systems perspective of parenting: The child, the family and the social network.* Pacific Grove, CA: Brooks/Cole.

Rohrer, L. M., Cicchetti, D., Rogosch, F. A., Toth, S. L., Maughan, A. (2011). *Developmental Psychology, 47*(1), 170–181. doi: 10.1037/a0021305.

Rugaber, C. (2012, September 7). *U.S. economy adds 96,000 jobs, rate falls to 8.1%. Associated Press.*

Schore, A. N. (2010). The right brain implicit self: A central mechanism of the psychotherapy change process. In J. Petrucelli (Ed.), *Knowing, not-knowing and sort-of-knowing: Psychoanalysis and the experience of uncertainty* (pp. 177–202). London, UK: Karnac.

Shaw, D. S., & Vondra, J. I. (1995). Attachment security and maternal predictors of early behavior problems: A longitudinal study of low income families. *Journal of Abnormal Child Psychology, 23,* 335–356.

Shonkoff, J. P. (2009). Investment in early childhood development lays the foundation for a prosperous and sustainable society. In R. E. Tremblay, M. Boivin, and R. Peters (Eds.), *Encyclopedia on Early Childhood Development* [online]. Montreal, Quebec: Centre of Excellence for Early Childhood Development and Strategic Knowledge Cluster on Early Child Development (1–5). Retrieved from http://www.childencyclopedia.com/documents/ShonkoffANGxp.pdf

Shonkoff, J. P., Boyce, W. T., & McEwen, B. S. (2009). Neuroscience, molecular biology, and the childhood roots of disparities: Building a new framework for health promotion and disease prevention. *The Journal of the American Medical Association, 301,* 2256–2259.

Shonkoff, J. P., Garner, A. S., Siegel, B. S., Dobbins, M. F., McGinn, L., Pascoe, L., & Wood, D. L. (2012). The lifelong effects of early childhood adversity and toxic stress. *Pediatrics, 129*(1), 232–246.

Short, K. (2011). The Research; Supplemental Poverty Measure. The U.S. Department of Commerce, The U.S. Census Bureau, Washington, D.C.

Social Security Administration. (2010). Monthly statistical snapshot, May 2010. Retrieved from http://www.socialsecurity.gov/policy/docs/quickfacts/stat_snapshot/#table3

Stossel, J. (2014). The free market is the best antidote to reduce poverty. Reason.Com, October 8, 2014. Retrieved from http://reason.com/archives/2014/10/08/poverty

Toth, S. L., Cicchetti, D., Rogsoch, F. A., & Sturge-Apple, M. (2009). Maternal depression, children's attachment security, and representational development: An organizational perspective. *Child Development, 80*(1), 192–208.

Totsika, V., & Sylva, K. (2004). The home observation for measurement of the environment. *Child and Adolescent Mental Health, 9*(1), 25–35.

U.S. Census Bureau. (2007). Annual Social and Economic Supplement. Retrieved from http://pubdb3.census.gov/macro/032008/pov/toc.htm

U.S. Department of Commerce. (2012). How the Census Bureau measures poverty. The U.S. Census Bureau. Washington, D.C.

Van IJzendoorn, M.H., & Bakermans-Kranenburg, M.J. (2003). Attachment disorders and disorganized attachment: Similarity and different. *Attachment and Human Development 5,* 313–320.

Weinberg, B.A. (2001). The incentive model of the effect of parenting income on children. *Journal of Political Economy, 109*(2), 266–280.

CREDITS

- Fig. 5.4: Source: http://www.dss.virginia.gov/files/about/sfi/2011_nfsc/plenaries/virginia_strengthening/NEFSC_Opening_Plenary_Presenation_9.26.11_FINAL_NO_NOTES.pdf.
- Table 5.2: Source: https://www.census.gov/hhes/www/poverty/data/threshld/.
- Fig. 5.5: Source: http://www.heritage.org/sites/default/files/~/media/images/reports/2013/08/sr140/cp-fed-spending-numbers-2013-page-9-chart-2.jpg.
- Fig. 5.6: Source: http://marketbusinessnews.com/wp-content/uploads/2017/06/Welfare-State-Pros-vs-Cons.jpg.

CHAPTER SIX

Social Policy and Education

SOCIAL POLICY AND EDUCATION

Education of children is one of the primary functions of a society. It could be stated that the overall success of a society depends on an educated population to carry on the functions of that society. In order to meet the demands of economic stability, an educated citizenry with competent skills is needed (Carnevale, Smith, & Strohl, 2010). In recent years, the U.S. economy has required a high degree of technology, a competency not needed a few generations ago. As technology expands exponentially and economies become more global in focus, U.S. children must be educated and highly competent to compete in the world market.

Over the past several decades, U.S. parents and educators have sounded an alarm that all is not well in American schools (Klein, 2011). This alarm was echoed by persons of different social and political backgrounds and beliefs, although for different reasons. One position on the poor standing of American education is the belief that spending needs to be increased, teachers need to be rewarded for outstanding teaching, and classrooms need to be smaller. An opposite view is that spending is unrelated to outcomes, there is no relation to teacher merit pay and student performance, and curriculum standards should be determined by local school boards. This chapter will address these seemingly paradoxical positions and attempt to offer some thoughts that could bridge the gap between the disparate points. The chapter organization will first review the historical perspective of American education and how it arrived in its current place.

THE HISTORY OF AMERICAN PUBLIC EDUCATION

Schooling is a very recent phenomenon in human history. For the most part of human existence, children learned behavior and skills needed to be successful in a hunter-gatherer society through play and initiative (Gray, 2013). There was no need for formal or structured education. Children were free to learn by active exploration and acquired skills naturally for making tools, learning about plants and animals that could be eaten, and taking initiative. Play was the essential element of the hunter-gatherer societies in all aspects of children's lives, and work had not yet been invented.

With the invention of agriculture, human life, particularly the penchant for play, gave way to the concept of work (Gray, 2013). Agriculture changed the nomadic life to one in which people stayed with the land, leading to ownership and permanent housing. Work took over the place of natural play and initiative as the way to learn and was characterized as boring and a drudge. Much of the agricultural work was done by children and continued generation after generation. Over time, a division in classes of landowners versus non-landowners established a hierarchical system in which children were at the bottom. According to Gray, children's natural tendency to learn though play was squelched. This period of time is referred to as the **Middle Ages,** and the hierarchal system is referred to as **feudalism.**

With the rise of industry and the **bourgeois state**, the role of children in society changed again. All sense of childhood was lost, and children were treated similarly to slaves (Gray, 2013). Beginning in the 16th century, schooling gradually developed as an alternative to the harsh treatment of children. In Europe, the call for compulsory education of children was partly due to the rise of Protestant religions that emphasized salvation, which was dependent on reading and understanding the Bible. In Germany, for example, most of the early schools were run by the Lutheran Church.

In America, many of the colonies were established because of a desire for religious freedom. Reading and understanding the Bible were considered very important (Mintz, 2012). Churches became the center for education in the colonies, although not in uniform, because different colonies consisted of different ethnic and religious groups. From the 1600s to the 1800s, there was no compulsory education in colonial America. Education was generally for the affluent class; persons of lower status did not receive formal education (Pulliam & Van Patten, 2006).

Colonial education took place in churches, homes, libraries, and clubs (Mintz, 2012). After the Revolutionary War, President George Washington addressed the need to educate the masses. New England, settled by the Puritans, greatly influenced education in the colonies. Being able to read the Bible was an essential concern and meant that churches were one of the first public places for educational instruction. The Massachusetts Bay School Law of 1642 required that parents teach their children how to read and write (Pulliam & Van Patten, 2012). Failure at executing this law, however, resulted in additional laws to address the needs of education, such as the Old Deluder Act of 1647, which required that communities with more than 50 households provide education for children. While this law had good intentions, it failed to be equitable for all children, as it mainly educated the elite for future leadership.

The oldest school was the Boston Latin School, established in 1635, which taught Latin and Greek, and was essentially the place to be for the affluent and future leaders (Conroy, 2000). Classes were held in the home of the headmaster and later in the home of Daniel Maude. The first institution of higher education was Harvard, established in 1636. During subsequent decades in the 1640s and 1650s, compulsory education began to spread to other Northern colonies. In the South, many children were educated in their homes because of the general view that education was a private matter. Affluent children also attended private schools, and some parents even sent their children to England for schooling. The South was more dispersed in population and less concentrated, which further decreased the impetus for public education (Arthur, 2000).

Early schooling consisted of much of the harshness that children experienced in the fields. Schoolmasters, not always well prepared for the task at hand, believed that schools were meant to keep children on task, and children were frequently beaten when they failed to be compliant (Gray, 2013). Play was seen as a deterrent to learning and was not encouraged. Boys and girls generally did not receive the same education, as boys were given more advanced curriculum. Boys were taught how to read and write, because both were important in executing documents. Initially girls were only taught to read, because they were not expected to be as efficient in matters of business as boys.

The need for an educated citizenry began taking hold by Thomas Jefferson's presidency (Pulliam & Van Patten, 2012). Jefferson supported a bill, *Bill for the More General Diffusion of Knowledge*, which would have supported public education. However, because many persons still felt education should be provided by private means, an abridged bill, *Act to Establish Public Education*, finally passed and became law under James Madison's presidency in 1796. The educational system still was not fully opened to women until after some educational institutions were set up primarily for them, such as the Litchfield Female Academy (Pulliam & Van Patten, 2012).

The 19th century presented new challenges for U.S. citizenry that could not be addressed through the existing educational system (Mintz, 2012). Immigrants began coming to America in droves, creating an immediate need to acculturate them into the American workforce. This influx of immigrants from Europe was especially apparent in large metropolitan areas in the Northeast. In order to be productive citizens, immigrants needed to be able to work, and the best way to integrate them in the workforce was through learning the language, customs, and social expectations in America.

Some have argued that, as schooling evolved from this early period, it retained its work focus in that children were controlled in most aspects of school (Gray, 2013). In this way of thinking, schooling is the endpoint of a progression that started with a harsh authoritarian focus. Schooling can be seen as a type of work in that children put in roughly the same amount of time as adults. They become identified by the school years, such as being a freshman or senior. Some would point to the fact children are forced to attend school, and it is not something they naturally or freely choose to do. Nevertheless, the view that education of children was feasible for a strong economy was too powerful of a belief for legislators to be swayed by variant philosophical points of view.

The philosophy of education in its early form in America was influenced by the work of John Locke and Jean-Jacques Rousseau (Pulliam & Van Patten, 2012), who believed that a child's mind was a **tabula rasa**, or blank slate, which could be shaped by experiences. The implication of Locke's ideas about education, however, produced a top-down system in which parents and teachers had to guard themselves against careless modeling and interaction with children in negative ways that might have a lasting impact. While Rousseau had beliefs that overlapped with Locke, he differed on the concept of how children learn. In place of a blank slate, he believed that children possessed an inner curiosity and that this internal process mediates learning.

Later, John Dewey and other writers helped educational philosophy to further evolve (Neil, 2005). For Dewey, education was the thread that held together a society, given that all persons die, thus passing on the knowledge of each generation to the next. He was critical of authoritarian models of education and believed that there is more to learning than simply passing on knowledge from scholars to children. True education would take into account not only a body of existing knowledge but would also incorporate the actual experiences of children.

By the Civil War, most states had enacted laws for public education, and for the most part, schools were operated on a local level without interference from the federal government (Pulliam & Van Patten, 2012). Several events directly affected the future of the federal government's role in public education. First, business leaders and politicians expressed concerns that the U.S. needed an educated citizenry to keep in step economically with other nations. The second major event was the Supreme Court case of *Brown v. Board of Education* (1954), leading to the desegregation of schools, which overturned the separate but equal ruling in *Plessy v. Ferguson* (1896).

Brown v. Board of Education was a combination of five cases that were before the Supreme Court in 1952 (Dudley, 1994). These cases were subsumed under the name *Brown v. Board of Education*. The major argument was that the **separate but equal law** violated the equal protection under the law clause in the Fourteenth Amendment. It was argued that separate but equal did not lead to optimal development of Black children. The Court did not reach a conclusion in 1952 but reheard the case in 1953. Before the Court could take up the case again, the Chief Justice, Fred Vinson, died and was replaced by Earl Warren, who presided over the decision in 1954 that made school segregation illegal. The Court ruling allowed for each state to present a plan of how it would comply.

Gradually, the federal government became more involved in education (Pulliam & Van Patten, 2012). The passage of the National Defense Education Act of 1958 signaled a more active role in providing funding for promoting higher standards in math and science. With the **War on Poverty** in the 1960s, the federal government committed itself more firmly to establishing national standards. Head Start began in 1964 to provide quality preschool readiness for children below the poverty line and has continued to the present. In the late 1970s, the Education for All Handicapped Children Act was another direct intervention of the federal government into the educational system.

No Child Left Behind (NCLB)

NCLB, the reauthorization of the Elementary and Secondary Education Act of 1965 and 1994, was passed by a bipartisan vote of the U.S. Senate and the House of Representatives and signed into law by George W. Bush in 2002. The goals of NCLB were to ensure accountability by annually administering standardized testing, holding teachers accountable for student outcomes, and rewarding schools with high achievement while punishing schools that fall below expected standards (NCLB, 2001). Proponents of standardized testing believe that it allows for more objective assessment of student learning than would come from schools and teachers. In addition, it was believed that it would level the playing field for minorities and poor children and, therefore, close the achievement gap.

Accountability was a central theme for NCLB, which set up a timetable for student testing. For grades three through eight, testing of students in math and reading was to begin in 2005–2006 and annually thereafter. By 2007–2008, students in elementary, middle, and high school had to be tested once. The National Assessment of Education Progress testing program, which drew from a sample of fourth and eighth grade students nationally, would compare results across states. Schools had yearly expectations of standards and failing to meet them for two and/or more successive years could result in 1) educational assistance from the Department of Education or, 2) students could choose to attend another school that met their expectations and this transfer would be paid for by the school system. In some sparsely populated areas of the country, a transfer outside the school district might be necessary (Hombo, 2003). For schools that persisted in not meeting the expectations, more stringent measures would be taken.

Under the NCLB law, teachers hired through Title I funding had to be certified to teach the subject matter (Fuller, Gesicki, Kang, & Wright, 2006). New standards also applied to paraprofessionals who would need to have completed at least two years of college or be evaluated to show proficiency in the subject material by the 2005–2006 school year. To enhance learning opportunities for low-income students in grades K–3, competitive grants were offered to schools through the **Reading First** program. While some schools and educators lauded NCLB, others not only openly criticized it but believed that it was inadvertently discriminatory, since some school systems with greater diversity had more roadblocks in meeting the guidelines (Fulleret et al., 2006).

NCLB gave the states until 2013–2014 to be 100% compliant with all aspects of NCLB. The percentage of schools that were able to meet the annual benchmarks in 2010 was only 62% (McNeil, 2011). With the increasing sense of failure to meet the benchmarks, many school districts sought ways to opt out. Others believed that stringent accountability was needed and that more time was needed to attain the desired results.

One of the major problems for noncompliance is the **high-stakes testing**, or testing that links to decision making regarding school policy. High-stakes testing are transparent and hold schools to strict accountability. In a recent study, Au (2007) reviewed 49 qualitative studies on the relation between high-stakes testing and curriculum. He found that high-stakes testing reduces the curriculum to the test content and limits the materials that teachers present to students. The overall effect is to compartmentalize learning and reduce student achievement to the narrow focus of the tests. It creates a top-down approach in which those in positions of power are able to control classroom content.

High-stakes testing may present a problem for special needs children. Some educators believe that special needs children may not receive the accommodations they need in order to be successful in high-stakes testing (Albrecht & Jones, 2003). Some educators believe that the need for more attention should be addressed and that guidelines for special needs children's inclusion in high-stakes testing should be reevaluated. According to Albrecht and Jones, the outcome for these children may be lower self-esteem, a greater sense of failure, and even feeling responsible for their school's poor showing on these tests.

Some researchers have found that NCLB may inadvertently reduce the performance of some children and enhance the performance of other students along racial lines (Krieg, 2011). NCLB tests students according to racial groups. To meet annual yearly standards, a certain percentage of students in each racial group must be proficient on the high-stakes testing. If specific groups of students fail to meet expectations on the high-stakes testing, resources may be taken away from higher-performing students and given to lower performing students. This shift in resources to lower performing students may involve curriculum, teacher, and funding changes. Some educators have warned that reducing resources for the most proficient students may create a "**proficiency ceiling,**" namely, a reduction of the potential of higher-achieving students (Brown & Clift, 2010, as cited in Krieg, 2011). Researchers have compared schools that meet AYT expectations on high-stakes tests and those that do not. For example, high-proficiency groups who attend a school with a group that is low proficiency will score lower on high-stakes tests than high-proficiency students in a school in which there are no low-performing students. The shifting of resources away from the high-proficiency students is believed to be a major factor in their lower scores. Other researchers have investigated schools targeting particular students who fall below proficiency and noted that they make the most improvement in test scores (Springer, 2008, as cited in Krieg, 2011). According to Krieg, even schools that had no racial groups below proficiency may still shift resources from a high-proficiency group to a group that minimally passed in order to prevent future failing scores.

According to Krieg (2011), one of the stated goals of NCLB, reducing the achievement gap between racial groups, may actually be accomplished inadvertently by lowering the test scores of the most proficient students. The danger in this circumstance is that, over time, focusing less on the proficient students may put them at a disadvantage in higher grades to meet proficiency. A survey of teachers found that the majority were in favor of accountability standards but were concerned about the unintended reduction in the quality of education (Murnane & Papay, 2010). Krieg (2011) suggests that to remedy the outcome that students at the highest proficiency level will suffer, NCLB might change its guidelines to require a percentage increase in all groups.

The Forum on Educational Accountability released a report calling for massive changes in the accountability systems (Klein, 2007). It calls for a revamping of a system that measures accountability largely through tests, and suggests increasing the scope to include professional development and outreach to parents. This proposal would shift some of the Title I funding from student transfers and monitoring to teacher professional development. In addition, it proposes to reduce the penalties to schools for not meeting expectations by requiring specific guidelines for improving parental involvement.

Analysis of the costs of implementing NCLB shows that they are generally more than funds available, particularly for states with high numbers of students below proficiency (Duncombe, Lukemeyer, & Yinger, 2008). Since NCLB must meet state standards and does not set separate standards, the consequence of having to make efforts in testing may contribute to states setting low standards. According to Duncombe et al., much of the high cost of NCLB and the failure to achieve proficiency results from educating disadvantaged and special needs children.

AMERICAN EDUCATION IN CRISIS

Laws passed by Congress and signed into law became the official policy for American education (See Table 6.1). While the federal government has been highly involved in education since the early 1990s, quality education tends to be more spotty and a matter of local schools and teachers in contrast to a nationally consistent standard across all schools (Moyer, 2012). No one seems particularly happy with American education, regardless of his or her political views. Conservatives complain that progressives have been in charge of most of the policy decisions in the past several decades, and quality of education has generally declined. Progressives believe that conservatives have blocked efforts to increase funding and have initiated curricula fights that have not enhanced quality, such as the 2009 contentious stalemate in Texas over teaching creationism alongside evolution.

Some Problems in Education

The answer to the question "What's wrong with American education?" depends on who is asked. There is no consistent answer, and no recent efforts have successfully impacted student outcomes. Some recurring problems, regardless of the overall education model, can be delineated. First, there is a high teacher attrition rate (Jalongo & Heider, 2006). The vast majority of teachers hired each year are not for new positions but to replace teachers who have left the profession in the preceding year. It is estimated that about 46% of teachers leave the profession after five years. Attrition rates have increased over the past decade, which means that teachers, overall, have less experience than in the past. Causes for leaving the profession are many, but teachers are under pressure for their students to learn and do well on standardized tests. Many have oversized classrooms and poor resources, which lead to burnout.

Second, schools need a close and supportive relationship with parents, which requires ongoing efforts (Jalongo & Heider, 2006). In many cases, working with parents depends on disparate factors that are unique to the community. Parental involvement enhances student learning as evidenced by higher academic achievement of students and higher graduation rates (Elish-Piper, 2009). Communicating with parents through newsletters, internet streaming, sponsored parent-child activities, and other means of forming a school community with parents would help in creating the partnership needed for effective parental involvement.

TABLE 6.1 Important laws and court cases affecting American education

IMPORTANT LEGISLATIVE LAWS
The Massachusetts Law of 1647—Every town of 50 families must provide a school for children.
The Massachusetts Education Law of 1829—Towns of more than 500 are required to provide public education.
The Land Grant 1862—Public land donated to build public institutions of higher education to teach agriculture and mechanic arts.
Michigan State Supreme Court 1874—Allowed Kalamazoo to levy taxes for education.
Civil Rights Act 1875—Banned segregated schools; overturned by Supreme Court in 1883.
Hatch Act of 1887—Created network of agricultural experiment stations attached to land grant institutions.
The Second Morrill Act 1890—Additional funding for land-grant colleges; leads to creation of 16 historically Black land grant-colleges.
Plessy v. Ferguson 1896—Made separate but equal under the law.

(continued)

TABLE 6.1 (*Continued*)

IMPORTANT LEGISLATIVE LAWS
Alvarez v. the Board of Trustees of the Lemon Grove (California School District) 1931—Prohibited placing Mexicans students in a separate school.
Servicemen's Readjustment Act of 1944—Known as the GI Bill, provides assistance for veterans to attend college.
McCollum v. Board of Education 1948—Supreme Court rules that schools cannot allow release time during the day for students to participate in religious activities.
Brown v. Board of Education of Topeka 1954—Strikes down the separate but equal law.
Browder v. Gale 1956—Supreme Court rules that segregated seating on a bus is unconstitutional.
Engel v. Vitale 1962—Schools cannot require students to pray to an official prayer created by the state.
Murray v. Curllet 1963—Schools cannot require the reading of passages from the Bible.
Civil Rights Act 1964—Prohibited discrimination on the basis of race, color, sex, religion, or national origin.
The Elementary and Secondary Education Act (ESEA) 1965—Provided federal funds for low-income students.
The Indian Education Act 1972—Focused on unique needs of Native American students.
Lau v. Nichols 1974—Schools must provide equal opportunities to all students, including LEP students.
Plyer v. Doe 1982—Supreme Court rules that Texas cannot bar undocumented children from public education.
Individuals with Disabilities Education Act (IDEA) 1990—Adds autism and brain injury to the eligibility list.
Georgia Preschool for All 1995—First state in the union to adopt such a program.
No Child Left Behind 2001—Replaces the Bilingual Act of 1968, student testing and penalties for schools that fail standards.
The American Reinvestment and Recovery Act of 2009—Ninety billion dollars to prevent layoffs.
Common Core State Initiative 2009—Set consistent standards for what children should know.

Third, schools produce students with poor literacy skills who tend to either drop out or must take remedial courses for college (Jalongo & Heider, 2006). Reading comprehension for many students is below expectations and contributes to poor academic performance and high school dropout rates. Poor reading skills are one of the main concerns in the high school dropout rate, which currently stands nationally at approximately 4% (Muskal, 2013). While a 78% graduation rate seems far too low, it actually represents a substantial increase since 2009. Hard pressed to find definitive changes in education policy that might explain the increase in graduation rates, the Department of Education hypothesized that the poor economy may discourage some teens from leaving school for work. This explanation, however, is inconsistent with reasons generally given for students dropping out of high school, namely poor academic performance and behavioral and emotional problems (Rumberger, 2013). Also, it should be noted that students who fail to complete high school have the highest unemployment rates of any group. Graduation rates tend to vary according to regions of the country and racial and ethnic groups (See Table 6.2).

TABLE 6.2 Graduation rates by lowest and highest states and racial and ethnic groups

LOWEST GRADUATION RATES	HIGHEST GRADUATION RATES
Nevada—57.8%	Wisconsin—91.1%
District of Columbia—59.9%	Vermont—91.4%
GRADUATION RATES BY RACE	
African American—66.1%	Asian/Pacific Islanders—93.5%
American Indian and Alaska Native—69.1%	White—83%
Latino—71.4%	

Adapted From: http://articles.latimes.com/2013/jan/22/nation/la-na-nn-high-school-graduation-rate-increasing-20130122

Fourth, efforts at reforming education have produced few tangible results (Jalongo & Heider, 2006). The **Elementary and Secondary School Education Act of 1965 (ESEA)**, which addressed deficiencies in education and has been reauthorized a number of times, the latest of which was in 2001 in NCLB, has failed to increase graduation rates and the standing of U.S. students when compared with international students. The achievement gap still exists despite the focus on improving education for poor and minority students. Expenditures for each student have more than doubled since the ESLA went into effect in the 1960s, while scores on math and science have remained relatively flat. The average American family spends about $120,000 for its children's education and many parents are dissatisfied with public school education, feel alienated from the decision-making process, and feel helpless to do anything about it.

Much of the increase in expenditure in education has resulted from hiring new staff (National Center for Educational Statistics, 2012). The 2013 budget has an increase of 25 billion dollars just for new school personnel, most of which are not teaching positions (White House, 2012). Since 1970, student enrollment from kindergarten through twelfth grade increased by approximately 8%, while, during the same period, expenditure increased by 138%. Support staff now makes up the largest piece of the staff pie, with teachers slightly under 50% (National Center for Educational Statistics, 2012). Over the last decade, there has been an increase of about 3% in administrative positions over teaching positions. Since the 1950s, teacher positions, as a total of the education staff, have decreased by 30%.

Student/teacher ratios are generally believed to be important in improving student outcomes. In reviewing student/teacher ratios since the 1950s, it can be noted that, in the 1950s, the ratio was 27.5 students for each teacher, and in 2012, the ratio had significantly dropped to 15.2 (National Center for Educational Statistics, 2012). The research is mixed on whether class size affects outcome and mainly depends on the way data are interpreted. For example, one side of the argument would point out the positive effects from **Student Teacher Achievement Ratio (STAR)** (Achilles et al., 2008) testing, but others would point out that these benefits are not permanent (Rivkin, Hanushek, & Kain, 2005). Revamping the school personnel by eliminating some non-teacher jobs would not affect the student-teacher ratio. In summation, the trend for low student/teacher ratios has been in effect since the 1950s with no substantial difference in student outcomes.

It is interesting that, as America frowns over its standing in the world in terms of math and language, the past decade has seen a significant increase in students applying for college, particularly among Black and Hispanic students—an increase of 30% and 57%, respectively, from 2000–2007 (U.S. Department of Labor, Bureau of Labor Statistics, 2012). The increase in college enrollment has not come with increased budgetary resources, which has meant that colleges have become more selective. As selectivity becomes the norm, more minority- or low-income students may be less likely to be successful in college. Future projections for the type of education needed for the jobs that are anticipated to increase all show a requirement for some education beyond high school (U.S. Department of Labor, Bureau of Labor Statistics, 2012). For example, NCLB became law in 2002 and, with support from conservatives and progressives, was viewed with high expectations that it would transform American education (Calkins, Ehrenworth, & Lehman, 2012). The basic premise of testing children to see what they know and holding teachers and schools accountable would appear, at first glance, to be the antidote to failing schools. It has been anything but that, and is opposed by parents, teachers' associations, and labor unions. The law required that states meet specific standards in reading and math by 2014. More than half of the states were waived from meeting this deadline and others applied for waivers. The replacement program for these states is the **Common Core Standards**.

Common Core

The Common Core Standards were adopted in 2009 and are expected to be approved in all states. The basic focus is to align kindergarten through twelfth grade education with consistent learning expectations so that students will be better prepared for college and careers (Calkins et al., 2012). Funded by the Bill and Melinda Gates Foundation, the standards were set by governors of both parties and a panel of experts. The core standards focus on content learning as well as specific skills (Forgione, 2012). The standards seek to promote critical thinking rather than methods that rely on rote memory. While 45 states signed on voluntarily, not all states have embraced the Common Core standards and can opt out. The five states that did not sign on are: Alaska, Texas, Virginia, Minnesota, and Nebraska. Nebraska's resistance to adopting the standards is mainly in response to state law regarding the role that the Nebraska Department of Education has in developing and implementing the state curriculum for Nebraska's teachers. To get funding from the Obama administration in the **Race to the Top Program**, states had to accept the standards. Those opposed to the Common Core standards feared the loss of control of local school districts, and, in some cases, the new standards would be lower than those that were in place (Calkins et al., 2012).

Proponents for Common Core point out a number of reasons for the standards, including different and even inconsistent standards in various states, addressing the mobility of families who frequently move to a different state, aligning education with job skills, and the globalization of the job market (Calkins et al., 2012). Assessment of students will take place in grades three through eight and high school by implementing the Race to the Top Assessment Program. Funds will come from the federal government to states adopting the Common Core to determine how the assessment will be developed. The assessment instrument must consist of 85% of the Common Core standard, and 15% can be specific to state standards. The Common Core assessment is in language arts and math, and the states are free to assess other subjects.

One of the reasons for Common Core is the globalization of the workforce (Calkins et al., 2012). Critics point out that one size does not fit all. Critics also say that the advertisement on national TV to sell the idea to the public was a great campaign but more rhetoric than reality. For example, critics point to the rhetoric on the Common Core's website, which states that the federal government did not initiate or set the curriculum for the standards. In addition, the two main emphases are math and language arts. Critics point out that most of the work on the standards was not done by state educators and governors but by ACHIEVE, Inc., a Washington, D.C., nonprofit funded by the Bill and Melinda Gates Foundation (Hrenchir, 2015). Furthermore, critics claim that most of the states that have adopted the standards did so out of fear of losing the federal money for Race to the Top.

Critics further claim that the curriculum in math and language arts will be determined by agencies and nonprofits in Washington, D.C., with no local control (Hrenchir, 2015). While reading classical literature has been an essential focus of literature in most schools, Common Core will encourage informational and nonfiction reading. Proponents of Common Core believe that content reading will be more helpful to students in developing **critical thinking** (Porter, McMaken, Hwang, & Yang, R., 2011). However, critics are concerned about who selects the readings and whether the readings are one-sided in ideology, which would not facilitate critical thinking (Calkins et al., 2012).

Critics charge that the requirement to have 70% nonfiction content will force schools to make choices that would reduce appropriate content in other classes (Calkins et al., 2012). Critics also point out there are no definitive evaluations that determine that informational reading has an advantage to reading nonfiction. Furthermore, many critics believe that a major drawback is the unrealistic goal that all students can meet standards for college entrance (Borowski, 2013). Many students may be better served by vocational and technical training.

Although Common Core claims not to be a curriculum, critics point out that if the standards determine what students should know, it also, to some degree, would determine the curriculum. According to Eitel and Talbert (2012), the Common Core standards and the national assessment of students will direct much of the curriculum. Proponents believe that a single set of standards will be better for students than a patchwork of different standards now in place that produce differences in outcomes (Common Core States Standards Initiative, 2012). The lack of trial runs on Common Core means that the effectiveness is unknown.

Many critics believe that the math standards are below current standards (Borowski, 2013). For example, the Common Core standards will teach algorithms and adding and subtracting triple digit numbers in the fourth grade instead of the second grade, as it is now taught. Long division will not be taught until sixth grade. The earlier grades will focus on learning math concepts rather than working with actual problems. Critics point out that, because of the national test, schools will not be able to deviate from the national guidelines (Stotsky, 2012). Proponents state that the standards may be changed and even improved on (Common Core States Standards Initiative, 2012); critics point out that it would be very unclear who has the authority to change the standards since they are copyrighted by the National Governors Association (NGA) and the Council of Chief State School Officers (CCSSO) (Stotsky, 2012).

According to Stotsky (2012), states were so eager to adopt the standards for fear of losing Race to the Top money that they did not accurately assess the rigor of the standards. According to Stotsky, the language arts component makes teachers responsible for teaching material that they were not trained to teach, namely nonfiction, informational material. It would also require that college training would have to reflect this different focus and, therefore, require substantial changes. Long-term effects would be the reduction in **analytical thinking**. Nonfiction and informational literature generally is written from a single point of view and does not compare to the complexity, subtlety, and irony often found in fiction.

Proponents of the Common Core state that it is developmentally appropriate for young children and outlines what kindergarten children should know to be on track (Common Core States Standards Initiative, 2012). One of the math components is to teach kindergartners math concepts using the "**Just the Facts**" program. They learn basic addition of how numbers are related to quantities through a song format. Children are placed in groups where they can talk about math concepts to each other, and teachers follow the group work by discussing what they have just learned. In addition to math, kindergarteners must master the language arts components. In place of stories in which children are asked to talk about themselves in the context of the story, teachers will ask **text-dependent questions** (TDQs) in which children will use the text to answer the questions from the reading. One of the main purposes for the shift in language arts is to introduce new words. Proponents of Common Core believe that children will benefit from this foundation of learning and thinking about math concepts (Common Core States Standards Initiative, 2012).

TABLE 6.3 Developmentally appropriate practice (NAEYC)

BASIC PRINCIPLES FOR DEVELOPMENTALLY APPROPRIATE PRACTICES INCLUDES:
1. What is appropriate for age?
2. What is appropriate for individual children?
3. What is culturally appropriate?
THESE PRINCIPLES LEAD TO THE FOLLOWING OUTCOMES IN TEACHING:
1. Creates a community of learners
2. Focuses on development and learning
3. Develops appropriate curriculum
4. Evaluates outcomes in development and learning
5. Works cooperatively with families

Adapted From: Copple, Bredekamp, and Gonzalez-Mena, 2009

Some early childhood education leaders, however, take a different view of guidelines for kindergarteners and express caution in implementing Common Core relative to developmentally appropriate practice (Copple, Bredekamp, & Gonzalez-Mena, 2009). According to this view, developmentally appropriate practice is based on two principles that are absent from Common Core: 1) children are different, and each child's individual needs must be addressed, and 2) each child must be encouraged and supported in his/her individual goals in learning. Furthermore, determining guidelines for all children to meet undermine their individual needs, which may reflect ethnic and cultural components. They would also argue that having standards for kindergarten students is different from having specific guidelines that eliminate individual focus.

There are other concerns in implementing Common Core for middle-and high-school students. For example, some educators have raised questions about one of the main purposes of Common Core, which is that it will prepare all students for college and/or careers. Educators have called into question if all preparation for careers is the same as preparation for college. In other words, do all students need the same education even if they are seeking different careers? Critics argue that careers and college preparation are vastly different with little overlap (Solman, 2013). Employers generally want tech savvy workers with communication and interpersonal skills, who have real-world experiences with community-based learning. The vast majority of workers would not need or even ever use advanced math in their careers or jobs. It could be argued that many students fail high school, because they are taught skills that they lack interest in, and they know that they will never use them in their jobs. According to Solman (2013), educators fear that schools will eliminate art and technical career courses and replace them with more advanced math courses. Little is addressed in Common Core about how schools will address struggling students and keep them on track. Common Core does acknowledge that not all students will be able to master the material and achieve at the desired level. Proponents argue that Common Core offers suggestions and support, such as teacher resources for struggling students (Common Core States Standards Initiative, 2012).

FUTURE DIRECTIONS IN EDUCATION

Before exploring future directions in education, it must be noted that Donald Trump ran for president on a theme to improve education, and his first budget reflected his desire to reform education (Evers & Alger, 2017). His budget called for a reduction of expenditures in two programs, TRIO and GEAR UP, that are aimed at improving college admission for at-risk high school teens. While this budget cut was lambasted by progressives, it was based on studies that show that neither program was effective in improving high school graduation rates and college entrance for highly at-risk teens. According to Evers and Alger, other non-effective programs were reduced or cut in the Trump budget, including School Improvement Grants (SIG), which gave funds to schools that were low performing to improve math and science scores and increase high school graduation rates. As noted by Evers and Alger in 2017, the program, which was drastically increased under the Obama administration, has cost taxpayers more than seven billion dollars and has failed to improve academic performance. It will be interesting to see how the Trump administration will affect future developments in education. This much is known: he will cut programs that are ineffective regardless of the sentimental reasons for continuing them. How current educational policies like Common Core will fare under the Trump administration remains to be seen.

While Common Core offers the advantage of consistency across the educational domain, it may not address the needs of both the most gifted and the least gifted students. It may also de-emphasize creativity, an important aspect of learning espoused by Sir Ken Robinson (2009). According to Robinson, all educational systems developed during the Industrial Revolution and were designed by those at the top of the educational hierarchy to create systems that perpetuated themselves. The educational systems continue today by educating students in batches by age. Many students are not challenged by such a system, and to keep them in class, Robinson believes that schools promote overuse of medication. Robinson believes that schools anesthetize students with medication rather than allowing their creativity to drive the education process. He criticizes contemporary educational models as being a production-line mentality. According to Robinson, the challenge is not how to raise the bar of achievement, but how to respond to each child's way of learning. He believes that it is hard to develop a system that essentially starts from the ground up rather than from the top down. According to Robinson's perspective, problems with the Common Core would be similar to critics from National Association for the Education of Young Children (NAEYC), namely, the educational system needs to meet the unique needs of children. A one-size-fits-all approach would only reproduce the mediocre system already in place.

Robinson (2009) is not turning the educational system over to the whims of children, but suggests that a model such as a Montessori classroom, in which children are free to engage in a variety of self-chosen activities, could be a starting point for a new paradigm. His ideas promote an **agency-based approach** to education based on individual choice rather than compulsion. An agency-based education model provides students with a pursuit of truth from original sources. Parents are acknowledged as the main guide in their children's education. The agency-based approach is based on the view that a top-down hierarchical educational system benefits children from higher economic backgrounds. In the current education system of NCLB, some children learn that they cannot compete and, therefore, give up on education. According to this perspective, the Common Core initiative has not articulated how it can be used for individual students and, likely through standardized testing, will merely perpetuate the same failed systems in place now.

A SYSTEMS/DIALECTICAL PERSPECTIVE OF EDUCATION

In applying a systems/dialectical approach to education policy, the first concern that emerges is the lack of systemic and holistic thinking. For example, while the overall assumption of accountability of students and schools as the core in implementing education policy is generally accepted as appropriate, many critics believe that accountability in NCLB is a linear system that fails to reflect the complexity of education in America (Dawoody, 2008; Houston, 2007). Holding schools accountable simply by student test scores is linear and fails to grasp the complexity of education. According to Dawoody (2008), NCLB attempts to predict the future from a limited set of variables that lack adaptability to changing circumstances. Dawoody believes that the budget process is a central component in the linear accountability, which is based on long-term projections that do not account for interacting components. This system will then tend to perpetuate itself rather than change in response to different circumstances, which may, at times, need to change in structure.

According to Dawoody (2008), the flawed logic of NCLB is that poorly performing school districts will be penalized by the withdrawal of funds, which will then mean that local support must fill this shortfall. Because local support will not help meet the problem of low test scores or lower test scores the next year, this will reduce federal support even further. Dawoody would replace this faulty pattern with a complexity model referred to as the Agent-Based Model (Gilbert, 2008, as cited in Dawoody, 2008), which is an interactive system comprising the federal government, the states, and the school districts. Each of the three interacting systems would be autonomous and capable of influencing the entire system. Instead of a linear approach, Dawoody believes that a **nonlinear interacting system**, a mutual causal model, would mean that, as input comes into the system from outside, it would have reverberating effects throughout and alter or restructure processes. Reorganization would be a constant and allow the system to be relevant for inevitable unpredictability.

The tendency to think linearly permeates most of Western thought. Everything from decisionmaking to mathematics has been influenced by the linear thinking of Newton (Dawoody, 2008). However, cause and effect thinking is not descriptive of the world we live in, which lacks predictability and renders long-term planning ineffective. Dawoody believes that the answer to this dilemma is in short-term planning and budgeting. In an Agent-Based Model, NCLB funding would not be based on single causes, such as test results, but have measures that included the larger network. Such a system would recognize that taking resources from one group to give to another would have dire circumstances on the entire system.

Another benefit in systems/dialectical thinking is to curtail the blame game, which is now the *modus operandi* of administrators, educators, and government. Consequently, a top-down approach flourishes in the blaming environment, because it separates those who are actually carrying out the educational edicts from those who are creating them. The ones at the top can blame those at the bottom for not delivering, while the ones at the bottom can blame those at the top for creating impossible guidelines. Using coercion at least forces attempts at compliance but undermines the objective of broadening and deepening education. One can only ask if this approach is the best way to ensure higher educational outcomes for all. Learning is not enhanced by means that increase stress and punishment. Children have to know that their test scores are central to the schools' proficiency. Students are also singled out according to racial subgroups, which could mean that some groups would be considered problematic for the school to achieve its goals. The accountability aspects leave much to be desired. Schools with only one subgroup that fails to meet proficiency are treated in the same way as schools in which all groups fail to meet proficiency. All students, including special needs and English language learners (ELL), are expected to meet the same standards, which may not be realistic.

Other concerns are raised in a top-down heavily bureaucratic system, such as creating input from those who implement the system. The current system may have an even greater problem in that it may not promote the U.S.'s standing among other industrialized nations. For example, the best way to compete with other countries, such as China, may not be in setting standards so that all students can achieve them. Rather the U.S. education system may be better served by focusing on growth and enhancement at all levels of learning. In others words, a system should focus on the broader picture of what children need to learn and how data can be used to improve efforts to arrive at the goal, while, at the same time, allowing for structural changes that might be required to fulfill this assessment.

A systems/dialectical perspective would be concerned with how children learn. It would, first of all, recognize that children learn at different speeds and through different means (Romanelli, Bird, & Ryan, 2009). Schools have to be concerned with children's development, which goes far beyond the intellectual to include their physical, social, and emotional well-being. The question becomes, "What contributes to the development of the whole child?" According to Ginsberg (2007), children are growing up in a hurried society in which parents and even preschools are abandoning the time dedicated to free play. Ginsberg believes that children need a full repertoire of activities, including academic learning, but parents and teachers should also be mindful of the significant contribution that play makes to the development of the child.

Free play enhances the development of the brain by allowing the child to fully explore the environment and creatively interact (Ginsberg, 2007). Play helps children develop resilience that will be needed later in trying circumstances. Child-driven play helps children make decisions, think in new ways, and pursue their own interests (McElwain & Volling, 2003, as cited in Ginsberg, 2007). While adults frequently play with children, there is less benefit to the child in terms of developing leadership skills and taking initiative than when children determine their play activities (Hurwitz, 2003, as cited in Ginsberg, 2007). In short, play activities tend to mediate other aspects of the child's development.

Rather than increasing play time and activities even in kindergarten, the trend has been a gradual decrease in play time and an increase in time for academic subjects (Pellegrini & Bohn, 2005). Compliance with NCLB has left the amount of time children have for play even more reduced and increased the time for math and reading. Sedentary learning may benefit some children, but overall, it might have significant effects on others, particularly boys. While touting the benefits of free play, Ginsberg (2007) understands that too much unstructured time is detrimental to children. The main point of focus is how much free play time is optimal for development. While there are many factors related to the increased diagnosis of childhood mental illness, it is likely that the hurried lifestyle that develops early and the reduction in free play as the child moves through the grade school years could significantly impact adolescent depression and other mental disorders (Ginsberg, 2007).

Because of the increase in single-parent families and families in which both parents work, there is less time for children to be engaged in unstructured play (Barker, Semenov, Michaelson, Provan, Snyder, & Munakata, 2014). At the same time, children are, more than ever, expected to excel academically, especially in science, mathematics, and language arts, and many parents begin pushing their child's academic prowess early. Because of poor access to the out-of-doors, many children spend much time in front of the TV or computer. Many children live in apartment buildings that may have a swimming pool, but few other places where children can play.

Along with the reduction in free play has been a general reduction in children's contact with nature. In a more agrarian time, children in the U.S. spent much of their time outside. Contact with nature has similar effects as free play in that a lot of free play takes place outside. With the reduction of space for children to be outside and the fear that many parents have that their children may be abducted, children have few unsupervised experiences in the "woods." Researchers have found that experiences with nature increase bonding, as evidenced by higher levels of **oxytocin,** the attachment hormone (Welberg, 2008). Oxytocin is also related to more positive social and interpersonal interactions with others.

As mentioned above, Ken Robinson (2009) has written extensively about the failure of education worldwide. Robinson believes that children have much greater abilities than they display, because the process of education is too limiting. The potential of each student is not being maximized through educational systems. A key element of education should be allowing students to be wrong.

TABLE 6.4 Challenges to education

1. **Creative potential.** All persons have creative ability, and when they discover it, there is a tremendous impact on their overall achievement.
2. **Freedom and control.** Freedom is not about letting go; it is about knowledge and involves innovation.
3. **Cultural Changes.** Persons must respect the cultural changes and values that drive creative thoughts and ideas.
4. **A Systemic Approach.** Creativity and cultural education are not subject material but should drive education. A balanced approach of curriculum, teaching methods, interaction with parents, and assessment should be used.

Adapted From: Robinson, 2009

Because most educational systems discourage children being wrong, Robinson believes that they are also stifled from developing new ideas and concepts. Thus, schools universally fail to inspire creativity, and educators turn education into boring, repetitive, dumbed-down materials that call for rote memory. He believes that the educational system with certain subjects at the top, such as math, science, and language arts, worked well for the 19th century Industrial Revolution, but not for today.

The American educational system is organized much like a factory, in which students move through the grades according to age with a corresponding curriculum. Convergent thinking dominates the educational landscape with little focus on divergent thinking, which, according to Robinson (2009), is a prerequisite for creativity. Furthermore, Robinson believes that standardized testing as a measure of what children learn is another symptom of the real problem. It is not enough to revise the present system; according to Robinson, it should be transformed by changing the operating paradigm.

The paradigm shift for Robinson (2009) is, first of all, a change in how educators view intelligence; that is, to acknowledge that intelligence is diverse and multi-dimensional. The narrow focus on intelligence is nowhere more evident than in NCLB. According to Robinson, instead of promoting greater achievement, divergent thinking, and creativity, the present educational systems does the very opposite. The specific intelligence of some students is not recognized, because they fail to achieve in math, science, or language arts. Consequently, these students form the opinion that they are not smart and, over time, act out that belief. To some degree, Robinson believes that children who develop this sense of failure are also more likely to be diagnosed with Attention Deficit Hyperactivity Disorder, which is a convenient way for authority figures to control children's behavior. According to Robinson, instead of forcing students into one paradigm, which sets standards that apply across the board that align with college entrance requirements, educators should adopt a diverse curriculum that allows for a wide range of individual choice and interest.

According to Robinson (2009), a main stumbling block in fully understanding intelligence is that most people do not associate it with creativity. Creativity links things together that are not present, except in the imagination. For Robinson, creativity is the highest form of intelligence. While engaged in creative acts, persons use media, such as music, paint, or words, which gives them a sense of satisfaction. Many people are never able to find that passion because of the way subjects are presented in school. Intelligence is based on diversity, according to Robinson; unfortunately, schools focus on conformity and linearity. A systemic view promotes looking at how things are different so that knowing how things really are can follow.

In applying a systems/dialectical perspective, a number of dialectical positions emerge. First is the argument for and against a Federal Department of Education. There are generally three arguments for a Federal Department of Education: federal intervention in education is needed; it has been successful in improving education; it is an appropriate extension of the Constitution (Murray, 2008). Proponents for the Department of Education believe that, although education is not specifically mentioned as a responsibility of the federal government, it provides some consistency in education across state lines to ensure that all persons receive a quality education. Proponents would also point out that the Department of Education has developed support for education through loan programs, increasing graduation rates and improving outcomes for minorities, children below the poverty level, and special needs children (Murray, 2008). Laws such as the National Defense Education Act of 1958 and the Supreme Court ruling in *Brown v. Board of Education* were necessary to change the course taken by states and local school districts. Proponents point out that test scores in basic skills have improved since 1978, evidence that the Department of Education not only was needed to intervene to protect the rights of all children but also to permanently monitor and promote quality education. On the other hand, Murray points out that critics of the Department of Education believe that the intervention in the 1950s and 1960s was justification to correct the violations, but not necessary as an ongoing entity. They point out that the baseline year of 1978 used for comparison was the lowest point in testing scores, and that the increases seen from 1978 is just a return to the same level prior to the federal government's involvement. Furthermore, programs such as Title I, created for the purpose of improving minority and poor children's scores, have done little to achieve their stated goals. In addition, critics point out that the most influential advances in education did not come from the Department's initiatives but from external sources. Critics note that parents are left out in the heavily bureaucratic federal system, and initiatives such as Common Core should be set up by states or local districts and not by the federal government. In summation, critics point out that the government has spent a great deal of money, but none of the programs cited for the establishment of the Department of Education has been successful.

KEY TERMS

Schooling	No Child Left Behind (NCLB)	Critical thinking
Middle Ages	Reading First	Analytical thinking
Feudalism	High stakes testing	Just the Facts Program
Bourgeois state	Proficiency ceiling	Text-dependent questions
Colonial education	The Elementary and Secondary School	Agency-based approach
Tabula Rosa	Education Act (ESEA)of 1965	Non-linear interacting system
Separate but equal	Student Teachers Achievement Ratio	Oxytocin
War on Poverty	Testing (STAR)	
	Common Core Standards	
	Race to the Top Program	

STUDY QUESTIONS TO ACCOMPLISH THE LEARNING OBJECTIVES

1. Briefly trace the history of education in the U.S. Determine if the purpose of education has changed.

2. Discuss some important court cases on education. Discuss how the court has played a role in changing the educational landscape.

3. Define NCLB. Briefly describe the pros and cons of NCLB. Evaluate the effectiveness of NCLB

4. List arguments that public schools are failing. Evaluate why efforts to improve public schools failed. Justify your belief that public schools are failing or, on the other hand, that they are effective.

5. List the basic components of Common Core. Determine if Common Core is an improvement over NCLB. Justify your answer.

6. Discuss the major criticism of Common Core for kindergarten students. Evaluate whether Common Core meets the learning needs for kindergarten students.

7. List the NAEYC criteria for developmentally appropriate practices and how they lead to positive outcomes.

8. Discuss Sir Ken Robinson's criticisms of the American educational system, and evaluate Robinson's suggestions for improving education. Formulate how his ideas would work in the present systems or how a new system would have to be created.

9. Discuss the accountability system in NCLB and Common Core. Analyze whether accountability is different or essentially the same in the two systems.

10. Determine if a systems/dialectical perspective improves educational outcomes. Justify your answer.

DEBATE ACTIVITY FOR STUDENTS

Consider the following proposition: Educational standards should be set by local school boards with parental input.

- Review refereed literature on this topic. Do a library and Internet search to find relevant material. Investigate some of the additional readings.

- Develop three arguments for the proposition.

- Develop three arguments against the proposition.

- How do the arguments relate to other systems, such as the community or culture?

- Is there common ground?

- What are the long-term consequences of taking action?

- What new or common-ground solutions should be offered? If no common ground, what new position could emerge from a dialogue between the two positions?

- How is the new position superior to the original positions?

ADDITIONAL READING RESOURCES

14 Crucial Pros and cons of No Child Left Behind Act. (2015). *ConnectUS: The Global Issues Blog.* Retrieved from http://connectusfund.org/14-crucial-pros-and-cons-of-the-no-child-left-behind-act

Bleiberg, J., & West, D.M. (2015). In defense of the Common Core Standards. *Center for Technology Innovations at Brookings,* March 2014. Retrieved from https://www.brookings.edu/wp-content/uploads/2016/06/Bleiberg_West_Common-Core-State-Standards.pdf

Bogenschneider, K. & Johnson, C. (2015). Family involvement in education: How important is it? What can legislators do? *The Policy Institute for Impact Seminars.* Retrieved from https://www.purdue.edu/hhs/hdfs/fii/wp-content/uploads/2015/06/fia_brchapter_20c02.pdf

Farris, S. E. (2012). The perception of school board members and their role in improving college and career readiness, *On Line Theses and Dissertations,* 64. http://encompass.eku.edu/edt/64

Toward a Definition of Creativity. (2010). Wisconsin Task Force for Creativity and Education, February 19, 2010. Retrieved from https://www.education.com/reference/article/towards-definition-creativity/

Urban, W.J., & Wagoner, J.L. (2011). *American education: A history* (4th ed.). New York, NY: Routledge.

REFERENCES

Achilles, C.M., Bain, H.P., Bellott, F., Boyd-Zaharias, J., Finn, F., Folger, J., … Word, E. (2008), Tennessee's Student Teacher Achievement Ratio (STAR) project. Retrieved from http://hdl.handle.net/1902.1/10766 UNF:3:Ji2Q+9HCCZABw3csOdMNdA== HEROS, Inc.;Helen Pate Bain and Carolyn Cox, Co-Chairs;Jayne Boyd-Zaharias, Executive Director [Distributor] V1 [Version]

Albrecht, S., & Jones, C. (2003). Accountability and access to opportunity: Mutually exclusive tenets under a high-stakes testing mandate. *Preventing School Failure, 47,* 86–91.

Arthur, L. L. (2000). A new look at schooling and literacy: The colony of Georgia. *Historical Quarterly, 84*(4), 563–588.

Au, W. (2007). High-stakes testing and curriculum control: A qualitative meta-synthesis. *Educational Researcher, 36*(5), 257–268.

Barker, J. E., Semenov, A. D., Michaelson, L., Provan, L. S., Snyder, H. R., and Munakata, Y. (2014). Less structured time in children's daily lives predicts self-directed executive functioning. *Frontiers in Psychology,* 2014, doi: 10.3389/fpsyg.2014.00593

Borowsky, J. (2013). Ten reasons to oppose Common Core. FreedomWorks, July 23, 2013. Retrieved from http://www.freedomworks.org/content/top-10-reasons-oppose-common-core

Brown v. Board of Education of Topeka. (1954). 347 U.S. 483.

Calkins, L., Ehrenworth, M., & Lehman, C. (2012). *Pathways to the Common Core.* Portsmouth, NH: Heinemann.

Carnevale, A. P., Smith, N., & Strohl, J. (2010). Help wanted: Projections of jobs and educational requirements through 2018. Georgetown University, Center for Education and the Workforce. Retrieved from http://cew.georgetown.edu/jobs2018

Common Core State Standards Initiative. (2012). Implementing the Common Core State Standards. Retrieved from http://www.corestandards.org/

Conroy, M. (2000). School choice: Or is it privatization? *Educational Researcher, 29*(7), 15–30.

Copple, C., Bredekamp, S., & Gonzalez-Mena, J. (2009). *Developmentally appropriate practice.* (3rd ed.). Washington, D.C.: NAEYC.

Dawoody, A. R. (2008). A complexity response to funding public education. *The Innovative Journal: The Public Sector Innovative Journal, 13*(3), 1–9.

Dudley, M. E. (1994). *Brown v. Board of Education, (1954).* New York, NY: First Century Books.

Duncombe, W., Lukemeyer, A., & Yinger, J. (2008). No Child Left Behind Act: Have federal funds been left behind. *Public Finance Review, 36*(4), 381–407.

Eitel, R. S., & Talbert, K. D. (2012). *The legal aspects of the common core standards, race to the top and conditional waivers.* Pioneer Institute. Retrieved from http://pioneerinstitute.org/download/the-road-to-a-national-curriculum/

Elementary and Secondary School Education Act. (1965). Retrieved from http://www.k12.wa.us/esea/

Elish-Piper, L., & Piper, M. E. (2009). Parents' involvement in reading. *Illinois Reading Council Journal, 37*(4), 56–62.

Evers, M. E., & Alger, V. E. (2017, July 12). Trumps' educational cuts aren't devastating: They're smart. *The Washington Post.* Retrieved from http://www.latimes.com/opinion/op-ed/la-oe-evers-alger-trump-education-cuts-good-20170612-story.html

Forgione, P. D. (2012). Coming together to raise achievements: New assessment for the Common Core standards. Center for K–12 Assessment and Performance Management at ETS.

Fuller, B., Gesicki, K., Kang, E., & Wright, J. (2006). Is no child left behind working? The reliability of how states track achievement. *Policy Analysis for California Education.* Retrieved from http://www.edpolicyinca.org/publications/no-child-left-behind-act-working-reliability-how-states-track-achievement

Ginsberg, K. R. (2007). The importance of play in promoting healthy child development and maintaining strong parent-child bonds. *Pediatrics, 119*(1), 182–191.

Gray, P. (2013). *Freedom to learn: Why unleashing the instinct to play will make our children happier, more self-reliant, and better students for life.* New York, NY: Basic Books.

Hombo, C. (2003). NAEP and no child left behind: Technical challenges and practical solutions. *Theory into Practice, 42,* 59–65.

Houston, P. D. (2007) The seven deadly sins of No Child Left Behind. *Phi Delta Kappan*, June, 2007, 744–749.

Hrenchir, T. (2015). Five failures of common core claimed by opponents. *Newsmax*, April 22, 2015. Retrieved from http://www.newsmax.com/FastFeatures/common-core-failures-opponents/2015/04/22/id/640076/

Jalongo, M. R., & Heider, K. (2006). Editorial teacher attrition: An issue of national concern. *Early Childhood Education Journal, 33*(6), 379–380.

Klein, A. (2007). Critics of NCLB ask Congress to overhaul it. *EducationWeek,* February 23, 2007. Retrieved from http://www.edweek.org/ew/articles/2007/02/23/25nclb.h26.html?print=1 3/5/2007

Klein, J. (2011). The failure of American schools. *The Atlantic,* June 2011. Retrieved from https://www.theatlantic.com/magazine/archive/2011/06/the-failure-of-american-schools/308497/

Krieg, M. E. (2011). Which students are left behind? The racial impact of the No Child Left Behind Act. *Economics of Education Review, 30*(4), 654–664.

McNeil, M. (2011). Are 82% of schools failing under NCLB warned? *Education Week*, August 3, 2011.

Mintz, S. (2012). Education in the American colonies. Retrieved from http://www.digitalhistory.uh.edu/database/article_display.cfm?HHID=36

Moyer, B. (2012). Messing with Texas textbooks. Retrieved from http://billmoyers.com/content/messing-with-texas-textbooks

Murnane, R. J., & Papay, J. J. (2010). Teachers' views on No Child Left Behind: Support for the principles: Concerns about the practice. *Journal of Economic Perspectives, 24*(3), 151–166.

Murray, C. (2009). *Real education: four simple truths for bringing America's education back to reality.* New York, NY: Three Rivers Press.

Muskal, M. (2013). U.S. high school graduation rates hits highest in decades. *Los Angeles Times*, January 22, 2013. Retrieved from http://articles.latimes.com/2013/jan/22/nation/la-na-nn-high-school-graduation-rate-increasing-20130122

National Center for Educational Statistics (2012). The condition of education. Retrieved from http://nces.ed.gov/programs/coe/

Neil, J. (2005). John Dewey: The modern father of experiential education. Retrieved from https://wilderdom.com

No Child Left Behind. (2001). PL- 107–110.

Pellegrini, A. D., & Bohn, C. D. (2005). The role of recess in children cognitive performance and school adjustment. *Educational Research*, January/February, 13–19.

Plessy v. Ferguson. (1896). 163 U.S. 537.

Porter, A., McMaken, J., Hwang, J., & Yang, R. (2011). Common core standards: The new U.S. intended curriculum. *Educational Researcher, 40*(3), 103–116. doi:10.3102/0013189X11405038.

Pulliam, J. D., & Van Patten, J. J. (2012). *The history and social foundations of American education.* (10th ed.). Upper Saddle River, NJ: Pearson.

Rivkin, S. G., Hanushek, E. A., & Kain, J. F. (2012). Teachers, schools, and academic achievement. *Econometrica, 73*(2), 417–458.

Robinson, K. (2009). *The element: How finding your passion changes everything.* New York, NY: Viking.

Romanelli, F., Bird, E., & Ryan, M. (2009). Learning styles: A review of theory, application, and best practices. *American Journal of Pharmaceutical Education, 81*(3), 47.

Rumberger, R.W. (2013). Poverty and high school dropouts: The impact of family and community on dropout rates. American Psychological Association. Retrieved from http://www.apa.org/pi/ses/resources/indicator/2013/05/poverty-dropouts.aspx

Solman, P. (2013). Are College and Career Skills Really the Same? *PBS NewsHour.* Retrieved from http://www.pbs.org/newshour/rundown/2013/06/are-college-and-career-skills-really-the-same.html

Stotsky, S. (2012). *Common core standards devastating impact on literary study and analytical thinking.* The Heritage Foundation. Retrieved from http://www.heritage.org/research/reports/2012/12/questionable-quality-of-the-common-core-english-language-arts-standards

U.S. Department of Labor, Bureau of Labor Statistics. (2012). Occupational Outlook Handbook, 2012–2013. Retrieved from http://www.bls.bov/ooh/about/projections-overview.htm

Welberg, L. (2008). Trust in oxytocin. *Nature Reviews Neuroscience, 9,* 500. doi:10.1038/nrn2446.

White House. (2012). Investing in future: Returning teachers to the classroom. Retrieved from http://www.whitehouse.gov/sites/default/files/Investing_in_Our_Future_Report.pdf

CREDITS

CHAPTER SEVEN

Social Policy and Family Development

LEARNING OBJECTIVES

At the end of the chapter the student will be able to:

✓ Define marriage and family and explain why a definition is necessary for social policy;

✓ Recall arguments for and against DOMA, analyze both sides of the arguments, and compare and contrast the effectiveness of these arguments:

✓ Identify steps in the process of establishing an amendment to the Constitution. The student will recognize arguments on both sides of the Parental Rights Amendment and be able to compare and contrast the effectiveness of the arguments;

✓ Define the term family structure, summarize the argument for the connection of family structure to family functioning, and justify the formation of social policies based on family structure;

✓ Define gender wage gap and defend that it exists;

✓ Understand issues related to stepfamilies, and evaluate social policies affecting step-families;

✓ Label issues related to adoption, and analyze the factors involved in successful foster care placements that lead to adoption;

✓ Understand the role that unwed fathers have with their children, and discuss the implications for social policy;

✓ Summarize research finding of cohabitation, and evaluate the effects on marriage; and

✓ Paraphrase the arguments for and against non-traditional adoptions and explain how social policy is affected by non-traditional adoptions.

SOCIAL POLICY AND FAMILY DEVELOPMENT

Social policy for families tends not to be addressed with the same level of consistency as social policy for children. While many social policy issues directly affect families, there is little coordinated linkage between issues. Instead, family social policy tends be a smorgasbord of efforts that may even be contradictory. No doubt the changing scene of family structure and diversity of family roles dampened attempts to develop an overarching guide or framework for present and future social policy. While attempts are made at various levels of government to remediate conditions of individuals, the lack of an overall family social policy guide means that many issues are unaddressed or done so haphazardly (Newman, 2006). Consequently, long-term outcomes for a family social policy will likely depend on how certain issues are defined. For example, same-sex marriage will depend on how marriage is defined, parental rights will depend concomitantly on how child and adolescent rights are defined, and policies regarding abortion will depend on a definition of when life begins.

Many family social policy issues are suspended between different ideological belief systems. As pointed out earlier, this dialectic is necessary to critically evaluate equally valid opposing points of view. If a traditional family focus is taken, social policy would emphasize different aspects than if a family revisionist position is taken. Likewise, if the government is viewed as the best way to provide basic needs for all persons, especially in providing for preventative measures for families at risk, the policies that create and maintain a support system would be instituted. This chapter will address various points of view on social policy related to family development, such as the definition of marriage, gay and lesbian marriage, parental rights, adoption, and stepfamilies. While volumes could be written on each of these topics, the emphasis in this chapter is to highlight the dialectical issues related to the topics.

MARRIAGE

Defining Marriage and Family

Defining marriage may seem rather easy at first, and perhaps it was decades ago, but today defining marriage is no simple task. Much of the discussion that follows will imply a specific definition of marriage. In fact, defining marriage will delimit the content of what constitutes marriage, who can and cannot marry, determine gender or partner roles and social relationships, influence state and federal laws, and create a host of other issues. The definition below is intended to be broad enough to resist reflecting a particular ideology of marriage. **Marriage** is defined as a contract or union of spouses who pair bond for the purpose of psychological and sexual intimacy and cooperate to share resources and may have offspring or adopted children. This contract is recognized through state law and may also reflect religious and cultural rituals. While marriage in some cultures can be arranged, marriage in the U.S. tends to be freely chosen by the partners (Crossman, 2017). This definition is rather broad and includes general ideas that are prevalent in American society. A caveat is that any definition of marriage may actually reflect the historical time in which it is made rather than a definitive definition that will withstand the changing historical context.

A similar caveat is necessary in defining family, and for this reason, a definition void of biases for preconceived parameters is necessary. Because the family is a social construct and unit, it can be defined in a vast array of meanings. The meaning chosen here is to reduce the tendency to align with preconceived notions. A **family** is defined in accordance with the U.S. Bureau of the Census as, namely, a group consisting of two or more persons residing in the same household who are related biologically or by adoption (U.S. Bureau of the Census, 2006). This definition is distinct from **household,** which refers to two or more persons who share the same dwelling. According to this definition, a household would not always be considered a family but not the reverse (Newman,

2006). The family as a social group is a bond that typically transcends other bonds and has the presumption of permanence. Generally, relationships created in a family provide greater emotional, financial, social, and intellectual sharing of ideas than other relationships (Anderson, 2014). Families develop **rituals** and **routines** that make family relationships more meaningful than other relationships (Fiese, Tomicho, Douglas, Josephs, Poltrock, & Baker, 2004).

While the above definitions of marriage and family are broad, neither includes some types of relationships. For example, marriages in the U.S. are **monogamous,** meaning that they consist of two persons, which excludes different types of group marriages, such as **polygamy**, one man and two or more women, or **polyandry**, one woman and two or more men (Newman, 2006). However, families are not required to have two partners and may consist of one adult and children, referred to as single-parent families. Marriage has primarily been referred to as between a man and a woman, although that part of the definition is missing in the above, and more will be discussed about gender and marriage later in the chapter. Because marriage is state regulated and not federally mandated, laws governing marriage vary according to states. For example, some states allow for common-law marriage, which is based on the length of the cohabitation, while other states, such as California, do not. Distant kin may be allowed to marry in some states, and the age at marriage also varies according to state laws. In addition, the word family has a more inclusive meaning for nonbiological persons to whom we have an emotional bond. The term used for describing these nonrelated family relationships is **fictive kin** (Newman, 2006).

Gay and Lesbian Marriage

The definition of marriage has taken on a new meaning now that gays and lesbians are able to legally marry, generally referred to as **same-sex marriage**. Since marriage and divorce laws are governed by the states, there is a no federal statute that can bring uniformity to this issue. **Traditional marriage** in the U.S. refers to the marriage of one man and one woman. This point of view contends that marriage existed before recorded history and predates statutes to regulate it. At present in the U.S., same-sex unions are legal in all 50 states due to the Supreme Court rule in *Obergefell v. Hodges* in 2015. Prior to that ruling, 37 of 50 states declared that marriage was between one man and one woman. Early court challenges to laws denying same-sex marriage, such as *Baker v. Nelson* in 1971, were rejected with a firm reaffirmation that marriage was between one man and one woman.

By 2013, 13 states had legalized same-sex marriage, beginning first with Massachusetts in 2004. From 2003 to 2008, the overall divorce rate in Massachusetts declined significantly and was the lowest in the nation in 2008 (Silver, 2010). Whether this decline was related to the increase in marriage of same-sex couples relative to the number of total divorces is unknown. Before the Supreme Court ruling, the majority of states (37) in the U.S. had banned same-sex marriage, although public support had shifted to favor same-sex marriage. After the Supreme Court ruling, the U.S. joined 19 other countries that allowed same-sex marriages. Some noted countries of the 20 that do allow same-sex marriage are the Netherlands, Belgium, France, Canada, Spain, and Sweden (Lavers, 2013). While estimates of the cost of same-sex marriage for governments is in dispute, in the U.S. it is estimated that same-sex marriage may cost the federal government an estimated $898 million in mandatory and discretionary spending (Marcellino, Nelson, & Anthony, 2009).

The Supreme Court ruling in *Obergefell v. Hodges* was based on the Fourteenth Amendment to the Constitution that not allowing same-sex marriage violated the rights of gays and lesbians equal protection under the law (Masci, Brown, & Kiley, 2017). According to a Pew research report at the time the ruling was made, the majority of Americans supported same-sex marriage, 57% for and 39% against. As of July 2017, the level of support for same-sex marriage has increased to 62% overall, although different cohorts in American society differ in their support (Masci et al., 2017). For example, 85% of persons with no religious beliefs favor same-sex marriage compared to 68% for White Protestants, 67% of White Catholics, 44% for Black Protestants, and 35% for White Evangelicals. In terms of age cohorts, millennials' support it at 75%, compared to the lowest support cohort being those over 72 years of age at 41%. What the above figures from the Pew Research Center reveal is that, like abortion and other lightening rod issues, the debate is not over and will continue to be a debated issue.

TABLE 7.1 Court rulings on the constitutionality of DOMA

Windsor v. United States—June 26, 2013. Supreme Court ruled that Section 3 of DOMA was unconstitutional.
Gill v. Office of Personnel Management—Case filed on behalf of a number of lesbian couples to receive comparable benefits as heterosexual couples. The ruling in *Windsor* applies to this case.
Commonwealth of Massachusetts v. Department of Health and Human Services—Case brought by the Attorney General of Massachusetts that Section 3 in DOMA was unconstitutional. Ruling in *Windsor applies* to this case.
Golinski v. Office of Personnel Management—Case brought on behalf of same-sex employees for equal benefits. Decision in *Windsor* extends to this case.
Pedersen v. Office of Personnel Management—Case brought on behalf of same-sex employees for equal benefits.
Dragovich v. U.S. Department of Treasury—Case filed in 2010 in California to include spouse in health care benefits. A judge on the Ninth Circuit Court of Appeals ruled that Section 3 under DOMA was unconstitutional and that the tax law in California restricting same-sex couples from inclusion in health care benefits was unconstitutional.

The lead up to the Supreme Court ruling slowly emerged over a number of decades. Academic literature took up the cause of same-sex marriage in the 1990s and reopened the question from the civil-rights perspective (e.g., Eskridge, 1992). Although little progress was imminent from academic literature, the groundwork was laid for formidable changes that would come later. While the general public was not swayed by academic arguments, there was enough concern about challenges to the traditional view that Congress acted in 1996 to pass Defense of Marriage Act (DOMA). DOMA, under Section 3, refused to acknowledge same-sex marriage on the same level as heterosexual marriage and denied same-sex partners federal tax and Social Security benefits. In February 2011, the Obama administration proclaimed that it would no longer defend DOMA in court. This decision gave new life to same-sex marriage advocates and opened the door for challenges that would not be defended by the administration. One major case was in California in *Perry v. Schwarzenegger*, which challenged Proposition 8, a referendum passed by voters declaring that marriage was between one man and one woman. A district court judge ruled that Proposition 8 was unconstitutional, which was stayed by the Ninth Circuit Court of Appeals. In June 2013, the U.S. Supreme Court ruled in *Windsor v. United States* that Section 3 of DOMA was unconstitutional, which extends to other similar cases.

The Argument for DOMA

Proponents for DOMA argued that marriage is an essential component of society and that same-sex marriage will undermine this foundation. The argument is also based on what is believed to be in the best interests of children. They point out a preponderance of research that shows the importance of two biological parents of different genders. They believe that promoting marriage does not deny any other type of relationship; it merely defines what is and what is not marriage. Redefining marriage to include same-sex marriage would, therefore, not be in the best interest of children who depend on the family for socialization and psychological health. Their argument is that same-sex marriage would deny that children do better with a mother and father and the unique roles that each play in the development of children. According to a number of researchers who investigate the roles that mother and fathers play in the development of children, they conclude that mothers cannot compensate for the father's role and vice versa (Moore, Jekielek, & Emig, 2002; Popenoe, 1996). Further, researchers have found that teenage girls reared without fathers are at greater risk for early sexual activity (Ellis, 2003). Researchers have found that children raised by gay and lesbian parents have greater likelihood of engaging in gay or lesbian behavior (Stacey & Biblarz, 2001). Because children are such an important part of family life, supporters of DOMA believe that same-sex marriages do not produce offspring and, therefore, will always be considered an alternate family form. The limits for producing biological offspring that are 50% of each parent would mean that same-sex families would never have the same biological composition as a heterosexual couple with offspring.

Other concerns raised by supporters of DOMA included weakening taboos about other types of marriage. For example, they asked "What would keep a group of persons from marrying if they love each other and share intimacy?" Some have labeled this the "slippery slope argument" against same-sex marriage, because it would create additional civil rights arguments for any number of other possible types of marriage (Keenan & Associates, 2013). Supporters of DOMA believed that marriage must be viewed as a privilege and not a right. Persons do not have a civil right to be married, and the government can choose to give this privilege to some and not to others. The view further held that limiting marriage to one man and one woman is not discriminatory. Some believed that same-sex marriage will ultimately undermine marriage because of this ambiguity in definition (Kurtz, 2004).

The Argument against DOMA

While civil unions and domestic partnerships have been in place in many states for some time, many gay and lesbian activists believed that same-sex relationships continue to be discriminated against. What was needed, from their perspective, were the same rights and privileges as heterosexual relationships. In their view, DOMA was a biased law that perpetuated inequitable relationships and myths about gay and lesbian relationships. Proponents for same-sex relationships believed that DOMA was unconstitutional and not based on sound evidence that same-sex marriages should be prohibited.

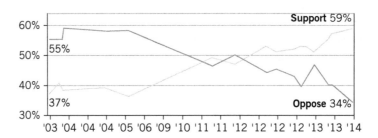

FIGURE 7.1 Public support and opposition to same-sex marriage
Note: 2012 and previous: Do you think it should be legal or illegal for gay and lesbian couples to get married?
Source: This Washington Post-ABC News poll. *The Washington Post*. Published on March 5, 2014, 12:01 a.m.

The opposition to DOMA pointed out that marriage has not always been defined as a union of one man and one woman, as the DOMA advocates claimed (Silver, 2010). For example, there are both historical and current occurrences in which other forms of marriage exist, including polygamy, communal living, and the use of mistresses and prostitutes (Silver, 2010). According to this view, the definition of marriage evolves in response to changing societal changes. A recent survey found that the majority of Americans favored same-sex marriage (Jones, 2013).

This change in the increase in the support for same sex marriage may, in part, be due to the lessening of religious influence on beliefs and behaviors in American society (Jones, 2013). Further, linking marriage to religious and moral considerations as a primary agent in marriage was viewed by same-sex advocates as inappropriate, because the state gives the church the power to perform marriage ceremonies and not vice versa.

Proponents of same-sex marriage believed that the concerns about the well-being of children in gay and lesbian families were not well founded. They pointed to a growing body of research that demonstrated that gay and lesbian families not only have strengths but produce children with greater academic and social skills than heterosexual families (Gartell & Bos, 2010). Proponents point out that the rush to judgment against same-sex families was not based on definitive research findings. They argued that same-sex marriages might allow for more children who are currently waiting for adoption to find homes before they time out.

Other benefits of same-sex marriage included increases in withheld federal income taxes and revenues from the sale of marriage licenses, which may significantly increase local government budgets. Proponents of same-sex marriage believed that these benefits would offset estimates that federal benefits to same-sex couples would be costly. In addition, psychological health may be improved, which would be another cost savings benefit to society.

While the debate about DOMA and same-sex marriage has receded into the background after the Supreme Court ruling, it continues to be a bone of contention in many states. For example, in March 2017, the Tennessee legislature introduced a bill (House Bill 892 and Senate Bill 752) that would eliminate all same-sex unions in the past and prohibit future marriages (Freedom for All, 2017). To date, this bill has not been enacted into law. In North Carolina, a bill was signed into law that lifted protection for LGBT persons, particularly in restricting restrooms sharing with transsexuals (Tchekmedyian, 2017). This law was repealed in March 2017 by Governor Roy Cooper.

Mississippi passed a law in 2016 that allows businesses to refuse services to LGBT persons on the basis of religious beliefs, but not affecting any state or federal constitutional rights guaranteed to all citizens (Berman, 2016). The bill also had a provision that government employees could recuse themselves from engaging in services that violated their religious beliefs. It is expected that advocates for traditional marriage will continue to push for measures to reverse or limit same-sex unions. Like opposition to abortion, it will continue to crop up in various ways.

FAMILY SOCIAL POLICY

The important role of the parent in the life of the child is immeasurable and assumed to be the most influential relationship for the development of attachment and socialization into society. Sometimes, this role is considered private in that parents have vast freedom to enact the parenting role in any way they desire. On the other hand, contemporary parents feel a lessening of this role due to various governmental policies and programs. Efforts on the part of the government to limit **parental authority** can be met with severe negative reaction (Dixon, Graber, & Brooks-Dunn, 2008). While many industrialized nations have initiated laws banning corporal punishment, beginning first with Sweden in the early 1980s, there continues to be resistance to laws prohibiting parents from spanking children in the United States. For example, a bill introduced in the California Assembly prohibiting parents from spanking their children created such a groundswell of opposition that it died before coming to a vote (Hanson, Jr., 2008).

An underlying issue in social policy is whether the policy should be individually or group focused (Bogenschneider, 2006). If policy is group focused, the family is of paramount importance in developing and applying the policy. Over the past four decades, the family has changed, and to some degree, social policies affecting families have lagged behind. Since policies are generally targeted toward individuals and, in the case of the family, targeted toward children, the once dominant role of the family in protecting children has eroded.

Parental Rights

There has been a growing concern in U.S. society that parents have decreasing influence in their children's lives, partly because of laws that give children rights to engage in behaviors or activities without parental knowledge or consent. The movement for a **Parental Rights Amendment** to the Constitution, which aims to protect children from being controlled by governmental influences that might be contrary to parental values or wishes and has been discussed for years, was reintroduced in the Senate on August 2, 2017, by Lindsay Graham (Reynolds, 2017). The Amendment also protects parents from international interference in the form of the **United Nations Convention on the Rights of the Child (UNCRC)**. Although signing the Convention occurred in 1995, it has not been ratified by the U.S. government, which some believe would subject family law in the U.S. to international control. Among others things, ratifying it would mean that laws regarding children, including juvenile crime and even homeschooling, would have to be reviewed internationally.

TABLE 7.2 Sections of the parental rights amendment

Section 1: Parents have the right to direct the rearing of their children.
Section 2: No governmental body may infringe on the rights of parents without due cause.
Section 3: No treaty or national or international governmental body can infringe on this right.
Section 4: Current law regarding end of life or abortion will not change.
Section 5: Prohibits judges from using international law to rule on parental rights.

Adapted From: http://www.parentalrights.org/index.asp?Type=B_BASIC&SEC=%7B4771B53E-D345- 4753-BEF4-68C1CA71CE13%7D

Proponents for the Parental Rights Amendment claim that there is a history of law and court cases supporting the primary position of parents in the rearing and socialization of children over and above governmental interference. For example, in *Pierce v. Society of Sisters* (1925) and later in *Wisconsin v. Yoder* (1972), the primary role of the parent in the rearing and socialization of children was firmly emphasized. More recently, the Supreme Court once again supported parental rights in 2000 in *Troxel v. Granville*, which ruled that the Washington State grandparent visitation statute did not take precedence over parental rights. A success in the evolution of parental rights occurred in July 2013 at the state level when the Illinois State Supreme Court ruled that a state law that required parents or guardians to be notified 48 hours before a minor could have an abortion procedure was constitutional. While this law had been on the books for approximately a decade, it had not been enforced. Advocates for parental rights believe that this ruling may have ramifications for other states and national policy.

Prior to the reintroduction of the Parental Rights Amendment by Senator Graham, it had been introduced in three other Congresses (Parental Rights Amendment, 2014). The proposal must pass both chambers of Congress by a two-thirds margin vote and, upon passage, goes to each state to ratify. To become an amendment to the Constitution, three-fourths of the states, or 38 legislatures, must ratify it. Proponents believe that ratification of the Amendment is necessary, because rights of parents are slowly vanishing. For example, if children are allowed to make their own decisions about contraception, abortion, the morning-after pill, and other current initiatives without parental knowledge, proponents of the Amendment believe that parental influence over their children will decrease.

As the influence of parents lessens in making important decisions, proponents of the Amendment believe that children will be more vulnerable to negative influences and make decisions that will adversely affect them in the future (Parental Rights Amendment, 2014). For example, a law that allows children to make what is really an adult decision, such as abortion or taking the morning-after pill, puts them at greater risks to make impulsive and irrational decisions influenced more by their peers than adults, without understanding the consequences of their actions. Proponents for the Amendment are bolstered by much research that shows that teens who have open communication with their parents fare better on many variables, including academics, drug usage, sexual promiscuity, smoking, and delinquent acting out (Parental Rights Amendment, 2014). Laws that promote secrecy between parents and children, particularly those that allow children to make decisions without parental knowledge, actually undermine children's development. For this reason, proponents of the Amendment believe that it is necessary to bolster parental involvement with their children. They contend that the family is the safety net for the children and that the government is not.

Proponents for parental rights believe that the general legal climate in the U.S. is stacked against parents (Parental Rights Amendment, 2014). They believe that children are removed from homes and placed in foster homes without good reason, and parents have little recourse. The fear is that Child Protective Services and Family Courts do not strictly adhere to the primacy of the rights of parents to raise their own children. Since there is no law that addresses the primacy of the rights of parents, and some believe that there is no standing in the constitution for parental rights, proponents believe that it is necessary to establish once and for all parental rights in the Constitution.

Opponents to the Parental Rights Amendment contend that a constitutional amendment is not necessary and may be dangerous to children, because it may make it more difficult for governmental agencies to intrude in abusive families (Stevenson, 2009). Investigating claims of abuse against parents may be much harder to do, and parents can hide behind the Amendment. Stevenson (2009) believes that existing laws are adequate and other Amendments in the Constitution, notably the Fourth and Ninth, are adequate to cover parental rights issues. In addition, Stevenson believes that schools and families need to work together, and there should be mutual trust between the school system and families. The Amendment would erode this trust and sway the balance of power toward parents. Some have held that the Amendment would cause an increase in litigation that could have damaging effects on the quality of education and child development in general (Head, 2011). The bottom line in the opponent's argument is that public education could be undermined by the Amendment, because parents would have an established right to direct all aspects of their children's lives, including education. Since many parents are unhappy about public education, it might cause a groundswell of opposition to public education.

Opponents to the Amendment are quick to point out that parents already have the right to parent their children, unless they are breaking the law (Stevenson, 2009). Opponents charge that conservatives, homeschoolers, and Christian groups are the main proponents of the Amendment, and therefore, it does not appeal to the majority of people. Opponents cite support from organizations, such as Planned Parenthood, National Teachers Association, and People for the American Way.

The underlying factor in this debate is the influence that ratifying the UNCRC would have on the family's ability to parent its own children. A recent Zogby poll (2010) found little support for the UNCRC and a bolstering for support of the Parental Rights Amendment. The fear is that government workers could override parents on any issue related to their children. The consequences of the state's intrusion in the family at the behest of the children or others outside the family would be that parents would constantly be on guard against possible innocuous complaints that, nevertheless, would have to be defended against. Parents would have little authority to influence school procedures, and the state would dictate acceptable discipline techniques for children.

Universal Declaration

The Universal Declaration of Human Rights was adopted by the United Nations in 1948 and reflected widespread reaffirmation of the rights and equality of all persons in all nations (Glendon, 2004). The United Nations, which was enrolled in 1945 following World War II, established a number of commissions, one of which was the Human Rights Commission with Eleanor Roosevelt as the first chairperson (Universal Declaration of Human Rights, 2008–2017). Under her leadership, the Universal Declaration of Human Rights was established in 1948. All member nations unanimously voted in favor of the declaration, and it continues throughout the world as a basic contract between governments and people.

While the ideas of freedom and individual rights are still voiced by governments and leaders in the United States and most other countries, some believe that this basic contract between the government and its constituents is declining and, in some cases, is outright disregarded (Marshall & Smith, 2006). Glendon (2004) believes that persons have devolved into believing that human rights are a kind of smorgasbord where one can pick and choose which rights they want to emphasize. Over time, this perception of human rights gave way to the view of human rights in terms of classes of people, such as women's rights and children's rights. Some scholars believe that the United Nations Commission on Human Rights has become less relevant to the very reason it was formed and should be revamped (Schaefer & Kingham, 2006). The criticisms reflect a growing tendency to reduce support for the Commission, which includes member nations that are guilty of gross human rights violations. Calls are continually being made to hold countries accountable for human rights violations. While the Universal Declaration on Human Rights continues to be a very important document, enforcement of the provisions of the document needs to be tightened.

Parenting Education

Another area in which parents and society conflict is whether or not parents need training to provide optimal development for their children. **Parenting education** has been around for many decades and usually is the result of parents failing in some way in their parenting role and needing remedial help (Yousefi, 2016). Parents are frequently referred to parenting education classes after coming before the court in a child abuse incident. Fulfilling the requirements of the court means that many parents are involved under duress and have no choice. The question is whether parents would seek parenting education on their own to become better parents. The ancillary query is whether participating in parenting education improves parenting or is largely ineffective in actually changing or improving parenting behaviors. Programs of parenting education differ according to the need of parents with some families needing **transition to parenthood** training and others needing therapy for the whole family.

One of the major concerns is whether it is possible for researchers to translate what is known about effective parenting into training that can help parents from various backgrounds and capacities (Yousefi, 2016). A study by Pinquart and Teubert (2010) found that a program of parenting education with expectant parents was effective, but the effect size, which differed according to circumstances surrounding the initiation of training, gender, type of training, and goals, was rather small.

FAMILY STRUCTURE

Family structure, as noted elsewhere, is a major component in understanding public policy relating to families. Cohabitation, single-parent families, and families of divorce are often viewed as causes for the decline of family functioning (Sharma, 2013). The cure is generally believed to be a return to the traditional family, which means the nuclear family with a mother, father, and biological children. The dialectic here is that one side supports traditional families and the other side embraces diverse family types. The next section will address the arguments each side makes.

The Family Is a Diverse Institution

It is no surprise to anyone that the family has been changing for decades. Perhaps one of the major changes is in the number of women who are the breadwinners of the family. According to Pew Report (Wang, Parker, & Taylor, 2013), women are the main source of income in approximately 40% of households. Instead of viewing changes in the family as disruptions, this perspective portrays the family as complex in nature. Approximately 7 million women are currently unpartnered in the U.S. In these families, women can be overwhelmed with parenting and working without a built-in support system. Two factors contribute to this change for women: they are more accepted in the workforce, and families headed by women are much more common. Women's desire to work full-time versus part-time has also increased in recent years. At present, about 24% of women earn more than their husbands, still a minority of families but significantly more than in the 1960s (Wang et al., 2013).

Some findings dampen enthusiasm that women may continue to out-earn their male partners. For example, recent research found that marriage rates have decreased for women who earn more than their potential partners, and that wives who are better educated than their husbands are less likely to work than women who are less educated than their husbands (Rampell, 2013). The fact that women with greater education are less likely to work is, perhaps, a new trend in marriage composition and may be one of the continuing factors that create the gap between men and women's pay deferential. In addition, in marriages in which the wives make more than their husbands, the risk of divorce is higher, and women are more dissatisfied with marriage. In newlywed couples, there seems to be greater tolerance for women making more money than husbands, as evidenced by a higher percentage of couples in which the wives earn larger salaries (Rampell, 2013).

The wage-earning gap between men and women has been closing since the 1970s. Today, an average of all incomes reveals that women make about 83% of the income of men (Brown & Patten, 2017). Since women today have more advanced educational degrees, it would seem that the gap would have closed more. One of the main reasons for the gap continues to be the presence of dependent children in the home. Women spend more time in child care, which affects their availability to participate as freely as men in the workforce. In addition, women continue to lag behind men in top-level administrative positions and as chief executive officers. In 2012, a smaller portion of women was hired in new jobs compared to men which also saw the gap increase from approximately 98% to 90% for women in the 25 to 34 age range (Brown & Patten, 2017). One explanation for this decline in female employment is the recession. Women are less likely to continue looking for jobs than men, and in the competition for new jobs, women are less likely to be as aggressive. Married women may also feel that taking care of the home is their priority.

Some economists take a different view of the wage gap between men and women, noting that many traditional female jobs pay less than traditional male jobs, and men tend to have more seniority in positions that employ both men and women (Greszler & Sterk, 2014). Because they have greater seniority, men, on average, tend to make more money for the same job. New hires, however, tend to not have this pay differential. When these factors are considered, there is very little difference in the wages of men and women, with men making only slightly more than women.

Another factor affecting working women is the type of jobs available (Greszler & Sterk, 2014). With the downturn in manufacturing a few years ago, more men lost jobs than women, but in the past few years, the trend has favored male employment. The most recent trend is a decline in jobs in the public sector, which employs women in greater numbers than men. Future trends, however, may change to benefit women, because they significantly outnumber men in obtaining college degrees (Rampell, 2013).

Stepfamilies

Folklore in American childhood literature paints a negative picture of **stepfamilies**, particularly of the stepmother, which, unfortunately, lingers on in social policy (Mason, 2003). At the same time, that biological relationships have been strengthened, stepfamilies' relationships continue to be loosely defined, and the parenting roles of stepparents are, at best, ambiguous (Mason, 2003). Biological parents have great advantages over stepparents, who have few rights, including custody in the event of the biological parent's death. There is also no stipulation that stepparents support stepchildren during or after the marriage if it ends in divorce. The number of children affected by stepfamilies grows every year as a result of the high divorce rate and unwed mothers who marry. Since stepfamilies are formed without prior long-term planning, most persons in stepfamilies have to adjust to a situation that they may not have anticipated or even desired. The Pew Research Center (2011) also found that, when asked about closeness in their families of origin compared to their present-day families, persons raised in stepfamilies remembered the experience as being more distant if there were stepparents.

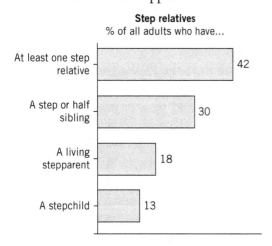

FIGURE 7.2 Steprelatives

Note: Only those who have ever been married were asked if they have stepchildren; however, the percentage reported in the table is based on all respondents. *Source*: Pew Social & Demographic Trends survey (Oct 1-21, 2010; *n*=2,691)

While stepfamilies exist in all strata of society, there are common characteristics that set them apart from other families. A person who experienced a stepfamily tends to be less than thirty years old, poorly educated, and a racial minority (Pew Research Center, 2011). Younger persons in contemporary society may reflect the changing demographics of increased unmarried partners and marriages to nonbiological parents. The higher incidences of unwed pregnancy and divorce among minorities may account for the higher incidences of stepfamilies (Pew Research Center, 2011). Living in a stepfamily not only means having stepparents but also an increase of exposure to stepsiblings, which can be a major source of stress.

In addition to persons feeling more distant in stepfamilies, researchers have found that the level of emotional (Floyd & Morman, 2001) and financial support for stepchildren in families (Gray & Brogdon, 2017) is less than that for biological children. Similarly, researchers have found that, in extended kin relationships, such as stepchildren and step-grandparents, there tend to be less supportive and satisfying emotional relationships (Gray & Brogden, 2017). This tendency to provide financial and emotional support for biological offspring has been labeled in the literature **discriminative parental solicitude** (Daily & Wilson, 1980). From an evolutionary psychology perspective, the tendency to support biological offspring represents investment in ones' own genetic material. This

reduced support for nonbiological children continues throughout the lifespan. The conclusion from this point of view is not that stepparents are unable to perform the role of parent, but that they do not perform it as well as a biological parent. Some family experts believe that the lack of adequate policies associated with stepparenting are so deeply rooted that the best policy is to minimize them altogether (Popenoe, 1993).

State governmental policies regarding, for example, marriage and divorce tend to place the stepparent on the same status as that of a stranger living in the home (Mason, 2003). On the other hand, federal governmental policy through Temporary Assistance for Needy Families (TANF) and Social Security do not make distinctions on the basis of stepparenting. Until recently, the Federal Employee's Retirement System had a long history of excluding stepchildren and adopted children from receiving benefits. At best, the stepparent can be looked at as having some status as a provider, however limited that might be, but falling far short from the same status as a parent.

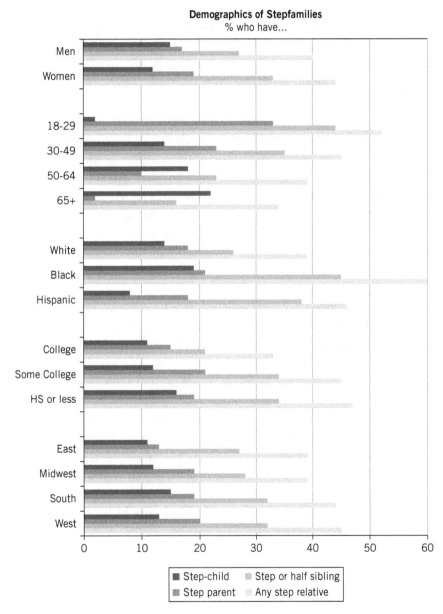

FIGURE 7.3 Demographics of stepfamilies

Note: Hispanics are of any race, Whites and blacks include only non-Hispanics. Only those who have ever been married were asked if they have stepchildren, however, the percentages reported in the table are based on all respondents.

Source: Pew Social & Demographic Trends survey (Oct 1-21, 2010; n=2,691)

Some family experts accept the view that the family is changing and that stepfamilies are merely part of the changing family landscape (Mason, 2003). Consequently, stepfamily dynamics are neither denied nor affirmed. There is some safety and distance in viewing family formation as voluntary, and therefore, private and not privy to intrusion from the outside. Still other family experts believe that laws should be enacted that will give stepparents who function as parents the same rights as biological parents. For example, in current law, at the death of the biological parent or in the event of divorce, the stepparent has no legal rights for custody or visitation (Mason, 2003). For stepparents who already function as parents, the well-being of children may be well served when the stepparents have rights to continue parenting after the death of the biological parent. Enhancing the rights of the stepparent may have some effect on the rights and obligations of the noncustodial parent. A clarification of these issues would need to be explicitly stated in any revision of laws relating to the rights and obligations of stepparents. If the role and support level of the stepparent is such that it competes with the support of the noncustodial parent, specific guidelines must be in place to minimize an adversarial relationship. Some researchers say that since many noncustodial fathers do not support their children after divorce, or support them only minimally, stepfathers who do fill in this gap left vacant by the biological father should have legal avenues that allow them ease in assuming the parenting role (Mason, 2003). While adoption by the stepparent has always been an option when noncustodial parents voluntarily abnegate their parenting roles, recognizing the support of stepparents and increasing their rights could also be accomplished short of adoption.

Not only do stepfamilies have difficulty with parenting roles and divorce but there are also considerable problems regarding inheritance (Mason, 2003). Stepfamilies without standing lack legal protection for inheritance, because such families are not considered families. Even when there is a legal will that lists stepchildren as beneficiaries, there is no guarantee that the court will rule for stepchildren. Some researchers take the position that it is time for a shift away from the rational view that families have two parents and embrace the view that contemporary families are not served well by this view.

State laws generally focus on maintaining the tie with the noncustodial parent and believe that this right should not be terminated except in certain circumstances involving actual or potential harm to the child. Some have posed that, at the marriage of the biological parent to a nonbiological person, a new type of adoption could take place at the time of marriage (Engel, 2003). This automatic adoption could offer legitimacy to the stepparent-stepchild relationship from the beginning while at the same time not terminating or lessening the role of the noncustodial parent. The underlying tenet to this perspective is that the two-parent system may not be an adequate concept for contemporary family formations; some family forms would be benefited from a multiple-parent arrangement rather than the traditional two-parent family.

Adoption

Currently there are approximately 500,000 children in foster care in the U.S. who are eligible for adoption; about 50,000 of them will be in foster care for at least five years (Zill, 2011). Children in foster care have been removed from their biological parent(s) and cared for under the auspices of the state. According to Zill, the cost of maintaining these children in foster homes is in excess of nine billion dollars. The majority of children of both genders in long-term foster home placements have disciplinary problems, and more than half of adolescents have criminal or arrest records. This proclivity for aggressive and disruptive behavior leading to criminal acts carries over into adulthood. There is recent evidence that a significant number of persons in prison were part of the foster placement program in their formative years, costing the government another five billion dollars (Nunn, 2012). Given that only 10–15% of children in foster placements are adopted, it means that foster home placements are equivalent to a breeding ground for a plethora of problems.

Children in foster care are at risk for a host of problems, which may be one of the reasons that many children continue in foster care long term (Zill, 2011). Another reason that children tend to linger in foster care rather than be adopted is that state and federal laws give preference to biological parents' rights for reunification pending their completion of specific treatment requirements. The federal government has taken steps to increase adoption by providing incentives such as a tax credit and stipends for poor families. According to Zill, some believe that policies regulating adoption should make it less cumbersome by reducing paperwork and streamlining the **parent(s) reunification** efforts. Other factors related to lower adoption rates include the reduction of international adoptions. International adoption rates have declined from a high of almost 23,000 in 2004 to less than 10,000 in 2011, and they are expected to continue to drop as a result of Russia's cancellation of its international agreement with the U.S. (Wicker, 2013). Given that 60,000 Russian children have been adopted by U.S. parents, and 300 adoptions were pending in the State of Mississippi alone at the time of the freeze, a large dent will be made in the number of international adoptions. Recent estimates for international adoptions are at the lowest point in 35 years (Jordan, 2017). Recommendations for policy changes can be found in Figure 7.6.

In recent years, one of the efforts to make more children available for adoption has been the broadening of categories of persons wanting to adopt (Goldberg, 2015). For example, some of the groups that have been given priority rights in adoption include gay and lesbian families and single-parent families. The inclusion of these various groups has been met with challenges from those who have a traditional view of the family.

The **traditional view of adoption** supports the belief that children have the right to a mother and a father; allowing children to be adopted in diverse family structures that do not have two married parents deprives the child of the best developmental outcomes (Goldberg, 2015). In addition, the traditional view supports the belief that gay and lesbian relationships are not as stable as heterosexual relationships and, therefore, would be damaging to children (ACLU, 1998). This view also points to some studies that show that children in gay and lesbian relationships are more likely to have sexual diffuse issues, a lack of focus in sexual identity, than other children (Patterson, Fulcher, & Wainright, 2002).

TABLE 7.3 Policy recommendations for adoption

1. Change U.S. federal law that would allow every child access to the adoption assistance benefits.
2. For Native Americans, allow direct access to Title IV-E.
3. Eliminate the fair hearing process for Title IV-E eligibility.
4. All children in foster care should be eligible for Medicaid.

Source: www.nacac.org/policy/subsidy.html

The opposing point of view contends that gays and lesbians make good parents (Farr & Patterson, 2013). They believe that the crux of the issue is not a right to parent, but who can provide the parenting that the child needs (ACLU, 1998). In addition, children raised by gay and lesbian couples tend to believe more in diversity than other families—a finding that is not viewed in a negative way (Patterson, 2013). Instead, believing in diversity and having tolerance for various family forms may make one more socially and culturally competent.

While the supporters of the traditional view want to limit adoption to families with two parents, the supporters of the **nontraditional view** believe that both children and families are enhanced when a diversity point of view is taken (Patterson, 2006). Unfortunately, longitudinal studies have not been conducted to compare how children in foster care who are not adopted and those who are adopted by a wide range of families fare in adulthood.

An alternative to foster care has been **family preservation**, which keeps the child in the family and is involved in an array of treatment modalities (Roberts & Everly, 2006). The idea behind family preservation is that biological families overall provide better support for children than non-related group or individual settings. Those who favor family preservation over foster care focus on the length of time in foster care, which is a little over two years, and the high costs, including administration of the program and payments to foster home providers. Roberts and Everly also point out that about half of children entering the foster care program have reunification with parents as the goal, while only about one-fourth have the goal to be adopted. This statistic alone, they reason, is enough to support enhancing the family environment. Most families who have the children removed because of neglect or abuse have other problems. A family preservation approach addresses not only neglect and abuse but other problems, such as marital discord, poor economic conditions, inadequate housing, and health care.

Another statistic that family preservationists favor is the condition of children 18 to 21 who age out of foster care without being reunited with their families or adopted by nonbiological parents (U.S. Department of Health and Human Services, 2011). These children have poor adjustment to adulthood, tend to not graduate from high school, and are poorly qualified to support themselves. These aged-out children of foster care tend to be the lost children who as young adults are on their own without supportive family ties and who have little other support.

Family preservationists believe that there are a number of advantages to keeping children in their families over foster care (Roberts & Everly, 2006). First, family preservation emphasizes stability for children over time better than foster care. Second, when children cannot be reunited with their families of origin, restructuring adoption processes to reduce the time spent in foster care and also reducing the number of children who age out of foster care would improve the overall experience of foster care and adoption. Family preservationists believe that more care should be given to the timeline to reduce some of the negative consequences of foster care.

TABLE 7.4 Children in, entering, and exiting foster care, 2015

IN—September 30, 2015, an estimated 427,910 children in foster care. ƒ
ENTRIES—During 2015, 269,509 children entered foster care. ƒ
EXITS—During FY 2015, 243,060 children exited foster care. ƒ
TRENDS—The number of children in foster care on September 30, 2015, (427,910) remains lower than those in care on the same day in 2006 (510,000). However, 2015 saw an increase in these numbers as compared to 2014 (415,129)

(Adapted from Foster care Statistics 2015 http://www.care welfare.gov)

Birth Records

Generally state policies regarding the availability of birth records for adoptees vary, with a minority of states allowing adoptees easy access and most only limited access or no access (Fleming, 2005). Recently, the governor of the State of Washington signed a bill that allows adoptees to have access to their birth records if born prior to 1993 and their birth parents do not object (National Public Radio, 2013). Along with Washington, a number of other states, such as Minnesota and Maryland, have pending legislation.

Unwed Fathers' Rights

Unwed biological fathers have limited legal rights regarding adoption of their children (Fetrow, 2014). If the parents cohabited during pregnancy and lived together, a few states have laws that require the agreement of the father for adoption (Carlson & McLanahan, 2006). If the parents did not cohabit during pregnancy and never lived together, the father's approval of the adoption is not required, and he will not be informed of the intent for adoption. However, he can challenge the adoption by a court proceeding that will determine the best placement for the child. The onus is on the father to prove his parenting status with the child. The determination is almost always made on the parental actions of the unwed father and not on his biological status. He has to involve himself in the daily life of the child and fulfill the role generally expected of all fathers (Carlson & McLanahan, 2006).

Cohabitation

Cohabitation is when two adults live together as a couple but are not married. Researchers believe that cohabitators vary in their reasons for living together, and this variation is important for outcomes associated with cohabitation (Smock & Manning, 2004). Depending on how cohabitation is defined, it can be viewed as a boost to marriage, an alternative to marriage (Smock, 2000), or an alternative to singlehood (Rindfuss & VandenHeuvel, 1990). If cohabitation is viewed as a step in the dating process that will ultimately lead to marriage, either with the current partner or a future partner, there is no adversarial relationship with marriage, and cohabitation serves a purpose as a preparation for marriage. The negative consequences of cohabitation, particularly as they relate to the care of children, would be minimized. In addition, cohabitation as a prerequisite for marriage would not tend to increase the number of stepfamilies created when single mothers marry someone other than the father of their child.

If, on the other hand, cohabitation is viewed as an alternative to marriage, as is the pattern in Sweden and other European nations, the greater increase in cohabitation means a decrease in marriage (Smook, 2000). Traditionalists assume that a decrease in marriage and a concomitant increase in cohabitation would be highly correlated with the problems associated with single-parent families. This assumption is made because cohabitators tend to break up, have shorter relationships, and are more likely to mate with other partners (Smook, 2000).

Another possibility is to view cohabitation as an alternative to singlehood. This view means that single persons are not ready to be married, but also are not satisfied with being single (Rindfuss & VandenHeuvel, 1990). This view also would be less threatening to traditionalists, because they could think of the arrangement as a choice to be in a relationship, so that relationship is valued over singlehood. Persons are not cohabiting so much as an alternative to marriage, but because they prefer a more committed relationship over non-committed singlehood.

Currently in American society, the number of cohabitators has increased to record levels (Stepler, 2017). In the 1950s, more than three-fourths of women were married by their twenty-fifth birthday. The census data for 2009 reveal that married households have fallen below 50%. The number of children living in households with two parents continues to drop from the 1970s and, in 2010, accounted for about two-thirds of families. The number of unwed households has increased to approximately 45% in 2010 (U.S. Census Bureau, 2010). The surprising fact is the increase in persons over 50 years of age who are cohabitating. According to Stepler, 23% of all cohabitators in 2016 were over 50 years old. Generally, policies for cohabitators have lagged behind in providing the same rights as for married couples. However, by 2010, there were 10 states that had civil union laws that virtually gave cohabitators the same rights as married couples. In general, over the past four decades, the prerequisites for family formation have changed so that marriage is only one option among many for creating a family.

Traditionalists would argue that debunking the laws that protect married couples by allowing cohabitators to have the same rights and privileges not only undermines the institution of marriage but also puts children at risk for less than optimal development (Kohm & Groen, 2005). According to Kohm and Groen, traditionalists point to a host of literature that show advantages in psychological health, academic achievement, and social adjustment for children with two parents. Traditionalists are concerned that, as married and non-married families continue to exist side-by-side with non-married gaining ground, the distinctions that research has made will erode to the degree that all family types will be lumped together. Traditionalists view the breakdown of distinctions in family form so that no form is considered the benchmark represents a decline in both the family and the individuals that make up families.

These changes in family form are viewed by non-traditionalists as more about having a choice to decide on an alternative that is more appealing to couples than marriage (Smook, 2000). The reduction in marriage is viewed more as a positive change and suggests that researchers should curtail the need to have a benchmark family for comparison. Non-traditionalists believe that marriage has become merely one option among many, although, paradoxically, the majority of adults view marriage as the ideal. Figure 7.8 shows the result of public opinion polls about marriage, and, surprisingly, the majority still holds marriage in high regard, although some categories such as sex outside of marriage show changes of opinion.

Although divorce rates continue to decline, acceptance of divorce and unmarried cohabitation continues to increase (Stepler, 2017). Clearly, public opinion has changed in what constitutes a marriage and family, but the place of marriage as being desirable for couples is still an important value. The definition of family has been broadened to include cohabitators, especially if children are involved. In fact, when children are included, persons more readily acknowledge it as a family. Non-traditionalists believe that this change in public opinion has occurred at a faster rate than the laws or social policies affecting families (DiFonzo, 2011). Consequently, those who feel discriminated against because of laws that limit or exclude them from formal recognition as a couple or family are resorting to the courts for retribution. Non-traditionalists believe that the courts are ruling in more favorable ways for diverse families rather than strictly following predetermined laws, as in the past. One of the main guidelines currently used in determining custody and other matters is not so much biological ties as what is in the best interest of the child. According to Cott (2000, as cited in DiFonzo, 2011), the majority of cases that come before judges do not adhere to definitions of family relationships in law, and judges have to rule on other criteria. The term **functional norms** refers to the process of making legal decisions on the basis of the nature of the relationships rather than formal legal guidelines.

TABLE 7.5 Attitudes on marriage

GALLOP POLL		
2006	Married or plan to be married	91%
	Will never marry	4%
	My marriage rating	A
2009	Affairs are morally wrong	92%
	Unwed birth morally wrong	45%
	Unmarried sex morally wrong	40%
	Divorce morally wrong	30%
2013	Affairs are morally wrong	91%
	Unwed birth morally wrong	36%
	Unmarried sex morally wrong	33%
	Divorce morally wrong	24%

Adapted From: http://www.gallup.com/poll/117328/marriage.aspx

Traditionalists admit that the definition of the family is becoming more diverse, but believe that it is still important to make clear distinctions between various family forms, and to conduct research that compares and contrasts these family forms (Kohm & Groen, 2005).

Traditionalists also believe that the answer to what is in the best interest of the children is far outweighed on the side of the traditional biological family. The average short length of the cohabiting relationship and the lack of legal standing compared to a married couple combine to make cohabitation a risk for most children. Although some recent research found that long-term cohabitation does not harm children, most cohabitation does not last beyond five years.

Traditionalists believe that the well-being of children is not safeguarded in cohabiting relationships (DiFonzo, 2011). Traditionalists believe that it is better for children to have two biological parents with both parents involved in parenting. Non-traditionalists believe that marriage is not the answer for family problems (DiFonzo, 2011). They take the view that cohabitation is here to stay, and that efforts to support marriage may have detrimental effects if other circumstances are ignored, such as poverty, educational level, and employment of parents. Non-traditionalists would also point out that the lack of marriage is more common in some segments of the population and carries a racial and economic valence that needs to be understood and addressed (DiFonzo, 2011). Marriage for the sake of marriage without addressing these social issues would only add to the problem. For example, poor families are more likely to suffer stress related illnesses, child abuse, domestic violence, and substance dependency.

KEY TERMS

Marriage

Family

Household

Ritual

Routine

Monogamous

Polygamy

Polyandry

Fictive kin

Same-sex marriage

Traditional marriage

Defense of Marriage Act (DOMA)

Parental authority

Parental Rights Amendment

United Nations Convention on the

   Rights of the Child (UNCRC)

Parenting education

Transition to parenthood

Family structure

The wage-earning gap

Stepfamilies

Discriminative parental

   solicitude

Parents' reunification

Traditional views

Nontraditional views

Family preservation

Cohabitation

Functional norms

STUDY QUESTIONS TO ACCOMPLISH THE LEARNING OBJECTIVES

1. What are the definitions for "marriage" and "family"? Why are definitions important for social policy? Determine how changing family definitions affects social policy.

2. What are arguments for DOMA? What are arguments against it? Which argument is most influential? Evaluate whether this issue has become stagnant.

3. What are components of the Parental Rights Amendment? Determine the effectiveness of the Parental Rights Amendment.

4. What does family structure refer to? Why is family structure such an important factor in family social policy?

5. Discuss arguments on the gender gap in wages. Analyze which arguments are most compelling.

6. Discuss parenting issues in stepfamilies. What kind of social policy might address these issues? On the basis of what you know about stepfamilies, determine a stance on social policy.

7. Discuss issues related to adoption in foster care. Evaluate if adoption is a good option for children in foster care.

8. Should unwed fathers have guaranteed rights for children they father? Defend the idea of keeping unwed fathers in contact with the mother and child.

9. Discuss incidences of cohabitation in society. Justify viewing cohabitation on the same level as marriage.

10. Discuss traditional and nontraditional views of adoption. Determine if there is common ground between the two positions. Determine which position has the most support. Justify your belief.

DEBATE ACTIVITY FOR STUDENTS

Consider the following proposition: There is no need for the Parental Rights Amendment.

- Review refereed literature on this topic. Do a library and Internet search to find relevant material. Investigate some of the additional readings.

- Develop three arguments for the proposition.

- Develop three arguments against the proposition.

- How do the arguments relate to other systems, such as the community or culture?

- Is there common ground?

- What are the long-term consequences of taking action?

- What new or common-ground solutions should be offered? If no common ground, what new position could emerge from a dialogue between the two positions?

- How is the new position superior to the original positions?

ADDITIONAL READING RESOURCES

Moore, S. (2014). The real pay gap. The Heritage Foundation. Retrieved from http://www.heritage.org/poverty-and-inequality/commentary/the-real-pay-gap

Nam, C.B. (2004). The concept of the family: Demographic and genealogical perspectives. *Sociology Today,* Fall 2004. Retrieved from http://www.ncsociology.org/sociationtoday/v22/family.htm

Schaefer, (October, 2015). Obstacles here and abroad for non-traditional families. *Nonprofit Quarterly,* Retrieved from https://nonprofitquarterly.org/2015/10/16/obstacles-to-adoption-here-and-abroad-for-non-traditional-families/

Sharma, R. (2013). The family and family structure classification redefined for the current times. *Journal of Family Medicine and Primary Care, 2*(4), 306–310.

Smith, E.L. (2017). Unwed fathers - protecting your rights: Preventing your infant from being adopted without your consent. The Spruce. Retrieved from https://www.thespruce.com/unwed-fathers-protecting-your-rights-26237

REFERENCES

ACLU (American Civil Liberties Union). (1998). In the child's best interests: Defending fair and sensible adoption policies. Retrieved from http://www.aclu.org/lgbt-rights_hiv-aids/childs-best-interests-defending-fair-and-sensible-adoption-policies

Anderson, J. (2014). The impact of family structure on the health of children: Effects of divorce. *The Linacre Quarterly, 81*(4), 378–387.

Baker v. Nelson (1971). 191 NW2d 185. Minnesota.

Berman, M. (2017). Mississippi Governor signs law allowing businesses to refuse services to gay people. *The Washington Post.* Retrieved from https://www.washingtonpost.com/news/post-nation/wp/2016/04/05/mississippi-governor-signs-law-allowing-business-to-refuse-service-to-gay-people/?utm_term=.df57b4bb6eee

Bogenschneider, K. (2008). *Family policy matters: How policymaking affects families and what families can do about it.* (2nd ed.). New York, NY: Routledge.

Brown, A., & Patten, E. (2017). The narrowing, but persistent, gender gap in pay. The Pew Center, April 3, 2017. Retrieved from http://www.pewresearch.org/fact-tank/2017/04/03/gender-pay-gap-facts/

Carlson, M. J., & McLanahan, S. S. (2006). Strengthening unmarried families: Could enhancing couple relationships also improve parenting? *Social Service Review, 80*(2), 297–321.

Crossman, A. (2017). The definition of marriage in sociology: Types, characteristics and the social function of the institution. *ThoughtCo*, May 11 2017. Retrieved from https://www.thoughtco.com/marriage-3026396

DiFonzo, D. H. (2011). How marriage became optional: Cohabitation, gender and the emerging of functional norms. *Rutgers Journal of Law Public Policy, 8*(3), 521–672.

Dixon, S. V., Graber, J. A., & Brooks-Dunn, J. (2008). The roles of respect for parental authority and parenting practices in parent-child conflict among African American, Latino, and European American Families, *Journal of Family Psychology, 22*(1), 1–10.

Ellis, B. J. (2003). Does father absence place daughters at special risk of early sexual activity and teenage pregnancy? *Child Development, 74*(3), 801–821.

Engel, M. (2003). United States degrades stepfamilies. National Stepfamily Resource Center. Retrieved from http://www.stepfamilies.info/key-advocacy-issues.php

Eskridge, Jr., W. N. (1993). A history of same-sex marriage. *Virginia Law Review, 79,* 1419–1513.

Farr, R. H., & Patterson, C. J. (2013). Coparenting among lesbian, gay, and heterosexual couples: Associations with adoptive children's outcomes. *Child Development, 84*(4), 1226–1240.

Fetrow, K. L. (2014). Unwed fathers' rights regarding adoption. Retrieved from http://www.adoptionbirthmothers.com/unwed-fathers-rights-regarding-infant-adoption/

Fiese, B. H., Tomicho, T. J., Douglas, M., Josephs, K., Poltrock, S., & Baker, T. (2004). A review of 50 years of research on naturally occurring routines and rituals: Cause for celebration? *Journal of Family Psychology, 16*(4), 381–390.

Fleming, C. B. (2005). The open records debate: Balancing the interests of both parents and adult adoptees. *William & Mary Journal of Women and the Law, 11*(3), 461–480.

Floyd, K., & Morman, M. T. (2001) Human affection exchange III. Discriminative parental solicitude in men's affectionate communication with their biological and nonbiological sons. *Communication Quarterly, 49,* 310–327.

Freedom for All. (2016). Tennessee bill to nullify and void same sex marriages will cost the state $9 billion. Retrieved from http://www.freedomforallamericans.org/tennessee-bill-to-nullify-and-void-same-sex-marriages-will-cost-state-9-billion/

Gallop Poll. (2013). Marriage. Retrieved from http://www.gallup.com/poll/117328/marriage.aspx

Gartrell, N., & Bos, H. (2010). U.S. National Lesbian Family Study: Psychological adjustment of 17-year-old adolescents, *Pediatrics, 126*(1), 1–11.

Glendon, M. A. (2004). The role of the law in the Universal Declaration of Human Rights. *Northwestern Journal of International Rights, 2*(1), 1–19. Retrieved from http://scholarlycommons.law.northwestern.edu/cgi/viewcontent.cgi?article=1008&context=njihr

Gray, P. B., & Brogdon, E. (2017). Do step- and biological grandparents show difference in investment in emotional closeness with the grandchildren? *Evolutionary Psychology, 15*(1). doi.org/10.11771/147404917694367/

Greszler, R., & Sterk, J. (2014). Equal pay for equal work: Examining the gender gap. The Heritage Foundation, May 22, 2014. Retrieved from http://www.heritage.org/jobs-and-labor/report/equal-pay-equal-work-examining-the-gender-gap

Goldberg, J. (2015, October 27). Why family matters, and why traditional families are still the best. *The Los Angeles Times.* Retrieved from http://www.latimes.com/opinion/op-ed/la-oe-1027-goldberg-family-structure-20151027-column.html

Hanson, Jr., R. (2008). Joint legislative newsflash update. Child and Family Protection Association. Retrieved from http://www.childandfamilyprotection.org/AB755Newsflash080129.html

Head, T. The Parental Rights Amendment (PRA). Retrieved from http://civilliberty.about.com/od/equalrights/qt/parental_rights.htm

Jones, J. M. (2013). Same-sex marriage support solidifies e 50% in U.S. Retrieved from http://news.gallup.com/poll/162398/sex-marriage-support-solidifies-above.aspx

Jordan, M. (2017, April 13). Overseas adoptions by Americans continues to decline. *The New York Times.* Retrieved from https://www.nytimes.com/2017/04/13/us/overseas-adoptions-decline.html?mcubz=3

Keenan, et al., (2013). United States Supreme Court issues ruling on DOMA and Proposition 8 cases. Retrieved from http://www.keenan.com/news/brief/2013/BRF_20130627_SCOTUSMarriage_KA.pdf

Kohm, L. M., & Groen, K. M. (2005). Cohabitation and the future of marriage. *Regent University Law Review, 17,* 261–277.

Kurtz, S. (2004, February 2). The end of marriage in Scandinavia. *Weekly Standard.*

Lavers, M. K. (2013). Virginia lawmakers seek to repeal same-sex marriage ban. *The Washington Blade.* Retrieved from http://www.washingtonblade.com/2013/02/16/non-discrimination-bill-among-topics-discussed-at-alexandria-townhall/adam_ebbin_insert_c_washington_blade_by_michael_k_lavers/.

Marcellino, A. G., Nelson, K., & Anthony, C. H. (2009). H.R. 2517 Domestic partnership benefits and obligations act of 2009: As ordered reported by the House Committee on Oversight and Governmental Reform on November 18, 2009. The Congressional Budget Office, Washington, D.C.

Marshall, J., & Smith, G. (2006). Human rights and social issues at the U.N.: A guide for U.S. policymakers. *The Heritage Foundation*, August 31, 2006. Retrieved from http://www.heritage.org/global-politics/report/human-rights-and-social-issues-the-un-guide-us-policymakers

Masci, D., Brown, A., & Kiley, J. (2017). 5 Facts about same-sex marriage. Pew Research Center, June 26, 2017. Retrieved from http://www.pewresearch.org/fact-tank/2017/06/26/same-sex-marriage/

Mason, M. A. (2003). The modern American stepfamily: Problems and possibilities. In M. A. Mason, A. Stolnick, and S. D. Sugarman (Eds.), *All our families: New policies for a new century* (2nd ed.) (pp. 96–116). New York, NY: Oxford University Press.

Moore, K. A., Jekielek, S. M., & Emig, C. (2002). Marriage from a child's perspective: How does family structure affect children, and what can we do about it? *Child Trends Research Briefs,* June 2002, 1. Retrieved from http://www.childtrends.org/files/MarriageRB602.pdf.

Newman, D. W. (2006). *Families: A sociological perspective.* New York, NY: McGraw-Hill.

National Public Radio. (2013). New law opens birth certificates sparks questions. December 24, 2013. Retrieved from http://www.npr.org/2013/12/24/256853037/new-aw-opens-birth-certificates-sparks-questions

Nunn, B. (2012, June 24). Statistics suggest bleak futures for children who grow up in foster care. *Amarillo Globe News.* Retrieved from http://amarillo.com/news/local-news/2012-06-24/what-comes-next

Patterson, C. J. (2006). Children of lesbian and gay parents. *Current Directions in Psychological Science, 15*(5), 241–244.

Patterson, C. J., Fulcher, M., & Wainright, J. (2002). Children of lesbian and gay parents: Research, law and policy. In B. L. Bottoms, M. B. Covera, and B. D. McAuliff (Eds.), *Children, social science and the law,* (pp.176–199). New York, NY: Cambridge University Press.

Parental Rights Amendment (2014). Parentalrights.org. Retrieved from http://www.parentalrights.org/index.asp?Type=B_BASIC&SEC=%7B4771B53E-D345-4753-BEF4-68C1CA71CE13%7D.

Perry, v. Schwarzenegger (2009). No C 09-2292 VRW.

Pew Research Center. (2011). A portrait of stepfamilies. January 13, 2011. Pew Research Social and Demographic Trends. Retrieved from http://www.pewsocialtrends.org/2011/01/13/a-portrait-of-stepfamilies/

Pierce v. Society of Sisters (1925). 268 U.S. 510 (1925)

Pinquart, M., & Teubert, D. (2010). Effects of parenting education with expectant and new parents: A meta-analysis. *Journal of Family Psychology, 24*, 316–332.

Popenoe, D. (1996). *Life without father: Compelling evidence that fatherhood and marriage are indispensable for the good of children and society.* New York, NY: The Free Press.

Popenoe, D. (1993). American family decline, 1960–1990: A review and appraisal. *Journal of Marriage and the Family, 55*, 327–342.

Rampell, C. (2013). Women and marriage at Princeton. *Economix: Explaining the Science of Everyday Life.* April 1, 2013. Retrieved from Economix—Explaining the Science of Everyday Life Search APRIL 1, 2013, 2:18 PM 94 Comments Women and Marriage at Princeton.

Rindfuss, R. R., & VandenHeuvel, A. (1990). Cohabitation: A precursor to marriage or an alternative to being single? *Population and Development Review 16*, 703–726.

Roberts, A. R., & Everly, G. S. (2006). A meta-analysis of 36 crisis intervention studies. *Brief Treatment and Crisis Intervention, 6*(1), 10–21.

Schaefer, B., & Kingham, J. (2006). The United Nations Human Rights Council: Repeating past mistakes. *The Heritage Foundation.* Retrieved from http://www.heritage.org/report/the-united-nations-human-rights-council-repeating-past-mistakes

Sharma, R. (2013). The family and family structure classification redefined for the current times. *Journal of Family Medicine and Primary Care, 2*(4), 306–310.

Silver, N. (2010). Divorce rates higher in states with gay marriage bans. *FiveThirtyEight.* Retrieved from http://www.fivethirtyeight.com/2010/01/divorce-rates-appear-higher-in-states.html

Smock, P. J. (2000). Cohabitation in the United States: An appraisal of research themes, findings, and implications. *Annual Review of Sociology 26*, 1–20.

Smock, P. J., & Manning, W.D. (2004). Living together in the United States: Demographic perspectives and implications. Population Studies Center at the Institute for Social Research University of Michigan. Report #04-555.

Stacey, J., & Biblarz, T. J. (2001). (How) does the sexual orientation of parents matter? *American Sociological Review, 66*(2), 159–183.

Stevenson, D. G. (2009). The parental rights amendment: Bulletin #67. National Home Education Legal Defense. Retrieved from http://www.nheld.com/BTN67.htm

Tchekmedyian, A. (2017, March 30). North Carolina governor signs repeal of controversial bathroom law. *The Los Angeles Times*. Retrieved from http://www.latimes.com/nation/nationnow/la-na-north-carolina-bathroom-bill-20170330-story.html

Troxel v. Granville (2000). 530 U.S. 57 2000.

U.S. Bureau of the Census. (2010). Household and Families. Retrieved from https://www.census.gov/prod/cen2010/briefs/c2010br-14.pdf

U.S. Bureau of the Census (2006). Statistical Abstracts of the United States. Retrieved from http://www.census.gov.compendia/statab/2006/2006edition.html

U.S. Department of Health and Human Services. (2011). Administration for Children and Families Adoption and Foster Care Reporting System Report #10-17. Retrieved from http://oig.hhs.gov/reports-and-publications/oas/acf.asp

Wang, W., Parker, K., & Taylor, P. (2013). Breadwinner moms: Mothers are the sole or primary breadwinner in four-in-ten households with children. *PewResearch Social and Demographic Trends*. Retrieved from http://www.pewsocialtrends.org/2013/05/29/breadwinner-moms/

Wicker, R. (2013, July 23). Russia's adoption freeze: Is a humanitarian solution within reach? *The Washington Times*. Retrieved from http://www.washingtontimes.com/news/2013/jul/23/russias-adoption-freeze/

Windsor v. United States (1974). 419US 938.

Wisconsin v. Yoder (1972). 406 U.S. 205 1972.

Yousefi, S. (2016). How do parenting lessons benefits parents and children. Novak Djovokic Foundation, Feb 2, 2016. Retrieved from https://novakdjokovicfoundation.org/how-do-parenting-lessons-benefit-parents-and-children/

Zill, N. (2011). Adoption from foster care: Aiding children while saving public money. Brookings. Retrieved from http://www.brookings.edu/research/reports/2011/05/adoption-foster-care-zill

Zogby Poll. (2013) Americans strongly oppose U.N. threat to parental rights. Retrieved from http://www.citizenlink.com/2010/11/08/zogby-poll-americans-strongly-oppose-u-n-threat-to- parental-rights/

CREDITS

CHAPTER EIGHT

Social Policy and Child Abuse and Neglect

LEARNING OBJECTIVES

At the end of the chapter, the student will be able to:

✓ Describe the stages of child abuse and analyze how they are related to the incidences;

✓ Summarize arguments supporting a belief in the reduction of child abuse occurrences;

✓ Define corporal punishment and general reasons for not using it as a discipline technique with children;

✓ Define child neglect and evaluate if more focus should be on reducing it;

✓ Define child sexual abuse and break down the strategy that I used to prevent it. Design a model that could be used to inform social policy about child sexual abuse;

✓ Know the effects of child abuse on the child's brain and how it might affect social policy;

✓ Define mandatory sentencing for sexual abuse and evaluate if it and other sexual abuse laws are effective deterrents to committing sex crimes.

CHILD ABUSE AND NEGLECT

Child abuse and neglect is defined by both the federal government and by state laws for both criminal and civil purposes. The Child Abuse and Prevention and Treatment Act (CAPTA) (2010) defines abuse as "any recent act or failure to act on the part of a parent or caretaker, which results in death, serious physical or emotional harm, sexual abuse or exploitation, or an act or failure to act which presents an imminent risk of serious harm" (p. 1). Neglect is sometimes categorized separately and refers to a host of parental behaviors in which proper attention is not given to the child leading to child endangerment. Behaviors range from not providing for health concerns of the child to tacit allowance of the child's use of drugs and alcohol (CAPTA, 2010). Laws regarding child abuse and neglect are applied to parents or immediate caregivers but not to nonfamily members who are not occupying a position of caregiver. The rate of child abuse and neglect of substantiated cases in California in 2012 was 8.9 per 1,000 (Needell et al., 2012). Child abuse and neglect are categorized into four types, including physical, neglect, sexual, and emotional abuse (Giovannoni & Becerra, 1979). These types may be broadened to include abandonment or, in some cases, neglect because of the substance abuse of the parent. These categories are not mutually exclusive, and overlapping occurs.

Child abuse and neglect is a major problem for children in the United States. Estimates are that more than 3.4 million children are abused in the U.S. every year, the highest number of abuse among industrialized nations (ASPCC, 2017). Children of all races and ethnic backgrounds are represented as victims of abuse and neglect, but some differences are noted. The number of children who die from abuse has increased over the past 15 years and now stands at approximately 2,000 per year (U.S. Department of Health and Human Services, 2011). The alarming fact is that the majority of child deaths because of abuse occur to children younger than four years of age. In addition, many children die from abuse that is not given as an official cause of death. The probability of severe injury and death from child abuse increases dramatically, perhaps as much as 50 times, when children are raised in non-biological homes (Schnizer & Ewigman, 2005). Abuse tends to continue across generations since approximately 30% of children who were abused as children later abuse their own children (ASPCC, 2017). Not only is abuse of children physically and emotionally damaging to children, but it is also an economic burden on society, with an annual cost of about 125 billion dollars a year (Fang, Brown, Florence, & Mercy 2012).

The U.S. was slow to protect children from abuse, and only after public outcry over the beating of a child by foster parents in 1875 was a law enacted to protect children. It was not until the 1960s that states took child abuse seriously and enacted laws to further protect children (Myers, 2008). This surge of attention to the plight of children followed the publication on child abuse that coined the phrase **battered child syndrome**. Pediatric radiologists became important in identifying severe abuse resulting from the parent shaking the child and causing neurological damage, such as subdural hematoma, retina hemorrhage, and cerebral edema.

TABLE 8.1 Frequency of abuse and neglect

Neglect	62.8%
Physical abuse	16.6%
Sexual abuse	9.3%
Emotional/psychological abuse	7.1%
Medical neglect	2.0%
Other	14.3%

Adapted from: http://www.americanhumane.org/children/stop-child-abuse/fact-sheets/child-abuse-and-neglect-statistics.html

In recent years, much has been written about the decline in the number of substantiated child abuse and neglect cases (Finkelhor & Jones, 2004). A number of factors contribute to the decline in the overall number of cases, including a focus on prevention and treatment, rapid response to missing children reports, and neighborhood notification programs. According to Finkelhor and Jones, it is necessary to identify the reason for the lower numbers, because otherwise, there may be a false impression of the safety of children in U.S. society, given the fact that the U.S. rate is higher than other industrialized nations.

One possible reason for the decline in child abuse and neglect cases investigated by Finkelhor and Jones (20004) was reporting standards by Child Protective Services (CPS). They reviewed state reports on substantiated cases to determine if CPS standards were more conservative, that is, not labeling some cases of abuse that had been labeled as such in the past. Their investigation found that a survey of all states revealed that the same percentage of substantiated cases was reported annually, with no evidence that a more conservative labeling of abuse occurred.

Finkelhor and Jones (2004) concluded that there was more than likely a decline in the number of cases because of a drop in the number of sexual abuse cases. They point out the decline in crime rates for the period and improved home environments for children. It would be expected that as the home environment improves, the well-being of children would also improve. The decline in sexual abuse of children is also represented by the amount of focus and attention given to this form of maltreatment. When rates decrease, there is support for the social policies that led to the decrease. Policymakers feel encouraged that their efforts were rewarded and continue in the effort to further reduce occurrences. Further concerns regarding reporting of abuse should address the differences in the collecting and sharing of data from CPS and law enforcement agencies. Data from CPS tend to be gathered inconsistently across districts, which become somewhat problematic in complying and making sense of the data.

PHYSICAL ABUSE

Physical abuse is damage to the child inflicted by the parent or caregiver that causes physical injury (ASPCC, 2017). Whether the parent intended to damage the child is irrelevant. A wide range of parental behaviors can result in injury to the child. Most often the parent tries to discipline the child and takes measures that cause the injury, which can range from a mild bruise to broken bones and even death.

Spanking (Corporal Punishment)

The method of **spanking (corporal punishment)** as a type of discipline has been highly correlated with abuse, although spanking as such is not considered abusive (ASPCC, 2017). Since spanking involves hitting a child, there can be a fine line between appropriate spanking and abuse. While few experts in child and family development or therapists who work clinically with child problems and parenting promote spanking as a means of discipline, the vast majority of parents admit to spanking their children, especially young children (Straus, 2000). Research on spanking reveals that children can be affected beyond any physical injury they may receive. Physical punishment of a child is one of the oldest parental means of discipline and a way to gain control of the child's annoying behavior. Recent studies show that there are long-term negative effects of being spanked, but no research shows long-term positive effects (Walton, 2012). One of the most common effects is **depression,** which can be a lifelong condition. Of major concern, according to Walton, is that children learn from being spanked that aggression gives advantages and solving problems, most notably, can be accomplished through aggressive means. Perhaps the most damaging effect is the damage to the parent/child relationship. Children are not as trusting or bonded to parents who spank them. Children may resent parents for spanking them, but seemingly are unaffected in other ways. However, the long-term effects are less supportive to helpful relationships with parents, siblings, coworkers, and partners.

New brain imaging research bolsters older research that found negative outcomes from physical abuse. For example, researchers have found that children who are abused physically have reduced gray matter and slightly lower intelligence quotients (IQs) (Afifi, Mota, Dasiewicz, MacMillan, & Sareen, 2012). Their brains also produce lower amounts of dopamine, similarly to persons with addiction disorders, and they are prone to depression, anxiety disorders, substance abuse, and alcoholism and, to some degree, suicidal ideation throughout the lifespan. A recent study found that the association between mental illness and being spanked as a child is significant, accounting for from 2% to 7% of mental illness, including depression, and **mood disorders** and **anxiety disorders** (Afifi et al., 2012). Afifi and associates focused on less severe physical punishment, such as non-abusive spanking in a large national sample of subjects in the U.S.

Not everyone agrees that non-abusive spanking is related to mental disorders in children and has lifelong consequences. For example, Robert Larzelere and Brett Kuhn (2005) reviewed 26 research studies on non-abusive spanking and found that physical punishment was only negative when it was the only form of punishment or not applied appropriately. Larzelere and Kuhn contend that appropriate non-abusive spanking following noncompliant behavior to other disciplinary tactics includes one or two swats across the buttocks with an open hand followed by the parent, whose emotions are under control, providing an explanation for the spanking and assuring the child of the parent's love. Larzelere and Kuhn refer to this type of spanking as **conditional spanking**, which they believe does not damage the child emotionally. Furthermore, Larzelere and Kuhn believe that all forms of disciplinary actions of the parent are related to later behavioral misconduct, and, in this regard, spanking is no different than other methods. In addition, they believe that comparing children who were spanked against children who were not spanked, and perhaps did not need parental intervention, is comparing apples and oranges. Instead researchers should only compare children who need disciplinary intervention. They found that there is no difference in outcomes between other forms of discipline and spanking when an intervention was needed by the parents. While Larzelere and Kuhn raise interesting questions, those who oppose spanking would question how many parents actually use conditional spanking and would point out that the majority of child abuse occurs when parents are disciplining a child. Opponents believe that few parents use spanking when they are not angry and few rationally explain the reason for the spanking to their child (Walton, 2012).

Beaten or Hit with Objects Causing Physical Damage

Physical abuse causing bodily harm results from being hit, grabbed, slapped, shaken, pushed, hit with an object, and other similar parental behaviors (Strauss, 2001). While children from all types of backgrounds can be physically abused, the probability is greater in certain types of families. Families in poverty with low levels of education, families with mothers who smoke, single-parent families, and children born with low birth rates all predict higher rates of abuse (Schnitzer & Ewigman, 2005). In addition, disabled children have an increased probability of being abused.

Most experts believe that physical abuse is underreported because definitions and reporting of abuse vary (Lynne, Gifford, Evans, & Rosch, 2015). Underreported cases of child abuse fit a particular profile, which includes the child being White, living with his/her parents, being young in age rather than adolescent, and having head or stomach injuries. In underreported cases of head or stomach injuries, children are more likely to die from their injuries than those with similar injuries from accidental causes. Generally, the probability of being abused increases with age, but the more severe abuse occurs with young children.

As mentioned above, abusive behavior toward the child affects the growth of gray matter in the developing brain. Brain imaging shows that gray matter increases from early childhood until about age 10 when **pruning** and **myelination** occur (Sowell et al., 2003). Stress and trauma such as from parental abuse can cause a disruption in the brain development of the child through specific brain systems including the **hypothalamic-pituitary-adrenal (HPA) axis**, **sympathetic nervous system (SNS)**, and **serotonin** (Watts-English, Fortson, Gibler, Hooper, & DeBellis, 2006). Long-term emotional responses and the formation of memory and learning are heavily influenced by these three brain systems. While IQ differences of abused children compared with children who were not abused have been found, some studies have found no differences (Pollak et al., 2010). In adults, research has not demonstrated a significance difference in IQ scores based on being abused as a child. Numerous studies have investigated the relationship of abuse and memory impairment with mixed results. Most studies on the cognitive outcomes of physical abuse do not control for co-existing morbidities, which means that the results of poor cognitive effects, including learning and memory, may be caused by other factors (Navalta, Polcari, Webster, Boghossian, & Teicher (2006). It is likely that memory impairment is found only with a concomitant circumstance of **Post-Traumatic Stress Disorder (PTSD)** (Samuelson, Krueger, Burnett, & Wilson, 2010). In addition, a number of studies have reported that visual and attention issues are related to physical abuse and neglect, but the studies fail to control for confounded variables.

A large number of studies have investigated emotional processing in children who have been physically abused or neglected. These findings suggest that children who were physically abused or neglected tend to react to anger directed at them and to recognize angry facial expressions, while their recognition of other emotional expressions is blunted (Fries & Pollak, 2004). Research shows that emotional processing of abused and neglected children is less adequate in childhood, but the deficits disappear by adulthood (Ochsner & Gross, 2005).

Signs of Physical Child Abuse

Physical child abuse usually leaves bruises in areas of the body not normally bruised in play, including the face, head, buttocks, and abdomen (Springer, Sheridan, Kuo, & Carnes, 2007). Injury to these parts of the body can cause severe damage, such as retinal detachment, swelling and blood hemorrhage in the brain, and broken bones. Other telltale signs of child abuse can be the found by analyzing the bruise. Frequently, the shape of an object used by the parent can be found on the child's body, such as the imprint of a belt or hand. Sometimes the injury is not apparent during visual inspection but, nevertheless, can be just a severe as a noticeable injury. Because physical injury is common in children, and, at times, unusual accidental injury may resemble abusive injuries, persons interacting with the child may be ambivalent about the cause of the injury. Consequently, a thorough investigation beginning with the child's past and present behaviors can help clarify an accurate understanding of the reasons for the injuries (Springer et al., 2007).

In some cases it is difficult to determine the age or reason for the injury, such as denture marks or burns (Wagner, 1986). Some children of abuse have bite marks on various parts of their bodies, usually hidden by clothing. Adult bite marks can be distinguished from child bite marks by size (Wagner, 1986). Burn marks are difficult to determine from natural injury. However, burns resulting from parental or caretaker action tend to differ from accidental burns, which may occur on extremities such as arms or legs and are more likely to be from hot liquid spills or touching hot objects.

One of the most serious injuries from abuse is to the head, which is related to **subdural and retina hemorrhages** (Reece & Sege, 2000). Head injuries are frequently correlated with hospital treatment, either as an emergency room visit or as hospitalization, and are more likely to lead to death than other types of injuries (Reece & Sege, 2000). Head injury, such as skull fracture, can occur from any cause including accidental falls. Because children with head injuries may be asymptomatic, many injuries may go unnoticed. Retina hemorrhages, which may also go unnoticed and untreated, can be distinguished by general pattern from accidental injury.

TABLE 8.2 Symptoms of physical abuse

PHYSICAL SYMPTOMS OF CHILD ABUSE INCLUDE:
1. Black eyes and facial bruises
2. Broken bones that would appear to be non-accidental
3. Bruise marks in the shapes of objects or fingers
4. Bruises in unusual places
5. Damage to the head
6. Burns that differ from splashes
7. Choke marks on the neck
8. Cigarette burns
9. Marks around the wrists or ankles
10. Bite marks
11. Whelp marks

In addition to physical signs of abuse, the abused child may show behavioral changes in mood, compliance, and emotionality (Al Odhayani, Watson, & Watson, 2013). The child's regular routines of play, interacting with others, and alone time may be disrupted. The child may attempt to avoid being home and make excuses to be with friends. Although child physical abuse occurs from many reasons, it can be related to parents' unrealistic expectations of their child and demanding responses from the child that are beyond his/her developmental level. Children sometimes speak of odd or eccentric parental behavior to classmates and teachers, which can be a sign of domestic instability often associated with abuse. Descriptions of parental behavior by the child at school or with friends that indicate mood swings or erratic decision making may also indicate that a parent is mentally ill or a substance abuser. Vague, nondescript, and various explanations for the injury given by the child or caregiver are other red flags that abuse may have occurred. Children who are physically abused may have absences from school and be withdrawn and preoccupied when at school. They may not have appropriate peer interactions, exhibiting either withdrawn or aggressive behavior. They may also show signs of restlessness and anxiety, mimicking symptoms of attention-deficit hyperactivity disorder (ADHD). While these descriptions alone do not represent abuse, coupled with other indicators they should not be summarily ignored or dismissed (Al Odhayani et al., 2013).

NEGLECTED CHILDREN

Neglected children also have distinct behavioral, psychological and physical characteristics that distinguish them from non-neglected children (Norman, Byambaa, De, Butchart, Scott, & Vos, 2012). It is not uncommon that neglected children may have vitamin deficiencies, tooth decay, and worn or poorly sized clothing. They tend to be chronically hungry and lack attention to proper hygiene. They are fatigued from poor nutrition and tend to lack energy to complete tasks. They typically lack adult supervision and are exposed to dangerous situations. While these conditions may emanate from other causes, care must be given to determine if neglect is implicated.

Child neglect is the most frequent form of child maltreatment accounting for approximately two-thirds of referral cases and the most ignored in the literature (Wilson & Horner, 2004). Scholarly articles and theory development on neglect and the effects on children are ignored in both popular media and academic publications. The paucity of literature may be due to the nature of neglect or the ignoring of the needs of the child, which can be difficult to identify objectively. This much is known, however, that the youngest children are the most victimized. Neglect is deeply rooted in parenting behaviors typical of mentally ill or substance-abusing parents (Hamilton & Bundy-Fazioli, 2013). Neglect is viewed as a chronic parental behavior that reoccurs often. Parents are engaged in a chronic pattern of inadequate protection and supervision of their children. Families that lack two parents, have work schedules that leave children alone for hours at a time, and fail to provide effective discipline at times when they do interact with their children are more likely to have neglected children. The single stressed-out mother is the poster child for what neglect looks like, although families of all backgrounds can be guilty of neglect. While the main focus of neglect is on the mother, little is written about father absence on neglect (Wilson & Horner, 2004). These families tend to be poor and live in undesirable neighbors. Families in which neglect is usually found have multiple problems and tend to need public support on a variety of fronts. Addressing the parenting issue of failure to protect the child is only one method of intervention.

Also included in neglect is allowing the child to participate in dangerous activities that defy common sense (Wilson & Horner, 2004). For example, parents involved in the use and distribution of drugs may inadvertently provide the opportunities for the child to engage in such activities. While the parent may not directly encourage the child in these harmful and illicit activities, the fact that they are not protected from engaging in them is neglectful. Whether the parent actually intends the neglectful behavior is a moot point, because the negative consequences for the children would be the same. Ultimately, neglect is viewed as any behavior on the part of the parent that abnegates the parenting role and requires that the child make decisions or engage in activities that may be beyond his or her developmental level (Wilson & Horner, 2004).

One of the ways parents of neglected children have been described is demoralized, or a kind of numbness and a giving up of effort to make things better (Wilson & Horner, 2004). This moral apathy has roots in alcohol and drug addiction, as well as abject poverty. Parents with a combined income of less than $15,000 a year are 44 times more likely to neglect their children when compared to parents making more than $30,000 a year. Neglecting parents abuse alcohol and drugs for different reasons, but regardless of the reason, the connection of substance abuse to neglect of children is strong. Some parents may be antisocial while others may abuse alcohol and drugs as a coping mechanism for mental illness. When parents are impaired for whatever reason, they do not provide adequate supervision or attention to children (Wilson & Horner, 2004).

Not all neglecting parents, however, are impaired through alcohol or drug use or are mentally ill. Some are preoccupied with jobs or other activities and spend little time interacting with their children (Ochsner, 2012). While **dual-career couples**, defined as both parents invested in career development and advancement and receiving a great deal of satisfaction and personal fulfillment from their jobs, may provide for the physical and material needs of their children, they could be at risk for neglecting their children's need for interaction and emotional support. Busy parents may lack the time and energy to engage their children in mutual activities (Wilson & Horner, 2001). These cases typically would not be reported to child protective services and would not be included in statistical reports. Wilson and Horner point out that neglect in affluent families takes a decidedly different route than neglect in poor families, yet the outcomes on children may be similar. In affluent families, child care is usually accomplished through hired nannies or private child care. While it cannot be argued that the use of child care professionals is in any way neglectful, depending on the circumstances, spending little time with a parent and the majority of time with paid care may raise the risk attachment disorder (Belsky, 1986).

Other underlying factors in child neglect are children exposed to domestic violence and children who live in neighborhoods in which there is an elevated concern for one's safety and security. Families in which **domestic violence** is a frequent occurrence may be at greater risk for neglect of children (Radford & Hester, 2006). Typically, when the mother is in an abusive relationship, there tends to be a concomitant failure to protect children who are either abused or neglected themselves.

While neglect is often associated with the post-birth environment, there is substantial evidence that the prenatal period can be characterized by neglect (Solis, Shadur, Burns, & Hussong). For example, pregnant women who do not provide for a positive **prenatal environment** free of alcohol or smoke exposure are either intentionally or non-intentionally neglectful of their children. Typically, a woman's behavior toward the care and needs of her child before birth parallels behavior after the birth. The consequences of a women's prenatal behavior are addressed in another chapter.

Effects of Neglect on the Child

While there is little focus on child neglect, it is well established that neglect has a profound effect on children. Researchers have found that infancy and early childhood are particularly vulnerable time periods (Hildyard & Wolfe, 2002). For infants, neglect may affect the development of attachment, as measured by the Bayley Scales of Infant Development. Children of neglect may also have cognitive deficits and memory problems. Emotional neglect, in which parents fail to provide for basic psychological support, is more difficult to detect, because there are no physical evidence or standout behaviors that prick the attention of others. The **failure to thrive syndrome**, in which infants fail to develop according to age expectations, results from the lack of warm and supportive contact with caregivers (Hildyard & Wolfe, 2002).

FIGURE 8.1 Neglected child.

Research on neglect consistently finds that children have anxious attachment with their parents, which develops very early and is pervasive throughout life (Erickson & Egeland, 2002). Generally, the effects of abuse rest on several factors, including the age of the child at the time of the neglect, factors that are considered protective, the duration and severity of the neglect, and the quality of the parent-child relationship. One of the major causes of reduced brain growth is inadequate nutrition, resulting in cognitive and language delays. For children zero to three, there is a need for repeated language to develop vocabulary. When the caregiver ignores the babbling and other vocal attempts to get the caregivers attention, development of language will be delayed. Studies have found that neglect is a greater factor in reduced language acquisition than other forms of abuse (Gaudin, 1993).

Emotional effects of neglect are correlated with distant and distrustful relationships with parent caregivers (Erickson & Egeland, 2002). This lack of trust in intimate relationships may also be related to the inability to understand the emotions of others and to lack empathy. Neglected children may lack both confidence in their social ability and have reduced capacity for understanding the feelings of others. They may appear apathetic in situations in which others have very strong emotions. Their responsiveness to emotional input may be shallow and inappropriate, resulting in poor peer relationships. Low self-esteem, juvenile delinquency, drug and alcohol abuse and addiction, and poor academic achievement are other noted outcomes of neglect (Goldman, Salus, Wolcott, & Kennedy, 2003). According to Goldman et al., children who experience neglect often are described as having **global neglect**, or deficits in a number of spheres. Global neglect is related to smaller brain growth in young children, which affects brain size. While these effects appear and are noticeable early in development, the negative effects persist throughout the lifespan.

3-Year-Old Children

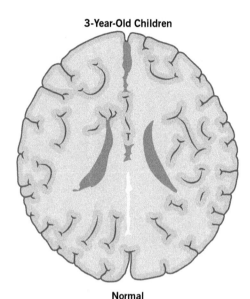

Normal

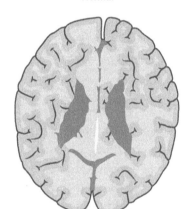

Extreme Neglect

FIGURE 8.2 Brain image of severe neglect

Neglect is also felt on a societal level as economic risks (Greder & Brotherson, 2001). Neglect of a young child is highly correlated with later juvenile delinquency, adult crime, mental and emotional illness, substance abuse, and domestic violence. Furthermore, the inability to maintain steady employment in adulthood may be a long-term effect of neglect. The economic cost of treatment over the lifespan of children of neglect is far greater than the cost of prevention (Greder & Brotherson, 2001).

Risk Factors

While neglect occurs across the family demographic board, some families experience more risk for neglect than others (Ernst, Meyer, & DePanfilis, 2004). As risk factors increase, the probability of neglect will increase, especially if there is a decrease in protective factors. Many children live in an environment, such as poor, unsafe, and overcrowded neighborhoods, that contributes to neglect. Living in unsafe and dangerous neighborhoods is related to a host other risk factors, such as poor nutrition, exposure to lead, lack of outdoor activities, and gang infestation. While no single risk factor is the cause of neglect, the greater the accumulation of factors, the higher the probability of neglect (Ernst, Meyer, & DePanfilis, 2004). Although a poor environment is highly correlated with neglect, when many protection factors are present, such as strong parent-child relationships, positive and supportive marital partners, and community support, these families can function at a high level.

Family variables related to neglect include the presence of domestic violence (Kantor & Little, 2003). Victims of domestic violence may also lack the ability to protect the child from being abused and neglected, often referred to as the **failure to protect**. Research indicates that children are well aware of the domestic violence even when parents think otherwise (Bragg, 2003). Family stress, particularly referred to as **chronic stress**, subjects parents to ongoing anxiety and fear, which is then acted out in their role relationships. This includes the parent-child relationship, which results in reduced parenting efficiency. Families experiencing chronic stress have less ability to respond appropriately to stress than other families, and even minor unexpected events can cause maladaptive responses.

Family variables, including positive and open communication patterns, the expression of empathy, and problem solving ability combine to reduce the probability of neglect (Corcoran & Nichols-Casebolt, 2004). Families with active and engaged fathers, regardless of the environment in which the family lives, tends to produce better overall outcomes in children and be a protective factor against neglect. These positive relationship skills enhance cohesion and family emotional bonding.

Characteristics of parents are important variables in the risk for neglect. For example, parents with mental or emotional problems fit a general profile for greater risk of neglecting their children. In addition, parents who were themselves abused as children and were reared in unstable and chaotic families are more likely to neglect their children (Tolan, Sherrod, Gorman-Smith, & Henry, 2004). Parents who had problems with their parents and had histories of running away or removal from the home and placement in foster care have higher incidences of neglect and abuse as adults. This connection to the parent's past issues is reflected in all types of abuse and neglect.

Other factors involving parents who contribute to neglect include substance abuse, the age and gender of the parent, and past arrests by the police (Stowman & Donahue, 2004). In addition, women are more likely to neglect children, especially young poorly educated mothers. Research studies have found that parents who abuse substances are more likely to engage in all forms of child abuse and neglect (Kelley, 2002).

Young children, children with special needs, and children with behavioral problems are the most likely to be neglected (Goldman, Salus, Wolcott, & Kennedy. 2003). Children with special needs require more attention and parental support than other children, which may result in increasing the parents' stress and anxiety. This can result in neglectful behaviors that are meant to restore the parents' emotional equilibrium.

Prevention and treatment can be aimed at the child, the parents, or the family. Because families who abuse their children have multiple problems, a family approach to both prevention and treatment may be the most effective (Thomlison, 2004). A systems paradigm in which behaviors of individual members are viewed as mutually caused and maintained provides a comprehensive model for reducing the number of abuse and neglect cases and simultaneously treating such families. Family therapy based on systems theory has a long clinical history of addressing dysfunctional families. Thomlison notes that ongoing treatment and support, which takes place in the perpetrator's home, has been found to be an effective strategy.

EMOTIONALLY ABUSED CHILDREN

While emotional abuse is often linked with other types of abuse, especially neglect, it is important to recognize it as a distinct category. It is most often given less attention than other forms of child abuse (Glaser, 2002). According to Glaser, the definition of emotional abuse is somewhat unclear, and researchers have more trouble studying it. Coupled with the tendency to treat children in the least restrictive manner, the diagnosis and treatment of children who are emotionally abused has lagged behind other forms of abuse. Furthermore, Glaser states that emotional abuse is viewed as a specific type of a harmful interaction pattern with the parent without physical contact. In contrast to child sexual abuse, which tends to be secretive, emotional abuse of a child is openly observable.

Child abuse in any form interferes with the normal emotional processing of daily experiences. Emotional abuse often leads to cognitive deficits in processing information (Kim & Cichetti, 2010). Children who experience emotional abuse during their formative years account for about one-third of all children (Varese et al., 2012). These children experience a number of negative consequences throughout their lifetime, including lower educational levels, criminal behavior, and mental and social maladjustment (Young & Widom, 2014). The link between emotional abuse and mental health issues later in life is strong.

CHILD SEXUAL ABUSE

Sexual abuse of children is broadly defined as any act or threat of act of sexual aggression toward a child where there is an age differential, regardless of whether the child gives consent (Broman-Fulks et al., 2007). Incidences of sexual abuse are difficult to determine, because many cases are reported some time after the abuse occurs. According to research, as much as 75% of child sexual abuse is not reported until after at least a year (Broman-Fulks et al., 2007). According to the Centers for Disease Control (CDC) (2014), approximately 25% of girls and 16% of boys are sexually victimized before the age of eighteen. According to research, a child's probability of being raped is approximately three times the probability that an adult will be raped (Berliner & Elliott, 2002). When compared to all reported sexual assaults, child sexual assault accounts for more than two-thirds of all cases. When survey data of incidences of child sexual abuse are compared, there is little consistency in findings; this suggests that a major hurdle in understanding the extent of child sexual abuse is disparate methods of collecting data (Gardner, 1989). Reporting of child sexual abuse has increased in the U.S. because of mandatory reporting by professionals who come in contact with families and children. Currently, approximately 10% of reported cases of child abuse and neglect are child sexual abuse (Berliner & Elliott, 2002).

Contrary to popular belief, the majority of child sexual abuse cases are not committed by pedophiles or persons who are sexually excited by and seek out children for sexual gratification. Male juveniles account for approximately 36% of cases of sexual victimization (Crimes Against Children Research Center, UNH, 2010). In addition, most cases of rapes are committed by an acquaintance, friend of the family, or family member. Researchers have found a link between sexual perpetrators whose victims are adults and children. For example, researchers, using a polygraph methodology in interviewing sexual offenders, found that more than 80% of child sexual abusers also raped adult females and, conversely, at least one-half of those found guilty of raping adults had also sexually abused children (Crimes Against Children Research Center, UNH, 2010).

Reporting of child abuse varies, which, to some degree, accounts for inconsistencies in the finding. For example, researchers using clinical samples tend to conclude that there are higher familial sexual abuse cases than for researchers using non-clinical samples (Crimes Against Children Research Center, UNH, 2010). Differences in the gender of children who are sexually abused have generally been found by researchers. In addition, states collect data differently, which accounts for some discrepancies. Sexually abused boys tend to be older than girls and are more likely to be abused by non-family females. Over the past number of years, researchers believe that the occurrences of child sexual abuse have decreased due to more attention to sexual abuse and more consistent means of punishing perpetrators (Finkelhor & Jones, 2004). Children who live in homes with biological parents are less likely to be victims of sexual abuse than children in single-parent or stepfamily homes. Victimization occurs in a variety of settings, including the home, and may occur spontaneously or be planned by the perpetrator for some time. **Grooming the victim,** as will be discussed below, is one of the maneuvers used by perpetrators. The use of force does occur often, which may have detrimental emotional outcomes (Crimes Against Children Research Center, UNH, 2010).

As stated above, child sexual abuse is generally reported long after the fact, with accidental disclosure being the most common form of disclosure for young children (Finkelhor & Jones, 2004). Researchers have found that it is not uncommon for young children who are victims of sexual abuse to wait until adolescence or adulthood to disclose (Copeland, Keeler, Argold, & Costello, 2007). Frequently, the disclosure is made accidently or unintentionally by the child confiding in a friend who tells a parent. A classic study by Sorenson and Snow (1991) with a large sample found that there are four basic stages that disclosure takes. First, the child is in denial and denies the abuse to others. Second is disclosure followed by recantation in which the child recants the denial. Lastly, the fourth stage is the reaffirmation of the abuse. Recanting the abuse tends to be based on pressure from an adult. The most effective way for disclosure to happen is for the child, or adult, for that matter, to be asked directly about being abused.

Sex Trafficking of Children

Sex trafficking of children is generally seen as a problem in developing countries and not in the U.S., but recent statistics show that it is occurring at higher numbers than previously believed within the U.S. (Hardy, Compton, & McPhatter, 2013). Affecting from 200,000 to 300,000 children in the U.S., sex trafficking has become a major concern. Sex trafficking of children does not have to include force, fraud, or coercion, because children can be manipulated by other tactics of power and dominance. A sex trafficker of children is defined as anyone who uses or exploits children to engage in sexual behavior, including family members, peers, pimps, and acquaintances. A pimp-oriented sexual exploitation of a child usually involves massage services and pornography (Reed, 2011, as cited in Hardy et al., 2013). Children of sex traffickers are transported across the U.S. to perform various sex-related acts. A complicated circumstance is that many sexually exploited children become attached to their traffickers, which reduces their ability to free themselves and also leads to them supporting their trafficker when arrested. Sexually exploited children through trafficking usually suffer from a number of emotional problems, including anxiety, depression, drug and alcohol addiction, and dissociative disorders. It is also evident that sex trafficking of children leads to faulty belief systems, poor decision making, and relationship dysfunction (Lloyd, 2011, as cited in Hardy et al., 2013).

Effects of Child Sexual Abuse

Children who are sexually abused come from chaotic and unstable families. Researchers have to take care with complex analysis to ferret out the effects of sexual abuse from the effects of the chaotic family (Putnam, 2003). The effects of child sexual abuse vary according to a number of variables, including the type of abuse and degree of severity (Putnam, 2003). For example, not all sexual abuse includes being touched. In most cases of child sexual abuse there are negative consequences, because the experience lacks consensus; it changes the relationship with the perpetrator, who is often a family member or known to the child, and engages the child in activity that is age inappropriate. Children are not developmentally ready for a sexual experience and one that is forced or non-consensual produces negative and even traumatic side effects. Some of the most common effects found from clinical and nonclinical samples include depression and Post-Traumatic Stress Disorder (PTSD).

While children do not ordinarily link sexual abuse with emotional difficulties, studies find that there is a direct correlation (Putnam, 2003). Children who were sexually abused will score higher on depression measures than children who were not sexually abused. In addition, according to Putnam, They also are more likely to be suicidal, experience greater levels of anxiety, and have lower levels of self-esteem. Depression associated with childhood sexual abuse stems from internalizing the experience, which also leads to a lower sense of self-esteem and self-worth. Children may feel that they somehow are responsible for the abuse, and instead of blaming the perpetrator, they turn it inward on themselves, which is sometimes referred to as **survivors shame.**

Children of sexual abuse who develop depression may also suffer from poor eating habits and not getting enough sleep. Eating disorders, such as **bulimia** and **anorexia**, can develop because of an over-emphasis on the body (Thompson & Wonderlich, 2004). Body image and concern about appearance may be disguised ways to attempt to control more negative and unacceptable emotions (Thompson & Wonderlich, 2004). Consequently, the emotional disorders may continue throughout the lifespan in the form of eating disorders, sleep deprivation, confusion, disorientation, and anxiety disorders.

Childhood sexual abuse can prevent and hinder the development of normal friendships and relationships with peers (Putnam, 2003). Generally, the impairment of forming and maintaining relationships depend on the severity of the abuse. The longer the abuse occurred and the severity of the abuse is directly related to the degree of emotional dysfunction. The effect on future relationship formation can be very great, especially the reticence of developing intimate relationships.

Childhood sexual abuse can result in a severe anxiety disorder known as PTSD, which is characterized by flashbacks of previously negative experiences that affect present coping and appropriately response to stimuli (Schmahl, Vermetten, Elzinga, & Bremner, 2003). This re-experiencing of the events causes muted and sometimes avoided responses to normal experiences. Although PTSD affects both children and adults, symptoms vary according to a number of variables. While PTSD can be caused by a variety of conditions, one that that does not have to happen, that does not happen automatically, and can and should be avoided is sexual abuse. Researchers have focused in recent years on the long-term effects of trauma and its relationship to the development of PTSD (Schmahl, Vermetten, Elzinga, & Bremner, 2003). There is also concern that traumatic events, such as sexual abuse, may alter the developmental trajectory of abused children. Although a number of circumstances are related to the development of PTSD in children, none is more egregious than sexual abuse. Most experiences related to PTSD occur from physical harm, which can be re-experienced periodically from stimuli that would be considered innocuous. Although most people develop symptoms of PTSD soon after the traumatic event, some do not present with symptoms until some future date. The sexual abuse of a child is most damaging when it occurs over time, when the perpetrator is part of the family's inner circle, and when it involves physical touching or rape. Some findings suggest that adults who developed PTSD as children from physical and sexual abuse have increased levels of cortisol when reviewing traumatic situations in an experimental setting (Schmahl, Vermetten, Elzinga, & Bremner, 2003).

Neuroscientists have found that child sexual abuse alters genetic patterns, suggesting that it may be possible in the future to identify various mental or emotional disorders through analyzing genetic patterns and formulate treatment modalities according to these patterns (Ressler, Burgess, & Douglas (1988). There is also evidence that different types of traumatic events may have different effects of gene activity. For example, one recent study cited by Ressler et al. compared persons who develop PTSD from abuse with persons who developed PTSD from other causes, and found differences in the activity of genes. The group that developed PTSD from abuse was more likely for genes related to the nervous and immune systems to be affected, while PTSD associated with other causes showed greater alteration in gene death and the rate of growth of genes.

Studies confirm that later effects of sexual abuse affect females more than males. For example, Filipas and Ullman (2006) found that females blame themselves for the abuse and use more coping strategies of denial than do male victims of sexual abuse. In addition, females report more symptoms of PTSD than males, especially when the disclosure of the abuse was delayed. The researchers also generally found that disclosing the abuse to others did not elicit negative reactions.

The effects of PTSD caused by sexual abuse of children, as described by Browne and Finkelhor (1986), included four steps. First, the child is traumatically sexualized, meaning that the natural development of sexual behavior has been interrupted, and the child may have difficulty with sexual expression throughout the lifespan. Second, the sexually abused child may feel betrayed by family members, particularly if there appeared to be little effort to protect the children from the abuse. It is not uncommon that girls will feel betrayed by their mothers. Third, the reaction of others to the disclosure or knowledge of the abuse may be negative stereotyping that affects the self-esteem of the child. Fourth, sexually abused children often feel powerless to stop the abuse and may, in fact, give up resistance, since they see no way to prevent or stop it.

PTSD effects have been described in several different models. According to Kerr (2011), **PTSD** reflects either a single traumatic event labeled as **Type I**, or long-terms effects referred to as Type II. Type I can reflect single traumatic events that are psychologically damaging although they occur only one time. On the other hand, **Type II PTSD** typically develops from long-term repeated abuse in which the child suffers ego damage.

Intrafamilial Sexual Abuse (Incest)

Most cultures have laws forbidding sexual intercourse between close kin, although there is some variation. In the past, the incest taboo referred to sexual relations between a parent and a child, but now encompasses a broader meaning of sexual relations within the family, including step relationships, referred to as intrafamilial (Glasser & Kolvin, 2001). Four decades ago, sexual abuse of a child within the family was considered rare, but based on ongoing research, it is now believed to be a major family and social problem (Denov, 2004).

Female Sexual Perpetrators

The common view that the male is the perpetrator of sexual abuse and the female is the victim obfuscates the reality that some victims are male. Male victimization tends to go unnoticed, and female perpetrators tend to be less identified or punished (Denov, 2003). According to Denov, researchers and clinicians alike pay little attention to females as perpetrators. A few researchers have raised unanswered questions about the process and occurrence of female sexual abuse. Traditional sexual scripts for males and females in which males are viewed as aggressors and females as passive in sexual relations further reduce efforts to focus on female abuse. Women are viewed in all societies as being less aggressive, emotionally supportive of others, and having greater caretaking skills. Not only does the cultural script minimize females as sexually aggressive, but it also casts doubt that abuse perpetrated by women is as harmful as abuse perpetrated by men. As cited in Denov, the literature on female perpetrators comes mainly from analyzing case material and self-report studies. This analysis found a higher likelihood of perpetration of child sexual abuse for females than case material. This difference in case material and self-reports may emanate partly from the influence of cultural sexual scripts in the court system, which tends to ignore cases involving women as perpetrators. Sexual abuse by women is viewed as being less reported by victims than sexual abuse by males. Researchers have also found that abuse by females is less reported by both male and female victims (Denov, 2004). Overall, fewer cases are prosecuted by the court systems, and when a case is prosecuted, females are given considerably lower sentences.

Gender biases in sexual abuse cases were found in a study conducted by Hetherton and Beardsall (1999, as cited in Denov, 2004). The research consisted of two groups of professionals, social workers and law enforcement personnel, who were given the same case scenario with males and females as the perpetrators. Both groups were consistent in concluding that female abuse was less severe and needed less intervention than the male abuse. No doubt this pervasive gender bias attitude contributes to fewer cases reported and prosecuted.

Mandatory Reporting of Abuse

Professionals who work with children are required to report suspected child abuse and neglect. The professionals in the majority of states and provinces include medical personnel, school personnel, therapists, social workers, child care workers, and law enforcement personnel (Child Welfare Information Gateway, 2012). Since **mandatory reporting of sexual abuse** is governed by state law, some states require additional persons than those mentioned above. For example, in California, mandatory reporting is required for personnel in businesses or groups that provide activities for children, such as camps or recreational facilities (Child Welfare Information Gateway, 2012). In approximately 18 states and Puerto Rico, all persons are required to be mandatory reporters in addition to professionals working with children. All states allow anyone to report suspected abuse. Most states suspend **privileged communication**, communication between a professional and a client that is confidential, in the case of abuse. The attorney-client confidential communication is most often allowed by states. Generally, the disclosure of the name of the person reporting abuse is kept confidential in most states, but some have special provisions for the release of the name.

Perpetrators

Much has been written and hypothesized about perpetrators, with disparate points of view and ongoing discussion. It is clear from the preponderance of research literature that most child sexual perpetrators are not pedophiles and do not have a sexual preference for young, prepubescent children (Glasser & Kolvin, 2001). Instead, child sexual perpetrators tend to have the capacity for sexual abuse of children in addition to other sexual deviant behavior, such as rape of adult females. What this means is that sexual exploitation of children, except for a small minority of abusers who prefer young children as sexual objects, represents a wider and more pervasive problems in society.

One of the questions that is commonly asked is: Does a link exist between being abused as a child and committing acts of abuse as an adult, or the **victim-to-perpetrator paradigm**? A substantial body of literature has addressed the victim-to-perpetrator paradigm to understand the overall phenomenon of sexual abuse and victimization. While large in scope, there still exists debate over the meanings of the findings that link victimization and perpetrators (Glasser & Kolvin, 2001). For example, there are more girls victimized than boys, but few female perpetrators. Some studies, however, conclude that the number of male victims may be much larger than reported, because most experts believe that males tend to underreport sexual abuse. As cited in Glasser and Kolvin, most studies find that approximately 30% of perpetrators were victims of sexual assault as children, while only 11% of non-abusers were abused. In addition, researchers also find that children who are victims of sexual abuse tend to be raised in chaotic and dysfunctional homes, which may contaminate a direct link to the victim-perpetrator model. Generally speaking, however, the victim-perpetrator link tends to be supported for males but not for females.

Sexual Abuse and Recidivism Rates

Sexual offender recidivism rates, the rate at which offenders commit other sexual crimes after prosecution, range between 10% and 15%, although some abusers have higher rates (Harris et al., 2003). According to Harris et al., researchers have identified two types of sexual offenders, those engaging in deviant sexual activities and those with antisocial personality disorder, the latter of which commit the most heinous sexual crimes. Contributing factors for persons who commit sexual crimes are deviant sexual behavior, hostile and unstable family background, inability to form appropriate long-term affectionate bonds, and accepting attitudes toward sexual aggression.

Sexual Predator Laws

Although the majority of sexual abuse cases are committed by someone known to the victim, much effort on the part of the state and federal governments has been made to curb stranger sexual abuse, which tends to be more heinous and usually involves abduction, rape, and murder (Heide, Beauregard, & Myers, 2009). Child abductions receive much media attention and outcry from parent advocacy groups. Federal legislation, both to prevent future sexual abuse and to punish offenders, has been enacted on the federal level over the past twenty years.

One of the most well-known laws is referred to as **Megan's Law**, which allows for registration of sex offenders and community notification of their residences (Megan's Law: Sex Offenders Registration and Exclusion Law, 2001). The federal law was entitled the Jacob Wetterling Sexual Abuse Act of 1994. Megan's Law, which resulted after Megan Kanka was lured from her home by a neighbor who had previously been convicted of sex crimes, has been bolstered by other legislation to make it a stronger deterrent for perpetrators. This legislation includes the Adam Walsh Child Protection and Safety Act of 2006 (para. 1), which enlarged reporting jurisdictions, including Native American citizens, and increased the number of sexual crimes for registration. The purpose of this is act is to follow in the community discharged sexual offenders after they have served time. The registry, consisting of online state websites, includes the offender's name, place of residence, and sexual offenses. Failure to comply with the law, which includes updates of present status, is a federal crime.

Jessica's Law was passed by the state legislature in Florida and subsequently in several other states after the abduction and murder of Jessica Lundsford by a known sexual offender who lived next door. This law made lewd acts against a child under the age of 12 a life felony, established mandatory prison sentences of 25 years, lifetime electronic monitoring, and lifetime probation after serving time (Jessica's Law Now, 2014).

The question often arises regarding the effectiveness and constitutionality of sexual offender laws. Recidivism rates for persons convicted of sex offenses, which are generally lower than the general population, range from 15% to 20% depending on a number of factors, including the type of offense and the treatment offered (Aos, Miller, & Drake, 2006). Prison sentences without treatment have not been found to be effective in reducing recidivism (Aos et al., 2006). Repeat offenders, especially male pedophiles, are the most likely to commit additional crimes. Not only are recidivism rates high for offenders who target strangers, but they commit the most heinous sex crimes. Most experts believe that early detection and treatment are the most effective in reducing sexual crimes and decreasing recidivism rates (Worling, Litteljohn, & Bookalam, 2010). Studies have found that prison time does not reduce the risk of committing future sexual crimes, while cognitive-behavioral treatment does reduce the risk (Aos et al., 2006).

Researchers have begun to compile data on sexual offenses to determine what factors are effective in reducing the occurrence of such crimes and the recidivism rates. Recent research by Prescott and Rockoff (2008) found some interesting and incongruous findings. For example, while community notification laws may deter some persons from committing sexual crimes, they seem to increase the recidivism rate of those who commit crimes. The researchers hypothesized, without empirical evidence, that because of their "status" as sex offenders, sex offenders tend to be unemployed, live in poor and unsafe housing, and lack a supportive social network. In other words, sex offenders are already at the bottom on the social ladder and, therefore, there would be few additional costs to continuing sexual exploitation of others. Prescott and Rockoff further hypothesized that life in prison may be more rewarding than life in a rejecting society.

TABLE 8.3 History of laws and sexual abuse

• Jacob Wetterling Crimes Against Children Sexually Violent Offender Registration Act—1994
• The Pam Lychner Sexual Offender Tracking and Identification Registration Act—1996
• Megan's Law—1996
• Jacob Wetterling Improvements Act—1997
• Perfection of Children From Sexual Predators Act—1998
• The Campus Sexual Protection Act—2000
• Prosecutorial Remedies and Other Tools to End the Exploitation of Children Today (PROTECT) Act—2003
• Adam Walsh Child Protection and Safety Act—2006
• Department of Justice, Office of the Attorney General, Applicability of the Ex-Offender Registration and Notification Act
• Keeping Internet Devoid of Predators (KIDS) Act
• Kids of 2008

Prescott and Rockoff (2008) are not alone in their concerns about the full effect of sex offender laws on rates of sex crimes and related crimes. According to Lancester (2011), sex offender laws fail to accomplish their purposes of reducing the occurrence of sex crimes and providing appropriate treatment for offenders. One of the main reasons for this failure, according to Lancester, is the unwieldy size of the state and federal registries, which now exceed 700,000 names. Because the federal registry is a joining of the state registries and is governed by state laws, there are differences in the types of offenses that make up the registries across states. In some states, a person's name appears on the registry for urinating in public, for minors engaging in consensual sex or sexting, and for sexually explicit messaging with peers through social media such as Facebook. Other states include only persons who have engaged in forcible rape or other acts of sexual exploitation or violence. This inconsistency raises the question of the arbitrariness of sex offender laws and whether some persons are inappropriately identified as sex offenders. In addition, **mandatory sentencing** and **civil commitment laws** in some states have provisions that offenders deemed inappropriate for release after the original sentence has been served may be retained indefinitely, or if released, must have an electronic monitor for life. Further, some states, such as California, prohibit sex offenders from public access to areas frequented by children and restrict their places of residence.

Opponents to the extensive sexual offender laws believe that they are unfair, excessively punish, and violate basic human rights (Lancester, 2011). They advocate for repealing the most restrictive laws beginning with public restrictions. In addition, opponent advocates recommend that registries be open to law enforcement officials but not to the general public. According to Lancester, public registries marginalize offenders and encourage recidivism, believing that offenders have little to lose by continued offenses. In addition, opponents to sexual offender laws believe that the evidence supporting such restrictions is not verified by research data. The one-size-fits-all approach to sexual offenders belies the fact that offenders are not a homogenous group. Advocates for strict laws point out that while registry laws may not reduce the occurrence of sex crimes, they have been effective in making arrests after crimes have been committed (Lancester, 2011).

False Allegations

Not all allegations of sexual abuse are true, and some researchers have noted a range of approximately 5% false reports in recent years (Young, 2014). One reason for the number of false reports may be due to the increase in mandatory reporting and greater attention to sexual educational settings. However, since many abused children do retract their accusations, the actual number of false reports is hard to determine. Gardner (1989) hypothesized that the **parental alienation syndrome**, in which one parent demonizes the other parent, most likely the father, to the child during times of conflict between the parents, such as in custody battles, only further confuses and obviates the situation.

Another ongoing issue is the actual investigation of the accusation. For example, one of the most flagrant problems is when the investigator conducting the interview with the child asks leading questions (Kinnear, 2007). Unless investigators are specifically trained to interview children, their own biases may prevent an open and realistic conclusion. The use of anatomical dolls can also produce false reporting and requires considerable training not to bias the child's responses. The court proceeding may cause a child to relive the abusive situation; videotape or transcripts of the child's statements could protect the child from further damage. Court proceedings tend to be protracted, and the child may be on the stand a number of times, including during cross-examination. The effect on the child who testifies in court is also heavily influenced by whether the case has a positive outcome or negative outcome. If the perpetrator is found guilty, the outcome for the child tends to be positive.

Treatment of Sexual Abuse

Initially, one of the most important functions for CPS is to remove the child from the situation in which abuse is occurring (Filipas & Ullman, 2006). A decision is made by CPS as to whether the child can remain in the family. Frequently, removing the child may be required if the abuser is a family member who lives at the same address as the child. If the offender is a parent, detailed information about that parent, including past history of abuse, is necessary to determine future plans. The non-abusing parent must also be evaluated to determine the extent of his/her knowledge of the abuse and whether the parent failed to protect the child. If either the offender or the child is removed from the home, visitation becomes an important issue to determine. Investigators must also decide if the offender has potential to be rehabilitated.

The abused child has a reduced ability to trust others, especially when the abuser was a close trusted family member (Filipas & Ullman, 2006). The inability to trust is further eroded when the non-abusing parent withholds support and fails to fully believe the child's accusations. When a nonfamily member is the abuser, the child may still feel betrayed by parents not protecting him/her from this acquaintance (Filipas & Ullman, 2006). The abused child will feel a multiplicity of emotions, including blaming himself/herself, self-identity problems, and fear and anxiety. In response to these emotions, the child may react in a number of ways that can result in various therapeutic interventions. Some children may publicly act out sexually, such as masturbating frequently. Curtailing this inappropriate public behavior and dealing with the over-sexualized behavior is essential for reducing the likelihood of the child being a sexual perpetrator in the future.

Other treatment issues revolve around the relationship between the mother and the victim (Filipas & Ullman, 2006). The mother-victim relationship is the key to family reunification. If this relationship lacks support, or if the abuse caused a relationship distancing to occur, repair is needed before reunification can commence. The risk of future re-victimization is reduced when the mother-victim relationship is cohesive. Generally speaking, the mother-victim relationship refers more to the mother-daughter dyad than to the mother-son dyad.

A SYSTEMS/DIALECTICAL PERSPECTIVE OF CHILD ABUSE AND NEGLECT

Applying a systems/dialectical perspective to child abuse and neglect begins with an understanding of the systems from which the abuse emerged. Abusive systems have reverberating effects throughout a person's life course (National Academy of Sciences, 2014). Since the negative effects continue throughout the lifespan, finding systemic ways to prevent and treat child abuse is an ongoing challenge. Research and treatment endeavors must take a holistic approach to address the biological, physical, psychological, and cognitive dimensions of child abuse (Guterman, Lee, Lee, Waldsfogel, & Rathouz, 2009). Designing studies that address the complexity of child abuse took a new direction in the fragile families longitudinal studies (McLanahan, Tach, & Schneider, 2012).

These studies provide evidence of the interlocking systems at play both in the problem formation and in all the treatment modalities that are involved.

In applying a systems/dialectical perspective, one of the core principles is contradiction (Montegomery & Baxter, 1996). Contradiction means that there are elements that are opposite to each other, such as the revealing-concealing and the openness-closeness dialectics that characterize much of communication. Children and adults as well, who are involved as a victim or perpetrator, are caught up in the reveal-conceal contradiction. The contradiction is fed by experiencing shame related to the abuse (Limandri, 1989, as cited in Dindia, 2008). This contradiction of feelings is especially strong for sexually abused children, because on the one hand, they might think others would disapprove of them as perhaps causing their abuse, and on the other hand, they would point the finger at someone without empirical evidence that abuse actually occurred. To be open about the abuse will also forever change this relationship with the alleged perpetrator and their relationship with other family members.

We must also keep in mind that according to Montgomery and Baxter (1996), the contradiction is not simply a dialectic between two points, such as to reveal or to conceal, but involves many diverse elements, which they referred to as multivocality. This dialectical process is continuous and results in ongoing change. According Dindia (2008), it is impossible to be fully open or fully closed, which means that the dialectical contradiction is never fully resolved. In terms of child abuse, especially child sexual abuse, full disclosure may never occur because of the opposing force of concealment (Summit, 1983, as cited in Dindia, 2008). This could explain how children who disclose their sexual abuse may also recant their story with this process occurring numerous times.

Sorenson and Snow (1991, as cited in Dindia, 2008) proposed a spiral process to explain how children disclose sexual abuse. Most often, children follow a sequence of first denying that abuse occurred, followed by partial disclosure, full disclosure, recanting, and reaffirming. Children are more likely to deny the abuse if questioned by an authority figure, such as a parent. This process emphasizes that children disclose their sexual abuse in a nonlinear manner (Dindia, 2008).

If one took only a systems point of view, the entire system and roles that persons play in the system would be analyzed. To some theoretical scholars, a systems view of abuse and neglect might deemphasize power and gender relationships and, therefore, provide only a partial explanation. A dialectical perspective added to the systems perspective would provide greater explanatory power and broaden the scope for treatment options.

KEY TERMS

Child abuse and neglect
Battered child syndrome
Physical abuse
Spanking (corporal punishment)
Depression
Anxiety disorder

Hypothalamic-pituitary-adrenal (HPA) axis
Sympathetic nervous system
Serotonin
Post-Traumatic Stress Disorder (PTSD)
Subdural and retina hemorrhage

Failure to protect
Chronic stress
Child sexual abuse
Grooming the victim
Survivor's shame
Bulimia
Anorexia

Mood disorder

Conditional spanking

Pruning

Myelination

Mandatory reporting
of sex abuse

Privileged communication

Victims to perpetrator
paradigm

Sexual offender
recidivism rates

Jessica's Law

Mandatory reporting
of sexual abuse

Neglected children

Dual-career

Domestic violence

Prenatal environment

Failure to thrive

Megan's Law

Jessica's Law

Mandatory sentencing

Civil commitment laws

Parental alienation

Civil commitment laws

Victim to perpetrator

Type I PTSD

Type II PTSD

Interfamilial abuse

Parental alienation
syndrome

Mother-victim relationship

Emotionally Abused
Children

Sex Trafficking of Children

Mandatory sentencing

Megan's Law

Privileged communication

STUDY QUESTIONS TO ACCOMPLISH THE LEARNING OBJECTIVES

1. Discuss the four basic stages of sexual abuse. Analyze how these stages could be helpful in reducing child abuse.

2. Have cases of child abuse and neglect declined in recent years? Explain and defend your answer.

3. Define physical or corporal punishment. Discuss the link between physical punishment and abuse. Should measures be taken to curtail spanking as a form of discipline of children? Justify your answer.

4. Define child neglect. Evaluate why neglect of children is less likely to be prosecuted than other forms of abuse. Should more effort go into reducing the occurrence of neglect? Defend your answer.

5. Define child sexual abuse. Determine if prevention and treatment efforts of child abuse is on the right track. Generate ideas for future social policy for child abuse.

6. Discuss the effects of child sexual abuse. How does sexual abuse affect the child's brain? Evaluate current social policy for child sexual abuse.

7. Discuss the difference in female and male sexual victimization. Should more effort be placed on reducing acts committed by female perpetrators? Defend your answer.

8. List the drawbacks for mandatory reporting of sexual abuse. Do the drawbacks outweigh the positive effects? Explain your answer.

9. Identify sexual predator laws. Summarize whether sexual predator laws are helpful, or do they do more harm than good, given that sexual predators do not commit the bulk of sexual abuse?

10. What are false allegations in sexual cases? Judge efforts that could be made to reduce the occurrence of false allegations.

DEBATE ACTIVITY FOR STUDENTS

Consider the following proposition: Treatment for sexual perpetrators, such as in Coalinga State Hospital, is a waste of taxpayer's money.

- Review refereed literature on this topic. Do a library and Internet search to find relevant material. Investigate some of the additional readings.
- Develop three arguments for the proposition.
- Develop three arguments against the proposition.
- How do the arguments relate to other systems, such as the community or culture?
- Is there common ground?
- What are the long-term consequences of taking action?
- What new or common-ground solutions should be offered? If no common ground, what new position could emerge from a dialogue between the two positions?
- How is the new position superior to the original positions?

ADDITIONAL READING RESOURCES

Bugental, D. B., Ellison, P. C., Lin, E., Rainey, B., Kokotovic, A., & O'Hara, N. (2010). A cognitive approach to child abuse prevention. *Psychology of Violence, 1*(S), 84–106.

Gerhoff, H. T. (2013). Spanking and child development: We know enough now to stop hitting our children. *Child Development Perspective, 7*(3), 133–137.

Kidd, K. K. (2010). Sexual offender laws and prevention of sexual violence or recidivism. *American Journal of Public Health, 100*(3), 412–419. doi: 10.2105/AJAPH.2008.153254

Losel, F., & Schmuker, F. (2005). The effectiveness of treatment for sexual offenders: A comprehensive media analysis. *Journal of Experimental Criminology 1*(1), 117–146.

Mann, R. E., & Barnett, G. D. (2013). Victim empathy interventions with sexual offenders. *Sexual Abuse: A Journal of Research and Treatment, 25*(3), 283–301.

Strauss, M. A., Gelles, R. (Eds.). (2017). *Physical violence in American families: Risk factors and adaptations in 8,145 families.* New York, NY: Routledge.

REFERENCES

Adam Walsh Child Protection and Safety Act. (2006). The National Conference of State Legislatures. Retrieved from http://www.ncsl.org/research/civil-and-criminal-justice/adam-walsh-child-protection-and-safety-act.aspx.

Afifi, T. O., Mota, N. P., Dasiewiez, P., MacMillan, H. L., & Sareen, J. (2012). Physical punishment and mental disorders: Results from a nationally represented U.S. sample. *Pediatrics, 130*(2), 184–192.

Al Odhayani, A., Watson, W. J. & Watson, L. (2013). Behavioral consequences of child abuse. *Canadian Family Physician, 59*(8), 831–836.

American Society for the Positive Care of Children. (2017). Child abuse statistics. Retrieved from http://americanspcc.org/child-abuse-statistics/

Aos, S., Miller, M., & Drake, E. (2006). Evidence-based adult corrections programs: What works and what does not. Olympia, WA: Washington State Institute for Public Policy.

Bragg, H. L. (2003). Child protection in families experiencing domestic violence. U.S. Department of Health and Human Services, Administration for Children and Families, Administration on children, Youth and Families, Children's Bureau, Office of Child Abuse and Neglect, Washington, D.C.

Belsky, J. (1996). Parent, infant, and social-contextual antecedents of father-son attachment security. *Developmental Psychology, 5*, 905–913.

Belsky, J. (1986). Infant day care: A cause for concern? Zero to Three, *6*(4), 1–7.

Berliner, L., & Elliott, D. M. (2002). Sexual abuse of children. In J. E. B. Myers, L. Berliner, J. Briere, C. T. Hendrix, C. Jenny, T. A. Reid, *The APSAC handbook on child maltreatment* (2nd ed.) (pp. 55–78). Thousand Oaks, CA: Sage.

Broman-Fulks, J., Ruggiero, K. J., Hanson, R. F., Smith, D. W., Resnick, H. S., Kilpatrick, D. G., & Saunders, B. S. (2007). Sexual assault disclosed in relation to adolescent mental health: Results from the national survey of adolescents. *Journal of Clinical Child and Adolescent and Psychology, 36*(2), 260–266.

Browne, A., & Finkelhor, D. (1986). Initial and long-term effects: A review of the research. In D. Finkelhor (Ed.), *A sourcebook on child sexual abuse* (pp. 143–179). Beverly Hills, CA: Sage.

Centers for Disease Control and Prevention. (2014). Together for girls: Scope of the problem—sexual; violence against girls. Retrieved from http://www.cdc.gov/violencePrevention/sexualviolence/together/index.html

Child Abuse Prevention and Treatment Act (CAPTA) Reauthorization Act of 2010 (P.L. 111–320), § 3.

Child Welfare Information Gateway. (2012). Mandatory reporters of child abuse and neglect. Washington, D.C.: U.S. Department of Health and Human Services.

Copeland, W. D., Keeler, G., Angold, A., & Costello, E. J. (2007). Traumatic events and post-traumatic stress in childhood. *Archives of General Psychiatry, 64*, 577–584.

Corcoran, J., & Nichols-Casebolt, A. (2004). Risk and resilience: Ecological framework for assessment and goal formulation. *Child and Adolescent Social Work Journal, 21*(3), 211–218.

Crimes against Child Research Center, UNH (2010). Trends in children's exposure to violence, 2003–2011. Retrieved from www.unh.edu/ccrc//

Erickson, & Egeland. (2002). Child neglect. In J. E. B. Myers, L. Berliner, J. Briere, C. T. Hendrix, C. Jenny, T. A. Reid, *The APSAC handbook on child maltreatment* (2nd ed.) (pp.3–20). Thousand Oaks, CA: Sage.

Ernst, J., Meyer, M., & DePanfilis, D. (2004). Housing characteristics and adequacy of the physical care of children: An exploratory analysis. *Child Welfare, 85*(5), 437–452.

Denov, M. S. (2004). The long-term effects of child sexual abuse by female perpetrators: A qualitative study of male and female victims. *Journal of Interpersonal Violence, 19*, 1137–1156.

Fang, X., Brown, D. S., Florence, C. S., & Mercy, J. A. (2012). The economic burden of child maltreatment in the United States and implications for treatment. *Child Abuse and Neglect, 36*(2), 156–165.

Filipas, H. H., & Ullman, S. E. (2006). Child sexual abuse, coping response, self-blame, post-traumatic stress disorder, and adult sexual revitalization. *Journal of Interpersonal Violence, 21*(5) 552–572.

Finkelhor, D., & Jones, L. M. (2004). Sexual abuse in the 1990s: Evidence for possible causes. Juvenile Justice Bulletin. U.S. Department of Justice, Office of Justice Programs, Office of Juvenile Justice and Delinquency Prevention.

Fries, A. B., & Pollak, S. D. (2004). Emotion, understanding, in post-institutionalized Eastern European children. *Developmental Psychopathology, 16*(2), 355–369.

Gardner, R. (1989). Differentiating between bona fide and fabricated allegations of sexual abuse of children. *Journal of the American Academy of Matrimonial Lawyers 5*, 1–25.

Gaudin, J. (1993). Child neglect: A guide to intervention. National Center for Child Abuse and Neglect, U.S. Department of Health and Human Services, Administration for Children and Families.

Glasser, M., & Kolvin, I. (2001). Cycle of child sexual abuse: Links between being a victim and becoming a perpetrator. *The British Journal of Psychiatry, 179*(6), 882–894.

Goldman, J., Salus, M. K., Wolcott, D., & Kennedy, K. Y. (2003). A coordinated response to child abuse and neglect: The foundation for practice. Office of Child Abuse and Neglect, Children's Bureau.

Greder, K., & Brotherson, M. J. (2001). Stress and coping: Low-income mothers feeding their children. National Council on Family Relations, 42(2), F5–F8.

Giovannoni, J. M., & Becerra, R. M. (1979). *Defining child abuse*. New York, NY: The Free Press.

Hamilton, T. A., & Bundy-Fazioli, K. (2013). Exploring the complexities of child neglect: Ethical issues of child welfare practice. *Journal of Social Work Values and Ethics, 10*(2), 13–24.

Hardy, V. L., Compton, K. D., & McPhatter, V. S. (2014). Domestic minor sex trafficking: Practice implications for mental health. *Journal of Women and Social Work, 28*(1), 1–11.

Harris, G. T., Rice, M. E., Quinsey, V .L., Lalumiere M. L., Doer, D., & Lang, C. (2003). A multisite comparison of actuarial risk instruments for sex offenders. Center for Addiction and Mental Health University of Toronto, Correctional Services of Canada.

Heide, K. M., Beauregard, E., & Myers, W. C. (2009). Sexually motivated child abduction murders: Synthesis of the literature and case illustration. *Victims and Offenders, 4*(1), 58–75.

Hildyard, K. L., & Wolfe, D. A. (2002). Child neglect: Developmental issues and outcomes. *Child Abuse & Neglect, 26,* 679–695.

Jessica's Law Now. (2014). Retrieved from http://jessicaslawnow.wordpress.com/about-jessicas-law/

Kantor, G. K., & Little, L. (2003). Defining the boundaries of child neglect: When does domestic violence equate with parental failure to protect? *Journal of Interpersonal Violence, 18,* 138–155.

Kelley, S. J. (2002). Child maltreatment in the context of substance abuse. In J. E. B. Myers, L. Berliner, J. Briere, C. T. Hendrix, C. Jenny, and T. A. Reid (Eds.), *The APSAC Handbook on Child Maltreatment* (2nd ed.) (pp. 105–117). Thousand Oaks, CA: Sage.

Kerr, L. (2011). Dissociation in late modern American society: Defense against soul? ProQuest.

Kim, J., & Cichetti, D. (2010). Longitudinal pathways linking child maltreatment, emotional regulation, peer relations, and psychopathology. *Journal of Child Psychology and Psychiatry, 51,* 106–116. doi: 10.1111/j.1469-7610.2009.02202.x

Kinnear, K. L. (2007). *Childhood sexual abuse: A reference book* (2nd ed.). Santa Barbara, CA: ABC-CLIO.

Lancester, R. N. (2011). *Sex panic and the punitive state.* Berkeley, CA: University of California Press.

Larzelere, R. E., & Kuhn, B. R. (2005). Comparing child outcomes of physical punishment and alternative disciplinary tactics: A meta-analysis. *Clinical Child and Family Psychology Review, 8*(1), 1–37.

Lynne, E. G., Gifford, E. J., Evans, K. E., & Rosch J. B. (2015). Barriers to reporting maltreatment: Do emergency medical professionals fully understand their role as mandatory reporters. *North Carolina Medical Journal, 76*(1), 13–18. doi: 10. 18043/ncm.76.1.13

Megan's Law: Sex Offenders Registration and Exclusion Law. (2001). Office of the Attorney General, State of California, Department of Justice.

Myers, J. E. B. (2008). A short history of child protection in America. *Family Law Quarterly, 42*(3), 449–463.

Navalta, C. P., Polcari, A., Webster, D. M., Boghossian, A., & Teicher, M. H. (2006). Effects of childhood sexual abuse on neuropsychological and cognitive function in college women. *Journal of Neuropsychiatry and Clinical Neuroscience, 18*(1), 45–53.

Needell, B., Webster, D., Armijo, M. et al. (2012). Child Welfare Services Report for California. Retrieved from http://cssr. berkeley.edy/ucb_childwelfare

Norman, R. E., Byambaa, M., De, R., Butchart, A., Scott, J., & Vos, T. (2012). The long-term effects of child physical abuse, emotional abuse and neglect: A systematic review and meta analysis. *PLOS Medicine.* Retrieved from http:// journals.plos.org/plosmedicine/article?id=10.1371/journal.pmed.1001349

Ochsner, K. N., & Gross, J. J. (2005). Review of the cognitive control of emotion. *Trends in Cognitive Science, 9*(5), 242–249.

Ochsner, T. J. (2012). The impact of dual-career marriage on role confleict and satisfaction. University of Portland, Master's Thesis. Retrieved from http://pilotscholars.up.edu/cgi/viewcontent.cgi?article=1073&context=cst_studpubs

Pollak, S. D., Nelson, C. A., Schlaak, M. F., Roeber, B. J., Wewerka, S. S., Wiik, K. L., … Gunner, M. R. (2010). Neurodevelopmental effects of early deprivation in post-institutionalized children. *Child Development, 81*(1), 224–236.

Prescott, J. J., & Rockoff, J. E. (2008). Do sex offender registration and notification laws affect criminal behavior? Retrieved from http://ssrn.com/abstract=110066

Putnam, F. W. (2003). Ten-year update review: Child sexual abuse. *Journal of the American Academy of Child and Adolescent Psychiatry, 42*(3), 269–278.

Radford, L., & Hester, M. (2006). Mothering through domestic violence. *British Journal of Social Work, 37*(4), 770–772.

Reece, R. M., & Sege, R. (2000). Childhood head injuries: Accidental or inflicted? *Archives of Pediatric and Adolescent Medicine, 154,* 11–15.

Ressler, R. K., Burgess, A. W., & Douglas, J. E. (1988). *Sexual homicide: Patterns and motives.* Lexington, MA: Lexington Books.

Samuelson, K. W., Krueger, C. E., Burnett, C., & Wilson, C. K. (2010). Neuropsychological functioning in children with post-traumatic stress disorder. *Child Neuropsychology, 16*(2), 119–133.

Schmahl, C. G., Vermetten, E., Elzinga, B. M., & Douglas-Bremner, J. (2003). Magnetic resonance of hippocampal and amygdale volume in women with childhood abuse and borderline personality disorder. *Psychiatry Research, 122*(3), 193–198.

Schnizer, P., & Ewigman, B. (2005). Child deaths resulting from inflicted injuries: Household risk factors and perpetrator characteristics, *Pediatrics, 116,* 687–693.

Solis, M. J., Shadur, J. M., Burns, A. R., & Hussong. A. M. (2012). Understanding the needs of children whose parents abuse substances. *Current Drug Abuse Review 5*(2), 135–147.

Sorensen, T., & Snow, B. (1991). How children tell: The process of disclosure of child sexual abuse. *Child Welfare, 70,* 3–15.

Sowell, E. R., Peterson, B. S., Thompson, P. M., Welcome, S. E., Henkenius, A. L., & Toga, A. W. (2003). Mapping cortical change across the human life span. *Nature Neuroscience, 6*(3), 309–315.

Springer, K. W., Sheridan, J., Kuo, D., & Carnes, M. (2007). Long-term physical and mental health consequences of childhood physical abuse: Results from a large population-based sample of men and women. *Child Abuse and Neglect, 31*(5), 517–530.

Straus, M.A. (2001). *Beating the devil out of them: Corporal punishment in American families and its effect on children.* Piscataway, NJ: Transaction.

Straus, M. A. (2000). Corporal punishment and primary prevention of physical abuse. *Child Abuse and Neglect, 24*(9), 1109–1114.

Stowman, S.A., & Donahue, B. (2005). Assessing child neglect: A review of standardized measures. Aggressive and Violent Behavior, 10, 491–512.

Thomlison, B. (2004). Child Maltreatment: A risk and protection factor perspective. In M. W. Fraser (Ed.), *Risk and resilience in childhood: An ecological perspective* (2nd ed.) (pp. 89–131). Washington, D.C.: National Association of Social Workers Press.

Thompson, K. M., & Wonderlich, S. A. (2004). Child sexual abuse and eating disorders. In J. K Thompson (Ed.), *Handbook of eating disorders and obesity* (pp. 679–694). Hoboken, NJ: Wiley & Sons.

Tolan, P. H., Sherrod, L. R., Gorman-Smith, D., & Henry, D. B. (2004). Building protection, support, and opportunity for inner-city children and youth and their families. In K. I. Maton, C. J. Schellenbach, B. J. Leadbeater, and A. L. Solarz (Eds.), *Investing in youth, families and communities: Strengths-based research and policy* (pp. 193–211). Washington, D.C.: American Psychological Association.

U.S. Department of Health and Human Services, Administration for Children and Families, Administration on Children, Youth and Families, Children's Bureau. (2011). Child Maltreatment 2010. Retrieved from http://www.acf.hhs.gov/programs/cb/stats_research/index.htm#can

Varese, F., Smeets, F., Drukker, M., Lieverse, R., Lataster, T. Viechtbauer ,W., … Bentall, R.P. (2012). Childhood adversities increase the risk of psychosis: A meta-analysis of patient-control: Prospective- and cross-sectional cohort studies. *Schizophrenic Bulletin, 38*(4), 661–671.

Wagner, G. N. (1986). Bitemark identification in child abuse cases. *Pediatric Dentistry, 8,* 96–100.

Walton, A. G. (2012, February 24). The long-term effects of spanking. *The Atlantic.* Retrieved from http://cdn.theatlantic.com/static/mt/assets/food/main%20thumb%20shutterstock_75783793.jpg

Watts-English, T., Fortson, B. L., Gibler, N., Hooper, S. R., & DeBellis, M. D. (2006). The psychology of maltreatment in childhood. *Journal of Social Issues, 62,* 717–736.

Wilson, D., & Horner, W. (2005). Chronic child neglect: Needed developments in theory and practice. *Families in Society: The Journal of Contemporary Social Services, 86*(4), 471–481.

Worling, J. R., Litteljohn, A., & Bookalam, M. A. (2010). Twenty-year prospective follow-up study of specialized treatment for adolescents. *Behavior, Science and Law, 28,* 46–57.

Young, C. (2014). Crying rape: False rape allegations exists and they are a serious problem. *Slate,* September 18, 2004. Retrieved from http://www.slate.com/articles/double_x/doublex/2014/09/false_rape_accusations_why_must_be_pretend_they_never_happen.html

Young, J.C., & Widom, C.S. (2014). Long-term effects of child abuse and neglect on emotional processing in adulthood. *Child Abuse and Neglect, 38*(8), 1369–1381. doi: 10,1016/j.chiabu.2014.03.008

CREDITS

CHAPTER NINE

Social Policy and Domestic Violence

LEARNING OBJECTIVES

At the end of this chapter, the student will be able to:

✓ Explain the belief that both the perpetrator and the victim of domestic violence are mentally ill;

✓ Understand Straus' position that both men and women are violent and how this position leads to a model of treatment;

✓ Identify the effects of domestic violence and postulate how these effects could be minimized thorough social policy;

✓ Outline the components of two models for understanding domestic violence, learned helplessness and conflict theory, and analyze the models to determine which model best describes the reality of domestic violence;

✓ Discuss how children are affected by domestic violence and interventions that could reduce these effects;

✓ Identify reasons why men are considered the perpetrators and women are the victims of violence and formulate a critique of this position;

✓ List arguments for broadening the definition of domestic violence to include female violence and discuss how this would shift the paradigm for explaining domestic violence;

✓ Label the components of a systems/dialectical perspective of domestic violence and determine if a systems/dialectical perspective is an improvement over other models.

SOCIAL POLICY AND DOMESTIC VIOLENCE

The previous chapter discussed child abuse and neglect and social policy. This chapter expands the topic of violence in the family to include the adult-partnered relationship and its influence on other relationships and events within the family. These forms of violence within the family include the physical, sexual, emotional, economic, and psychological. Recent attention to stalking and the use of cybertechnology have been included in a broader definition. To call greater attention to the incidences of **domestic violence** in American society, the Department of Justice proclaimed October 2009 as Domestic Violence Awareness Month, and to pledge greater cooperation of local, state, and federal law enforcement in reducing the incidences of domestic violence. The effects on the victims can be devastating long past the event and can lead to mental and emotional instability.

While the study of these forms of violence on family members has been undertaken for some time, there are still considerable gaps in knowledge about the risk factors for some groups of persons and the patterns associated with their occurrence.

Statistical data find that about one in three females (35.6%) and one in four (28.5%) males have been victims of violence by an intimate partner (Black et al., 2011). Both males and females have experienced some form of psychological violence by an intimate partner, and more than 50% have done so before their 25th birthday (Bureau of Justice Statistics, 2006). During the period of 1999 to 2004, approximately 22% of violence against women was committed by one's partner. Violence against one's partner occurs most often at home in the evening. While women of all races or ethnic groups are victims of domestic violence at about equal rates, separated women are more likely to be victimized than married women. Although women are victimized in urban and rural areas, the rate of victimization for urban women is greater than for rural women. During 2004, 2.2 million women called a hotline, and when women seek help, there is a reduction in the rate of abuse. For example, in 2004, there was about a 70% decrease in abuse when women contacted a shelter. Receiving services from a shelter reduced the rate of abuse in a follow-up when compared to women who did not seek services (Wolfe, Campbell, &Jaffe, 2012). Domestic violence is endemic and nearly three-fourths of persons acknowledged knowing a victim of domestic violence.

As stated elsewhere, the exact occurrences of domestic violence are hard to determine. Researchers have determined that the way information is gathered from spouses who are suspected of domestic violence is a key factor in obtaining correct information (Dryden-Edwards, n.d.). For example, direct questions about being hit may not generate correct information about the incident, while a more indirect questioning approach may produce more accurate information. Persons are less likely to admit to hitting their partners when asked directly, but would be forthcoming with information when asked an open-ended question.

Some domestic violence leads to **homicides** committed by married and unmarried partners at about the same rate (Bureau of Justice Statistics, 2006). About 30% of female homicides each year and 5% of male deaths result from partner violence. Abuse that leads to homicide generally has a long history of conflict in the relationship, and some escalation of the abuse has occurred. Such cases tend to be known by law enforcement and other social services agencies. Family and friends also have knowledge of the relationship stress that leads up to the homicide.

A frequent form of abuse that goes unnoticed is **male victimization**. Males are less likely to seek help and admit to being abused far less than females (Sorenson & Taylor, 2005). Female partners, as well as male partners, who tend to be highly controlling of their partners are more likely to abuse their partners than non-controlling partners. While male victimization tends to be far less severe than female victimization, the psychological and social damage is just as potent.

Husband battering was first discussed in the 1970s but continues today as a taboo subject. One of the first attempts to discuss husband battering was made by Steinmetz (1977), who used the Conflict Tactics Scale (CTS) to measure violence in intimate relationships. Her research concluded that husbands and wives had similar incidences of violence although varying in type. The Family Violence Research Program at the University of New Hampshire conducted a national enquiry into gender-related family violence and found that males and females engaged in relationship violence at the same rate (Straus, Steinmetz, & Gelles, 1980). While overall rates were comparable and, in some cases, female rates were higher in some categories of violence, it was clear from the studies that men engage in more severe forms of abuse. Subsequent research using larger samples, especially of minority groups, confirmed the initial research (Straus & Gelles, 1990).

The categories of violence from the Conflict Tactics Scale range from throwing something to beating up the partner (Straus & Gelles, 1990). It could be argued that these are vastly different forms of violence, occur for different reasons, and, consequently, are not comparable. On the other hand, some researchers have argued that when the categories of severe violence are pooled together, females actually engage in more severe violence than men (Stets & Strass, 1992). Another national study using the CTS was conducted in 1992 and, when compared to rates of violence in the previous two studies, it revealed that male violence had decreased significantly while female violence did not change (Stets & Strass,1992).

Some researchers have been very critical of the methodology using the CTS, because it does not consider the context, consequences, or severity of abuse (Kurzs, 1993). In addition, researchers point out that men tend to minimize their abusive acts, and women tend to overstate theirs (Jaffe, Lemon, & Poisson, 2003). Critics also raised the question of whether the abusive acts of women were in self-defense. Critics also point out that purely quantitative measures do not give the type of information that can determine antecedents to the abuse. Defenders of the CTS point to numerous other studies using other methodology that show similar results (Straus, 1999). They also emphasize that much of the survey data were actually gathered from females even though researchers made an effort to separate surveys filled out by males from surveys completed by females. Surveys completed by only females did not differ from the pooled surveys of both males and females.

The proponents of female battering contend that women do not initiate violence but do so in self-defense (Walker, 1984; Young, 2014). From this perspective, women are justified in their responses to being battered by taking actions, such as murdering the batterer. In other words, the definition of domestic violence that includes the view that women are violent only in self-defense prevents women from being considered murderers of their husbands. Men, for example, are not excused from being charged with murder for taking revenge against someone who has abused them in the past. This idea is partially supported by the finding that women are more likely to say that they use violence in response to the partner's violence, but it also gives support to the argument that women are more likely to use violence in self-defense (Saunders, 1986). However, other findings suggest that women were just as likely to initiate violence as men (Young, 2014). Typically, the argument that justifies female violence includes an array of male behaviors that might be offensive to women and is not just limited to male violence. Furthermore, by accepting the severity of injuries delineated between male and female violence, any act of female violence against a male could be justified.

Advocates for the view that women are victims of domestic violence and men are perpetrators point to the findings that men are six times more likely to cause physical damage than are women (Wolfe, Campbell, & Jaffe, 2012). Findings also reveal that women lose more time at work and are more psychologically damaged by abuse than men, especially with such conditions as depression and anxiety disorders. In addition, such knowledge as the above about the severity of abuse justifies the view that women are victims of domestic violence.

The other side of the argument would challenge the above paragraph, concluding that the assault should be the focus, not the injury (Wolfe, Campbell, & Jaffe, 2012). They would say that the focus on the injury not only minimizes female violence but actually supports it, since it would not define female violence that caused no injury as domestic violence. They would argue that the outcome would only identify domestic violence that causes injury; other forms of domestic violence would be ignored. Overall such a focus on males as perpetrators and establishing treatment centers, along with other ways of focusing on male violence, has reduced male violence. However, the lack of attention to female violence has resulted in no change in the level of female violence. This side would argue that prevention and treatment efforts should not cease and should be expanded to include female violence as well.

Researchers have noted that males tend to underreport being victims of abuse. Women are more likely to call police when they are victims, and the husband is more likely to be arrested (Stets & Straus, 1992). Because of this inconsistency in reporting abuse, only about 2% of women are arrested, and fewer than that are prosecuted (Brown, 2004). Some researchers have concluded that governmental surveys compared to independent researchers tend to show the widest gaps between male and female victimization (*Dutton vs. Nichols*, 2005).

A study by Canadian researchers Walsh and colleagues (2010) looking at both male and female perpetrators of domestic violence with a psychiatric disorder have similar profiles. This study also found that the styles of perpetrators generally given to male perpetrators can also be applied to females. For example, women who engage in a high level of violence against their partners in an intimate relationship also engage in violence outside the relationship. Furthermore, women whose violent episodes are infrequent and result in little injury to their partners are similar to males who display infrequent non-injury violence. While this study focused on psychiatric patients and might not represent all forms of domestic violence, it does give some insight into violence of males and females who engage in the most egregious forms of domestic violence.

In the U.S., the first national survey to determine the effects of abuse on men was recently conducted by Hines and Douglas (2011). The question can be raised regarding the assumptions going into the study, since it was sponsored by the Department of Mental Health, not the Department of Justice. In other words, researchers from the Department of Mental Health presuppose that violence toward men is a mental health concern, not a crime. Advocates for male rights on this issue would suggest that male victims are not treated with the same degree of concern as female victims. According to an international study by Mattingly and Straus (2008), more than 50% of males and females believe that, under certain circumstance it can be appropriate for females to slap their partners, while less than 30% believe that it can be appropriate for a male to slap a female. Kelly (1988) found that men are even more likely to be arrested than their abusing female partners when men call the police to report abuse against them.

Restraining orders are a typical means of creating distance between the perpetrator and the victim (Kelly, 1988). The perpetrator must stay a certain distance from the victim or risk being arrested for violating the restraining order. The vast majority of restraining orders are against men, some of whom are actual victims of the abuse; it means that they have limited or no access to their children and must relocate to a different residence, often at great cost (Kelly, 1988). In some states, such as Oregon, restraining orders can be issued on the basis of a potential victim's fear, rather than on specific threatening behaviors of the other party (Oregon Coalition against Domestic and Sexual Violence, 2017). Advocates for male rights as victims of domestic violence are calling for a redefinition that alters the concept of male-on-female violence to include both sexes.

Power and Control Wheel

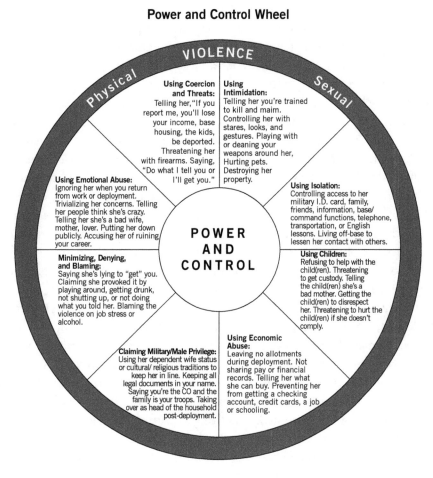

FIGURE 9.1 Power and control wheel

THE EFFECTS OF DOMESTIC VIOLENCE ON VICTIMS

Domestic violence usually refers to the physical and/or psychological damage inflicted by one partner in a relationship on the other partner (Rakovec-Felser, 2014). Different theories for the cause of domestic violence have been postulated, including a desire on the part of a partner to exert control, intimidation, or fear in his/her partner. **Conflict theory** has been used primarily by feminists to assert that a male may go to any length to isolate his partner from others who may gain awareness of the abuse or attempt to stop it (Zorza, 2006). Consequently, the abused partner is unable to take control of her life and, as a result, experiences social and psychological damage. The power and control wheel is rooted in the view that men have more power and are more privileged than women. In this view, men learn about being a batterer from a society that allows it, because women are considered second-class citizens (Zorza, 2006). The wheel of power is depicted with an inner hub of power and control and an outer realm of physical and sexual power, which is connected to internal spokes of the wheel. The inner spokes are comprised of intimidation, emotional abuse, isolation, minimization, children, male privilege, and economic abuse (Pence & Paymar, 1993).

The focus on women as the victims and men as perpetrators is justified by some researchers because of a number of factors. Although some researchers have found that the total acts of violence of men and women are approximately equal, significantly more women are at greater risk for physical injury than men (Serran & Firestone, 2004). Despite statistics to the contrary, some researchers hold that American society is still patriarchal and women are devalued (Serran & Firestone, 2004). Other researchers believe that this view of the victimization of women reflects a small number of incidences of wife battering but does not represent the vast majority of domestic violence, namely, that both males and females are violent at about the same rates (Dutton & Nicholls, 2005).

Conflict theory has been used by other theorists to explain domestic violence, including Murray Straus (1999). In developing the Conflict Tactics Scale, Straus postulated that any inequity in the marital relationship would be subject to control by the dominant partner, either male or female. Because of the hypothesis that the dominant partner of either sex would be more likely to maintain dominance by the use of violence, Straus departs from a purely gender-based view of dominance in relation to domestic violence. In addition, Straus focuses on a broader definition of abuse than wife battering and concludes that men and women have about the same rate of abuse, with men higher in some categories and women higher in others.

An early theory attempting to explain domestic violence was the belief that batterers were mentally ill (Yllo & Bogard, 1988). This explanation meant that both the perpetrator and the victim shared a type of illness in which the perpetrator used force and intimidation, while the victim tended to be masochistic and dependent. Researchers over time, however, did not find a close link between mental illness and abusing one's partner, because domestic violence is limited to the partner and not other people (Dutton, 2006). Likewise, the view that men are violent because of the inability to control their anger has not been widely accepted. According to Dutton, this view claims that men with **anger management** difficulties abuse their partners because of loss of control caused by drinking alcohol, other substance abuse, or emotional flooding that inhibits their ability to think rationally. The drugs lower the inhibition level and the anger emerges without the ability to control violence. This theory has limited support, because the batterer tends to choose the time, place, and person to exhibit his/her violent behavior. Researchers have found that the batterer is actually calm and controlled during the violent episodes, as opposed to being out of control. Other research indicates that women are generally the first to strike, which initially sets the violent episode in motion (Dutton, 2006).

A related theory to mental illness is the genetic or biological theory that postulates that trauma during development may account for the violence (Dutton & Starzomski, 1987). For example, physical trauma to the head has been found by some researchers to link with men who abuse their partners. The physical trauma results in brain damage, which interferes with normal cognitive functioning and the ability to control impulses (Dutton & Starzomski, 1987). When these men are met with crisis or conflict in a relationship, they are easily overcome with emotional impulses they cannot control and resort to violence. While this theory may have some relevance to some forms of abuse, the majority of domestic violent episodes are not explained by this theory.

Some researchers have referred to domestic violence as being the result of **learned helplessness** (Seligman, 1975); the victim is unable to leave the abusive relationship and has become dependent on a partner who subjects him or her to periodic abuse (Rakovec- Felser, 2014). A close corollary to learned helplessness is the belief that domestic violence creates a cycle resulting from increasing tension and stress, followed by the violent outburst, and then remorse by the perpetrator (Walker,

1984). This position may not take into account that there are other factors, such as social, economic, and cultural, that contribute to both the initiation and prevalence of abuse. In addition, contrary to the learned helplessness view, most research concludes that some women are reluctant to leave because of reprisals against their children and themselves, while other women make efforts to leave (DeKeseredy & Dragiewicz, 2007).

Some theories tend to emphasize the mutual nature of abuse. For example, systems theory, while not making the victim the cause of the abuse, views the nature of the partnership in which abuse occurs as the focus rather than individual members (Cahn & Lloyd, 1997). A systems analysis of domestic violence is that the relationship produces the abuse, and behaviors of both partners contribute, although at different levels. This view does not let the abuser off lightly but rather points out the interactional dynamic that leads to abuse. This model would criticize other perspectives that not only place blame on one party completely but demonize the abuser, while acknowledging no contribution from the victim. A systems perspective would eliminate the terms "perpetrator" and "victim" and replace them with the notion that abuse is occurring within the confines of a specific relationship. This perspective might also suggest that, because an abuser abuses in one relationship, he or she may not be abusive in another relationship. The mutual aspect of the abuse is frequently missing in most theories, because the focus is generally on the severity of the abuse, which typically points to a male perpetrator. Furthermore, a systems model of domestic violence would point out that, since men are also abused, the wheel of violence model and learned helplessness models do not apply, because their language and rationale presuppose a female victim.

A systems/dialectical perspective would not minimize female victimization, but would suggest that, contrary to other models, domestic violence occurrence is not homogeneous. Some domestic violence may occur, because the male partner views the female role as subordinate and the male role as privileged. However, there are many incidences of abuse in which both partners participate, albeit in different ways. To fully understand domestic violence, theoretical thinking must present a model that explains various relational factors that are intertwined (Bogard, 1999). For example, a woman who verbally abuses and slaps her partner, who then "loses" control and beats her up, may be different from the cool, calm, and collected wife batterer. A model that can incorporate disparate cases is more comprehensive than a model that merely fits perpetrators and victims into neat little boxes. A systems/dialectical model would suggest that gender alone is too narrow a focus for understanding the individual, familial, and societal contributions to domestic violence. Furthermore, data on domestic violence from all fronts suggest that there are two distinct forms, one resulting from male and female violence that occurs fairly evenly from both genders, and one resulting from severe wife beating.

Effects of Domestic Violence on Children

While much literature exists on the direct effects on children who are abused, a smaller body of research exists on the effects on children who observe domestic violence. However, in recent years, researchers have turned their attention to the short- and long-term effects of abuse on children (Kohl, Barth, & Hazen, 2005). One of the reasons for a focus on children as witnesses of domestic violence is that children tend to be present in abusive homes at about twice the rate of their presence in non-abusive homes (Fantuzzo & Mohr, 1999). Researchers have found that children who observe domestic violence conclude that witnessing violence can alter social relationships and, therefore, constitutes a type of abuse to the child (Somer & Braunstein, 1999). Although parents may think children are not aware of the violence, studies confirm that frequent marital abusive episodes have negative effects on children (Hague & Mullender, 2006). More children are present in families in the early years of marriage when most of the violence between partners occurs (Rennison & Welchan, 2000).

Researchers have identified witnessing abuse in a number of ways, including verbal without visual observation and seeing the effects of the abuse, such as the mother's black eye or bruises (Cunningham & Baker, 2004). While some studies have not made a distinction between hearing or seeing the abuse, the severity of the abuse tends to be the most important factor. Most recent studies have eliminated the term "witnessing" and adopted the term "exposure" to include all forms of direct and indirect risks from the child's awareness of domestic violence.

Although domestic violence can occur at any point in the lifespan, young couples are more vulnerable because of a higher incidence of alcohol and drug use, immaturity, and jealousy (Fantuzzo et al., 1997). Children under the age of five, who live in single-parent homes and below the poverty line, tend to often witness domestic violence in the home. According to Fantuzzo et al., while witnessing marital violence has generally not been given as a sole cause of long-term negative effects on emotional and psychological development of children, it has been viewed in combination with other co-existing risk factors. Moreover, much of the research of the effects of domestic violence on children has methodological problems, measures mother-only samples, or lacks clear theoretical models (Wolfe et al., 2003). Samples have been drawn mainly from shelters and data collected from mothers (McIntosh, 2003). These samples may not accurately depict the majority of times that children are exposed to partner violence.

Researchers have also tended to use check-list measures of behaviors of the child that do not correlate to the complexity of the family context (Wolfe et al., 2003). Variables such as the status of the family, intact versus single-parent family size, and family stress are inconsistently controlled by most researchers. It is also important to determine if the child witnessing the abuse has been abused, since these children might have more profound and negative reactions. Excluding and not controlling for variables reduces the predictability of such studies.

Some researchers have opted for a developmental model for determining the effects of a child witnessing domestic violence; such a model would allow for analyzing a multitude of factors that might also co-effect development (Wolfe et al., 2003). Researchers have often had difficulty separating the effects of direct abuse from indirect abuse, because the outcomes have been the same. In recent research, investigators are more interested in understanding the whole context in which the abuse is occurring (Wolfe et al., 2003).

The ecological theory of Bronfenbrenner (1986) is also a helpful module in understanding the social contextual factors associated with domestic violence. This model assumes that domestic violence would have an impact on the child in a number of ways. For example, children who witness domestic violence may be more prone to engage in abusive acts as adults (Jenkins & Bell, 1997). The impact on children results from children not only seeing the violence but learning that it can be an appropriate way to resolve differences in intimate relationships (Margolin & Gordis, 2003). Moreover, because approximately half of the children who witness domestic violence will also be maltreated, the effects of witnessing violence are compounded.

The effects of witnessing domestic violence on children are categorized into three patterns. First, children are affected behaviorally, emotionally, and socially (Hughes, Graham-Bermann, & Gruber, 2001). These children typically have poor coping skills and may develop a number of problems that affect their adjustment and interaction with others. Hughes et al. (2001) point out that, sometimes, behavioral problems are expressed through the withdrawal of oppositional behavior. The frequency of the violence and time between episodes are important variables in the severity of the effects on the child. Second, children who witness domestic violence tend to have problems in adulthood with depression and other emotional problems. Third, some researchers have found a link to cognitive deficits.

Studies linking the effects of domestic violence on children to intelligence quotient (IQ) have generally had methodological problems (Koenen, Moffitt, Caspi, Taylor, & Purcell, 2003). The association that some researchers have found between IQ and witnessing domestic violence has not controlled for the IQ of parents. A recent study attempting to eliminate the previous weaknesses in studies found that children exposed to domestic violence had a reduction of about eight IQ points; it also suggests that, as with other negative social factors, there are long-term effects in childhood development (Koenen, Moffitt, Caspi, Taylor, & Purcell, 2003).

The ongoing occurrence of domestic violence in the home undermines basic needs of children. For example, Chaffin et al. believe that the best outcome in children is when they are in a safe and supportive environment. Children need regular routines and a sense of normalcy and consistency. They need parents who are aware of their needs and have positive interaction patterns. Domestic violence reduces all of these factors, because parents are too focused on their own problems to adequately parent. The reduction of parenting effectiveness is true for both the perpetrator and the victim (Chaffin et al., 2004).

Children reared in homes in which violence between parents is frequent may over identify with one parent and see themselves in much the same way (Chaffin et al., 2004). For example, children who identify with the victim may believe that it is allowable to be dominated or abused by another person. On the other hand, identifying with the abuser justifies the use of force to get one's way in intimate relationships. In addition, domestic violence may also signal a loss of respect for both parents. Parents who are viewed as engaging in such violence behavior may be seen by children as somewhat defective or lacking in character, resulting in a minimizing of the parents' influence on children. It is more likely that children in this situation turn to other means of support, such as peers.

Ethnicity and Race and Domestic Violence

With the changing demographics in the U.S., there is a need to understand the role of ethnicity and race in domestic violence. At present, little research exists on minorities and the impact of domestic violence on minority families and children (Rennison & Planty, 2003). Most of the research that does exist on minorities and domestic violence focuses on social or cultural factors rather than specific familial circumstances (Pearlman, Zierler, Gjelsvik, & Verhoek-Oftedahl, 2003). For the most part, the focus on minority families has been on African Americans and Hispanics and has largely ignored Native Americans and Asian Americans (Lee, Sanders-Thompson, & Mechanic, 2002). The tendency among some researchers is to compare majority subjects with all minority subjects in one category. Generally ignored in studies on ethnicity and race are mixed-race persons (Raj & Silverman, 2002).

Researchers have found that race plays an important role in the prevalence of domestic violence. A study by Rennison and Welchans (2000) found that African American women had a 35% higher rate of domestic violence than the majority of women. The racial group with the highest rate of violence was Native American. Some studies have also included poverty as a variable, because minority women of all races tend to be overrepresented below the poverty line. In fact, Rennison and Planty (2003) found that when poverty was accounted for, there were no differences in domestic violence among women of different ethnic and racial groups.

Resilience in Children

Researchers have noted that some children are not affected by witnessing domestic violence (Hughes, Graham-Bermann, & Gruber, 2001), which has lead to investigations regarding why some children are unaffected. The term **resilience** has been applied to children unaffected by domestic violence and means that they are able to function normally despite the adverse situation. Resilience is viewed as evolving from individual traits and environmental resources that combine to reduce the **risks factors** (Richman & Fraser, 2001). Although little research exists exclusively on resilience and exposure to domestic violence, application from other relevant research on risk to violence is useful. **Protective factors**, ranging from the child's self-directed behavior to adult support, may have an impact on the severity of the effects from exposure to domestic violence. **Attachment style** is also an important variable in how domestic violence affects the child. For example, having a secure attachment with a caregiver acts as a protective factor for the child (Radford & Hester, 2006). Some studies have shown that the wider social network is important, because parents may not provide the emotionally supportive role that is needed (Radford & Hester, 2006). Child care workers, grandparents, and others with frequent contact with the child may help buffer the child from the severity of the abuse.

Individual traits that are related to resilience in children exposed to domestic violence include problem-solving skills, autonomy, and social skills (Iwaniec, Larkin, & Higgins, 2006). Resilient children have a greater sense of responsibility, overall high cognitive functioning, and bond with the non-abusing parent. According to Alvord and Grados (2005), other traits that are protective include positive thinking, taking initiative, and motivation. When children are able to self-regulate their responses to negative situations, it dampens the escalation of negative responses from others. An **easy temperament**, which is generally viewed as a lifelong stable trait, can provide a buffer against negative experiences. The age of the child has been noted by some researchers as being an important factor, because younger children are more prone to internalize and blame themselves (Alvord & Grados, 2005).

External factors that interact with **internal traits** are considered to be very important in resilience in children (Alvord & Grados, 2005). These factors include the family and social network, community, and culture. In terms of family, the style of parenting is an impactful variable. When parents are warm and supportive of children and discipline in a firm but flexible manner, children have greater resilience skills. Also of importance in the development of resilience is the amount of time that parents spend with their children and appropriate family organization and structure. Aside from parents and the immediate family, the extended family network can also affect the development of resilience in children.

The role of the teacher and impact on the child cannot be minimized in that the child may experience the teacher as a surrogate parent. Strong and positive relationships with peers at school increase self-esteem and self-efficacy, as can participation in extracurricular activities (Alvord & Grados, 2005). Community activities, such as recreational sports; social organizations, like boy or girl scouts; and other community involvement, help develop a sense of acceptance and belonging to a group, which might reduce the effects of exposure to parental violence. Culture may play an equally important role in resilience. Rates of domestic violence tend to be the same across different ethnic and racial groups, although Asian Americans show a lower rate than others. This rate may be underreported, however, because of the culture imperative not to divulge intimate details of the family to others (Burman & Chantler, 2005). Because minorities tend to have higher rates of poverty and poverty correlates to reported cases of abuse, it is assumed that minority children may be at greater risks for negative effects of domestic violence than other children. Exposure over a longer period of time may also affect children in poverty, because women in abusive relationships have fewer options than other women (Gewirtz & Edleson, 2004). The negative effects are exacerbated with multiple risk factors.

In summation, the development of resilience involves a number of factors, including supportive parenting; bonding with a parent; bonding with adults outside the family, such as teachers and caregivers; participation in school activities; and a community that recognizes domestic violence. Resilience is an ongoing trait that needs vigilance to reduce the risk factors that undermines it.

SOCIAL POLICY AND DOMESTIC VIOLENCE

Public policy on domestic violence is influenced by a number of agencies and foundations, one of which is the National Coalition Against Domestic Violence (NCADV) (n.d.). A major purpose of the NCADV is to influence legislative efforts in states and at the national level regarding the ending of domestic violence and supporting the rights of women to live free of fear and danger in their intimate relationships. Another agency, the National Network to End Domestic Violence (NNEDV) (n.d.), has a similar function as the NCADV (n.d.) of influencing legislation and the reauthorization of the Violence Against Women Act (VAWA) (n.d.), which was passed by both houses of Congress and signed by the president into law in March 2013. This law is instrumental in creating treatment options for women who are victims of dating violence; college women who are victimized; minorities, including Native Americans; immigrant women; women living in public housing; and lesbian, gay, bisexual, and transgendered victims.

The California Partnership to End Domestic Violence (CPEDV) (n.d.) aims to hold perpetrators accountable and create funding sources to provide ongoing services to victims of abuse. In addition, the CPEDV attempts to develop partnerships with other agencies and engage the civil and criminal court systems to better pursue justice for the victims of domestic violence. The CPEDV policy links domestic violence with gun violence because of the number of incidences in which gun violence is used or threatened to be used. The linking of domestic violence is based on statistics that relate to the increased possibility of a homicide from domestic violence when a gun is in the home. This policy especially attempts to join legislation in the California Assembly on domestic violence to promote the elimination of firearms from the home. Securing state and federal funds to combat domestic violence is another major policy purpose.

Prevention of domestic violence and the subsequent effects on children is a major endeavor of some public policy groups, such as *Futures Without Violence* (FWV) (n.d.). This policy-making group aims to reduce children's exposure to parental violence and supports the VAWA (2005). A specific component of that law, Children Exposed to Violence and Abuse, addresses the effects of domestic violence on children by training educational and child care personnel to recognize risk factors in children who may be exposed to domestic violence and can be referred to appropriate treatment services. In addition, FWV supports giving more attention to dating relationships in which violence occurs as a means of curtailing violence in relationships. Research demonstrates that dating violence continues after marriage, and one of the crucial components of violence in dating is attitudes about the acceptability of violence in resolving relationship problems. Children from ages eleven to nineteen would be the targets of educational material meant to change attitudes about the acceptability of violence. More focus would be on middle school children, since peer group influence is highest during these years.

While domestic violence generally occurs in the home and maintains privacy and secrecy in this way, FWV (n.d.) broadens its policy umbrella to include the workplace. Persons who work and are victims of domestic violence carry over much of the effects into the workplace. Stress, anxiety, and fear may affect their work performance by distracting them from job responsibilities. Some female victims miss work as a result of victimization but they may also receive verbally abusive calls while at work.

TABLE 9.1 California penal laws

SOME COMMON CALIFORNIA PENAL CODE SECTIONS REGARDING DOMESTIC VIOLENCE.
273.5 PC Spousal Abuse or Cohabitant Abuse—This establishes penalties for inflicting physical abuse on partner, resulting in injury.
243(e)(1) PC Battery—This law is similar to 273.5 PC Spousal Abuse or Cohabitant Abuse except no noticeable injury is necessary.
422 PC Terrorist Threats—This law prohibits making a threat to harm another in the home.
646.9 PC Stalking—Prohibits following or stalking so that a person might be fearful for his/her safety.
591 PC Malicious Destruction of Phone Lines—Disallows the removal or destruction of any electrical lines related to communications outside the family.
273.6 PC Violation of Domestic Violence Protective Order—Prohibits the violation of any restraining order.
12028.5 PC Family Violence/Firearms Seizure—This law allows the police to temporarily seize any weapon in plain view or discovered during a lawful search for up to 72 hours for its own protection or for the protection of others in the home.
12021(g) PC Restrictions on Firearm Possession—This law prohibits persons under a Restraining Order from obtaining a firearm, except in the case of settlement of community property.
6389 PC Relinquishment Of Firearms—Prohibits a person under a Restraining Order from owning a gun during the time the order is in effect except in the case of person who owns a gun by virtue of his/her job.

Adapted From: http://www.lapdonline.org/get_informed/content_basic_view/8887

The NCADV (n.d.) believes that violence against women and children results from the abuse of power and desire to dominate others. Furthermore, the NCADV believes domestic violence stems for the same desire to dominate as sexism, homophobia, classism, and anti-Semitism. The NCADV supports establishment of safe homes and shelters for women and children, in addition to eliminating the root cause of the desire to dominate others. Among the goals of NCADV are empowering women and children, and educating potential high-risk individuals and the public at large. All ethnic and racial groups are targeted in the effort to educate and inform persons of domestic violence. NCADV releases facts sheets and policy updates on domestic violence, including workplace violence, male victim violence, dating violence, effects on children, and domestic violence in minority communities. In addition, NCADV supports many community and national programs, including the *Remember my Name Project*, which is a list of the names of women and family members who have lost their lives during the year because of domestic violence.

Congressional legislation has been concerned about domestic violence, because many of the recipients of governmental programs, such as welfare, are victims of domestic violence. The Wellstone/Murray amendment in 1997 to the Personal Responsibility and Work Opportunity Reconciliation Act of 1996 (PRWORA) gave states the option to waive some of the requirements, such as work, for victims of domestic violence (Kogan, 2005). This amendment was meant to help battered women who do not meet the requirements to receive welfare cash funds. In short order, states adopted exceptions to their welfare law to continue benefits to battered women. Although this amendment was meant to provide needed assistance to battered women, Kogan documents the failure to achieve this purpose.

In reviewing social policy agencies there is a decided sameness in the definition of domestic violence; namely, that women and children are victims and men are perpetrators. There is little acknowledgement that women can be and, in fact, are violent. The types of prevention and treatment programs are geared toward protecting women and children. These assumptions and concepts affecting the defining of domestic violence are challenged by some researchers. For example, Kelly (2003) points out that one of the underlying assumptions to the definition is that it should not be altered, because it rests on long-established views of **patriarchy** and male privilege. Therefore, to challenge the definition of domestic violence and assert that women can also be violent is to challenge an established cultural definition. For this reason, Kelly and others believe that changing the definition will always be contested.

According to Kelly (2003), the limiting of a redefinition of domestic violence carries over to a discussion on methodology. A methodology that does not begin with the assumption of male privilege and control would not be allowed. Quantitative methodology is the preferred method of many domestic violence researchers, according to Kelly, because it does not challenge the supposition that men are violent and women are victims. Furthermore, the dialectic between **quantitative** and **qualitative research** is viewed by some as not contributing to an insightful dialogue on domestic violence.

Other considerations abound in the resistance to reframe defining domestic violence to include both males and females. Kelly (2003) points out that all of the funding for domestic violence prevention and treatment is for female victims. A redefinition would mean that new programs would have to be developed, and funds now used for female prevention and treatment programs may be diverted to fund programs for male victims. Diverting funds toward programs for men would be viewed as undermining the rights of women (Intimate Violence, as cited in Kelly, 2003). Kelly points out that, currently, the stance for most programs on domestic violence is to ignore and deny that females are also violent.

Mahoney's (n.d., as cited in Kelly, 2003) **separation assault theory of domestic violence** attempts to explain why women do not leave an abusive relationship. This theory postulates that women do not leave an abusive relationship, because leaving is not possible. In such a no-exit relationship, women are then justified in taking action against their partners, even to the extent of murder. Sometimes referred to as **battered wife's syndrome**, the wife who takes violent action against an abusing husband is appropriately acting in the only way she can to be free from the constant degradation of an abusive husband.

One of the most frequent ways for local governments to respond to domestic violence is in **mandatory warrantless arrest** of the perpetrator. Studies are fairly evenly divided on the effectiveness of mandatory warrantless arrests, but advocates for this policy persist in defending it (Kelly, 2003). The real issue is not so much whether mandatory arrests are the most effective policy, but that the public display of arrest implies public scorn and disapproval that other ways of addressing domestic violence would not. Furthermore, an arrest is a symbolic act that takes the abuser out of the privacy of the home and makes it a public act. Mandatory arrests also serve another purpose by taking the discretion of making an arrest away from the officer. The entire legal and judicial systems swing into action if the officer believes that arrest is warranted. The victim as well as the perpetrator have no discretion or choice to alter what comes next.

On the other hand, some researchers believe that mandatory arrests do not work for all persons, especially those living in poverty-level communities (Kelly, 2003). Poor communities with limited resources would benefit more from non-criminalized treatment procedures, such as shelters, and other treatment approaches. Both sides of the argument might agree that mandatory arrests might tend to deter some women from reporting abuse, because it might create more risk of danger than not reporting the abuse. Arresting the perpetrator may also cause economic instability in the family if the perpetrator is the only breadwinner.

The advocates against mandatory arrests would also say that while mandatory arrests may have protected many women, it did so at the expense of women having no voice to alter the legal process (Goodmark, 2009). Advocates against mandatory arrests would say that forcing all women into the same response to violence reduces individual freedom and decision making. From this perspective, women would be viewed as collective rather than individual, which deny women self-determination.

On the other hand, advocates for mandatory arrests point out that officers have less pressure from abusers or from victims who can attempt to sway their decisions (Goodmark, 2009). It also means that law enforcement and the courts were serious about domestic violence and would be an unequivocal message that domestic violence would not go unpunished. Women could rest assured that the perpetrators would have to determine if they wanted to continue with the abuse, given the punishment.

Advocates for mandatory arrests point to the need to proceed with prosecution even when the victim is afraid or refuses to participate for other reasons, which leads to the concept of **victimless prosecution** (Goodmark, 2009). The victim did not have to testify, since other evidence could be introduced by the prosecution. Victimless prosecution also undercut victims who recanted or wanted to testify in support of the perpetrator. Victimless prosecution paved the way for other prosecutor policies, including the **no-drop policy**—cases in which no maneuver can prevent a conviction (Goodmark, 2009).

Surveys of victims who called the police during a domestic violence experience revealed that when the perpetrator was a man, in almost half of the cases, the police asked him to leave the home, but no cases were reported when the female perpetrator was asked to leave the home (Intimate violence, as cited by Kelly, 2003). Kelly concluded that the police, like the general public, are greatly influenced by the limited definition of domestic violence.

Generally, the courts have also taken a limited view of domestic violence, such as in the case of *Thurman v. City of Torrington* (1985, as cited in Kelly, 2003). This case became the benchmark for a gender-based view of domestic violence in perpetuity. According to Kelly, the result of court cases such as *Thurman* was to reinforce the gender-based view of domestic violence and to support mandatory arrests and punishment of male perpetrators. In addition, all efforts to prosecute perpetrators of domestic violence focus on males rather than females.

Another reason for resistance to broadening the definition of domestic violence, according to Kelly (2003), is that the view of women being weak and defenseless does not fit with the view that women can also be aggressive. As a result, advocates for a limited definition of domestic violence can control the public debate. Furthermore, Kelly believes that not only is the public debate limited on domestic violence but the legal advantage that women have as victims allows them greater protection under the law and reduces legal protection for battered men. Kelly concludes that this gender bias regarding domestic violence is reflected in all levels of societal interactions. Perhaps the most disturbing circumstance is victim refusal to participate (Buzawa & Buzawa, 2003 as cited in Kelly, 2003). As in other situations regarding domestic violence, gender-specific considerations determine the expected outcome that would force prosecution of male perpetrators.

While defining and prosecuting domestic violence has taken a limited path, the same might be said for treatment, or **rehabilitation,** which is almost always the preferred response through laws and policies (Kelly, 2003). The policy to rehabilitate perpetrators appears to be inconsistent with a concurrent policy to incarcerate perpetrators. This confusion in policy is supported by the view that males need treatment and the crime of domestic violence is one of patriarchal and negative male attitudes. While studies tend not to support a treatment-oriented approach, advocates for the limited definition of domestic violence reinforce their view of the causes of domestic violence by creating treatment regimens that coincide. According to Kelly (2003), domestic violence prosecution never includes a discussion on female batterers.

Treatment programs consist of males taking responsibility for the violence and attending such treatment programs as anger management (Kelly, 2003). Generally, treatment programs concur with the accepted label that men are responsible for the violence, and women are victims. The Wheel of Violence referred to above became one of the paradigm prototypes for both conceptualizing domestic violence and treating perpetrators. Based on the assumption that men attempt to dominate women through the use of force, treatment programs consist of eradicating sexism. Kelly and others believe that treatment approaches for male perpetrators is a disguised way of convincing men that their limited definition based on patriarchy is the core position to take. Such treatment programs would be geared toward male perpetrators and their need to control anger. Any treatment programs that might lift the blame from males, such as couples therapy, would not be recommended as effective treatment. The treatment that males receive is laced with the view of male domination and female subordination. The goal of treatment is to "unlearn" cultural and societal indoctrination that women are less valuable than men. Men must learn new models of society to replace the old sexist models.

Both sides of this debate would argue that ending violence based on sexism is a desirable outcome (Kelly, 2003). The critics of the female victim model of domestic violence do not object to ending violence toward women, but do object to the limited definition and treatment objectives that fail to acknowledge female violence. When women use violence, the assumption is that they use violence in self-defense, do not initiate it, and consequently, do not need the same treatment regimen (Kelly, 2003).

The one-sided treatment approach is in no place more visible than in the establishing of shelters. While shelters have been around since the 1970s, the array of services in contemporary society is geared toward improving the lives of women and providing countless services that are also available to the general public (Kelly, 2003). Researchers have raised the question of whether shelters are effective given the methodological problems in the research (Gondolf & Fisher, as cited in Kelly, 2003). For example, measures of participant satisfaction, reoccurrence of violence, and rates of continued separation from the perpetrator are not viewed by some researchers as rigorous enough to determine the success of shelters. Some researchers believe that the recurrence of domestic violence rates after shelter services could be an important way to measure success of shelters, but generally fail to do so, because an adequate control group was not used. Critics of the use of shelters point to some risks for an increase in violence for shelter users. Advocates for shelters point out that as the increase in violence occurs when women are less serious about leaving and changing the dynamics of the relationship.

Critics of shelters and females as victims of domestic violence view shelters as confirming the assumption that women cannot be violent and that men need to be controlled (Kelly, 2003). In order to free victims from oppression, the shelter works to remove abused women from their oppressive relationships and helps them begin to establish new lives free from abuse. The shelter is viewed by advocates of female victimizations as a respite from the life of oppression that they have been forced to live (Kelly, 2003). While some shelters for males victims of violence have been established, the ongoing public support for such shelters has not materialized; the concept of males as victims of violence does not fit into the dominant paradigm of female victimization.

Kelly (2003) argues that the current policy regarding domestic violence does not adequately address the problem. Limiting the definition of domestic violence to male perpetrators and providing services that address only women denies the broader context of violence and, therefore, obscures the true picture of violence in intimate relationships. Kelly believes that what is needed now is a redefinition of domestic violence so that a new paradigm and treatment modality can emerge. What has hampered the development of theory is the lack of an appropriate dialectical process in which the dominant definition of domestic violence can be challenged. For example, domestic violence takes different forms and cannot be categorized into a neat package. Not even all batterers are homogenous; batterers batter for different reasons. Challenging the accepted view would provide more accuracy in understanding domestic violence and allow for more effective policies to emerge. The view that only men are violent must be challenged and a concomitant acknowledgement that women can be violent must be part of an expanded definition of domestic violence.

A SYSTEMS/DIALECTICAL PERSPECTIVE OF DOMESTIC VIOLENCE

An expanded definition of domestic abuse would allow for treatment to go beyond one-sided models, such as the Wheel of Violence Model. Advocates for a new model for conceptualizing domestic violence would allow for programs that are now established, such as improvement of poor verbal and social skills, methods of conflict negotiation, and mediation of differences, to be applied to all perpetrators, including female perpetrators. While it needs to still be acknowledged that some perpetrators do fit the definition of a male batterer and have sexist attitudes about women, and some may be psychopathic batterers devoid of empathy, it must also be understood that other forms of domestic violence occur and need equal attention. Perhaps more services at shelters should center on support of females and males to improve their personal and social lives.

The social policy dialectic regarding domestic violence pits advocates for the status quo against a broader view of violence that acknowledges male battering and the existence of female violence. As stated above, feminist theory is based on inequality of the sexes, which is grounded in the very core of society (Pence & Paymar, 1993). Society teaches men to be aggressive and women to be non-aggressive. Advocates for the status quo do acknowledge that women can be violent, but women's violence causes much less injury and is not a social problem with roots in oppression and lack of freedom to determine one's own life as is the case with men.

Advocates for a limited definition of domestic violence believe that treatment should be aligned with the **Duluth Model** (n.d.), which developed from a groundswell of interests after a number of incidences of domestic violence in Duluth, Minnesota. As stated above, the goal is to educate men about appropriate gender roles and how roles become toxic for victims of domestic violence. Educating men about the effects of sexist views on gender roles forms the crux of treatment for male perpetrators. In applying the Duluth model, there is no treatment for female perpetrators.

While the limited definition view regarding domestic violence tends to be the dominant model for most programs and treatment approaches, some aspects of violence cannot be applied to this model. For example, violence in gay and lesbian relationships has come under scrutiny in recent literature. The limited definition model for addressing same-sex violence in lesbian relationships, if explained by power and domination, would undermine the foundation for explaining male violence based on domination. If women can also be violent to each other, then, perhaps, they can also be violent with men. In addition, this position also has problems explaining violence toward children and occasional violence to other family members. The question also arises as to how frequently violence needs to occur in order to be addressed as a social issue. By not addressing female violence at all, a form of violence goes unacknowledged and muddles the social policy issue on domestic violence.

Advocates in support of the limited definition of domestic violence as the main policy foundation point out that the bottom line is that women are severely injured while men are not (Kelly, 2003). Much research using the CTS does not identify the context in which violence occurs. As a result, advocates for a limited definition state that the conclusion that women are as violent as men is a false assumption. Furthermore, they believe that funding for shelters and other forms of treatment for female victims and treatment for male perpetrators are the foundation for eradicating domestic violence.

A systems/dialectical perspective on domestic violence would also deplore sexism and any other belief system that contributes to female battering. It would also support means of reducing the effects of violence in homes and in society at large. While acknowledging the need to continue efforts to reduce female victimization, a systems/dialectical perspective would challenge the one-sided approach that now drives policy on domestic violence. Other forms of violence in the home must receive equal attention in social policy positions. Based on studies that conclude that mutual violence is often evident in families where the male is determined to be the perpetrator, a new understanding of the broader context of violence is justified.

Dutton and Nicholls (2005) believe that domestic violence occurs because of frustration, anxiety, and dysfunction in the development of relationship intimacy. Since violence occurs in similar frequency in lesbian relations, it can be assumed that gender domination is not the major factor. Acknowledging the idea of intimacy problems as the underlying cause of violence would redirect much of the attention in both prevention and treatment toward a relationship contextual paradigm.

KEY TERMS

Domestic violence
Homicides
Male victimization
Husband battery
Restraining order
Conflict Theory
Conflict Tactics Scale
Anger management
Learned helplessness

Ecological theory
Resilience
Risk factors
Protective factors
Attachment style
Easy temperament
External factor
Internal traits
Patriarchy

Quantitative research
Qualitative research
Separation assault theory
    of domestic violence
Victimless prosecution
Rehabilitation
No-drop policy
Duluth Model

STUDY QUESTIONS TO ACCOMPLISH THE LEARNING OBJECTIVES

1. Explain the view that both the victim and the perpetrator of domestic violence are mentally ill. Defend your position.

2. On what basis does Murray Straus conclude that men and women commit equal acts of violence? Compare and contrast the different points of view. Compose a theoretical frame that would justify Straus' position.

3. List the effects of domestic violence on the victim. Illustrate how these effects are present in daily living. Generate ideas for minimizing these effects.

4. Define learned helplessness and conflict theory. Discuss which theory, conflict theory or learned helplessness, best accounts for research findings in domestic violence. Support your conclusion with research findings.

5. How are children affected by domestic violence? What social policy initiative could be developed to address these issues?

6. Discuss how some children are less affected by domestic violence than others. What factors contribute to resilience? Relate your conclusions to a theoretical model.

7. Review arguments that men are perpetrators and women are victims of domestic abuse. Critically analyze this conclusion, and evaluate the veracity of this position.

8. Recall arguments that domestic violence should be defined broadly to include female violence. Explain the basis for these arguments.

9. Identify the current treatment model for domestic violence. How appropriate is the current treatment approach for domestic violence? Discuss the weaknesses.

10. How does a systems/dialectical position view domestic violence? Explain the pros and cons of this approach? Judge whether it is an improvement over other models.

DEBATE ACTIVITY FOR STUDENTS

Consider the following proposition: The definition of domestic violence should be broadened to include verbal and emotional abuse of one's partner.

- Review refereed literature on this topic. Do a library and Internet search to find relevant material. Investigate some of the additional readings.

- Develop three arguments for the proposition.

- Develop three arguments against the proposition.

- How do the arguments relate to other systems, such as the community or culture?

- Is there common ground?

- What are the long-term consequences of taking action?

- What new or common-ground solutions should be offered? If no common ground, what new position could emerge from a dialogue between the two positions? How is the new position superior to the original positions?

REFERENCES

Alvord, M. K., & Grados, J. J. (2005). Enhancing resilience in children: A proactive approach. *Professional Psychology: Research and Practice, 36*, 238–245.

Black, M. C., Basile, K. C., Breding, M. J., Smith, S. G., Walters, M. L., Merrick, M. T., ... Stevens, M. R. (2011). *The National Intimate Partner and Sexual Violence Survey (NISVS): 2011 Summary Report.* Atlanta GA: National Center for Injury Prevention and Control, Centers for Disease Control and Prevention.

Bograd, M. (1999). Strengthening domestic violence theories: Intersections of race, class, sexual orientation, and gender. *Journal of Marital and Family Therapy, 25*, 275–289. doi: 10.1111/j.1752-0606.1999.tb00248.x.

Bronfenbrenner, U. (1986). Alienation and the four worlds of childhood. *Phi Delta Kappan*, February, 430–436.

Brown, G. (2004). Gender as a factor in the response of the law-enforcement system to violence against partners. *Sexuality and Culture, 8,* 1–87.

Bureau of Justice Statistics. (2006). Intimate Partner Violence in the U.S. 1993, 2004, 2006.

Burman, E., & Cantler, K. (2004). There's no place like home: Emotional geographies of researching race and refuge provisions in Britain. *Gender, Place & Culture, 11*(3), 375–397.

Burman, E., & Chantler, K. (2005). Domestic violence and minoritisation: Legal and policy barriers facing minoritised women leaving violent relationships. *International Journal of Law and Psychiatry, 28* (1), 59–74.

Cahn, D. D., & Lloyd, S. A. (Eds.). (1997). *Family violence from a communication perspective.* Thousand Oaks CA: Sage.

California Partnership to End Domestic Violence (CPEDV). (n.d.). Retrieved from http://www.cpedv.org/

Chaffin, M., Slovsky, J. F., Funderburk, B., Valle, L. A., Brestan, E. V., Balachova, T., … Bonner, B. L. (2004). Parent-child interaction theory with physically abusive parents efficacy for reducing future abuse reports. *Journal of Consulting and Clinical Psychology, 72*(3), 874–884. doi:10.1037/0022-006X.72.3.500.

Cunningham, A., & Baker, L. (2004) What about me? Seeking to understand a child's view of violence in the family. London, Canada: Centre for Child & Families in the Justice System.

DeKeseredy, W. S., & Dragiewicz, M. (2007). Understanding the complexities of feminists' perspective on women abuse: A commentary of Donald G. Dutton's rethinking domestic violence. *Violence Against Women, 12*(8), 874–884.

Dryden-Edwards, R. (n.d.). Domestic violence. MedicineNet.com. Retrieved from http://www.medicinenet.com/domestic_violence/article.htm

Duluth Model. (n.d.). Retrieved from http://www.theduluthmodel.org/training/wheels.html

Dutton, D. G. (2006). *Rethinking domestic violence.* Vancouver, Canada: UBC Press.

Dutton, D. G., & Nicholls, T. (2005). The gender paradigm in domestic violence research and theory: Part I—The conflict of theory and data. *Aggression and Violent Behavior, 10*(6), 680–714.

Dutton, D. G., & Starzomski, A. J. (1987). The abusive personality and the Minnesota Power Wheel. *Journal of Interpersonal Violence, 12*(1), 70–82.

Fantuzzo, J. W., & Mohr, W. K. (1999). The Future of children: Prevalence and effects of child exposure to domestic violence. *Domestic Violence and Children 9*(3), 21–32.

Fantuzzo, J. W., Boruch, R., Beriama, A., Atkins, M., & Marcus, S. (1997). Domestic violence and children: Prevalence and risk in five major U.S. cities. *Journal of the American Academy of Child and Adolescent Psychiatry, 36,* 116–122.

Futures Without Violence (FWV). (n.d.). Retrieved from http://www.futureswithoutviolence.org/

Gewirtz, A., & Edleson, J. L. (2004). Young children's exposure to adult domestic violence: The case for early childhood research and support (Series Paper #6). Retrieved from http://www.uiowa.edu/~social wk/publications.html

Goodmark, L. (2009). Autonomy feminism: An anti-essentialist critique of mandatory interventions in domestic violence. Retrieved from http://works.bepress.com/leigh_goodmark/6

Hague, G., & Mullender, A. (2006). Who listens? The voices of domestic violence survivors in service provision in the United Kingdom. *Violence Against Women, 12*(6), 568–587. doi: 10.1177/1077801206289132.

Hines, D. A., & Douglas, E. M. (2011). Symptoms of post-traumatic stress syndrome disorder in men who sustain intimate partner violence: A study of help-seeking and community samples. *Psychology of Men and Masculinity, 12*(2), 112–127.

Hughes, H. M., Graham-Bermann, S. A., & Gruber, G. (2001). Resilience in children exposed to domestic violence. In S.A. Graham-Bermann and J. L. Edleson (Eds.), *Domestic violence in the lives of children: The future of research, intervention, and social policy* (pp. 67–90). Washington, D.C.: American Psychological Association.

Iwaniec, D., Larkin, E., & Higgins, S. (2006). Research review: Risk and resilience in cases of emotional abuse. *Child & Family Social Work, 11*(1), 72–82.

Jaffe, P. G., Lemon, N. K. D., & Poisson, S. E. (2003). *Child custody and domestic violence: A call for safety and accountability.* Thousand Oaks, CA: Sage.

Jenkins, E. J., & Bell , C. C. (1997). Exposure and response to community violence among children and adolescents. In N J. Osofsky (Ed.), *Children in a violent society.* (pp. 9–31) New York, NY: Guildford.

Kelly, L. (1988). *Surviving sexual violence.* Cambridge, MA: Polity Press.

Kelly, L. (2003). Disabusing the definition of domestic violence: How women batter men and the role of the feminist state. *Florida State University Law Review, 30,* 791–855.

Koenen, K. C., Moffitt, T. E., Caspi, A., Taylor, A., & Purcell, S. (2003). Domestic violence is associated with environmental suppression of IQ in young children. *Development and Psychopathology, 15,* 297–311.

Kogan, J. (2005). The failure of the Wellstone/Murray option to provide meaningful assistance to survivors of domestic violence. *Journal of Student Social Work, 4,* 36–43.

Kohl, P. L., Barth, R. P., & Hazen, A. L. (2005). Child welfare as a gateway to domestic violence services. *Children and Youth Services Review, 27,* 1203–1221.

Kurz, D. (1993). Physical assaults by husbands: A major social problem. In R. J. Gelles and D. R. Loseke (Eds.), *Current controversies on family violence* (pp. 88–103). Thousand Oaks, CA: Sage.

Lee, R. K., Sanders-Thompson, V. L., & Mechanic, M. B. (2002). Intimate partner violence and women of color: A call for innovations. *American Journal of Public Health, 92*(4), 530–534.

Margolin, M. G., & Gordis, E. B. (2003). Co-occurrence between marital aggression and parents' child abuse potential: The impact of cumulative stress. *Violence and Victims, 18,* 243–258.

Mattingly, M. J., & Straus, M. A., (2008). Violence socialization and approval of violence: A world perspective on gender differences and American values. A presentation at the Annual Meeting of the American Society of Criminology, St. Louis, MO, November 13, 2008.

McIntosh, J. (2003). Children living with domestic violence: Research foundations for early intervention. *Journal of Family Studies, 9*(2), 219–234.

National Coalition Against Domestic Violence (NCADV). (n.d.). Retrieved from http://www.ncadv.org/

National Network to End Domestic Violence (NNEDV). (n.d.). Retrieved from http://nnedv.org/

Oregon Coalition against Sexual and Domestic Violence. (2017). Restraining and Protective Orders. Retrieved from https://www.ocadsv.org/resources/browse/276

Pearlman, D. N., Zierler, S., Gjelsvik, A., & Verhoek-Oftedahl, W. (2003). Neighborhood environment, racial position, and risk of police-reported domestic violence: A contextual analysis. *Public Health Report, 118*(1), 44–58.

Pence, E., & Paymar, M. (1993). *Education groups for men who batter: The Duluth Model.* New York, NY: Springer.

Radford, L., & Hester, M. (2006). *Mothering through domestic violence.* London, UK: Kingsley.

Raj, A., & Silverman, J. (2002). Immigrant South Asian women at greater risk for injury from intimate partner violence. *Research and Practice, 95*(3), 435–437.

Rakovec-Felser, Z. (2014). Domestic violence and abuse in intimate relationship from public health perspective. *Health Psychology Research, 2*(3), 1821. Retrieved from http://doi.org/10.4081/hpr.2014.1821

Rennison, C. M., & Planty, M. (2003). Nonlethal intimate partner violence: Examining race, gender, and income patterns. *Violence and Victims, 18*(4), 433–443.

Rennison, C. M., & Welchans, S. (2000). Intimate partner violence. Bureau of Justice Statistics Special Report, U.S. Department of Justice, Office of Justice Program.

Richman, J. M., Fraser, M. W. (2001). *The context of youth violence: Resilience, risk and protection.* Westport, CT: Praeger.

Saunders, D. G. (1986). When battered women use violence: Husband abuse or self-defense? *Victims and Violence, 1*(1), 47–60.

Seligman, M. E. (1975). *Helplessness: On depression, development and death.* San Francisco, CA: Freeman.

Serran, G., & Firestone, P. (2004). Intimate partner homicide: A review of the male proprietariness and the self-defense theories. *Aggression and Violent Behavior, 9*(1), 1–15.

Somer, E., & Braunstein, A. (1999). Are children exposed to interparental violence being psychologically maltreated? *Aggression and Violent Behavior, 4,* 449–456.

Sorenson, S. B., & Taylor, C. A. (2005). Female aggression against male intimate partners: An examination of social norms in a community-based sample. *Psychology of Women Quarterly, 29,* 78–96.

Steinmetz, S. K. (1977). *The cycle of violence: Assertive, aggressive and abusive family interaction.* New York, NY: Praeger.

Stets, J., & Straus, M. (1992). *Gender differences in reporting marital violence: Physical violence in American families.* New Brunswick, NJ: Transaction.

Straus, M. (1999). The controversy over domestic violence by women: A methodological, theoretical and sociology of science analysis. In X. B. Arriaga, and S. Oskamp (Eds.), *Violence in intimate relationships* (pp. 19–44). Thousand Oaks, CA: Sage.

Straus, M. A., & Gelles, R. J. (1990). *Physical violence in American families.* New Brunswick, NJ: Transaction Press.

Straus, M. A., Steinmetz, S. K., & Gelles, R. J. (1980*). Behind closed doors: Violence in the American family.* Garden City, NY: Anchor.

Violence Against Women Act: Factsheet. (n.d.). Retrieved from http://www.whitehouse.gov/sites/default/files/docs/vawa_factsheet.pdf

Walker, L. E. (1984). *The battered woman syndrome.* New York, NY: Springer.

Walsh, Z., Swogger, M. T., O'Connor, B. P., Schonbrun, Y., & Stuart, G. L. (2010). Subtype of partner violence perpetrator among male and female patients. *Journal of Abnormal Psychology 119*(3), 563–574.

Wolfe, D. A., Campbell, M., & Jaffe, P. G. (2012). *Growing up with domestic violence.* Cambridge, MA: Hogrefe.

Wolfe, D. A., Crooks C. V., Lee, V., MacIntyre-Smith, A., & Jaffe, P. G. (2003). The effects of children's exposure to domestic violence: A meta-analysis and critique. *Clinical Child and Family Psychology Review, 6*(3), 71–187.

Yllo, K., & Bogard, M. (1988). *Feminist perspective on wife assault.* Newbury Park, CA: Sage.

Young, C. (2014). The surprising truth about women and violence. *Time,* July 25, 2014. Retrieved from http://time.com/2921491/hope-solo-women-violence/

Zorza, J. (Ed.). (2006). *Violence against women: Victims and abusers, legal issues, intervention and treatment* (Vol. II). Kingston, NJ: Civic Research Institute.

CREDITS

Social Policy and Technology

SOCIAL POLICY AND TECHNOLOGY

The socialization of children and the family moving through the lifespan are not only influenced by processes within the family but can be affected by the technological development of society. Prior to the 1950s, American families mainly lived on family farms in agrarian communities, and family farms were the norm. Many rural communities lacked amenities that are taken for granted today, such as running water, central heat, and even electricity. Television was in its infancy, and the thought of more advanced technology was not even a fantasy in most people's minds (Brinkley, 2013). Slowly, TV, personal computers, the Internet, video games, cellular phones, iPods, and **social media** such as Facebook have transformed American media, which, in turn, have had a dramatic effect on child and family development.

This chapter will detail how **social technology**, types of media that are used to communicate ideas, art, literature, and personal and public communication, affect children and families (Cohen, 2011). The chapter will be limited to the most influential media today in the lives of children and families. A few decades ago this endeavor would have been incomplete without a discussion of the effects of newspapers and books on children and families. In contemporary America, influential media is so much more immediately available that to some degree newspapers and books have taken a back seat. The discussion will center on the effects of TV, movies, video games, the internet, iPods, iPads, and Facebook. The regulation of social technology through the development of social policies will be reviewed and examined dialectically.

In reviewing the impact of various social technologies on children and adolescents, including movies, TV, rock music and MTV, advertisements, video games, the Internet, and computers, Villani (2001) found that these forms of media are related to an increase of aggression in children. Children exposed to social media tend to engage in more risky behavior, such as earlier sexual activity, smoking, and drug and alcohol use. They also tend to be overweight and have sleep and eating disorders. Generally, most research has found similar negative findings regarding the effects of social media on children. While older forms of media have been researched for many years, new forms, such as Facebook and iPods, are only beginning to be assessed (Mack, Behler, Roberts, & Rimland, 2007). The first topic below will address the effect of television on the development of children.

TELEVISION

Television has been around since the 1940s and has operated mainly as a private industry supported by advertising (Saelens, Sallis, Nader, Broyles, Berry, & Taris, 2002). TV programs tend to reflect viewer interests, and when programs are not supported by a large audience, there is little reason to continue the program. The federal government, under the auspices of the **Federal Communication Commission (FCC)**, controls the frequencies that broadcast media use and broadcast companies must apply for a license (Pecora, Murray, & Wartella, 2009). Cable TV does not use public broadcast frequencies and is less regulated by the federal government. While the FCC regulates the use of frequencies, there is less control over programming content, although some prohibitions exist regarding certain types of offensive programming. Advertising on TV programs was altered by the **Children's Television Act of 1990** by placing limitations on the time allotment for advertising during children's weekday and weekend TV viewing.

Television viewing by children is a given in American society. The question is not so much whether children are exposed to TV, but what is their age when they begin watching, how much time do they spend watching, and to what types of programming are they exposed (Pecora et al., 2009)? One of the disconcerting facts is how often young children watch TV. For example, almost half of children younger than two years of age watch TV on a daily basis

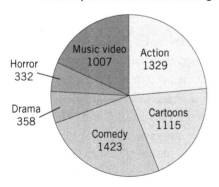

What types of TV shows & movies do kids spend the most time watching?

Music video 1007
Action 1329
Horror 332
Drama 358
Cartoons 1115
Comedy 1423

FIGURE 10.1 Kids and television

and three-fourths have watched some TV. Generally, parents say they are in the same room with an infant while he or she watches TV. As children age, the contact with TV becomes profound. By age six, children are spending approximately two hours a day watching TV. While this amount of time may not seem excessive, it is longer than the amount of time reading or being read to by a parent or playing outside (The Annenberg Public Policy Center of the University of Pennsylvania, 1997). The majority of six-year-old children turn the TV on for themselves without parental involvement, change channels, and watch DVDs. When children have TVs in their bedrooms, there is less supervision; children tend to watch more TV and often watch programs not suitable for them (Dennison, Erb, & Jenkins, 2002). Children with their own TVs in their rooms generally have more sedentary lifestyles and experience more negative consequences (Jordan & Robinson, 2008).

Research on the effects of watching TV on child development has consistently found certain negative outcomes. Among the negative outcomes is the likelihood of being obese or overweight (Institute of Medicine of National Academy, 2006). Food and drink marketed to children on TV commercials are high in calories and sugar content and low in nutrition. Low-income and unsupervised children tend to watch TV, also resulting in a greater probability of being obese. Researchers have found that the effects of TV watching and the relationship to obesity are directly related to amount of hours of viewing TV a day (Robinson, 1999).

Noting than treatment for obesity in children has produced little outward change, Robinson (1999) proposed a unique idea, which has continued to set the standard for addressing obesity in children. He believed that both conventional prevention and treatment per se for childhood obesity does not work. Instead, he proposed a direct model aimed at the two components for increased occurrence of obesity: reduced physical activity and increased amounts of poor nutrition foods. The intervention tracked TV watching and other sedentary activities, but did not replace them with physical activities. The results showed that by reducing the amount of TV watching and other sedentary activities, the level of obesity as measured by **the body mass index (BMI)** was significantly reduced. Robinson claimed that a causal relationship between reduced sedentary activities and obesity existed.

A study conducted by Matheson and associates (2004) focused primarily on children's amount and type of food intake during TV watching. The study found that, during weekdays, children consumed slightly less than 20% of their daily intake while watching TV. On the weekends, the daily consumption was approximately 25% of their daily intake. The sample was made up of two groups of different ages in order to compare younger and older children. The results indicated that there was no significant difference between the kind of food, particularly food high in fat, eaten during TV watching and meal times, but did find that, in younger children, eating while watching TV is associated with BMI.

A popular assumption is that children watch more TV when they spend more time inside partly because the mother fears for their safety when outside (Burdette & Whitaker, 2005). While the study by Burdette and Whitaker addressed the popular notion that a mother's fear of safety for her child in high-crime neighborhoods may directly affect the child's outside play time and, consequently, affect his/her weight, the study did not find a direct relationship between BMI and safe versus unsafe neighborhoods. Instead, the study found that children in unsafe neighborhoods did spend more time watching TV. While findings from another study on food intake while watching TV found similar results in that there tends to be no significant difference in BMI, it did conclude that children eat more protein and fruits and vegetables when the TV is not on (Coon, Goldberg, Rogers, & Tucker, 2001).

A major contributor to negative outcomes for children watching TV is the **exposure to violence**. Studies have found that by the age of 18, children have been exposed to 200,000 acts of violence, which generally go unpunished. Not only are children exposed to repeated violence, but most of it tends to be unrealistic (Strasburger, Wilson, & Jordan, 2009). Thus, violence is portrayed as achieving an end without appropriate consequences. In many cases, the violence is acted out by the main character or a character that the child can identify as a hero. Such mixture of fantasy with little corrective reality fails to give the child a proper framework for understanding violence.

"It's not dead, honey. You've just never seen it turned off before."

FIGURE 10.2 TV Violence

One side of the argument on the effects of violence on children is the view that, since everyone is exposed to **media violence** in the U.S. and only a small percentage of persons commit murder, the effects are negligible (Smith, 2006). Further, this argument is based on the view that persons, even children older than eight years of age, can distinguish fantasy violence from real violence. While this view might conclude that young children should be protected from violence, it would say that, overall, there is no evidence in daily life that viewing make-believe violence in movies and on TV changes the way persons interact.

This view would also pay attention to the **prosocial** benefits of media on children that tend to be underemphasized in the literature (Smith, 2006). This perspective would argue that if TV can teach children to be violent, as their opponents propose, the media can also teach prosocial behaviors. Prosocial behavior can be broadly defined as any behavior directed toward other persons that would be of some benefit to them, such as acts of altruism, cooperation, sharing, and openness to others of different ethnic or social backgrounds. A recent study of 2000 programs found that 73% of them had some content reflecting prosocial behavior and that these programs averaged about three prosocial acts per hour (Smith, 2006). These prosocial acts were more common in situational comedies and on children's networks such as *Disney* and *Nickelodeon* than other networks. Some children's programming, such as *Dora the Explorer* and *Sesame Street,* have high content in prosocial behavior.

The alternate view of this argument would state that the preponderance of evidence is that children viewing violence in media is a risk factor in the same way that smoking cigarettes is a risk factor for lung cancer (Wilson et al., 2002). It would say that viewing violence does not make persons violent, but it does increase the possibility that, at some point in their lives, they may resort to violent behaviors. This alterative view would say that while children's TV programming contains some prosocial behavior when compared to violence, prosocial loses by a large margin. For example, while prosocial acts occur at about four per hour, violent acts that children are exposed to occur at the rate of about 14 per hour (Wilson et al., 2002). Therefore, from this point of view, children are exposed to almost four times as much violence as prosocial acts. Advocates for limiting access to children watching violence on TV would also argue that children may be exposed to more violence than these statistics show. For example, not all children watch children's prosocial programming and may, in fact, be exposed to more TV violence and adult programming than is generally reported.

Advocates for learning prosocial acts from the media point to research in which children viewed a TV program that depicted a prosocial act and, after viewing, placed them in a situation in which they could imitate the same prosocial behavior (Smith, 2006). In comparing children who viewed the prosocial act with children who viewed a neutral act, children viewing the prosocial act were more likely to imitate it in a real situation than were the children who witnessed a neutral act.

Advocates for limiting violence on TV would answer the above by asserting that while some short-term effects of witnessing prosocial acts demonstrated that children can imitate those behaviors in real-life situations, they might also point out that prosocial acts are more difficult for children to grasp and tend to be heavier in dialogue than action (Wilson et al., 2002). Violent actions take place without dialogue or with dialogue that may have little influence on children. Furthermore, studies show that children younger than eight miss the moral lesson in programs, while those over ten tend to understand it. Consequently, younger children miss the meaning in the dialogue and are influenced much more by action, which is largely violent (McKenna & Osoff, 1998).

Beginning first in the 1950s, a major social policy issue about TV watching has been the concern about violence (Hamilton, 1998). One of the ways of addressing the concerns about TV violence has been a system of ratings. A **rating system** for violent, sexual, and vulgar content in movies and TV was created to help parents be more informed about the content of programming. Ratings established by the Motion Picture Association of America (n.d.) include G, PG, PG-13, R, and NC-17. They provide limited information about the actual content, but do offer a general designation for what the content may include. Some researchers believe that these ratings may even contribute to children having increased motivation to see movies that they think contains more adult type content and, therefore, undermine the ratings altogether.

A comparable rating system for TV programming was developed in 1997 (TV Rating Guidelines, n.d.). Like the rating system for movies, the TV rating system was based on the age of the viewer and consisted of TV-Y and TV-7. General audience ratings included TV-G, TV-PG, TV-14, and TV-MA. This rating system was deemed inadequate and quickly revised by adding new nomenclature, such as FV (fantasy violence) for children's programming. For the general public, new nomenclature was also added, such as V (violence), S (sex), L (language), and D (sexual dialogue). V-clip regulation has been standard on all TVs sold in the U.S. since 2000. Critics point out that although v-clips and TV ratings systems are standard on all TVs sold in the U.S., the majority of parents do not use them and would need a substantial incentive to increase usage (Kirkorian, Wartella, & Anderson, 2008).

Early Brain Development

Zero to three is the most important period for development (Tierney & Nelson, 2009). During this period, the brain is developing three-dimensional vision. Watching a dog catch a ball on a TV screen does not stimulate the brain in the same way as watching a real dog catch a ball. In seeing live action take place the brain can make sense out of these movements, while seeing the same images on TV does not produce the same effects. The live interaction produces learning, while TV watching may rewire the brain in a less productive manner. According to research conducted by Christakis and colleagues (2004), this rewiring of the brain may go unnoticed by busy parents. The rewiring occurs because of the quick constant changing of images, which are far different from the more continuous changes in real life. The effects of this rewiring will most likely show up in school-age children in the form of attention disorder.

The parent/child interaction in the early years is important for brain development (Tierney & Nelson, 2009). TV watching may reduce both the amount of time and the quality of time that parents and children interact. Studies have found that even background noise can have a detrimental effect on the parent/child relationship and the child's overall ability to learn (Kirkorian, Pempek, Murphy, Schmidt, & Anderson, 2009). For example, children raised in homes in which the TV is constantly playing have poorer reading and comprehension ability than children raised in homes of limited TV viewing.

Researchers have found that parents speak about 940 words per hour in interacting with a toddler, but with TV watching, this drops significantly. The parent/child interaction with young children has been referred to as a dance involving eye movement, tone of voice, and gestures, some of which are so intricate and minute that it takes watching a video tape of the interaction in slow motion to detect, but the human brain is able to make sense of it. This type of interaction is not possible in viewing a TV program.

The American Academy of Pediatrics (AAP (n.d.) released a policy statement that watching TV can be detrimental to children under the age of two. Recently, that position has been revised noting that some TV programming is geared for children of this age and watching with their parents rather than watching passively along may not be damaging (Kamenetz, 2016). Although it is difficult to determine with certainty what children recall from TV watching and how it will affect their development, some findings shed light on this overall effect (Kirkorian et al., 2008). For example, young children under the age of two tend to look at or gaze at objects that catch their interests. As children age, the amount of time gazing at TV programming increases; however, TV content that does not interest them tends to be ignored. Young children also show signs of being influenced by TV advertising by avoiding objects that received a negative emotional response from a TV personality, which indicates that they are capable of reacting to the emotions of others displayed on TV. When TV watching is excessive in childhood, and these children reach adolescence and young adulthood, there is greater likelihood of **antisocial behavior,** including criminal and aggressive acts.

After the age of two, children are able to learn some things from TV viewing that are helpful in language development and reading (Kamenetz, 2016; Kirkorian et al., 2008)). For example, some children's programming, such as *Sesame Street,* can improve literacy, math, and science skills in children older than two. These gains in vocabulary and other learning in young children from educationally focused programs are not seen when children watch adult content programs. Positive outcomes in enhancing learning of children from educational TV are especially important for low-income children.

Longitudinal studies on the relationship between **TV watching and aggressive behavior** in children found that TV watching affects aggression, and aggressive children watch more TV, which creates a type of circular pattern (Eron, 1963; Robertson, McAnally, & Hancox, 2016). Rejection by parents and parents whose own behavior approximates antisocial behavior are two intervening variables that affect the degree of influence on the child. Changing TV viewing habits as children age is not so much caused by increased cognitive development as it is caused by factors related to availability of TV programming.

The impact of movies on American society has a tremendous effect on social and interpersonal relationships (Hartstein, 2012). To some degree, children are also affected, especially in how they view social relationships. Children can be affected by unrealistic ideals that can lead to later life disappointments and poor self-esteem. Both boys and girls can be affected by unrealistic beliefs. According to Hartstein, one such belief affecting girls is referred to as the **"Princess Syndrome,"** the belief that happiness and success in life are dependent on a girl's physical attractiveness and pleasing personality.

Movie watching has been related to a number of specific negative behaviors (Huesmann, 2007). For example, the disproportionate number of people who smoke cigarettes in movies compared to real-life smoking no doubt influences adolescents to at least experiment with tobacco. The high exposure to smoking in movies increases by three times the probability of experimentation by adolescents who are frequent movie patrons over adolescents who are infrequent movie patrons. Few movies that display smoking ever address health issues related to its use or the public restrictions on smoking in restaurants or office buildings. Such cavalier treatment of smoking reduces any negative focus and implants the idea in the minds of children that it is "cool" to smoke.

Gender development in children is also affected by movies and TV (Johnson, 2015). Movies for young children are about **anthropomorphic characters** that look and behave like humans. For example, the animal lookalike characters stand erect, walk upright, and are able to talk with the best of them. Research indicates that anthropomorphic characters in movies and TV tend to parallel stereotypical gender roles in society. Some characters can also be transformed into other characters that have totally different qualities.

TABLE 10.1 Suggestions to reduce TV violence

SUGGESTIONS TO REDUCE THE EXPOSURE TO TV VIOLENCE
• Parents should periodically check what their children are watching on TV.
• Parents should establish house rules for watching TV.
• Parents should watch TV with their children and discuss the content.
• Parents should monitor and restrict news programs.
• Some programs with explicit violent content, such as *Criminal Minds*, should be prohibited for all children including adolescents.
• Parents should encourage their children in other ways of entertaining themselves, such as reading.
• Parents should create other ways of spending time together, such as in playing board games.

Adapted From: http://www.huffingtonpost.com/dr-gail-gross/violence-on-tv-children_b_3734764.html

Sexualization

A perhaps unintended consequence of the effects of TV watching and movies on children is an earlier interest in sexuality. Exposure to sexuality influences children to imitate what they see (Chirban, 2013). Sexual preoccupation may steer children toward deviant or premature sexual experiences. Children's informal vocabulary may become replete with sexual phraseology and expression. Adolescents who are exposed to sexually explicit content from frequent TV and movie watching have their first sexual experiences at an earlier age than other children.

The early initiation into sexual behavior is related to lifelong higher-risk sex, which is associated with more dissatisfaction in sex and higher incidences of sexually transmitted diseases (STDs) (Chirban, 2013). The premature exposure to sexual behavior can be related to the growing proclivity for sexual addiction in adults. Another risk factor from early exposure to sexual content is the probability of engaging in sexual violence. Sexual violence may be acted out toward others, or it may put one in a situation of being a victim.

A study at Dartmouth found that explicit sexual material not only leads to early entrance into adult sexuality but is related to low self-esteem (Parkes, Wright, & Sargent, 2012). Furthermore, such frequent sexual content reframes sexuality from the context of a stable intimate relationship to a priority in one's life. Researchers have found that the focus on casual sex is less rewarding than sex with one partner over a long period of time (Parkes et al., 2012). Adolescents who are preoccupied with sex struggle more with academic subjects, including math and logical thinking. The preoccupation with sexual thinking is associated with lower self-esteem in girls and more sexual aggression in boys. Healthy sexual development in children is retarded by excessive exposure to mature sexuality.

Gender identity first develops around the age of two and becomes increasingly influential as the child ages (Johnson, 2015). By middle school, children are occupied with a variety of concerns regarding their physical and social identities. Boys learn that the ideal male is physically strong, while girls are already attempting to lose weight to comply more closely with the ideal body physique. Studies have found that time watching TV and movies has negatively effect body image (Tiggermann & Pickering, 1996). More than half of middle school girls are unhappy with their body image, which increases to three-fourths by the end of high school (Brumberg, 1996). Even TV commercials that featured beautiful models tended to cause girls to be unhappy with their looks (Hargeaves & Tiggermann, 2002). Studies conclude that girls are as concerned about how they look as other characteristics, such as academic success.

Children's Direct Response to Media Stimuli

Some TV and movies that children are exposed to can be directly related to anxieties and fears, even when not intended to provoke such emotions (Kantor 2002). Feedback from parents in national surveys shows that children often respond with fear and anxiety after watching movies with scary plots and can be bothered by them for days. A growing body of research suggests that such immediate reaction to scary content may not be short-term effects only, but may continue to affect the child, such as with problems in sleeping (Gentile & Walsh, 2002). Sleep problems, classified as **sleep disturbance**, may affect both going to sleep and waking up during the night and needing to be consoled. A study with college students found that a substantial number still had fear reactions to movies seen in the past, even though many of them were from childhood (Harrison & Cantor, 1999). About 17% of the participants stated that the scary content from childhood movies affects the type of movies that see in the present. Because of their focus on visual input, younger children tend to be frightened more by scary faces and imagery, while school-age children are more frightened by scenes of bodily injury, and older children by plot content (Smith, Peiper, & Moyer-Guse, 2009).

Exposure to news stories of school shootings, terrorism, natural disasters, and accidental deaths can also increase fear and anxiety in children (Smith, Pieper, & Moyer-Guse, 2009). While the frequency of crime or other traumatic events has not increased, a single occurrence someplace in the world is now portrayed graphically on the TV screen. Children can be instantly transported into events by media and have firsthand experience that would have been impossible to witness a few generations ago (Smith et al., 2009). The result from the exposure to one incident, such as a child abduction, can increase the fear in children who will never experience it themselves. The global effect of news and event reporting, such as an outbreak of a dreaded disease in some remote part of the world, can seem like a very present danger to children in other parts of the world. The effects are exacerbated if the children live in close proximity to the event or if they are frequently exposed to it. Older children pay more attention to news stories and have greater anxiety, because they can generalize from a specific event to a broader context. Gender differences have been noted by researchers who have postulated that these differences arise from socialization. As girls age, they are more intensely affected by media than boys (Gerbner et al., 2002).

As cited elsewhere, the amount of time of the exposure to media is related to the strength of the effects (Kirkorian et al., 2009). To some extent, frequent watchers of TV and movies begin to see the world in a similar way. Consequently, if the type of media exposure is biased or limited in focus, a concomitant narrowing of perception of the viewer is most likely to occur. The general rule for parents is that the types of programming children are exposed to affects their internal perceptions of reality, which affects their relationships with others both behaviorally and psychologically.

VIDEO GAMES

Video games with violent content have been available to American children for several decades. The vast majority of children, particularly boys, play video games on a frequent basis. These games often set the player as the shooter and, therefore, as an active participant in the violence (Strasburger & Grossman, 2001). This active participation involves the player in the violent action rather than them serving as a bystander. The reward implicit in the games is for accomplishing violent acts, not for learning new information. Participants experience the same bodily reactions as if they were engaged in a violent confrontation, such as an increase in heart rate and blood pressure. Researchers in Sweden found that these bodily effects are not terminated with the cessation of playing but continue and may result in **stress-related outcomes** such as seizures (Vetenskapsradel, the Swedish Research Council, 2009). Research findings collaborate assumptions that active participation in violence mimics real-life violence. It increases violent thoughts and predisposes participants toward assessing the actions of others as aggressive. Participants' emotional balance is skewed toward negative thoughts and moods. In addition, researchers have found that adolescents who play video games are more likely to engage in violent acts than are angry adolescents who do not play video games

(Buckley & Anderson, 2006). Participating in violence after being exposed to violent video games is understood through an application of the **excitation transfer theory**, which states that the physiological response to the violence enhances negative emotional reactions.

The negative effects of video games reflect a wide range of outcomes, such as poor self-esteem from comparing oneself to the trim muscular human figures in the videos (Whitaker & Bushman, 2009). Of increasing concern is that video games are addicting and participants spend untold hours playing games. As in other forms of addiction, participants put time and energy into this activity while reducing other activities. Playing the games may excite the reward center of the brain but is followed by depressive and negative ruminating. Children who play video games excessively are approximately twice as likely to be depressed as children who do not play video games. The overall effect is a propensity for increased negative emotions and aggressive behaviors.

Researchers have found that adolescents who play video games for 28 hours a week are more likely to be diagnosed as depressed and have other negative outcomes, including decreased **social competency** (McGonagal, 2011). Social skills tend to be affected because heavy users of video games tend to have decreased empathy and poor sensitivity to the needs of others. Normal physical development requires at least two hours a day of rough-and-tumble play. Montagu (1986) believes that the lack of human touch may be a significant factor in precipitating the negative effects of video games and other forms of media. **Moral development** of children who are heavy users of video games may be compromised because they may be influenced to believe that violence is justified and necessary to resolve conflicts.

Children and adolescents who are frequent users of video games are more likely to have academic problems (Whitaker & Bushman, 2009). Playing video games may actually affect academic achievement by taking away from study time, but also may compensate for academic performance and, therefore, be both a cause and an effect of poor academic performance. Researchers concluded that when video games are available to children after school, the time spent in academic subjects is reduced. Unmonitored use of the computer by adolescents after school has similar effects as watching TV or seeing a movie.

Some studies have positive effects for less violent or educational video games (Ferguson, 2007). For example, playing video games can improve **visual/spatial functioning**. Some nonviolent games may benefit children by improving their ability to problem solve and critically evaluate situations. Games that involve strategies to win may help child to think logically (Granic, Lobel, & Engels 2014). Learning to think outside the box may be an added benefit to games in which players have to develop strategies to overcome obstacles. Video games may enhance learning, improve vocabulary and reading skills, and provide students with experiences with computer functioning that can directly relate to future employment. Other benefits may be improved planning, organizing, and management skills that are needed in a technological society.

SOCIAL MEDIA AND CHILD AND FAMILY SOCIAL POLICY

Children today are growing up with exposure to a much wider range of technological gadgets than ever before. This new media can be used in various ways and are associated with an array of negative outcomes (Strasburger, Wilson, & Jordan, 2009). According to recent research, children spend approximately seven hours a day with different forms of media, which is the largest amount of time for any activity in their waking hours. Much of this time is spent on new media, such as cell phones, Internet, and social websites (Jones & Fox, 2009). Children who have unsupervised access to the Internet can create profiles on MySpace and Facebook that parents might object to and can upload videos of all types onto these social websites. Most adolescents are bombarded with various forms of media, even when doing homework or studying for a test. Social media can also be used for negative purposes, such as harassing, stalking, or bullying. Researchers have found that the majority of adolescents who use social media revealed personal information about themselves that could be used against them and 23% uploaded photographs. As children age, they are much more likely to meet with a stranger they interacted with online (Berson & Berson, 2005).

More than half of adolescent users have more than one online address, and about 24% have different identities (Lenhart, Rainie, & Lewis, 2001). More than one-third of adolescents admit to lying about themselves or their age. More than 50% of adolescents say that they have posted negative things about others and have had negative things posted about them. More than 40% say they have been bullied on social media. Roughly half of adolescents 17 years of age have viewed some form of online sexually explicit pictures. Exposure to sexually explicit material on the Internet is related to more explicit sexual activity and conversations. For example, adolescents who are frequent users of sexual materials on the Internet are more likely to experiment with riskier sexual activity (Lenhart et al., 2001).

FIGURE 10.3 Social media.

The negative effects of social media tend to increase with increased use (Rideout & Hamel, 2006). Some studies have found that adolescents who excessively use social media, such as MySpace and Facebook, may have personality anomalies, including narcissistic and antisocial disorders. Some users may engage in **cyberbullying,** interacting in a threatening and a coercive manner, posting negative or critical pictures, or making false accusations. Cyberbullying is viewed by professionals as a form of violence directed toward a specific individual. Victims of cyberbullying are prone to having greater psychosocial disorders and engaging in riskier behaviors (Patchin & Hinduja, 2012). Adolescents are influenced by this type of media, because they tend to set norms that are also shared with others. The implication is that social media have been incorporated into a type of peer acceptance that reduces personal inhibitions (Strasburger, Wilson, & Jordan, 2009). While there has been public concern that sexual predators may be using the Internet to solicit for sex, which does happen, researchers have found that more solicitation comes from peer groups than from sexual predators. The propensity for cyberbullying seems to be increased for adolescents, because it tends to be anonymous, and parents and other adults are less aware of it than other forms of bullying (Dehue, Bolman, & Vollick, 2008). An international survey found that 77% of respondents felt that cyberbullying is a serious form of bullying and will take diligence to resolve (Patchin & Hinduja, 2012). The rates of cyberbullying have varied across different time frames and seem to be related to the age and status of the subjects. In no year was the percentage of abuse less than 20.8% (Patchin & Hinduja, 2012). Boys are not as likely to have ever experienced cyberbullying as are girls (16% vs. 28.6%). The widest difference in girls and boys in cyberbullying is that girls state that more hurtful comments are posted about them online (18.2% versus 10.5%). While boys post more hurtful comments and pictures, girls tend to post more gossip or rumors.

Other studies on cyberbullying outside the U.S. have found similar results (Mora-Meachan & Jägar, 2010). For example, a study of parents and their nine- to sixteen-year-old children conducted in twenty-five European countries found rates to be less overall than in the U.S. For example, only 3% of children admitted to sending hurtful comments to others online and 6% had received hurtful comments. In other research, when parents were asked if their children have experienced cyberbullying, the highest rate was India (32%), and the lowest rate was Italy (3%) (Mora-Meachan & Jägar, 2010).

A general finding from international studies is that childhood frequency of Internet use varies from country to country and, consequently, so does the risk (Livingstone & Haddon, 2012). Some low use and low-risk countries include Estonia, Lithuania, and Austria. In other countries, such as Bulgaria and Czech Republic, both the usage and risks are great. Haddon and Livingstone make a distinction between risk and harm, which are not the same thing. Risk refers to a possibility of harm, while harm refers to actual harmful behavior.

Facebook

Facebook is one of the most popular forms of communication for adolescents and young adults (Knorr, 2014). It is generally the way many people keep in contact on a daily basis, especially when separated by some distance. Adolescents post their daily activities, pictures, and videos of things that interest them, from academic subjects to political and religious beliefs. Unlike other social media, Facebook requires persons to post under their own names, and while this may encourage accountability for posts, women believe that it also undermines privacy. The disagreement on privacy rights of users, especially users under the age of 12, is between those who feel that adolescents should be protected from sexual predators and those who feel that open posting allows teens a wider range of influence. According to Knorr, it is believed that approximately 38% of children younger than 12 years of age are on Facebook. Approximately five million are younger than 10 years of age. While most children are unaware of the danger of being on Facebook, research reveals that the majority of parents are concerned, although some parents fail to take steps to fully address their concerns.

In a recent ruling on young adolescent users, Facebook has relaxed its rule on postings, allowing the posts of users under 12 to be accessible by everyone, not just ones' friends (Knorr, 2014). Those against such a loosening of the rules believe that retailers and other forms of advertising will bombard these younger users. In effect, it gives Facebook advertisers a new audience to address, which is driven by anticipated increases in revenues. According to Knorr, young adolescents do not have the impulse control to assess the merits of the types of manipulations advertisers of products would aim at them. The tracking of user posts would open the door for intrusive manipulation by targeting specific interests and products that adolescent users may not even want. Children under eight would stand a greater threat to such marketing because they are not sufficiently cognitively developed to distinguish between something that is real and something that is false. Furthermore, the argument goes that the privacy invasion of Facebook cannot be protected by the Children Online Privacy and Protection ACT (COPPA) (n.d.). In practice, COPPA puts the controls under parental auspices, which is only as effective as parents are in diligently keeping abreast of their children's Internet use.

While the argument tends to oscillate between the benefits and the dangers of children under 12 being on Facebook, others have taken a completely different tack. For example, Kleinberg (2012) takes the position that the natural role of Facebook for children should be educational, especially in the use of homework. He believes that parents, teachers, and students should congregate on Facebook. He suggests that students could upload particular areas of concern in their learning on Facebook, and others could respond to it. Such postings would create not only dialogue but unique ways to think outside the box. Since Facebook is international, the use could be expanded beyond the borders of one country. For example, children in one country could be involved in teaching children from another country a different language or consulting on difficult math problems. The suggestions by Kleinberg may be idealistic and beyond the general confines of Facebook. Persons tend to use Facebook as a divergence from other more structured activities. The very nature of the anonymity platform of Facebook belies a more purposeful use, and one is left with the recognition that it is what it is—a social, casual, and unstructured medium that resists more serious usage.

Cell Phones

Cell phone use and the resulting effects are still being assessed for children. Some studies have raised questions about children's cell phone use ranging from inappropriate use and contact to fears of brain tumors and cancer. Researchers Divan, Kheifets, Obel, and Olson (2008) in Denmark focused on the exposure to cell phones pre- and postnatally and behavior problems when the child was seven years of age, using a sample size of 13,000. Findings indicated that children at seven years of age have greater behavioral problems when they were exposed prenatally to cell phones versus postnatal exposure. Later analysis of this research by the authors with an increase of subjects to 28,745 found that children at age seven with behavioral problems had both pre- and postnatal exposure, rather than one or the other.

Another area of research on cell phone exposure and children is health. Generally, exposure to cell phone radio frequencies has been from exposure to transformers (Swerdlow et al., 2011). In a related study, Yoon-Hwan Byun and associates (2013) found a connection between mobile cell phone use and attention-deficit hyperactivity disorder (ADHD). Some researchers have focused more attention on the possible effects on the brain. Cell phone use by children and adolescents, in a study conducted by Aydin and associates (2012), focused on health issues related to absorption of radio frequency radiation during cell phone use, which has been associated with brain tumors and cancer. For the most part, no increase in brain tumors has been found for regular users, but mixed results have been found for excessive and long-term users. While Aydin and associates found no evidence for increased brain tumors from regular use, he also concluded that some risk could not be ruled out. Another study found that mothers' use of cell phones in 10-minute intervals while holding a newborn child disrupted heart rate rhythms and increased the beats per minute (Rezk et al., 2008). Researchers concluded that children residing near radar stations had poorer concentration and poorer memory than other children. Other studies on the effect of cell phone towers on children and adolescents have found a decrease in the level of **Phenylethylamine** (PEA), a bodily chemical compound similar to amphetamine. Conditions like depression and ADHD, for example, are associated with low levels of PEA (Buchner & Eger, 2011).

Some studies using rats as subjects have found that cell phone use creates **albumin** in the blood in the brain, which is usually not found in the brain of normally functioning persons, but is found in other parts of the body (Salford et al., 2003). This compromise to the brain by allowing compounds to cross the barrier is associated with increased physical and mental health dysfunctions).

In reviewing the research on **electromagnetic fields**, such as from cell phone exposure, Hedendahl (n.d.), a Swedish researcher, believes that there is ample evidence that a link does exist between exposure and health issues. Hedendahl seems to hedge on how supported her views might be given that most official conclusions point away from harmful effects.

Children and iPods and iPads

iPods and other hand-held devices are used by children for both entertainment and education. Some studies have shown that underperforming students can improve in self-efficacy when iPods are used as part of the curriculum (Choi, Jung, & Baek, 2013). A major benefit for using iPods is flexibility and can enhance learning even while the child is engaged in other activities. The overall effect is similar to having a mobile classroom. While the idea of the iPod as a mobile learning device is attractive, no studies have investigated whether this type of multitasking improves learning experiences.

In addition to iPods, **iPads** are also in current use in grade schools, high schools, and colleges (Hamilton, 2013). One large advantage of iPads is that they take the place of other hard copy materials and make it more versatile for student use. A study of medical students at the University of California at Irvine found a significant difference in scores of students who used iPads in their classes versus those who did not (Hamilton, 2013).

The Pearson Foundation (2012) conducted a survey on iPad use and found that students believe that they are very helpful. The survey also showed that ownership has increased from 7% to approximately 25%. The survey also found that about one-third of colleges were leaning toward obtaining them. It seems evident that scores in math and other subjects would be enhanced by the use of iPads when compared to textbooks.

Children and Sexting

Sexting is defined as interacting through mobile devises in a sexually explicit way, which may involve both written language and images (Livingstone, Haddon, Gorzig, & Olafsson, 2010). Sexting refers to a series of sexually explicit events and not limited to single events. Generally, research on this topic is lacking, and what exists has methodological problems (Ringrose, Gill, Livingstone & Harvey (2012). Ringrose et al. found that there are not simple solutions to understanding the reasons why children are sexting, but much of the motivation to participate is to be included in the group of peers. It creates a contradiction in that they feel compelled to voluntarily participate even though they may be simultaneously repulsed. If they want to be considered "cool" by their peers, they are not free to reject participating.

One of the main findings from research is that children face more problems in sexting from their peer group than from strangers (Ringrose et al., 2012). The real threat to their safety and emotional well-being is in the form of bullying, obscenity, and violence that tends to accompany sexting. To further complicate the concern is that children can be charged with crimes in the legal system, which could have long-term implications. Of particular concern is that nude images of children are considered pornography, which makes distributing and possessing them illegal. It is essential that guidelines for legal intervention be in place, which can separate out some of the salient points, such as whether the sexual content is coercive and exploitative or within a more normal range of adolescent pranks and experimentation. It is assumed that teens may not have an intention of harming or harassing their peers through sexting, and therefore, their behavior is less egregious than if there was an intention to harm. Unfortunately, there is little distinction in written law between the less offensive sexting or possession of nude photographs by teens and intentional and egregious child pornography by adults.

Legislation that sets the stage for policy formation regarding sexting teens is needed. Generally, if the sexting occurs between teens with permission for sharing nude photographs with each other and is not done to embarrass, harm the reputation, or for revenge, such as when dating teens break up, authorities use their discretion regarding prosecuting them (Crofts & Lee, 2013). The possibility of being charged with child pornography is present, however, even if the teen has permission to have a nude image of a peer on a cell phone.

Researchers have determined that gender plays a significant role in sexting (Ringrose et al., 2012). The age-old gender effects of a double standard where boys freely engage in sexting while girls are treated with derision is clearly shown in the literature. Gender may also play a role in the frequency of sexting and extent to which the sexting may be offensive.

SOCIAL POLICY AND TECHNOLOGY REGULATION

Social Policy and TV

The earliest policy addressing viewer needs and concerns about TV was determining programming that was the least objectionable (Hujanen, 2012). This period of time roughly covers the first few years of television and is euphemistically referred to as the "Golden Age of Television." While family comedy shows and various types of game shows dominated the evening TV schedule, some programming became more violent in content. The FCC has actively tried to protect children from viewing violence, sexual scenes, and vulgar and offensive language. One such endeavor was the creation of the safe **"harbor hours"** from 10:00 p.m. to 6:00 a.m. when children are considered less likely to watch TV (Blevins, 2011).

Legislation that was adopted and carried out by the FCC includes the **Children's Television Act (CTA) of 1990,** which addressed many concerns related to children and adolescent TV viewing. Advocacy groups led mainly by concerned parents, such as **Action for Children's Television (ACT),** began in the 1970s, and greatly affected the initiation of regulations by the FCC (Levinsky, 1999). One of the provisions was the establishment of minimal hours of core programming for children and adolescents, which was developed to meet their educational and informational needs. To enforce this regulation, the FCC stipulated that TV stations document their programming (FCC Issues New Rules for Children's Television Programming, n.d.). Although the purpose of the regulation was specifically to address the educational needs of children and adolescents, a report in 1999 by the Annenberg Foundation concluded that the actual amount of programming labeled educational decreased after CTA went into effect. The reason for the decrease was that many stations were only interested in requiring the minimal of hours per week and dropped many programs that were considered educational. An amendment to this regulation was added in 1999, which required three hours per week of educational programming with specific educational content. This regulation eliminated many programs that stations had labeled as educational without corresponding content (Mifflin, 1996).

A central kernel of the CTA was to provide adequate information about educational offerings to parents who could have more control over the type and content of programming their children were viewing (Mifflin, 1996). To facilitate parental knowledge of programming, the E/I icon on TV guides was required. In addition, TV stations were mandated to periodically submit reports on their educational programming.

The CTA also provided for greater control over commercial TV and advertising of products to children. **Program-length programming** is a program that is not separate from the advertising (Strasburger, Wilson, & Jordan, 2009). In other words, the entire program could be considered a commercial. This type of advertising carries the most vulnerability for children, because younger children do not distinguish between the program and the commercial, and it creates a strong desire for the product (Strasburger et al., 2009).

FCC regulations regarding children and TV viewing were again amended in 2004, which affected both **digital and analog programming** (Strasburger et al., 2009). The main focus of this regulation was to restrict the posting of website addresses that carried only advertising content.

Advertising pages on the website had to be distinguishable from other pages and could not be the home page of the website.

Social Policy and Social Media Regulation

Regulation of the Internet means that access to some websites is restricted in some way and to some users. Access to the Internet for children generally involves restricting access to certain websites (Lee & Chae, 2014). To address children's exposure to harmful material on the Internet, the **Children's Internet Protection Act (CIPA) of 2000** was enacted. This regulation placed restrictions on schools and libraries that received reduced rates for connectivity by requiring them to have safeguards that limited children's access to child pornography, and obscene and vulgar websites. CIPA also required that schools and libraries teach children the appropriate use of the Internet and monitor their online use.

A number of government regulations on the use and advertising of tobacco was aimed at reducing teenage smoking. One early initiative was adding an excise tax on cigarettes to make them cost more and, therefore, reduce the likelihood that teenagers could even afford to buy them (Smith & Foxcroft, 2009). Radio and television ads under the **Fairness Doctrine of the Federal Communications Commission,** established in 1967, also aimed at reducing teenage smoking by warning about the dangers of cigarettes. Specific laws, such as the Public Health Cigarette Smoking Act of 1970, forbade the advertising of socially acceptable images linked to cigarette smoking. Research is somewhat mixed on the effectiveness of these regulations, but according to Lewit, Coate, and Grossman (1981), the excise tax was particularly effective because of the increase in cost relative to the low purchasing power of teens, as compared to adults. The researchers also found evidence that banning positive cigarette ads from radio and television resulted in a significant reduction in teen's tobacco use rates.

Parental involvement with their children and adolescents encompasses the largest influence that media technology exerts. When parents watch TV or see a movie with their children, there is ample opportunity to engage in a dialogue about the meaning, purpose, moral, legal, and psychological implications of the plot (Phillips, Prince, & Schiebelhut, 2004). Children can share their views, ask questions, and, perhaps, reflect on analyses of the media event more than if they watched it alone. In addition, parents can use these times of co-watching of TV programs or movies to teach children lessons regarding unrealistic portrayals, and to help them recognize that everyday life does not consist of the frequency of one's contact with crimes or other trauma, as they occur on the screen (Phillips et al., 2004).

What is the overall effect of media technology on children's' development? The question has received less attention in the extant literature than the negative effects. Developmentally, children at early ages must learn to regulate their emotions and be competent in identifying basic emotions, such as sadness, happiness, and ambivalence Kirkorian et al., 2009). Media may play a large role in this development, as illustrated by research that shows that eight-year-old children are able to identify the emotions of characters in a program when retelling it (Huston et al., 1990). Some programming for children, such as *Sesame Street,* have developed specific material to help children identify emotions and improve emotional functioning. Some studies have found that children learn more about emotional content from educational programs than from those focused strictly on entertainment (Rideout & Hamel, 2006). According to Rideout and Hamel, no long-term studies have been conducted that support the proposition that media technology improves emotional development.

Media and Social Policy Debate

The underlying debate on the media is regulation. Should the media be regulated to reduce the negative effects? Does the **Freedom of Information Act** justify an open perspective on media? Would society be harmed more in the long-term if access to all forms of media was stricter? No one can deny the power of media in every aspect of human existence. People rely on media for information, maintaining contact, and consumption of products and services. Social media provide multiple purposes and opportunities for individuals to interact. Businesses use social media for advertising and informing about products and services. The use of social media for these various activities, however, is not without risk, some of which might be damaging to the business of the individual (Berger, 2011). The lack of regulation of social media creates anonymity and, therefore, an open opportunity for fraudulent or deceitful purposes. Persons with fake social media accounts can bully, threaten, or make false accusations without a great deal of concern or accountability. Businesses can create false accounts to praise their own products while lambasting their competitors. Some persons worry that having their personal information on social media gives unscrupulous persons the opening to steal their identities. Nevertheless, the debate rages on about the efficacy of regulation of media verses open and unrestricted access, giving persons the ability to choose and, thus, placing regulation in the hands of each individual.

One example of the debate involves regulation of news networks (Emery, 2014). On one side of the debate, people believe that more regulation is needed because news reporters can go too far and even violate the privacy of persons in gathering news. Furthermore, much of what passes for news is entertainment, which leaves people with a distorted view of events. As entertainment, news outlets are not guided by reporting the facts, and instead focus on reporting sensational stories to the public. The stories, coupled with the commercial enterprise of advertisements, tend to give viewers false and misleading perceptions. Another failing of news outlets from this perspective is opinion reporting, which again skews the facts and reduces objectivity since persons are influenced in how to think or feel about events.

People on the other side of this argument begin with the claim that the way to maintain freedom is to allow a free press (Debate.org, n.d.). They would further claim that when the government regulates the press, it is no longer free; now, perhaps, the government has arbitrarily limited its rights as a free and unencumbered entity. It would also postulate that freedom of speech is the bedrock of a free and democratic society grounded in the **Bill of Rights**.

In addition to the press and news outlets, debates over the regulation of language, explicit sexual content, and violence on TV and in movies has an ongoing presence (FCC, n.d.). The FCC has under its purview the purpose of regulating what would be considered offensive to persons. While the FCC functions as a broad sounding board, it has not clearly addressed its functions and has left unanswered questions. As this is being written, Congress is in discussion on a bill that would regulate indecency on TV by giving the FCC more authority to create restrictive regulations. The argument against regulation points out that regulations are already in effect and additional ones would only further erode individual choices (Gattuso, 2014). This perspective cites the support of the **American Civil Liberties Union (ACLU),** which leaves the choice of what children are exposed to up to parents rather than grant a broader reach of the government. It points out that parents are already equipped with rating blocks for both TVs and Internet. This perspective concludes that parents have at their disposal the means of protecting their children without further governmental intervention.

Advocates for greater control of the Internet argue that social media perform the role of a **public utility**, much the same as public utilities such as water supply and electricity (Kaplan & Haenlein, 2010). Since social media serve a public function of connecting individuals, they need regulating in order to protect those who use them against unscrupulous, unethical, or criminal activities. This perspective further argues that if websites, such as Google, are not regulated, they form a monopoly that has detrimental effects on individual rights to free markets. Because social media are indispensible, especially to adolescents and young adults, to function in a modern society in which one is linked with almost every aspect of society, advocates for regulation claim that it is required that safeguards and standards are consistent for all users (Tufekci, 2010).

On the other hand, opponents of the public utility argument point to a fundamental difference with utilities, such as water and electricity, on which a society depend to maintain daily activities; little change would actually occur if social media were terminated (Jamison, 2012). In other words, social media are not viewed as being essential to life and maintaining the economy. Opponents argue that regulations would have the opposite undesirable effect of creating a monopoly, such as in the case of water and electricity, rather than inhibiting monopolies (Thierer, 2012). Furthermore, this argument states that additional regulations would allow the government more control over the lives of people and businesses through advertising restrictions, which would undermine entrepreneurial initiatives and actually harm the economy. In addition, social media carry with it implications for the rights of free speech, which is guaranteed in the U.S. Constitution (Thierer, 2012). Social media websites can be held responsible for breaking laws in the same way businesses and individuals can be held responsible without creating an expansive set of new regulations.

KEY TERMS

Social media
Social technology
Federal Communications
  Commission (FCC)
Children's Television
  Act of 1990
The body mass index (BMI)
Exposure to violence
Media violence
Prosocial
Rating system
Zero to three
Antisocial behavior
TV watching and
  aggressive behavior
Princess syndrome
Anthropologic characters

Sexualization
Gender Identity
Sleep disturbance
Stress related outcomes
Excitation Transfer Theory
Social competency
Moral development
Visual/spatial functioning
Cyberbullying
Facebook
Cell phones
Phenylethylamine (PEA)
Albumin
Electromagnetic fields

iPods
iPads
Harbor hours
Action for Children's
  Television (ACT)
Program-length programming
Digital and analog programming
Children's Internet Protection
  Act of 2000 (CIPA)
Fairness Doctrine of the Federal
  Communications Commission
Freedom of Information Act
Bill of Rights
American Civil Liberties
  Union (ACLU)
Public utility
Sexting

STUDY QUESTIONS TO ACCOMPLISH THE LEARNING OBJECTIVES

1. List the negative effects of watching TV. List positive effects of TV watching for young children. Make an argument for the overall effect of TV watching on children.

2. Discuss the relationship between watching TV and obesity. Justify your answer.

3. Label the current ratings for TV programs and movies. Analyze the effectiveness of the current ratings for TV and movies. Determine if new restrictions should be imposed.

4. Discuss violence on TV and exposure to children. Calculate the effect of violence on brain development in young children.

5. Make an argument for greater restrictions on explicit sexual content on TV and in the movies. Compare with viable arguments from the opposing view.

6. List the positive outcomes for adolescents who frequently play video games. List the negative outcomes. Apply Excitation Transfer Theory to how adolescents are affected by violent video games.

7. Define cyberbullying, and defend that it is a real threat to the well-being of children.

8. Describe the effect that Facebook has on young children. Determine if it should be better regulated.

9. List the pros and cons of children using cell phones. Evaluate the health risk for long-term frequent use.

10. Review the debate on greater restrictions on social media. Judge whether there is a common ground in the arguments. Generate a social policy position based on the debate.

DEBATE ACTIVITY FOR STUDENTS

Consider the following proposition: Children allowed to use iPads as preschoolers would have an advantage in learning.

- Review refereed literature on this topic. Do a library and Internet search to find relevant material. Investigate some of the additional readings.
- Develop three arguments for the proposition.
- Develop three arguments against the proposition.
- How do the arguments relate to other systems, such as the community or culture?
- Is there common ground?
- What are the long-term consequences of taking action?

- What new or common-ground solutions should be offered? If no common ground, what new position could emerge from a dialogue between the two positions?

- How is the new position superior to the original positions?

ADDITIONAL READING RESOURCES

Good and bad effects of TV on children. (n.d.). Raise Smart Kids. Retrieved from https://www.raisesmartkid.com/all-ages/1-articles/13-the-good-and-bad-effects-of-tv-on-your-kid

Gordon, S. (2017). What are the effects of cyberbulling? *Verywell, August 9, 2017.* Retrieved from https://www.verywell.com/what-are-the-effects-of-cyberbullying-460558

Hartzog, W. (2015). Social media needs more limitations, not choices. *Wired.* Retrieved from https://www.wired.com/2015/04/social-media-needs-limitations-not-choices/

Margalit, L. (2016). What screen time can really do to kids brains. *Psychology Today, April 17, 2016.* Retrieved from https://www.psychologytoday.com/blog/behind-online-behavior/201604/what-screen-time-can-really-do-kids-brains

Naeem, Z. (2015). Health risks associated with mobile phone use. *International Journal of Health Sciences, 8*(4), V–VI.

Oaklander, M. (2015, July 27). Kindergartners watch more than three hours of TV a day. *Time.* Retrieved from http://time.com/3835891/child-obesity-kindergarten/

REFERENCES

American Academy of Pediatrics AAP) (n.d.). Media and children. Retrieved from http://www.aap.org/en-us/advocacy-and-policy/aap-health-initiatives/pages/media-and-children.aspx

Annenberg Public Policy Center of the University of Pennsylvania. (1997). *Television in the Home: The 1997 Survey of Parents and Children.* Philadelphia, PA: University of Pennsylvania.

Aydin, D., Feychting, M., Schuz, J., & Roosli, M. (2012). Childhood brain tumors and use of mobile phones: Comparison of a case-control study with incidences and data. *Environmental Health, 11,* 35. Retrieved from http://www.ehjournal.net/content/11/1/35

Berger, M. (2011). The freedom of information act: Implications for public health policy and practice. *Public Health Reports, 126*(3), 428–432.

Berson, I. R., & Berson, M. J. (2005). Challenging online behaviors of youth: Findings from an online analysis of young people in the United States and New Zealand. *Social Science Computer Review, 23*(1), 29–38. doi: 10.11770894439304271532

Blevins, J. L. (February 2011). Applying the U.S. safe harbor policy to television violence. *Journal of Children & Media, 5*(1), 37–52. doi:10.1080/17482798.2011.533486

Brinkley, A. (2013). The Fifties. The Gilder Lehrman Institute of American History. Retrieved from https://www.gilderlehrman.org/history-by-era/1945-present/civil-rights-movement

Brumberg, P. M. (1996). Standing in the spaces: The multiplicity of self and the psychoanalytic relationship. *Contemporary Psychoanalysis, 32,* 509–535.

Buckley, K. E., & Anderson, C. A. (2006). A theoretical model of the effects and consequences of playing video games. In P. Vorderer and J. Bryant (Eds.), *Playing video games, motives, responses and consequences* (pp. 363–378). Mahwah, NJ: Erlbaum and Associates.

Burdette, H. L., & Whitaker, R. C. (2005). A national study of neighborhood safety, outdoor play, television viewing, and obesity in preschool children. *Pediatrics, 116(3),* 657–662. doi:10.1542/peds.2004–244

Byun, Y-H., Ha, M., Kong, H. J., Choi, K-H., Burm, E., Choi, Y. et al. (2013). Epidemiological characteristics of mobile phone ownership and use in Korean children and adolescents. *Environmental Health Toxicology, 28* Article ID: e2013018, 8 pages EHT. http://dx.doi.org/10.5620/eht.2013.28.e2013018

Children's Internet Protection Act. (n.d.). Consumer and Governmental Affairs Bureau, Consumer Inquiries and Complaints Division. Retrieved from http://www.fcc.gov/guides/childrens-internet-protection-act

Children's Online Privacy and Protection Act COPPA. (n.d.). Retrieved from http://www.coppa.org/comply.htm

Children's Television Act of 1990. (n.d.). Federal Communications Commission. Retrieved from https://www.fcc.gov/guides/childrens-educational-television

Chirban, J. T. (2013). Age of un-innocence: Confronting difficult topics with kids. *Psychology Today.* Retrieved from http://www.psychologytoday.com/blog/the-age-un-innocence/201301/has-sexualization-struck-your-kids

Choi, B., Jung, J., & Baek, Y. (2013). In what way can technology enhance student learning? A preliminary study of technology supported learning in mathematics. A presentation at the Society for Information Technology and Teacher Education International Conference (SITE), March 25, New Orleans, Louisiana.

Christakis, D. A., Zimmerman, F. J., DiGiuseppi, D. L., & McCarty, C. A. (2004). Early television, exposure and subsequent intentional problems in children. *Pediatrics,* 133(4), 708–713.

Cohen, H. (2011). Social media definitions. Retrieved from http://heidicohen.com/social-media-definition/

Coon, K. A., Goldberg, J., Rogers, B. L., & Tucker, K. L. (2001). Consumption Patterns Relationships Between Use of Television During Meals and Children's Food. *Pediatrics,* 107(7). doi: 10.1542/peds.107.1.e7

Crofts, T., & Lee, M. (2013). Sexting, Children and Pornography. *Sydney Law Review, 35,* 85–109.

Debate.org. (n.d.). Does the Freedom of Information Act adequately promote government disclosure? Retrieved from http://www.debate.org/opinions/does-the-freedom-of-information-act-adequately-promote-government-disclosure

Dehue, F., Bolman, C., & Vollink, T. (2008). Cyberbullying: Youngsters' experiences and parental perception. *CyberPsychology Behavior, 11.* Retrieved from http://web.ebscohost.com.ezproxy1.sdu.edu/ehost/pdf?vid=4hid=1148sid=465317b-27ea-4062-87

Dennison, B. A., Erb, T. A., & Jenkins, P. L. (2002). Television viewing and television in bedroom associated with overweight risk among low-income preschool children. *Pediatrics,* 109(6), 1028–2035.

Divan, H. A., Kheifets, L., Obel, C., & Olson, J. (2008). Prenatal and postnatal exposure to cell phone use and behavioral problems in children. *Epidemiology, 19*(4), 523–529. doi: 101097/EDE.ObO13e318176dd47.

Emery, M. (2014). Regulating televised news: A new season for the public interest standard. *Notre Dame Journal of Ethics and Public Policy, 19*(2), 757–788.

Eron, L. D. (1963). Relationship of TV viewing habits and aggressive behavior in children. *Journal of Abnormal and Social Psychology, 67*(2), 193–196.

FCC. (n.d.). Issues New Rules For Children's Television Programming. *Wilmer Hale Publications.* Wilmer Hale. Retrieved from http://www.wilmerhale.com/

FCC. (n.d.). Program content Regulations. Retrieved from https://www.fcc.gov/media/over-air-reception-devices-rule#block-menu-block-4

Ferguson, C. J. (2007). The good, the bad, and the ugly. A meta analytic review of the positive and negative effects of violent video games. *Psychiatric Quarterly, 78,* 309–316.

Gattuso, J. (2005). The broadcast indecency: More regulation is not the answer. The Heritage Foundation. Retrieved from http://www.heritage.org/government-regulation/report/broadcast-indecency-more-regulation-not-the-answer

Gentile, D. A., & Walsh, D. A. (2002). A normative study of family media habits. *Journal of Applied Developmental Psychology, 23,* 157–178.

Gerbner, G., Gross, I., Morgan, M., Signorielli, N., & Shanahan, J. (2002). Growing up with television: Cultivation processes. In J. Bryant and D. Zillmann (Eds.), *Media effects: Advocates in media and research* (2nd ed.). Mahwah. NJ: Lawrence Erlbaum.

Granic, I., Lobel, R., & Engels, R.C.M.E. (2007). The benefits of playing video games. *American Psychologist 69*(1), 66–78. doi.org/10.1037/a0034857

Hamilton, I. (2013). UCI iPad program enters third year. *Orange County Register,* August 3, 2013. Retrieved from http://www.ocregister.com/articles/students-367087-year-third.html

Hamilton, J. T. (Ed.). (1998). *Television violence and public policy.* Ann Arbor, MI: University of Michigan Press.

Hargeaves, D. A., & Tiggermann, M. (2002). The effect of television commercials on mood and body dissatisfaction: The role of appearance-schema activation. *Journal of Social and Clinical Psychology, 20,* 287–308.

Harrison, K., & Cantor, J. (1999). Tales from the screen: Enduring fright reactions to scary media. *Media Psychology, 1,* 97–116.

Hartstein, J. L. (2012). Princess recovery: Raising empowered girls in a complicated world. *Psychology Today.* Retrieved from http://www.psychologytoday.com/blog/princess-recovery/201204/combating-princess-syndrome

Hendendahl, L. (n.d.). Children and electromagnetic radiation. Retrieved from http://www.eiwellspring.org/health/ChildrenAndEMF.htm

Hines, D. A., & Douglas, E. M. (2011). Symptoms of post-traumatic stress syndrome disorder in men who sustain intimate partner violence: A study of help-seeking and community samples. *Psychology of Men and Masculinity, 12*(2), 112–127.

Huesmann, L.R. (2009). The impact of electronic media violence: Scientific theory and research. *Journal of Adolescent Health, 41*(6suppl1), S6–13.

Huston, A. C., Wright, J. C., Rice, M. L., Kerkman, D., St. Peters, M. (1990). Development of television viewing patterns in early childhood: A longitudinal investigation. *Developmental Psychology, 26,* 409–420.

Institute of Medicine of National Academy (2006). Progress in preventing childhood obesity. How do we measure up? Retrieved from http://www.iom.edu/Reports/2006/Progress-in-Preventing-Childhood-Obesity—How-Do-We-Measure-Up.aspx

Jamison, M. (2012). Should Google search be registered as public utility? Social Science Research Network (SSRN). Retrieved from http://papers.ssrn.com/sol3/papers.cfm?abstract_id=2027543

Johnson, R.M. (2015). The evolution of Disney's princesses and their effect on body image, gender roles and the portrayal of love. *Education Specialist*, Paper 6. Retrieved from commons.lib.jmu.edu/cgi/viewcontent.cgi?article=1003&context=ed spec201019

Jones, S., & Fox, S. (2009). Generations online in 2009. Pew Internet Project. Retrieved from http://www.pewinternet.org/2009/01/28/generations-online-in-2009/#

Jordan, A. B., & Robinson, T. N. (2008). Children, television viewing, and weight status: Summary and recommendations from an expert panel meeting. *American Academy of Social Science, 615*(1), 119–132.

Kaplan, A. M., & Haenlein, M. (2010). Users of the world unite: The challenges and opportunities of social media. *Business Horizons, 53,* 59–68.

Kamenetz, A. (2016). The American Academy of Pediatricians lifts "no screens under the age of 2" rule. *nprEd*, October 21, 2016. Retrieved from http://www.npr.org/sections/ed/2016/10/21/498550475/american-academy-of-pediatrics-lifts-no-screens-under-2-rule

Kantor, J. (2002). The psychological effects of media violence on children and adolescents. Retrieved from http://yourmind-onmedia.com/wp-content/uploads/media violencepaper.pdf

Kirkorian, H. L., Pempek, T. A., Murphy, L. A., Schmidt, M. E., Anderson, D. R. (2009). The impact of background television on parent-child interactions. *80*(5), 1350–1359.

Kirkorian, H. L., Wartella, E. A., & Anderson, D. R. (2009). Media and young children's learning. *Future of Children, 18*(1), 39–61.

Kleinberg, S. (2012). Should children younger than 13 be on Facebook? Absolutely. *Chicago Tribune.* Retrieved from http://www.chicagotribune.com/features/tribu/ct-tribu-social-media-facebook-kids-20120607,0,3023829.story

Knorr, C. (2014). Sneaky ways advertisers target kids. Common Sense Media. Retrieved from http://www.commonsense-media.org/blog/sneaky-ways-advertisers-target-kids

Lee, S. J., Chae, Y. G. (2014). Balancing participation and risks in children's internet use: The role of internet literacy and parental mediation. *Cyberbullying, Behavior, and Social Networking, 15*(5), 257–262.

Lenhart, A., Rainie, L., & Lewis, O. (2001). *Teenage life online: The rise of the instant-message generation and the Internet's impact on friendship and family relationships.* Washington, D.C.: Pew Internet and American Life Project.

Levinsky, A. (1999). Unintended consequences. *The Humanist, 59*(6), 1–10.

Lewit, E. M., Coate, D., & Grossman, M. (1981). The effects of government regulations on teen smoking. *Journal of Law Economics, 14*(3), 273–298.

Livingstone, S., & Haddon, L. (2012). Theoretical framework for children's Internet use. In S. Livingstone, L. Haddon, and A. Gorzig (Eds.*), Risk and safety on the internet: Research and policy challenges in comparative perspective* (pp. 1–14). Bristol, UK: Policy Press.

Livingstone, S., Haddon, L., Gorzig, A., & Olafsson, K. (2010). Risks and safety for children on the internet: The UK report. *LSE.* London, UK: EU Kids online. Retrieved from http://eprints.lse.ac.uk/33730/

Mack, D., Behler, A., Roberts, B., & Rimland, E. (2007). Reaching students with Facebook: Data and best practices. *Electronic Journal of Academic and Special Librarianship, 8*(2). Retrieved from http://southernlibrarianship.icaap.org/content/v08n02/mack_d01.html??

Matheson, D. M., Killen, J. D., Wang, Y., Varady, A., & Robinson, T. N. (2004). Children's food consumption during television viewing. *American Journal of Clinical Nutrition, 79*(6), 1088–1094.

McGonagal, (2009). Video games: An hour a day is key to success in life. *Huffpost,* July 28, 2011. Retrieved from http://www.huffingtonpost.com/jane-mcgonigal/video-games_b_823208.html

McKenna, M., & Ossoff, E.P. (1998). Age differences in children's comprehension of a popular television program. *Child Study Journal, 28*(1), 53–68.

Mifflin, L. (1996, August 9). U.S. mandates educational TV for children. *The New York Times*, p. 6. Retrieved from http://www.nytimes.com/1996/08/09/us/us-mandates-educational-tv-for-children.html

Montagu, A. (1986). *Touching: The human significance of the skin*. New York, NY: Harper and Row.

Mora-Merchan, J., & Jäger, T., (Eds.). (2010). *Cyberbullying: A cross-national comparison*. Landau, Germany: Verlag Emprische Padagogik.

Motion Picture Association of America. (n.d.). What each rating means. Retrieved from http://www.mpaa.org/ratings/what-each-rating-means

Parkes, A., Wright, D., & Sargent, J. (2012). Are sexual media exposure, parental restrictions on media use and co-viewing TV and DVDs with parents and friends associated with teenagers' early sexual behavior? *Journal of Adolescence, 35*(6), 1121–1133.

Patchin, J. W., & Hinduja, S. (2012). *Cyberbullying prevention and response: Expert perspectives*. New York, NY: Routledge.

Pearson Foundation (2012). Survey on Students and Tablets 2012. Retrieved from http://www.pearsonfoundation.org/downloads/PF_Tablet_Survey_Summary_2012.pdf

Pecora, N., Murray, J. P., & Wartella, E. A. (Eds.) (2009). *Children and television: Fifty years of research*. Mahwah, NJ: Lawrence Erlbaum Associates.

Phillips, D., Prince, S., & Schiebelhut, L. (2004). Elementary school children's responses three months after the September 11 terrorist attacks: A study in Washington, D.C. *American Journal of Orthopsychiatry, 74*, 509–228.

Rezk, A. Y., Abdulqawi, K., Mustafa, R. M., Abo El-Azm, T. M., & Al-Inany, H. (2008). Fetal and neonatal responses following maternal exposure to mobile phones. *Saudi Medical Journal, 29*(2), 218–23.

Rideout, V., & Hamel, E. (2006). *The media family: Electronic media in the lives of infants, toddlers and preschoolers and their parents*. Palo Alto, CA: The Kaiser Foundation.

Ringrose, J., Gill, R., Livingstone, S., & Harvey, L. (2012). A qualitative study of children, young people and "sexting." *National Society for the Prevention of Cruelty to Children*. Retrieved from http://eprints.lse.ac.uk

Robertson, L. A., McAnally, H. M., & Hancox, R. J. (2013). Childhood and adolescent television viewing and antisocial behavior in early adulthood. *Pediatrics, 131*(3), 439–446.

Robinson, T. N. (1999). Reducing children's television viewing to prevent obesity: Randomized controlled trial. *Journal of the American Medical Association (JAMA), 282*(16), 1561–1567. doi:10.1001/jama.282.16.1657

Saelens, B. E., Sallis, J. F., Nader, P. R., Broyles, S. L., Berry, C. C., & Taris, H. L. (2002). Home environmental influence on children's television watching from early to middle childhood. *Journal of Developmental Behavioral Pediatric, 23*(3), 127–132.

Salford, L. G., Brun, A. E., Eberhardt, J. L., Malmgren, L., & Persson, B. R. (2003). Nerve cell damage in mammalian brain after exposure to microwaves from GSM mobile phones. *Environmental Health Perspectives, 111*(7), 881–883.

Smith, L. A., & Foxcroft, D. R. (2009). The effect of alcohol advertizing, marketing and portrayal of drinking behavior in young children: Systematic review of prospective cohorts, *BioMed Public Health, 9*, 51. doi: 10.1186/1471-2458-9-51

Smith, S. (2006). Altruism on American Television: Examining the amount of, and context surrounding, acts of helping and sharing. *Journal of Communication, 4*, 707–727.

Smith, S. L., Pieper, K. M., & Moyer-Guse, E. J. (2009). News, reality shows, and children's fears: Examining content patterns, theories and negative effects. In S. Calvert and B. J. Wilson (Eds.), *The handbook of children, media and development* (pp. 214–235). Malden, MA: Wiley-Blackwell.

Strasburger, V. C., & Grossman, D. (2001). How many more Columbines? What can pediatricians do about school and media violence. Presentation at the Annual Convention of the Pediatric Academic Society, Baltimore, Maryland, April 29, 2001.

Strasburger, V. C., Wilson, B. J., & Jordan A. B. (2009). *Children, adolescents, and the media* (2nd ed.). London, UK: Sage.

Swerdlow, A. J., Feychting, M., Green, A. C., Kheifets, L., & Savitz, D. A. (2011). Mobile phone, brain tumors and the interphone study. Where are we now? *Environmental Health Perspective, 119*(11) 1534–1538.

Thierer, A. (March, 2012). The perils of classifying social media platforms as public utilities. Working Paper Number 12–11, Mercatus Center at George Mason University.

Tierney, A. L., & Nelson, III, C. A. (2009). Brain development and the role of experience in early years. *Zero Three, 30*(2), 9–13.

Tiggermann, M., & Pickering, A. S. (1996). Role of television in adolescent women's dissatisfaction and drive for thinness. *International Journal of Eating Disorders, 20*(2), 199–203.

Tufekci, Z. (2010). Google buzz: The corporation of social commons. Retrieved from http://technosociology.org/?p=102

TV Parental Guidelines. (n.d.). Retrieved from http://www.tvguidelines.org/

Vetenstrapsradel (The Swedish Research Council). (2008, November 14). Violent video games affect boys' biological system, study finds. *SceinceDaily*. Retrieved from https://www.sciencedaily.com/releases/2008/11/081113101424.htm

Villani, S. (2001). Impact of media on children and adolescents: A 10-year review of the research. *Journal of American Academy of Child and Adolescent Psychiatry, 40*(4), 392–401.

Whitaker, J. L., & Bushman, B. J. (2009). A review of the effects of violent video games on children and adolescents, *Washington and Lee Law Review, 66*(3), 1034–1051.

Wilson, B. J., Smith, S. L., Potter, W. J., Kunker, D., Linz, D., Colvin, C. M., & Donnerstein, E. (2006). Violence in children's television programming: Assessing the risks. *Journal of Communication, 52*(1), 5–35.

CREDITS

CHAPTER ELEVEN

Social Policy and Ethnicity

LEARNING OBJECTIVES

At the end of this chapter, the student will be able to:

✓ Identify elements of Moynihan's report and determine if it explains the reasons for the demise of the Black family;

✓ Define the term "model minority" and determine if it should no longer be used;

✓ Identify components of the acculturation of Hispanics and generate a process that would make acculturation an easier process;

✓ Determine if Hispanic families are more family oriented than other types of families;

✓ List values that are traditionally linked to Native American persons and if these values can negatively affect their social, educational, and economic well-being;

✓ Summarize concerns about Native Americans and the use and abuse of alcohol and justify arguments to establish social policies related to Native Americans use of alcohol;

✓ Compare and contrast different ethnic groups according to their standing in education, economics, and stable family environment;

✓ Define the concept of affirmative action and debate whether it is still needed in today's society and support and defend a position.

SOCIAL POLICY AND ETHNICITY

In American culture, **ethnicity** is a term that generally refers to historical categories of race, including White, Black, Asian, Hispanic, and Native American. While these categories vary and essentially are invented by humans, the use of ethnicity as racial categories in linking to public policy issues tends to be reified and unchanging (Yanow, 2003). Several government agencies, such as the Census Bureau, collect and report each year on the number of persons assigned to each category. Rata and Openshaw (2006) claim that this tendency to categorize ethnicity leads to societal divisions that can be harmful and exclusive when applied to public policymaking. A discussion of ethnicity frequently refers to minority subpopulations within a larger population of White non-Hispanic persons. Projections for the next several decades suggest that this way of understanding ethnicity will change given that the White non-Hispanic population is expected to fall to below 50% of the total population (Chappell, 2017).

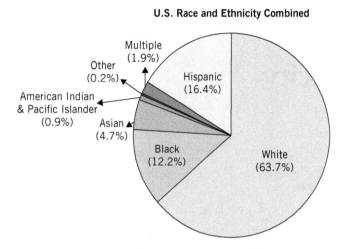

U.S. Race and Ethnicity Combined

FIGURE 11.1 U.S. RACE AND ETHNICITY, 2010
Data Source: 2010 US Decennial Census

Since 1997, the **Office of Management and Budget (OMB)** has categorized race in five basic groups: White, African American (Black), American Indian or Alaska Native, Asian, and Native Hawaiian or other Pacific Islanders (United States Census Bureau, 2017). An additional category, Some Other Race, was added over the past two decades to census reports for individuals who did not fit into one of the existing categories. The OMB's basic categories for the 2010 census defined the "White" category as persons from Europe, the Middle East, and North Africa. The census data are self-reported data, which allow for individuals to select a number of options. For example, individuals could select in a field of options, such as White alone or a combination of White with other races. In the 2010 census, 72% of individuals reported White alone and 3% reported White in combination for a total of 75%, or 231 million persons. Between the 2000 census and the 2010 census, the White alone population grew at a slower rate than the general population, 6% versus 9.7%. The White in combination category grew more than the White alone category, which saw a 37% increase, or 7.5 million persons.

The majority of the increase in the White in combination category involved Asians and African Americans (Hixson, Hepler, & Kim, 2011).

Hispanic origins were not considered a race in the 2010 census, because the designation of Hispanic can carry different races. In the 2010 census report, 9% of the total population, or 26.7 million persons of Hispanic origin, identified as White alone (United States Census Bureau, 2017). Hispanics who identified as White accounted for 70% of the increase in the White alone category. In addition, the Hispanics who identified themselves as White alone or White in combination in 2010 accounted for about 13% of the total population, compared to approximately 9% in the 2000 census, an increase of 4%, which was the largest increase of groups identifying themselves in the White in combination category. In general, the non-Hispanic White population declined in 15 states, including about half of the Midwestern states, while the South had lower rates of decline. The Southwestern U.S. had the largest population of Hispanic White alone or White in combination, including California, New Mexico, Texas, and Arizona (Hixson, Hepler, & Kim, 2011) .

In summation, over the 10-year period from 2000 to 2010, the census data reveal that the largest increase in the White population was because of the increase in White Hispanics coupled with the increase in White multiple race categories (Hixson, Hepler, & Kim, 2011). This data suggest that the major cause of the increase in White population is mainly due to its increase in diversity. The increase from 2000 to 2010 in White alone was 16%, White Hispanic accounted for 70%, and multiple races accounted for 14%. Although the number of persons living within the metro areas of the 20 largest centers in the U.S. declined in 19 of them, the non-Hispanic White alone group increased (Hixson et al., 2011).

The future projections for White alone and White in combination Americans are for a loss of their majority status within 30 years. This change will affect many aspects of American life, including kindergarten through twelfth grade education, politics, and the workforce. The shift in population demographics, with an increase in racial and ethnic diversity, is projected to affect political campaigns and elections; this shift was recently noted in the presidential election of 2012 with Obama receiving 78% of the non-White vote (Yen, 2012). Although the percentages of minorities voting for Hillary Clinton in the 2016 election against Donald Trump decreased, she still carried a huge majority of minority votes (Scott & Kirk, 2016). What it means to be a minority is changing, and race tends to be redefined in that there is an ever increasing number of persons who label themselves as multiple races. It is hypothesized that 50 years in the future, multiple race individuals will make up between 25 and 30 million persons compared to approximately eight million at present (Cohn, 2015). By 2028, it is estimated that minority adults ages 8-29 will outnumber young adult Whites. The increased number of Mexican immigrants and the high rate of births of Hispanic women will continue to drive up the minority population. Hispanic women have an average birth rate per female of 3.8 children. The increase in the number of children of school age is due to the higher birth rate of Hispanic mothers. If not for this rate, there would have been a decrease in the number of births over the number of deaths. As of 2012, minority infants under the age of one outnumbered White infants of the same age (Fry & Gonzales, 2008); by 2020, minority children will become the majority (Chappell, 2015).

Another factor is the shifting demographics of age as illustrated by the number of persons who are over the age of 65 (Suarez-Orozco, 2007). This increase in the older population is partially due to the Baby Boom period of 1946 to 1965. As the baby boomers begin to retire, they will also change the landscape of the U.S. by drastically increasing the number of persons over 65. Because of the forces already set in motion by immigration, birth rate of Hispanics, and increase in baby boomers, this projection of the effects of Hispanic population increase, according to Suarez-Orozco, will come true even if a slowing of these factors occurs.

CHANGING DEMOGRAPHICS RESULTING FROM IMMIGRATION

Over the past several decades, drastic demographic changes have occurred in the American Society (Cilluffo & Cohn, 2017). According to Cilluffo and Cohn, this trend will continue partly fueled by immigration. Immigration has always been contentious, but concerns about it escalated after the election of Donald Trump (American Immigration Council, 2016; Nowrasteh, 2016).

Legal Immigration Policy

Immigration policy in the United States is complex (Nowrasteh, 2016), but is based on several general principles, including admitting persons who have job-related skills, bringing families together, increasing the diversity of the population, and providing new beginnings for refugees (American Immigration Council, 2016). Immigration policy for reunifying families allows for a U.S. citizen to bring **immediate family relatives** who meet eligibility criteria. Admission is also allowed for

family preference systems, which admits more distanced family who also meet the eligibility standards for admission. The total number of family-based visas per year is estimated to be about 480,000, although it may exceed those numbers.

Persons are also admitted into the U.S. on the basis of having valuable skills needed to further the economy, which falls into two categories: **temporary visa classification** and **permanent immigration** (American Immigration Council, 2016). Temporary visas can be given to non-immigration workers to meet job skills for a specific periods of time. There are approximately 20 different types of visas classifications and the visa recipient must leave the country at the termination of the work, or their visa expires. Permanent immigration employment-based visas, which is limited to 140,000 a year and include spouses and unmarried children, fall into five categories, ranging from immigrants with extraordinary skills to unskilled other than seasonal or unskilled temporary.

Legal immigration from various countries is limited primarily to prevent an influx of immigration coming from any one country (American Immigration Council, 2016). At present, no more than 7% of all permanent immigrants can come from any one country. In addition, **refugees**, who are unable to return to their own countries due to political views, race, as well as other beliefs or circumstances. Another group of immigrants include those seeking **asylum** who are already in the U.S. and cannot return to their own country for the same reasons as refugees.

Others types of legal immigration include **Diversity Visa Program**, **Temporary Protected Status (TPS)** and the **Deferred Enforced Departure (DED)** (American Immigration Council, 2016). The Diversity Visa Program established in 1990 was intended to increase immigration from countries who historically have low immigration to the U.S., less than 50,000. Each year, 55,000 allocations are available for random entrance into the U.S. for persons who meet certain criteria for admission. No visas are allowed for regions sending more than 50,000 immigrants over the past five years. Temporary Protected Status refers to persons in this country temporarily who cannot return to their own country because of war, natural disasters, or other conditions considered to be temporary. Deferred Forced Departure is similar to Temporary Protected status but differs in that the executive branch of government makes the decision.

Illegal Immigration

Illegal immigration is dialectical and is heavily debated. The number of undocumented immigrants has steadily increased and today is estimated at more than 11 million, though that may be an underestimation (Gonzales & Raphael, 2017). It is also estimated that more than 2.1 million young undocumented children have been in the U.S. since birth and represent a particularly vulnerable population. Many of the children who were brought to this country by their parents are now adults and their trajectory to adulthood differs from legal status young adults and raises the possibility of mental health issues for immigrants.

The debate over illegal immigration is a heated policy matter. Those who are in favor of illegal immigration say that it is good for the economy (Krayewski, 2013). The core of this argument is that immigrants, legal or illegal, do jobs at lower wages than natural born citizens and that bolsters the economy. They also argue that the real culprits in damaging the economy are entitlements. While few illegal immigrants pay income taxes, other forms of taxes, such as sales tax, are paid by everyone. According to Krayewski, illegal immigrants contribute to few crimes, because otherwise, they would be subject to deportation. Since they desire to work, they tend to live under the radar of government scrutiny. Perhaps one of the most contested ideas is that persons have a natural right to immigrate. It is argued that this natural right to immigrate is more fundamental than a government's right to restrict it. Another argument for illegal immigration that appears to have support on all sides is that there are too many in the country to deport them. Deporting over 11 million persons would disrupt families, damage the economy by reducing the available workforce, and fracture society.

The election of Donald Trump as president of the U.S. changed the dialogue on immigration and underlying policies put in place by the Obama administration (Kulish, Yee. Dickerson, Robbins, Santos, & Medina, 2017). Although immigration was not thought of as a pivotal election issue, Trump made it a central theme of his campaign and tapped into a hidden concern shared by many citizens. One of the concerns was that immigrants reduce jobs for uneducated and poorly trained Americans (Nowrasteh, 2016). Not only does it take jobs away but reduces the income for all unskilled laborers since immigrants are willing to work for less pay. Many believe that immigrants misuse the welfare system, overburden schools, cause income inequality, and take health resources away from citizens by overusing medical facilities (Nowrasteh, 2016). Other concerns include an increase in crimes, especially involving drugs and sex trafficking. Throughout his campaign, Trump focused on America as a sovereign nation that must protect its borders by building a wall.

The Trump administration has kept immigration squarely in its crosshairs and has changed many of the Obama administration policies through executive orders (Alvarez, 2017). While the guidelines for the Obama administration was to focus on deporting only drug traffickers and gang members, the policy under Trump is to deport any illegal immigrant convicted of a crime. This policy is the same for all illegal immigrants convicted of a crime, regardless of how long they have lived in the U.S. and the depths of their familial roots in the U.S.

Another policy of the Obama administration was "**catch and release**;" those crossing the border illegally would be released because there was no facilities to house them until a court decision on their appeal for asylum could be processed (Kulish et al., 2017). Many of the illegal immigrants caught and released in this way would disappear but remain in the U.S. Two possible routes could be taken by the Trump administration: deport them back to Mexico while they wait for the court system and/or build more holding facilities. The Trump administration is also using "**expedited removal**" law dating back to 2002, which allows for deportation of an immigrant who has been in the country less than two months without going before a judge.

Several policies have received extensive media coverage. One of the most debated policies by the Trump administration is about **DACA (Deferred Action for Childhood Arrivals)** (Kulish et al., 2017). While the Trump administration officially suspended it, it is now in the hands of Congress. More than likely, some parts of DACA will remain, but the point of contention is whether or not it leads to amnesty (McCarthy, 2017). Another changing policy topic under the Trump administration that the media has paid much attention to is sanctuary cities, which do not turn over immigration status to Immigration Crime Engagement (ICE) of unauthorized persons arrested by the local police for committing a crime.

THE BLACK AMERICAN FAMILY

One of the first major publications concerning the American Black family was **Moynihan's report** (1965). This report painted a horrendous view of the Black community that, over the years, has had adherents and detractors. Moynihan particularly focused on ghetto violence, poverty, family breakdown, and single parenthood.

Many of these social problems are linked with the plight of urban poor, who tend to have low education achievement, poor career development, frequent incarceration, and high rates of drug addiction (Horowitz & Perazzo, 2012). While the Moynihan report was a landmark in identifying the concerns and needs of the Black urban poor, it failed to outline specific policy guidelines to improve outcomes. Many of the concerns raised have gotten worse, such as single parenthood. Other concerns, such as crime rates and incarceration, unemployment, and high school dropout rates, have also worsened over the intervening decades. For Moynihan, homes without fathers represented a recipe for poverty and poor educational attainment. Moynihan noted that unemployment and out-of-wedlock births tended to not be a direct positive association, since falling unemployment rates did not link with falling out-of-wedlock births. The birth of Black children to two-parent families in 1950 was approximately 53%, while today that figure has dropped to approximately 25%. According to the 2010 census report, almost twice as many children today are living in single-parent families (Horowitz & Perazzo, 2012). The number of children in two-parent families has dropped across all states in the U.S. While the rate of out-of-wedlock pregnancies over the past four decades has increased for all women, for Black women today, the rate is greater than 70%. The number of Black children born to two parents versus single mothers switched in favor of unmarried women for the first time in 1987 and continued to increased.

A number of explanations have been offered for the large number of Black children born to unwed mothers. One is that it is due to the high rate of incarceration of Black men; approximately 25% have been incarcerated or have some involvement with the criminal justice system by age 25 (Drake, 2013). This fact, coupled with the higher risk of young adult Black males dying from violent or criminal behavior, creates an imbalance in the number of females compared to males in the Black community. In addition, another explanation, according to Drake, is that Black women tend to be better educated and have greater employment, which means that there are fewer Black males who are potential partners. These explanations point to a vicious cycle in which Black children are born to unwed mothers and lack a stable male figure in their lives. Consequently, they grow up in poverty and complete the cycle by not finishing school or preparing themselves for high-paying jobs. Boys from these homes will experiment more with drugs and engage in behaviors that get the attention of law enforcement officers. On the other hand, these explanations help clarify how girls growing up in fatherless homes lack relationships with fathers and are not socialized into how a functional romantic relationship is maintained.

The **cycle of poverty** that exists in Black families tends to revolve around two points: The families lack the income of two persons, and working single mothers tend to bring home two-thirds less than two-parent working Black families (Anonymous, n.d.). When compared to two-parent Black families, 86% of children in single-parent families live in poverty, while only 14% of Black children in two-parent families live in poverty (Anonymous, n.d.). While poverty rates have increased for all families since 2010, it has increased more for female-headed single-parent families than for other families.

Moynihan's report (1965) set off a debate that, to some extent, divided historians and sociologists alike on the concerns regarding the Black family. Moynihan's report linked much of the concerns to the aftermath of slavery and discrimination thereafter. Because of **father-absent homes**, Moynihan believed that the Black family had developed into a female-centered family that, unfortunately, kept drifting deeper into dysfunction and poverty. His work was based on the writings of sociologist E. F. Frazier (1939), who based much of the problems with the Black family on the harmful effects of slavery. Noting that no enslaved person could enter into a contract, marriage was out of the question for Blacks during the period of slavery. This is not to say that marriage-like relationships did not exist among slaves. Slave families did exist, but since marriage was not legal, families could be split among different owners. Some visitations of partners occurred, according to researchers (Palmer, 2000), but the hierarchy of priorities was toward one's owner and not to the family as a unit. The threat of separation was always present for slaves, and approximately one-third of parents were separated from their children because of being sold to another plantation. A paradoxical situation arose in that encouraging slave families to be together aided in plantation owners' ability to keep persons enslaved; men were less likely to run away if they lived with their partners and children. Others have taken a different view of the sale of family slave members; they believe it was used as a way to diminish attachments and, therefore, made resistance to the demands of the owner less ominous.

In the intervening years after the **Civil War**, former slaves took refuge in finding lost family members and reuniting (Palmer, 2000). Newspapers and other public means of announcement were vehicles for finding former family members. While some persons formed new families during slavery, many retained ties or held to the belief that after the war they could be reunited with their families. As a result of the devastation to the southern economy, the federal government set up a bureau known as the **Freeman Bureau**, in existence from 1865 to 1872, which aided in family reunification and in helping former slaves and displaced Whites find shelter and the means to start their lives over. After the Civil War, former slaves were now able to legally marry and there is evidence that forming marital relationships was popular (Palmer, 2000).

While many agreed with Moynihan's overall perspective that slavery had destroyed the family, some took offense to his view that much of the present dysfunction in Black families was due to the female-headed structure. One of the most vocal critics of Moynihan and his views based on Frazier was Gutman (1976). According to Gutman, the majority of children born at the close of the Civil War had two parents, and there is ample evidence that these relationships had existed for some time. Moreover, his view was that this was a testament to the strength of the Black family and their resilience to withstand the horrible conditions of slavery.

Much has been written about the Black middle class, particularly noting that it has increased over the past several decades (Lang & Lehmann, 2009). It has also been noted that two-parent Black families tend to maintain family incomes that are above the poverty rates, while Black female heads-of-household tend to be below the poverty line. One indicator of economic success is the unemployment rate. As of July 2013, the unemployment rate for Blacks was 12.6%, roughly twice the rate for Whites, which has remained steady for decades. This differential is not easily explained, and a recent investigation into the disparity in employment rates between Whites and Blacks found that all models were equally unable to give a satisfactory answer. The report concluded that the racial discrimination model, however helpful it may be in understanding wage differentials between Blacks and Whites, does not explain unemployment (Lang & Lehmann, 2009). Other factors may affect the unemployment rates for Blacks, such as seniority in the job; persons without seniority tend to be Black and are most often let go in downsizing due to economic hard times.

Overall, Blacks make up about 11.6% of the labor force. Unlike White, Hispanic, and Asian groups, more Black women are employed compared to Black men (Lang & Lehmann, 2009). The number of Blacks with a college degree has grown faster than the number of Whites in recent years, but a gap still exists between the two groups. Public sector jobs are more frequently held by Blacks compared to Whites (20% vs. 14%, respectively), excluding self-employment. During the recent recession, Blacks had higher unemployment rates and slower rates of recovery than Whites. Unemployed Blacks take longer to find jobs than Whites, and the jobs they find are lower in pay. The unemployment rate for Blacks in 2011 was 16.7%, but by 2013, it was down to 13.6%.

The unemployment rate for youths also gives a good picture of economic concerns of Blacks (Lang & Lehmann, 2009). During the recent recession in November 2009, the unemployment rate for Black youths 16 to 19 years of age was approximately 49%. By 2011, there was some reduction in the unemployment rate, but it still was high and has continued to be high in 2013 (Meyer, 2013). Many Black teens gave up looking for jobs, which may be one reason for the drop in the rate coupled with the fact that enrollment rates in high school increased during this time frame. The inference is that the poor economy may have helped decrease the Black youth unemployment rate by eliminating many of the low-paying jobs that in the past may have enticed some students from staying in school. However, this explanation may lack credulity, because Blacks have lower employment rates at all educational levels. For example, Black youths with high school degrees still have an unemployment rate of approximately 16%, which is about twice that of White youths (Bureau of Labor Statistics, 2017). While many factors may coalesce to create this disparity in youth unemployment rates, logistics may also play an important role. Given that Blacks may reside in more depressed economic areas than Whites, the opportunities for employment in desirable settings may be more restricted. Having to commute to other locations may be problematic for youths who lack transportation. The longer the commute, the greater the problem in finding and holding down a job.

THE ASIAN AMERICAN FAMILY

The Asian alone population in the U.S. makes up less than 5% of the total population, but when viewed alone and in combination with other races, accounts for about 5.6% of the total (Humes, Jones, & Ramirez, 2011). Persons who self-select on the census as Asian include Chinese, Japanese, Filipino, Indian, Vietnamese, and Korean. Referring to themselves as "Asian," the term was first applied in the 1960s to replace the term "Oriental" (Chin, 1996). Immigrants from various Asian countries have come to the U.S. in waves for different purposes. In 1965, the passage of the Hart-Cellar Act was instrumental in changing immigration patterns for all persons of Asian background (Chin, 1996). Prior to this act, strict standards were set to control the immigration of Asian persons. One early wave of Asian immigration took place during the 1800s; it consisted of Chinese men who primarily came to the U.S. to work on the transcontinental railroad. A wave of Asian females followed to provide brides and partners for the men. Most Asian immigrants enter the U.S. from the West Coast and tend to remain in the Western U.S. Asian immigration from time to time was stymied by restrictive laws, such as the Asian Exclusion Act. More recent immigrants in the 21st century are from Vietnam, Cambodia, and the Pacific Islands (Chin, 1998).

Asian and Pacific Islanders accounted for over 18 million people, or roughly 6% of the population in the U.S. in 2012 (Humes, Jones, & Ramirez, 2011). Asians are also considered the largest growing ethnic group and tend to be better educated, more affluent, and family oriented (Pew Research Center, 2012). The average household income is slightly less than $70,000. Asian ethnic groups consist of Chinese, Indian, Filipino, Korean, Japanese, Pacific Islanders, and Vietnamese. The Pew Research Center found that Asians value marriage and family in higher numbers than the general population. They are more likely than the average American family to live in **multigenerational households**. Most Asian American families have two parents; female-headed families are a rarity. Furthermore, according to the Pew Research Center, **Intermarriage,** especially with White partners, is highest among Japanese and Filipino persons. Asian Americans, on average, have smaller families than other ethnic groups, especially Hispanic. The lower birth rate, combined with other demographics such as fewer out-of-wedlock births, means that the overall growth in the Asian American population rate is ever declining. The increasing number of Asian career women is expected to further slow the rate of births to Asian women. The Asian population trend now being set in Japan of more persons over 65 than under 15 years of age is expected to become the standard for the U.S. as well (Kotkin, 2012). Another trend in East Asian culture is the number of single Asian women. In some countries such as Taiwan approximately one-third of women between 30 to 34 are still single. While the marriage age has generally increased in industrialized countries, the age for first marriage in Asian countries is much higher and sure to influence Asian immigration to other non-Asian countries (Kotkin, 2012).

Asians and Education

Asian students tend to excel in all levels of academics, including grade school and college. In recent years, admission to prestigious colleges and universities has far exceeded the share of the total population. For example, while the Asian population in California is less than 15%, their enrollment at the two most prestigious universities in California and the nation in 2008, namely University of California, Los Angeles, and the University of California at Berkeley, was 40% at University of California, Los Angeles, and 37% at University of California at Berkeley (Perry, 2009). A report from the National Assessment of Educational Progress (NAEP) in 2014 on reading and math scores from tests taken by seniors concluded that Asians fared better than other groups. This report provided three levels of scores, basic, proficient, and advanced, across different demographic groups, coupled with the educational level of parents. Students with learning disabilities and English language learners were not included in this data. Scores were compared to 1992 data and found to be four points lower overall. Gaps in reading scores of Black and White students remained constant on reading indices, but math scores showed some improvement; however, the gap between White and Black and White and Hispanic students remained the same. This report also showed that scores in reading for Asian American students (generally limited to Chinese, Japanese, and Korean) were higher than for White students. Such findings have led some scholars to refer to Asian and Pacific Islanders as the **model minority**, a minority racial or ethnic group that achieves a higher educational, economical, and family stability status than the average for other minorities (Li & Wang, 2008).

While academic success is generally higher for Chinese, Japanese, and Korean students, some subgroups of Asian students do not out-perform White students. Newer immigrants groups, such as Vietnamese and Indonesians, have more difficulty with the English language and generally do not have as much academic success as older immigration groups (Li & Wang, 2008). Many reasons may exist for the differences in the academic success of these specific Asian students, but one factor may be the academic level of parents. Better educated Chinese and Japanese immigrants tend to come to the U.S. for work opportunities rather than for political asylum, as has been the case particularly for the Vietnamese. The added benefit of having college educated and economically stable parents is that they tend to promote the academic success of Chinese and Japanese students in primary and secondary education. Cambodian and Vietnamese immigrant children tend to be the first in their families to acquire a higher education degree.

Some researchers have noted a cultural component to the achievement of Asian and Pacific Island students (Chen & Stevenson, 1995). One finding demonstrated that Asian and Pacific Island students spend significantly more time studying and doing homework than other racial or ethnic groups (Kiderra, 2011). Asian and Pacific Island students spend less time on extracurricular activities and social media than do White students. These findings support the view that Asian students put more emphasis on achieving academically, and, as a consequence, have less social life development. In addition, the **Asian cultural imperative** to achieve and self-monitor one's self-improvement may shed light on why education has such value to Asian children. Their academic performance is culturally grounded in the desire to achieve, and there is the motivation to be the best they can be. This motivation to achieve is not as strong a cultural trait for White or Black families. While most American parents believe in the efficacy of education and the need to instill a desire to achieve academically, White, Black, and Hispanic parents lack the focus on early education that Asian parents consistently exhibit. Ingrained in many parents is the belief that young children should not be pushed too much because it might have opposite results. Some believe that preschool is for playing and that kindergarten begins the real focus on learning.

In Asian culture there is a greater sense of living up to one's responsibility as a parent and, consequently, the response from the child is to live up to the expectations of the parent (Hartlep, 2013). Good parenting that emphasizes providing for the opportunity for the child's self-development creates a cycle in which both the child and the parent act in accordance with each other's expectations, with good will toward each other. The Asian parent is an active co-participant in education, not a distant observer (Hartlep, 2013). This culture of co-participation with children by Asian parents extends to all socioeconomic levels, including low income. While these parents may not have the means themselves to properly supervise their children's schoolwork, they nevertheless provide an atmosphere in which other family members can take over this role. In addition, it should also be noted that there are fewer single-parent families formed by out-of-wedlock births among Asian women as compared to other racial and ethnic groups. Academic achievement, in particular, is a deficit in female-headed single-parent families.

There is another side to this debate, however, in that some question the term "model minority" as applied to Asians and Pacific Islanders (Hartlep, 2013). Hartlep points out that some research on Asians has not focused enough on differences in subgroups. Others have pointed out that the label of model minority is just another way to stereotype a minority group and subject it to a narrow frame of reference. It tends to hold up one minority group as an ideal while inherently criticizing other groups for not performing well. Instead of a desirable label, model minority carries with it impressions that may not apply to all persons in the group, which can lead to greater negative scrutiny. (Hartlep, 2013). Labeling of one minority group as a model may create animosity and competition with other minority groups, leading to further deterioration of the relationships among minority groups. One of the consequences of being a model minority is not being protected by governmental programs aimed at ensuring equal treatment under the law, such as affirmative action (McGowan & Lindgren, 2006). Another argument cited by McGowan and Lindgren is that the differences between Asian and other groups mainly reflect the educational level of the family and, therefore, not cultural or parenting practices, as has been proposed.

Some would argue that the parameters for determining a model minority are limited by the view that society generally holds for that minority. For example, in comparing educational attainment of immigrant groups, immigrants from Africa tend to have among the highest levels of education, with almost 50% holding a baccalaureate degree (McCabe, 2011). The level of education attainment for African immigrants and children born to them out-performs native-born Asians, is about two times the level of native-born Whites, and four times the level of native-born Blacks. In addition, immigrants from Africa tend to enter the job market in the U.S. at high levels, particularly in self-employed businesses. While African immigrants would seem to fit the criteria of model minority, unfortunately, the image of African countries being less developed carries a negative connotation that flags their accomplishments.

It has also been argued that creating a model minority was a political ploy meant to shield society from the evils of discrimination and undermine the argument that the effects of racism and discrimination are innocuous (Shankar, 2012). At its worst, the term tends to point blame on some groups, such as Blacks and Hispanics, for not being more successful. Instead of understanding or being sensitive to the unique experiences of each minority group, the term implies that all minorities are essentially the same and are in complete control of their destiny. According to Shankar, some point out that not only are minorities different in historical development but they also differ in present experiences and values. Even within minority groups there is variation in language and customs. The dropout rate for some Asian and Pacific Island groups, such as Vietnamese, are significantly higher than for White. Although Asian and Pacific Island students are overrepresented in some schools, they are also not admitted to others, while students not as qualified are admitted. Another concern for Asian and Pacific Island students is that sometimes they are merely assumed to be doing well because they are less identifiable in the classroom and do not appear to need extra attention. This lack of attention to Asian and Pacific Island students may paradoxically reward them for being mute and not expressing their concerns. Some have pointed out that parents of Asian and Pacific Island students tend to be less involved with the school system than other parents and, therefore, do not voice their concerns directly to school personnel.

Unanswered questions revolve around perpetuating a myth that has detrimental effects for all. Some questions of inequity exist that should be addressed. For example, while many Asian students struggle with English, schools typically do not consider them English language learners, and no programs exist for them to become more proficient (English Language Learners & Southeast Asian American Communities Fact Sheet, 2013).

LATINO/HISPANIC AMERICAN FAMILY

This section discusses Spanish-speaking persons in the U.S. who come from countries in South and Central America, Cuba, Mexico, Europe, and Spain. Both Latino and Hispanic are used interchangeably, but some Spanish descendants in the U.S. prefer to be called Latino (Austin & Johnson, 2012). For this reason, the terms will be used interchangeably in this section. In 2012, the Latino/Hispanic population in the U.S. stood at approximately 53 million persons, accounting for about 17% of the total population (Census Bureau, 2012). By 2060, the Hispanic population of the U.S. is estimated to become approximately 31%, or 128 million people. The majority, approximately 65%, of the Latino/Hispanic population in the U.S., is from Mexico, making the U.S. the second most populous Latino/Hispanic population in the world. Eight states in the U.S. have populations of persons of Hispanic origins in excess of one million. California has the highest number of Hispanic citizens, and Los Angeles has the highest increase of any city in the nation since 2010. In over 40% of the states, or 21 states, the Hispanic population is the largest minority population in the state. According to census data in 2012, Hispanic children are the fastest growing number of children under 18 in the U.S. Over 60% of Hispanic households have a married couple with children under the age of 18. Approximately three-fourths of families with children under the age of 18 speak Spanish in the home. The Hispanic population in the 2010 election accounted for roughly 8.4% of the total vote.

Latinos/Hispanics and Education

The percent of Hispanic adults in the U.S. who do not have a high school degree was about 34% in 2012, which is about 10% higher than the general population. In terms of higher education, slightly less than 15% of students enrolled in colleges in the U.S. identified themselves as Hispanic (U.S. Census Bureau, 2012). This statistic was helped by a single year of increase. In 2009 and 2010, the Hispanic college enrollment increased by 24%. In K-12, the number of Hispanic students comparable to other races and ethnicities has been increasing, and in 2012 was 25%, and 29% for nursery school (U.S. Census Bureau, 2012). While the share of high school graduates attending college dropped for White students in 2012, the number of Hispanic high school graduates attending college increased. It was the first time that college enrollment was greater for Hispanic high school students than for White students (49% vs. 47% respectively). While other groups decreased in enrollment in college, the number of Hispanics to attend college between 2011 and 2012 increased by 324,000. This increase is partly the result of fewer White students in the age cohort to attend college. The reason for the immense increase in Hispanic enrollment at all levels of education is the explosion in immigration and the high birth rate for Hispanic women (Fry & Taylor, 2013).

While 73% of White, 78% of Asian, and 63% of Black students enroll in four-year schools, only 54% of Hispanic students enroll (National Assessment of Educational Progress, 2014). A caveat exists, however, for Hispanic students and education. While enrollment numbers have greatly increased, the rate of matriculation is woefully low. The rate in 2010 for matriculation was 13% for Hispanics 24-29 years of age compared to 54% of Asians and 39% of Whites. One explanation for this disparity reflects the high number of Hispanics who have recently immigrated to the U.S. compared to other groups who are native born. Native-born Hispanics show about a 20% rate of matriculation for young adults ages 25-29 for four-year college degrees (National Assessment of Educational Progress, 2014).

A number of laws and court cases directly affected Hispanics and education. One of the major laws was the Elementary and Secondary Education Act of 1965. Although originally not directly aimed at Hispanics, it did open doors for minority students. This law, which was an integral part of Lyndon Johnson's War on Poverty, provided help for poor children. An amendment to this law in 1968, the Bilingual Act of 1968, was crafted toward Hispanic children to help them make clear transitions from Spanish to English. Generally, laws passed regarding the education of minority and bilingual children have been supported by the Supreme Court. *Plyler v. Doe* (1982) was a Supreme Court decision that provided equal opportunity for education to all children regardless of their legal standing. This decision was based on the belief that an educated citizenry is necessary for self-sufficiency and would reduce the dependency on the government. In a recent Supreme Court case involving a state's attempt to regulate immigration, the Court's decision was to strike down an Arizona law that restricted immigration (Cohen & Mears, 2012). The Court ruled firmly in favor of the federal government's authority to regulate immigration unimpeded by states; that is, states have no authority to create laws on immigration.

Another recent House of Representative's bill, *Help Separated Families Act of 2012*, focused on not disrupting families by separating children from parents who were in the U.S. illegally. This bill would ensure that children born in the U.S. of illegal parents would not suffer separation because the children were considered citizens and the parents were not citizens.

The Quality of Family Life and Divorce

Much has been written about the Hispanic community being pro-family and the structure of the home being two parents who take complimentary roles: the husband focused on work and the wife more focused on the home and children (Landale, Oropesa, & Bradatan, 2012). This view also tends to be supported by a lower divorce rate when compared to other ethnic groups, the strong influence of the Catholic Church, and the belief in self-sufficiency. The role of the Catholic Church has played an integral part in the value system of Mexican-American families. The divorce rate and the separated without divorce rate may both be affected by the connection with the Catholic Church. In the Catholic Church, marriage is a sacrament, and divorce is often obtained by annulment, a long procedure of levels of church bureaucracy in which the marriage is basically declared to have never existed. However, there is a caveat to this optimistic view of Hispanics and family structure. For example, while Hispanics have lower divorce rates when compared to other groups, they have higher rates of separation without divorce (Kreider & Simmons, 2003). When divorce rates are combined with separation without divorce, Hispanics have higher rates of family disruption than Whites. Consequently, family disruption tends to be high, leaving many children predominantly in the hands of female-headed homes. Studies have also found that the negative effects of divorce on children are not as great for Hispanic children than other ethnic groups (Padilla & Borrero, 2006).

What is known about how Hispanics view family structure from survey data is that almost three-fourths of Hispanics consider children's welfare to be enhanced when there are two parents in the household (Padilla & Borrero, 2006). Beliefs about abortion tend to be equally balanced, but

Hispanics tend to frown on having an abortion either because the mother is young or does not want the child. Only one in five believe that abortion should be legal on demand.

Historically, there is a paucity of research on Hispanic families, who, until recently, made up only a small portion of the U.S. population (Oropesa & Landale, 2004). One reason for this is that the Hispanic population in the U.S. is made up of a number of groups, including Cubans, Mexicans, Puerto Ricans, and South Americans. According to Oropesa and Landale, each of these subgroups has its own structure and, to some degree, values. Another factor that creates heterogeneity in these groups is the reason for coming to the U.S. The motivation for immigrating sets a point of value for their interaction affecting acculturation (Motel & Patten, 2015). The type of immigration, whether through legal immigration or undocumented by crossing the border, is linked with different expectations and involvement in the community. Another reason may be the increase of stress, particularly on the marital relationship, associated with immigration. The traditional structure of the family may be affected by this greater stress from immigrating and by the pressures of acculturation. As acculturation takes place, the cherished structure and gender roles associated with the traditional Hispanic family, particularly from Mexico, will remain intact. The observation that the Hispanic family has stable gender roles adds to the belief that the family is stable. It could be argued that gender roles as such may actually increase the divorce rate if persons in these marriages are under greater stress from changes, such as immigration to the U.S. (Oropesa & Landale, 2004; Motel & Patten, 2015). The intergenerational closeness, sometimes referred to as *la familia*, that binds Hispanic generations together over time for support may be at risk for immigrating families. The rate of acculturation may be different for different subgroups of immigrants and even within subgroups.

While all Hispanic groups share a common language, subgroups from different parts of the world tend to congregate in different regions of the country. Immigrants from Mexico tend to congregate in western and southern states, while Cubans reside in greater number in Florida, and Puerto Ricans in northeastern states (Oropesa & Landale, 2004). Recent trends show that Hispanics have increased two to three times in number in areas such as Alabama, Georgia, Tennessee, North Carolina, and Nebraska, states not noted for high Hispanic population. Hispanics concentrate in large metropolitan areas in the 20 most populous areas, including New York, Los Angeles, and Chicago.

Acculturation

Studies on Mexican Americans have found somewhat contradictory results. Some have found that **acculturation** may act to increase stress and anxiety, because spouses acculturate at different rates. The slower partner to acculturate may have more stress because of the increase in isolation that may result (Marsiglia, Booth, Baldwin, & Ayers, 2013). As acculturation occurs, immigrants are separated more for the traditional values that were important, namely a strong family tradition rooted in the values of Catholicism. Other researchers have found the opposite, namely that stress in marital relationships is amplified from acculturation (cited in Marsiglia et al., 2013). Family influence tends to remain intact for first, second, and third generations, and, while family does not become less important, a larger friendship network grows cumulatively for each generation. Some have predicted that divorce rates will gradually increase as acculturation increases. Of specific interest is how the second and third generations of immigrants accommodate themselves to American culture (Oropesa & Landale 2004).

Coping with divorce is an issue for any ethnic group. Some have postulated that divorce may be harder for immigrant Mexican males in this country than for females (Oropesa & Landale, 2004). It would generally be assumed that a female would have more dissatisfaction with a relationship based on traditional Mexican values in which she is more restricted. When her level of dissatisfaction reaches the breaking point, it is easier for her to leave the marriage and harder for the male to adjust. Divorce may be much more financially devastating for Hispanics because of the already low wages and a non-custodial father's inability to support the family after divorce (Marsiglia, Booth, Baldwin, & Ayers, 2013). The result is that many Hispanic families will be below the poverty line and supported by the government (ASPE Issue Brief, 2012). Furthermore, because the male may be less likely to support the family after divorce, his per capita income would be expected to be much higher than his former wife's income. Males who have attained greater education tend to not only maintain their levels of income after divorce but actually increase them. Females almost universally received custody of children. These economic and social trends after divorce are similar to the non-Hispanic White population. However, Hispanic women improve economically more after divorce than do non-Hispanic White women (Oropesa & Landale, 2004). Some of this difference may be due to Hispanic women relying more on their own earned income than Non-Hispanic White women. Overall, Hispanic women seem to cope better with divorce and the single-parent family aftermath than non-Hispanic White women. It may also be the case that stressors for Hispanic women are different than for other women due to their unique experiences.

The effect of divorce on Hispanic children still needs further analysis, but research tends to show that they are affected less than non-Hispanic White children (Amato, 2001). The generational support and influence in the Hispanic community may insulate Hispanic children from the negative trauma of divorce. The process of acculturation may, however, erode the impact of the supportive network for Hispanic children and means that, in time, divorce will be a more negative experience.

NATIVE AMERICAN FAMILIES

Native Americans and Alaska Natives are a diverse group and comprise about 530 tribes across the U.S. Native Americans comprise one of the smallest ethnic groups in the U.S. The 2011 census data reported that the current population of Native Americans is 5.2 million or about 1.7% of the total population. Since Native Americans tend to be of mixed race, only about 2.9 million are Native American and Alaska Native only and the remaining are of mixed racial backgrounds. Between the 2000 and 2010 census reports, the Native American and Alaska Native population increased by 26.7%, adding about 1.1 million. The three most populous states were California, Oklahoma, and Arizona, respectively. Fifteen states have a Native American and Alaska Native population of over 100,00, including California, Oklahoma, Arizona, Texas, New York, New Mexico, Washington, North Carolina, Florida, Michigan, Alaska, Oregon, Colorado, Minnesota, and Illinois. Slightly less than 20% of the population of Alaska Natives identify themselves as Native American and Alaska Native. The overall median age of the population (29) is less than the general median age of 37.2, which would mean that there is a larger pool of children under 18 years of age than the general population. Approximately 22% live on **reservations** or in government-designated areas. About 53% of families are two-parent families and the average age at marriage is roughly the same as the general population. A lower percentage of Native American and Alaska Natives own their homes as compared to the general population, and about 41% have a college degree compared to 44%. The median income is about $35,000 and the poverty rate is 28.4%, both of which differ significantly from the national population. The national rate for home ownership is approximately 65% compared to 54% for Native American and Alaska Natives. The rate of not having health insurance is almost double the national average of 15%. In most categories of health and well-being Native Americans and Alaska Natives lag behind the general population.

Values

While Native Americans share much of the same culture with the general population, and are analyzed with the same measures, there are a number of differences. These differences may appear as stereotypical information, but on a broader scale, they depict the cultural uniqueness of present and past Indian beliefs and customs (Boxer, 2009). While customs and values tend to set Native Americans off from the overall population, customs may even vary between tribes and geography. Native American and Alaska Native Americans may not be significantly different from other groups of Americans when they were raised in non-traditional Native American families. Those reared on reservations and by traditional Indian parents, however, tend to resemble the generalized view of Native American culture and values.

One of the major Indian values is to downplay individual accomplishments and not seek to promote oneself, especially to the detriment of another person (Boxer, 2009). Competition may be between groups, but one has a role to play in the group, rather than to seek attention for oneself. To live one's life in harmony with others is more desirable than to receive accolades for one's individual performance. The group's closeness and identity, such as the family, transcends even accomplishments in work or a career. In contrast to general values of assertiveness and leadership, Native Americans believe in being humble and making themselves small rather than large in the eyes of others. Private property and material possessions are an anathema to Indians, who believe more in giving away their possessions than accumulating them. More emphasis is placed on social interaction and living in close proximity with others, as opposed to living alone. Loyalty to the group is valued over being independent (Boxer, 2009).

Children are socialized differently in Native American families (Boxer, 2009). They tend to be treated with respect without corporal punishment. Children may be shamed or teased into compliance rather than punished. Being accepted in the group and acting appropriately are of highest priority. Parenting may involve the whole network, especially the grandparents. The code of honoring the family and being an integral part is taught to children from the very beginning. The elderly are expected to be influential in passing on the family traditions (Light & Martin, 1985).

Religion and spiritual experiences are more private than in the general American public where **community** is a typical shared experience (Boxer, 2009). American Natives experience religion though spiritual encounters in nature and events. Religious leaders emerge out of one's support for others rather than through promoting oneself. Like other experiences, living in the present is valued over either planning for the future or living with regret in the past (Boxer, 2009).

The belief that everyone had a place and a role in Indian culture meant that homosexuals and transgendered individuals were not condemned, as in traditional culture (Wilson, 2011). Persons who differed from the norm were believed to have special gifts and were valued for how they might contribute to the life of the community. It is interesting that a culture based on community would be more accepting of diversity than its counterpart, the traditional Westernized American culture, which was based on **individualism**. It would appear that acceptance of diversity might be more difficult if the culture was more homogeneous.

Native Americans and Alcohol Abuse

Much has been written about Native Americans and alcohol abuse. The facts tend to speak for themselves in that roughly 10% of its population die from an alcohol-related disease, such as cirrhosis of the liver. Almost 70% of those who die from alcohol-related diseases are men, and death generally occurs before the age of 50 (Associated Press, 2014). A troubling statistic is that 7% of the alcohol-related deaths were men under the age of 20. In addition, there has been a slow and continuous increase in **Fetal Alcohol Syndrome (FAS)** due to female drinking patterns. While more recognition of alcohol abuse has been made, treatment and especially prevention fall far short of making inroads into curtailing alcohol abuse among Native Americans. Since alcohol abuse is high, other related diseases, including drug abuse, cardiovascular disease, and suicide are also higher than the national average. Suicide rates are twice the national average and the highest risk occurs during the late teens/early adulthood period (Associated Press, 2014).

Life on the Reservation

One of the major problems of Native Americans living on reservations is the lack of employment. The largest single entity for jobs on the reservation is the government, which means that other more expansive careers are lacking. While the poverty rate is a little less than 30% nationally for Native Americans, the employment rate for residents on the reservations ranges between 38% and 63% (The National Center for Education Statistics, 2008). Many residents must work outside the reservation in order to gain economic viability.

Adequate housing has been an ongoing problem for Native Americans. Many households still lack running water, electricity, and even kitchen appliances (Fixico, 2006). Many live in overcrowded households with multiple generations living under the same roof. Such conditions increase the possibility of diseases and reduce the quality of life. The lack of adequate living environments may be related to the number of homeless Native Americans.

Health care is generally substandard on reservations. There is a shortage of doctors, pharmacies, and medical clinics in some communities (Fixico, 2006). Coupled with inadequate health care and acculturation to Anglo practices, Native Americans are at high risk for debilitating diseases, such as heart disease and diabetes. More than one-third of the Native American population will experience heart disease before the age of 65, which is twice the rate of White Americans. In addition, the rate of diabetes is more than twice the rate of White Americans.

As Native Americans have become more Westernized, they have slowly adopted different ways of living (Fixico, 2006). No small part of that has been in using modern technology, including social media. This creeping Western culture has not been as prominent on the reservation as to those who live and work off the reservation. The Native Americans living on reservations have carried on many of the traditions and values that have been closely aligned with Native American culture.

Social Policy and Native Americans and Pacific Island Natives

Two early policies, the *Northwest Ordinance of 1787* and the *Intercourse Act of 1790,* were meant to ensure that Indian land would not be confiscated or taken from them (cited in Boxer, 2009). Unfortunately, neither of these laws fully protected Indians from White invasion. The primary reason for uprooting Indian people was the push westward by White settlers. To justify this expansion, an egregious law, referred to as the *Removal Act of 1830,* was passed to provide a means for the U.S. government to trade land east of the Mississippi for land west of the Mississippi. It meant that Indians could legally be uprooted from their land in the east and relocated to land in the west.

SOCIAL POLICY AND RACE AND ETHNICITY

The general consensus on American social policy is that race and ethnicity have always played a hefty role in defining and carrying out social policy agenda (Lieberman, 2014). Governmental social policy has used race and ethnicity to address social and economic issues. For example, in providing a more equal access of minority admission to colleges and universities and job opportunities, **affirmative action**, which provided quotas for minorities, was believed to be a vehicle for eliminating lack of representation of minorities into the mainstream.

The merits of affirmative action have been debated since its inception. Many look at it as absolutely necessary to create what is generally referred to as an "equal playing field" for minorities and women. Without affirmative action, many persons who were able to attend prestigious universities would never have had the opportunity. It has increased diversity in educational institutions and in the workplace that heretofore did not exist. The argument for affirmative action is also based on the view that, without it, discrimination would have continued, and stereotyping of minorities would never have been addressed for the evil that it is. Furthermore, they argue that stereotypes in society apply to all races and genders, resulting in greater freedom and fewer imposed restrictions on all (Bergmann, 1996; Leef & Sterba, 2012).

Other arguments for affirmative action include making a case for centuries of discrimination toward minorities, especially Blacks, in which they have been denied the heritage of high-quality education, employment, and political standing (Leef & Sterba, 2012). Native Americans can also be included in the group of neglected Americans who have followed generations before them in poverty and low status as a result of discrimination. Without the full implementation of affirmative action, the rights of minorities would still be on the back burner. From this point of view, compensation for the wrongs of discrimination is an ongoing process and needs careful support (Bergmann, 1996).

In her very interesting and informative book, *Racism and justice: The case for affirmation action,* Gertrude Ezorsky (1991) defended affirmative action on the basis that it counteracted institutional racism. Without affirmative action, she argued that Blacks would have to exhibit extraordinary talents and abilities far beyond those of the majority of individuals. In the arena of employment, affirmative action requires that public announcements be made regarding a job opening. Furthermore, during hiring, job qualifications must be specific to the job announcement in order to prevent the hiring of a personal contact who may not have the skills necessary to function adequately in the job.

Derrick Bell (1987) believes that affirmative action actually helps Whites in the workplace, because in downsizing, seniority plays a huge role. Whites generally have greater seniority and they are able to retain their jobs, while newer hired minorities are not. According to Ezorsky (1991), while affirmative action is unable to help uneducated minorities who lack basic skills, it has been able to provide upward mobility to countless minorities who would have been overlooked in hiring. This argument concedes that in hiring some minorities, more qualified Whites may not have been hired, but justifies this on the basis of long-standing inequality. Furthermore, the continuation of affirmative action means that future generations of minorities will be able to participate and demonstrate that they are competent to do the job when given the opportunity.

The advocates for continuing affirmative action point to the existence of no other comparable system that would address the issues. Without affirmative action there is the fear that universities and employers will revert back to the old system. On the surface, the old system speaks to equality and hiring the most qualified, but underneath the rhetoric lies the slippage of minorities back into the shadows (Affirmative Action Overview, 2013; Leef & Sterba, 2012).

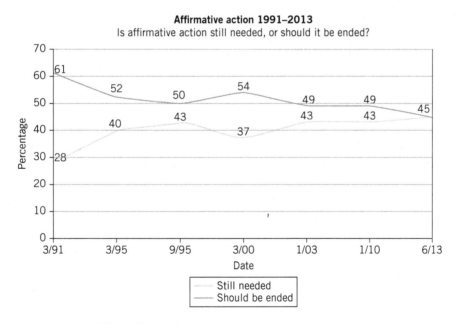

FIGURE 11.2 Affirmative action

On the other hand, advocates against affirmative action point out that the policy mostly benefits middle- and upper-middle-class Blacks, but not those on the lower end (Affirmative Action Overview, 2013). It can also be noted that affirmative action fails to help poor Whites and Asians and, in fact, discriminates against them, because they have no avenues to improve their lives. This argument hits squarely on the notion that affirmative action is discriminatory at its foundation in conception and practice (Leef & Sterba, 2012). Another point that the opposing side of the affirmative action debate takes is that, in some cases, the difference in minority scores and White or Asian scores is wide, leading to more qualified White and Asians students being denied admission (Affirmative Action Overview, 2013).

The advocates against affirmative action point out that even diversity is not enhanced, because different groups tend to promote their own agendas rather than meld into the whole (Affirmative Action Overview, 2013). For example, universities, in the name of diversity, will have a homecoming queen for each group or exclusive dormitories and clubs. From the advocates against affirmative action, the argument for diversity is seen as meaning that only minorities, or race, can create a diverse environment (Leef & Sterba, 2012). The implication is that all minorities are alike, one of the stereotypes that affirmative action was meant to squelch (Gratz, 2017). They further argue that affirmative action has just replaced the old racism with a new one, more subtle and egregious than the former. Proponents argue that racism is still alive and well and programs like affirmative action are the only buffer between minorities and the return to segregation. Those against affirmative action would say that if something has been tried for 25 years and has failed to end discrimination, perhaps it was not the best action in the first place (Affirmative Action Overview, 2013).

The advocates against affirmative action believe that students who are admitted to the university and receive preferential treatment in being hired for a job may always have that tainted view of not being there because they deserved to be (Leef & Sterba, 2012). If majority students and colleagues begin to question the qualifications of minority students, what has been set in motion by a policy that is supposed to create opportunity will have the opposite effect (Affirmative Action Overview, 2013).

Affirmative action has been made possible by court rulings and policies created by various businesses, schools, and agencies to combat discrimination (Leef & Sterba, 2012). The debate is not over, but tends to be less emotional. It is expected that in the near future we will see more action in the courts on both sides of the issue of affirmative action. A systems/dialectical perspective would look at the broader issues of discrimination from society as a whole and attempt to find the common ground between points of view—a common ground based on the acknowledgement that opposite points of view will each contain truths that should not be discarded.

KEY TERMS

Ethnicity

Office of Management and Budget

Moynihan's report

Father absent homes

Civil War

Freeman Bureau

Expedited removal

Diversity Visa Program

Permanent immigration

Multigenerational household

Intermarriage

Model minority

Asian cultural imperative

Acculturation

Reservation

Deferred Action for Childhood Arrivals (DACA)

Immediate family relative

Community

Individualism

Fetal Alcohol Syndrome (FAS)

Affirmative action

Cycle of poverty

Catch and release

Temporary Protected status

STUDY QUESTIONS TO ACCOMPLISH THE LEARNING OBJECTIVES

1. Outline components of Moynihan's report. Describe the strengths and weaknesses. Evaluate the adequacy of this report for understanding the causes of the breakdown of the Black family.

2. What does it mean that Asians are labeled the "model minority." Analyze the negative effects of this label. Argue for keeping or doing away with the label.

3. Discuss acculturation for Hispanics. Evaluate the pros and the cons of acculturation.

4. Discuss divorce in Hispanic families. Evaluate the concept that Hispanic families are more family oriented than other ethnic groups. Compare and contrast divorce in Hispanic families and the general population.

5. Define Native American values. Evaluate if these values place Native Americans at an economic disadvantage in American culture.

6. Determine if Native Americans have a greater problem with alcohol addiction than other Americans.

7. Generate significant social policy initiatives for Native Americans.

8. Compare and contrast immigrant groups on economic status and educational achievement.

9. Define affirmative action. Debate pros and cons for continuing affirmative action. Develop guidelines for using affirmative action that would not discriminate against others.

10. Compare and contrast immigrant groups on marriage and divorce. Evaluate how family life contributes to economic success of immigrant groups.

DEBATE ACTIVITY FOR STUDENTS

Consider the following proposition: Schools should adopt different disciplinary standards for minority students than majority students based on their history of discrimination and lack of privilege.

- Review refereed literature on this topic. Do a library and Internet search to find relevant material. Investigate some of the additional readings.

- Develop three arguments for the proposition.

- Develop three arguments against the proposition.

- How do the arguments relate to other systems, such as the community or culture?

- Is there common ground?

- What are the long-term consequences of taking action?

- What new or common-ground solutions should be offered? If no common ground, what new position could emerge from a dialogue between the two positions?

- How is the new position superior to the original positions?

ADDITIONAL READING RESOURCES

German, M., Gonzalos, M. A., & Dumka, L. (2009). Familism as a protective factor for Mexican origin adolescents exposed to deviant peers. *Journal of Early Adolescence, 29*(1), 16–42. doi: 10.1177/0272431608324475

Gewertz, K. (2007). Four decades later, scholars are reexamining "Moynihan Report." *Harvardgazette*, October 7, 2007. Retrieved from https://news.harvard.edu/gazette/story/2007/10/four-decades-later-scholars-re-examine-moynihan-report/

Knies, G., Nandi, A., & Platt, L. (2016). Life satisfaction: Ethnicity and neighborhoods: Is there an effect of neighborhood ethnic composition on life satisfaction? *Social Science Research, 60,* 110–124.

Newkirk II, V. R. (2017). The myth of reverse racism. *The Atlantic*, August 5, 2017. Retrieved from https://www.theatlantic.com/education/archive/2017/08/myth-of-reverse-racism/535689/

Ruffins, P. (2014). Beyond black and white: How the debate over affirmative action has evolved. *Diverse Issues in Higher Education*, April 9, 2014. Retrieved from http://diverseeducation.com/article/62756/

REFERENCES

Affirmative Action Overview (2013). National Conference of State Legislatures. Retrieved from http//www.ncsl.org/research/education/affirmative-action-overview.aspx

Alvarez, P. (2017). How Trump is changing immigration enforcement. *The Atlantic*, February 3, 2017. Retrieved from https://www.theatlantic.com/politics/archive/2017/02/trump-executive-order-immigration/515454/

Amato, P. R. (2001). Children of divorce in the 1990s: An update of Amato and Keith (1991) meta-analysis. *Journal of Family Psychology, 15*(3), 355–370.

American Immigration Council. (2016). How the U.S. Immigration system works, August 12, 2016. Retrieved from https://www.americanimmigrationcouncil.org/research/how-united-states-immigration-system-works

Anonymous. (n.d.). Poverty. Blackdeomographics.com. Retrieved from http//www.blackcdomgraphics.com/households/poverty

ASPE Issue Brief. (2012). Information on poverty and income statistics: A summary of 2012 current population survey data. Retrieved from http//www.aspe.hhs.gov/hsp/12/povertyand incomest/ib.shtu/

Associated Press. (2014). Alcohol causes 12 percent of native deaths. Retrieved from Cherokeephoenix.org/19753/article.aspx/

Austin, G., & Johnson, D. (2012). Hispanic or Latino: Which is correct? *Profiles in Diversity Journal*. Retrieved from http://www.diversityjournal.com/9724-hispanic-or-latino-which-is-correct/

Bell, D. (1987). *And we are not saved: The inclusive quest for racial justice.* New York, NY: Basic Books.

Bergmann, B.R. (1996). *In defense of affirmative action.* New York, NY: Basic Books.

Boxer, A. (2009). Native Americans and the federal government. History Today. Retrieved from http//www.historytoday.com/Andrew-boxer/native-america-and-federal-government/

Bureau of Labor Statistics. (2017). Employment and unemployment among youth, summer 2017. U.S. Department of Labor, Washington, D.C. Retrieved from https://www.bls.gov/news.release/pdf/youth.pdf

Chappell, B. (2015). For U.S. children, minorities will be the majority in 2020, Census says. *Southern California Public Radio,* March 4, 2015. Retrieved from https://www.npr.org/sections/ed/2016/07/01/484325664/babies-of-color-are-now-the-majority-census-says

Chen C., & Stevenson, H. (1995). Motivation and mathematical achievement: A comparative study of Asian Americans, Caucasian Americans and East Asian high school students. *Child Development, 66*(4), 1223–1234.

Chin, G. J. (1996). The civil rights revolution comes to immigration law. A new look at the immigration and nationality act of 1965. *North Carolina Law Review, 75,* 273.

Chin, G. J. (1998). Segregation's last stronghold: Race discrimination and the constitutional law of immigration. *UCLA Law Review, 46*(7).

Cilluffo, A., & Cohn, D. (2017). 10 demographic trends shaping the U.S. and the world in 2017. *Pew Research Center,* April 27, 2017. Retrieved from http://www.pewresearch.org/fact-tank/2017/04/27/10-demographic-trends-shaping-the-u-s-and-the-world-in-2017/

Cohen, T., & Mears, B. (2012). Supreme Court mostly rejects Arizona immigration law: Gov says "heart" remains. CNN Politics. Retrieved from http//www.cnn.com/2012/06/25/politics/scotus-arizona-law

Cohn, D. (2015). Future immigration will change the face of America. Pew Research Center. Retrieved from http://www.pewresearch.org/fact-tank/2015/10/05/future-immigration-will-change-the-face-of-america-by-2065/

Drake, B. (2013). Incarceration gap widens between Whites and Blacks. Pew Research Center. Retrieved from http//www.pewresearch.or/fact/tank/2013/09/06/incarceration-gap-between-white-and-black-widens/

English Language Learners & Southeast Asian Communities Fact Sheet. (2013). Retrieved from http://www.searac.org/sites/default/files/SEARAC_ELL_2013-1.pdf

Ezorsky, G. (1991). *Racism and justice: The case for affirmation action.* Ithaca, NY: Cornell University Press.

Fixico, D. L. (2006). *Daily life of Native Americans in the twentieth century—2006.* Newport, CT: Greenwood.

Frazier, E. F. (1939). *The Negro family in the United States.* Chicago, IL: University of Chicago Press.

Fry R., & Gonzales, F. (2008). A profile of Hispanic public school students: One-five and growing fast. Pew Research Hispanic Trends Project. Retrieved from http://www.pewhispanic.org/2008/08/26/one-in-five-and-growing-fast-a-profile-of-hispanic-public-school-students/

Fry, R., & Taylor, P. (2013) Hispanic high school graduation pass Whites in rate of college enrollment. Hispanic Trends Project, Pew Research Center. Retrieved from http//www.pewhispanic.org/2013/15/09/Hispanic-high-school-graduates-passwhite-in-rate-of-college-enrollment/

Gonzalas, R. G., & Raphael, S. (2017). Illegality: A contemporary portrait of immigration. *The Russell Sage Foundation Journal of the Social Sciences, 3*(4), 1–17. Retrieved from http://www.rsfjournal.org/doi/full/10.7758/RSF.2017.3.4.01

Gratz, J. (2014). Discriminating toward equality: Affirmative Action and the diversity charade. *Heritage Foundation,* February 24, 2014. Retrieved from http://www.heritage.org/poverty-and-inequality/report/discriminating-toward-equality-affirmative-action-and-the-diversity

Gutman, H. (1976). *The Black family in slavery and freedom 1750–1925.* New York, NY: Pantheon.

Hartlep, D. N. (2013). *The model minority stereotype: Demystifying success.* Greenwood, CT: Information Age.

Help Separated Families Act. (2012). H.R.612 B (112th).

Hixson, L., Hepler, B. B., & Kim, B. O. (2011). The White population: 2010: Census briefs. The U.S. Census Bureau, Washington, D.C.

Horowitz, D., & Perazzo, J. (2012). How the welfare state has devastated African Americans. Retrieved from http//www.discover the networks.org/viewsubcategory.asplid=1672

Humes, K. R., Jones, N. A., & Ramirez, R. R. (2011). Overview of race and Hispanic origins. 2011 Census Briefs, U.S. Census Bureau, U.S. Department of Commerce, Washington, D.C. Retrieved from http.www.census.gov/prod/cen2010/briefs/c2010br-12.pdf

Kiderra, I. (2011). Is there a "tiger mother" effect? *UC San Diego News Center.* Retrieved from http://ucsdnews.ucsd.edu/archive/newsrel/soc/5-4-11tiger_mother.asp

Kotkin, J. (2012). Decline of the Asian family. Drop in marriage, births, threaten economic ascendancy. Forbes online. Retrieved from http//www. Forbes.com/sites/joelkotkin/2012/10/23/the-decline-of-the-asian-family-drop-in-marriage-birth-threatens-economic-ascendancy/

Krayewski, E. (2013). 5 reasons to grant amnesty of illegal immigrants. *Reason.com.* February 7, 2013. Retrieved from http://reason.com/blog/2013/02/07/ed-krayewski-on-the-case-for-amnesty-for

Kreider, R., & Simmons, T. (2003). *Special Report on Marital Status: 2000,* C2KBR-30. Washington, D.C.: U.S. Bureau of the Census

Kulish, N., Yee, V., Dickerson, C., Robbins, L., Santos, F., & Medina, J. (2017, February 21). Trump's immigration policies explained. *The New York Times.* Retrieved from https://www.nytimes.com/2017/02/21/us/trump-immigration-policies-deportation.html

Landale, N. S., Oropesa, S., & Bradatan, C. (2012). Hispanic families in the United States: Family structure and process in an era of family change. In M. Tienda and F. Mitchell, *Hispanics and the future of America.* Washington, D.C.: National Academic Press.

Lang, K., & Lehmann, J. Y. K. (2009). Racial discrimination in the labor market: Theories and empirics. *The National Bureau of Economic Research, working paper #17450,* Washington, D.C.

Leef, G., & Sterba, J. P. (2012). Should universities continue "affirmative action" policies? *National Association of Scholars.* Retrieved from https://www.nas.org/articles/should_universities_continue_affirmative_action_policies

Li, G., & Wang, L. (Eds.). (2008). *Model minority myth revisited: An interdisciplinary approach to demystifying Asian American education experiences.* Greenwood, CT: Information Age.

Light. H. K., & Martin, R. E. (1985). Guidance of American Indian children: Their heritage and some contemporary view. *Journal of Indian Education, 25*(1), 1–7.

Lieberman, R. C. (2014). Race and ethnicity in U.S. social policy. In D. Berland, K.J. Morgan, and C. Howard (Eds.), *Oxford handbook of U.S. social policy.* Oxford, UK: Oxford University Press. Retrieved from http://www.oxfordhandbooks.com/view/10.1093/oxfordhb/9780199838509.001.0001/oxfordhb-9780199838509-e-025

Marsiglia, F. F., Booth, J. M., Baldwin, A., & Ayers, S. (2013). Acculturation and life satisfaction among immigrant Mexican adults. *Advances in Social Work, 14*(1), 49–64.

McCabe, K. (2011). African immigrants in the United States. Migration Information Source. Migration Policy Institute (MPI). Retrieved from http//www.migrationpolicy.org/article/africn/-immigrants-unitedstates/

McCarthy, A. (2017). Trump has not ended DACA. *National Review.* September 6, 2017. Retrieved from http://www.nationalreview.com/corner/451136/trump-has-not-ended-daca

McGown, M., & Lindgren, J. (2006). Testing the "model minority myth." *Northwestern University Law Review, 100*(1), 331–378.

Motel, S., & Patten, E. (2015). The 10 largest Hispanic origin groups: Characteristics, rankings and top countries. The Pew Research Center. Retrieved from http://www.pewhispanic.org/2012/06/27/the-10-largest-hispanic-origin-groups-characteristics-rankings-top-counties/

Moynihan, D. P. (1965). *The Negro family: The case for national action.* Office of Policy, Planning, and Research. Washington, D.C.: United States Department of Labor.

National Assessment of Educational Progress. (2014). Long term trends. National Center for Education Statistics, Institute of Education Sciences. Retrieved from nces.ed.gov/nationsreportcard/

National Center for Education Statistics. (2008). Status and trends in the education of American Indians and Alaska natives—2008. Institute of Education Sciences (IES). Retrieved from http//www.nces.ed.gov/pubs2008/nativetrends/ind_3_4.asp/

Nowrasteh, A. (2016). President Trump's immigration plan. *Caro Research Institute,* November 9, 2016. Retrieved from https://www.cato.org/blog/president-trumps-immigration-plans?gclid=Cj0KCQjw4eXPBRCtARIsADvOjY0Y_SGt0anjy04APAlxDydRPRMCOi0WOkYdsdR5cda2ph9ceCJDNkYaAkYxEALw_wcB

Orpesa, R. S., & Landale, N. S. (2004). The future of marriage and Hispanics. *Journal of Marriage and the Family, 66*(4), 901–920.

Padilla, A.M., & Borrero, A.E. (2006). The effects of acculturative stress on Hispanic families. In P. T. B. Wong and L. C. J. Wong (Eds.), *Handbook on multicultural perspective on stress and coping* (pp. 299–318). New York, NY: Springer.

Palmer, C. A. (2000). Defining and studying the modern African Diaspora. *Journal of Negro History, 85*(1/2), 27–32.

Perry, M. J. (2009). Post prop-209, Asian students benefit and are almost 50% of student body at Berkeley. *AEIdeals*. Retrieved from https://www.aei.org/publication/post-prop-209-asian-students-benefit-and-are-now-almost-50-of-student-body-at-uc-berkeley/

Pew Research Center. (2012). The rise of Asian Americans. Pew Research Social and Demographic Trends, June 19, 2012. Retrieved from httpl//www.pewsocialtrends.org/2012/06/19/the-rise-of-asians-america/*Plyler v. Doe.* (1982). 457 U.S. 202 (No.80–1538).

Rata, E., & Openshaw, R. (2006). *Public policy and ethnicity: The politics of ethnic boundary making*. London, UK: Palgrave Macmillan.

Scott, P., & Kirk, A. (2015).Hillary Clinton failed to win over Black, Hispanic, and female voters: The charts show why she lost the election. *The Telegraph*, November 11, 2016. Retrieved from http://www.telegraph.co.uk/news/2016/11/09/hillary-clinton-failed-to-win-over-black-hispanic-and-female-vot/

Shankar, S. (2012). Creating model consumers: Producing ethnicity, race, and class in Asian American advertising. *American Ethnologist, 39*(3), 578–591.

Suarez-Orozco, M. M. (Ed.). (2007). *Learning in the global era: International perspective on globalization and education*. Berkeley, CA: University of California Press.

U.S. Bureau of the Census (2017). Race. Department of Commerce, Washington, D.C. Retrieved from https://www.census.gov/topics/population/race/about.html

U.S. Bureau of the Census (2012). Profile America Facts for Features. Department of Commerce, Washington, D.C. Retrieved from httpl//www.census.gov/newsroom/releases/archives/facts_for_feaures_special_edition/cboz-ff19.htm/

U.S. Bureau of the Census. (2011). Profile America Facts for Features. American Indian Native Heritage Month, November 2011. Retrieved from http://www.census.gov/newsroom/releases/archives/facts_for_features_special_editions/cb11-ff22.html

Wilson, T. (2011). Changed embraces, changes embraced? Renouncing the heterosexist majority in favor of a return to two-spirit culture. *American Indian Law Review, 31*(1), 161–188.

Yanow, D. (2003). Constructing race and ethnicity in America: Category in public policy and administration. Armonk, NY: M.E. Sharpe

Yen, H. (2012). Census: White population will lose majority in U.S. by 2043. Associated Press, December 12, 2012. Retrieved from http://bigstory.ap.org/article/census-whites-no-longer-majority-us-2043

CREDITS

CHAPTER TWELVE

Postscript: The Future of Social Policy and Child and Family Development

Social policy has been at the forefront of legislation and the policy statements of nonprofit foundations from the beginning. Yet, attempts to understand and form universal principles that both describe and set appropriate parameters for future policy formulation are woefully weak. The discussion in this chapter may be as ineffectual as the previous attempts to make sense of, and plot a course for, social policy. This much is clear—social policies affecting children and families draw a huge audience. Wherever people gather, the discussions inevitably gravitate to child and family issues. Same-sex marriage, divorce, effects of divorce on children, abortion, fetal rights, education, redistribution of resources, diversity, and dozens of other topics directly or indirectly affect children and families. For the most part, these topics lack consensual agreement; discourse with varying opinions can be expressed in an open and civil manner or with emotional and irrational rhetoric. Many of these issues split almost 50–50 in public opinion, so that majority opinions can shift from one side to another in response to public events, crises, or confrontations. For example, the public majority on abortion rights had enjoyed a substantial gap over pro-lifers and still had a majority just after the Gosnell trial and the gruesome details of late-term abortions became public knowledge. However, in February of 2014, new data show that pro-life adherents had significantly narrowed the gap, and the vast majority of the public now supports greater restrictions on late-term abortions (Grossu, 2014).

While an idyllic view of debate deliberation of opposing views conjures up a Norman Rockwell painting depicting men in animated but friendly discussion at an old, candy-striped barber shop, the image that emerges today is quite different. The view today is more like opposing forces decked out in combat gear ready to blow away their "enemies." Both sides tend to be driven by strict **ideological beliefs** that preclude open and even respectful deliberation (Thomson, 2010). This is not to conclude that differences in themselves are unproductive or undesirable. Opinions are the stuff of people and represent subjective reality. Perhaps even what is believed to be objective reality is only the shared beliefs of a group of connected individuals. More often than not, political parties try to align themselves with an objective standard while painting the other party as out of touch or just plain unconcerned for the plight of certain segments of society, such as minorities or women. The unwritten credo is clear—if an otherwise good idea comes from the opposite side, it must be rejected, not on its own merits, but because it came from the other side (Conner & Jordan, 2010). Somehow the public tends to tolerate this kind of political dishonesty and not take it all that seriously but, unconsciously, is affected in its attitudes and predispositions for social activism.

POLARIZATION OF SOCIAL ISSUES

How the American political systems became so **polarized** is difficult to surmise. The roots of today's standoff go back at least four decades to the 1970s and result in less effort in solving many social and economic concerns (McCarty, Poole, & Rosenthal, 2009). The political system, no doubt, contributes to the polarization, because there is a need to categorize different groups of voters and, by doing so, frame a specific message for each one. It is true that some segments of the American society have tended to vote in blocks. For example, African Americans tend to vote Democratic, as evidenced by the most recent elections when over 90% voted for the reelection of Barack Obama and the candidacy of Hillary Clinton in 2016. Women also voted in larger numbers for Obama's reelection, despite the fact that under his administration, women lost ground economically, especially in the job market (Kessler, 2012). The "war on women" was a slogan used by the Hillary Clinton campaign to mobilize women to vote for her. Consequently, one could argue that persons are more affected by the message or ideology rather than the actual performance. Beliefs and attitudes fostered by political ideology tend to drive the outcomes more than actual performance (Conner & Jordan, 2010). As a result, Americans are polarized on a number of major issues, including the economy, health care, and the debt crisis (Stavins, 2011).

Reasons for the polarizations vary, but scholars look at several particular factors (Stavins, 2011). Some authors review demographic, social, or political analysis. For example, McCarty and associates (2009) postulated that primary elections tend to be geared toward a select group of voters who vote in primaries; they are the most vocal and the most polarized. The choices of candidates reflect these polarized voters. Not only are voters who cast ballots more selective of candidates who fit their belief systems, voting districts have become more homogeneous, reflecting either a liberal or a conservative view. Candidates for office from these districts have become more cognizant of the wishes of their constituents and, therefore, are more uncompromising in their legislative endeavors. Incumbents are favored in this system, because they cater to the cadre of voters who already put them into office. Those in office attempt to maintain their positions and do so in a manner that reinforces and reifies polarization.

Some writers have speculated that the changing media in America have directly contributed to polarization on social issues (Campante & Hojman, 2010). Various forms of media, movies, TV, the Internet, and even social media, such as Facebook and Twitter, offer information aimed at influencing persons' beliefs. Individuals now have more media outlets to choose from that support their own views and, therefore, lead to stronger individual beliefs that more readily enable polarization. Persons create and **eco-chamber** by selectively using the Internet to reinforce their own views of social and political issues.

Other factors that affect polarization are specific events or laws passed by one party without input from the other. A general backlash in voters occurs at times because voters feel unrepresented. A recent case in point is when two Northern California counties on the Oregon border voted to secede from California, because the voters believed that the California State Assembly and State Senate did not represent the views and beliefs of the citizens of those counties (Associated Press, 2013). These counties would certainly roll back many of the policies decided by California legislators that reflected the concerns and issues of large urban areas while ignoring the needs of rural families. Establishing policies that polarize citizens and then having those policies rescinded creates more activity in the social policy arena.

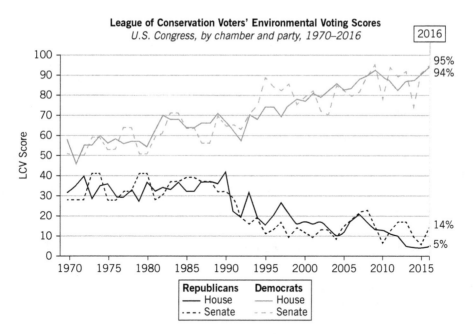

FIGURE 12.1 Polarization of congress
Source: League of Conservation Voters

Polarization tends to label some members of Congress as liberals and other members as conserva-tives. To some degree, the Democratic Party has the label of liberal while the Republican Party carries the connotation of being conservative (Levine, Fung, & Gastil, 2005). For many on the far left and far right, their respective parties are too much in the middle and they are compelled to exert force for the party to be ideologically pure. In terms of political parties, persons who label themselves independents have increased, though it might be expected that independents are really more conservative or liberal and largely follow these ideological paths.

Some authors take a more psychological point of view of both the cause and the remedy of polar-ization. For example, Conner and Jordan (2010) argue that polarization is caused by a "Convention Problem," or one in which there is no solution. Conner and Jordan believe that polarization is occurring in America, because "good people are doing bad things for good reasons" (p. 5). An increasing number of persons in American society are becoming politically active and are joining coalitions with like-minded persons. As like-minded persons interact about social policy issues, they develop stronger beliefs.

As pointed out by Conner and Jordan (2010), one's attitude about a social policy becomes more important than the depth of the knowledge; the primary endeavor of polarization is to create a certain attitude. This attitude becomes a type of filter that comes into play quickly as the person encounters real-life situations. Instead of having a full understanding of the merits of the informa-tion at hand, one makes snap decisions and comes to opinions about social policies through this filter. Because one's opinions form in this way, it means that he/she lacks real understanding of both his/her own view and the opposing view.

In developing their view that attitude is an important factor in polarization, Conner and Jordan (2010) reviewed literature on the associative neural network model and the connectionist network model. Both of the models conjecture that when stimuli enter a particular neural area of the brain, the entire network becomes activated. Repeated activation of this network will produce an entrenched pattern. It also means that if one has certain attitudes about a social policy, he/she will reinforce this attitude by experiencing an associated input. These neural networks are not destiny in that they do not predict all behaviors and are subject to change, but for persons who lack awareness and operate under the delusion that they know more than they do, it is aligned with a knee-jerk automatic reaction that leads to polarization.

The views of Schumpeter (1976), although over 40 years ago, provide additional insight to how persons make decisions on social policies. Schumpeter believed that persons regress to a lower form of thought processes when they engage in political discussion. The typical response to political activity for the average person is to be unprepared to engage because of lack of understanding even the facts before them, which prevents them for knowing and identifying a common ground with others. For this reason, persons are stuck in their own worlds and concerned only about their immediate circumstances. While Schumpeter's critique of the average person's ability to deliberate seems harsh, it is reflected in contemporary concerns that the average person is uninformed about political debate, and consequently, the necessary ingredient to effectively participate in social policy decision making (Fowler & Margolis, 2013).

Into the mix of trying to determine the root causes of polarization, Jonathan Haidt (2012) presents some interesting insights. His studies in moral psychology provide a window through which much of the concern on polarization can be viewed. For Haidt, from birth, persons are different in their moral judgments, which are expressed overtly as persons engage in moral reasoning related to personal, social, and political realities. In a research study that emphasizes this mechanism, Haidt and Graham (2009) found that persons who describe themselves as liberals tend to be driven by two moral principles: caring for oppressed persons and fairness. On the other hand, persons who describe themselves as conservative, tend to be concerned about these moral behaviors as well, but were more balanced in that they also care about traditions, loyalty to others, and authority. Haidt (2012) believes that this skewed moral concern by liberals costs them elections, because conservatives appeal to a broader range of moral concerns that people care about.

For Haidt (2012) being swayed by reasonable arguments takes a distant second place to making decisions based on intuition. Decisions are made quickly through intuitive means and reason is added later to justify the intuitive decision. In the experiments in his study, he found that most people can agree that a specific behavior is right or wrong, but cannot tell why they came to that conclusion. Giving reasons for a decision that was made quickly by intuition has evolved over time as a way to influence the thinking of other people. If everyone is making decisions through the same intuitive process, it means that no one has more moral authority than anyone else. In this view of morality and decision making, the playing field becomes equal.

The consequences of Haidt's (2012) research is that conservatism and liberalism are both legitimate and justifiable. He identifies them as the yin and yang, each having distinct understandings that the other should acknowledge and learn from. In accomplishing this goal of recognizing the interdependence of liberalism and conservatism, intuition and reason must be more closely aligned. What is missing from Haidt's analysis is how this integration of intuition and reason will take place.

What makes Haidt's (2012) position compelling is that he recounts his own struggle in moral decision making. He was raised in a Jewish home with a strong liberal ideology of which he was not fully aware. When he began his research in India, he was at first appalled by the patriarchal structure of the society and what he perceived to be the oppression of women. As he became more familiar with daily activity of persons in that society, he began to see that the patriarchal structure worked in that society. This experience opened him up to be able to see that different societies develop along different paths and not one path works for all societies. He views himself now as a centrist who can see the value in both conservative and liberal positions. The current reality that must be addressed in American social policies spawned by politics is that policies tend to be decided by force, intimidation, and political payoff rather than the true merits of the proposals. These ongoing polarized battles between conservatives and liberals do not, in the long run, solve the problems facing the nation. The present-day state of social policymaking affecting children and families reflects a crisis in purpose and goals. Is the goal meant to solidify power, trounce the opposing view, directly affect public opinion through misinformation and deception, and punish those with viable alternate views? The position taken in this book is that there should be another goal, namely, to never address issues from the point of view of right or wrong or best decision versus worst decision. The overall goal is to view all alternatives as representing specific values that are viable options and allowing for common-ground and/or new alternatives to emerge.

FIGURE 12.2 Polarization

A SYSTEMS/DIALECTICAL PERSPECTIVE

The major question facing social policy that affects children and families is how to foster positive solutions in an evolving system in which there is growth and change. In place of drawn battle lines, many call for **deliberation** and **dialogue**. Deliberation refers specifically to the process of formulating a problem-solving analysis of a social problem and moving toward solutions by understanding various ways of proceeding (Delli-Carpini, Cook, & Jacobs, 2004). This process of deliberation is one of mutual respect from stakeholders who offer different ideas. Dialogue is viewed more as a prerequisite for deliberation in that groups must come to the table and voice various viewpoints. The dialogue allows for understanding how each group frames the issue before deliberation can take place. Cultural values may, to some degree, affect the ideas presented and need to be accepted for what they mean to their group.

A systems/dialectical perspective offers an alternative **paradigm** to polarization. While both a systems/dialectical perspective and polarization would begin with different points of view, they would move in opposite directions. Polarization would bolster one's own perspective at the expense of the other position. This view would be reinforced by "demonizing" the other perspective without actually understanding that perspective. On the other hand, a systems/dialectical perspective postulates that starting at different points boosts the possibility of an effective outcome. It is not a panacea to solve every problem, but it does provide a frame of reference that permits debate to achieve an innovative outcome. Instead of moving against the other perspective, it seeks to understand fully both perspectives, creating openness to allow for the emergence of something new.

Polarization reduces a person's capacity for **divergent thinking** and increases either/or dichotomies. It makes the electorate less inclined to understand opposing views, because by nature, those views are considered to be inherently flawed. According to Sloman and Fernbach (2010), Americans have become so calloused toward a political process that aims at dividing persons into dissimilar clusters that the tactics politicians use no longer offend them. It is much like children who become so accustomed to the violence in the family that violence no longer is met with intense emotional reaction.

When political leaders and policymakers use strategies that polarize thinking, they are successful because of our basic **cognitive structure**. Rozenblit and Keil (2002) describe how persons reduce large comprehensive information down to impressions and attitudes, which provides the illusion that one knows more than he/she actually knows. Rozenblit and Keil labeled this phenomenon as "**the illusion of explanatory depth**" (p. 521). In other words, one's understanding of public policy issues is incomplete and never holds up completely under strict scrutiny. This lack of completeness in understanding is usually beyond one's awareness and is better seen by those with opposing views. It helps explain how polarization is a natural process that occurs to bolster faulty thinking. Rozenblit and Keil believe that complex information systems are not fully understood, because, while individuals may have knowledge of the function of parts, there is a failure to understand how parts actually work in connection with other parts to create the whole. The outcome is that individuals assume that they have a greater grasp on complex information than they actually do and, therefore, have the faulty feeling that they are right and other positions are wrong.

This way of selectively viewing information is in no place more evident than in the use of media. On one hand, it could be argued that TV and newspapers tend to make people less polarized, because material is presented from a more neutral point of view; viewers are then able to read into the content their own beliefs. However, it has become evident that modern-day media has had the opposite effect of increasing polarization. According to Dandekar, Goel, and Lee (2013), people tend to be influenced by new information that reinforces their beliefs and disregards other views. Consequently, changing one's belief patterns is extremely difficult to accomplish. In fact, there is evidence that presenting factual arguments that should challenge the opposite views only makes one adhere more intensely to his or her own beliefs. When one is confronted with information about a particular social policy issue, such as the effects of spanking on children, he/she will retain the information that supports current beliefs and disregard other points of view. An alternate idea to help break the tendency to polarize would be to have persons explain in greater depth how their theory of a particular social policy works. In this way, persons may become more aware of the gaps and inconsistencies in their own thinking and be more open to alternate explanations.

FIGURE 12.3 Political Polarization

When people know less than they think and have the faulty perception that they are right, that is polarization. And what can be done about it? Perhaps it is similar to the predisposition in some families for dysfunctional **triangulation**, which produces negative outcomes in individual members and the family as a whole but can be dealt with by individuals making efforts to remove themselves from the triangle. Because many of the social policy issues discussed in this book are very complex with viable competing views, the question arises about whether answers are readily available that can help with these uncertainties.

Sloman and Fernman (2010) provide some ideas for how to move through this impasse. One idea is understanding how individuals address opposing views. If opposing views are seen as wrong or out of touch, a typical reaction might be to dismiss them and not attempt a deeper understanding. Taking confrontational stands tends to lead to greater polarization. When one's position is challenged there is greater impetus to defend it, listen less to the alternate view, and sink deeper into the illusion that one's positions are the only right ways of thinking. Unfortunately, such a reaction leads to greater polarization and less overall cooperation.

A systems/dialectical perspective begins with the assumption that persons do not know what they think they know. In other words, humility is not a bad place to start. It might be very helpful if all sides in a debate actually spent more time in explaining how their ideas would actually improve the well-being of those for whom they are intended. More than likely, people will have difficulty making a sustained knowledgeable argument.

If the first step is a dose of humble pie, the second step is respect for opposing views. If one does not really know one's own point of view, he/she has even less knowledge of the opposing view or views. This stance is not dissimilar from how a therapist trained in family systems therapy works with a couple. Each partner views the relationship issues differently, even when describing the same events. The therapist's role is not to decide which partner is right or wrong and side with one over the other, but to recognize that this is a relationship with differences that needs to find some points of common agreement. Those areas of common agreement, however small and seemingly insignificant, become the basis for large-scale change.

Respect for the other involves eliminating labeling, blaming, or any negative characterizing of positions as inherently bad. One of the favorite games of politicians is to paint their opponents in a negative light, and compare that negative view with their own views that are supposedly wholesome. In couple's therapy, role-playing is sometimes used to help partners see how the other person feels. The goal in role-playing is not so much about understanding the verbal content of the partner's perspective, but in gaining an emotional awareness of being the partner. Role-playing succeeds only if each partner has the emotional experience of what the partner feels.

The idea of emotionally experiencing the partner leads to the third step of mutual cooperation. It can be assumed that those on different sides of social policies affecting children and families have a similar goal of improving the well-being of the target population. Much like a structural therapist who joins the family in order to change the system, those on opposite sides of a social policy issue must join together and be on the same team. The idea is to produce a win-win scenario.

Some child and family development social policy issues, such as abortion, the welfare state, child care, and education, tend to be lightning rods that quickly cause division and enmity. A systems/dialectical perspective is presented as an alternative theory to either/or thinking. It must be kept in mind, however, that systems/dialectical thinking is not without costs (Basseches, 2005). Systems/dialectical thinking requires challenging one's own beliefs with the same rigor as investigating the opposing point of view. It might mean giving way to uncertainty and being ambivalent when presented with "the truth."

Systems/dialectical thinking is a tool that allows for change to occur. It includes an understanding of the whole as well as the parts, which are frequently in confrontation with each other. It allows for novelty, an approach that closed logically oriented systems do not permit. One example is the field of education (Basseches, 2005). Perhaps education is a foundation for all other issues related to child and family development social policy. Education creates the formal logic and language by which social policy is understood and conceptualized.

An educational policy must be sufficiently open to supply students with a variety of viable frameworks to understand policymaking. Education should help individuals **differentiate** various points of view and be able to **integrate** and create new meanings. In the informational material and textbooks given students, there should be exposure to various viewpoints rather than one "right" point of view. All viewpoints should be open to critique and evaluation of their utility in the social arena. Just as valuable as analyzing various viewpoints is the ongoing **synthesis** of **multiple perspectives**. Education should not simply leave students in limbo, but should actively engage them in the synthesis and emerging of new ideas. The long history of literature and science is replete with **transformation** in theory and practice. Students should be involved in this ongoing transformation in which integration of ideas produces new and innovative concepts.

This author believes that if the ideas presented above are acted on, new solutions would emerge from a deliberation of different points of view. All of the issues discussed in this book, such as child care, well-being of children, family structure, poverty, technology, ethnicity, and others, are suspended between various points of view. Some of those have become reified and even squelch the recognition that other perspectives could offer any insight. One of these is the debate over the time spent by young children in non-parental child care. The debate was initiated by the publication of a study in 1986 by Jay Belsky. Belsky's findings that children younger than one year of age in center-based child care for more than 20 hours a week were at risk for insecure attachment with their mothers was met with harsh criticism. It was the first research that raised the possibility that center-based child care could have negative repercussions. Many reacted to Belsky's findings with an outrage that reflected a close-minded system in which the messenger of bad news was executed. Belsky (2009) defended himself by pointing out that policymakers should always be open to dissenting views, and policy should not be established on the basis of a single theoretical perspective. As a participant in the 15-year-long Study of Early Child Care and Youth Development (SECCYD), National Institute of Child Health Development (NICHD Early Child Care Research Network (ECCRN) with over 1,000 children in various child care settings, including center-based, Belsky believed that his position was at least partially vindicated. The study reiterated earlier research findings that the quality of the caregiver's relationship with the child is the main determinate in the child's response to child care. In addition, the study corroborated his earlier finding that time spent in child care has detrimental effects on children. Children exposed to child care early in life and for long periods are more aggressive and have greater behavioral problems than children who were not in child care. According to Belsky, despite an accumulating body of evidence documenting the negative findings, there has been little public knowledge of those negative effects, nor have professionals linked such behaviors to conduct problems. The longitudinal study also found that this negative behavior is related to the total time spent in child care for children younger than 4.5 years of age.

Policymakers might rush to make this study into a policy; according to Belsky (2009) they would be making a mistake in doing so. Belsky points out that the family is a major player in the child's life and carries more influence than child care. The quality of the relationship with parents, the structure of the family, and the psychological well-being of the mother are very important factors. Overall, the strength of the child care effect in comparison to the family is decidedly small. Belsky states emphatically that the problem has not been that the findings of the negative effects are small, but that among some of his peers, the findings have been ignored and marginalized. He emphasizes that research findings should not be ignored, however small the effect, because they do not fit the expected outcome. Such marginalizing of results is not only biased but contributes to polarization. According to Belsky, the more children who spend increasing time in child care, the more behavior problems will appear later in schools. Belsky states that the results of the study produced a disturbing finding that children who do not have a great deal of child care, but spend time with children who do, will display negative behaviors themselves. In other words, the behavior of aggressive children will influence other children to be aggressive.

On the basis of this very extensive ECCRN research project, the question is: What should drive policymaking in child care? The temptation is to decide what is the best option for parents and then promote this option while negating other options. For example, policy could decide to accentuate the positive findings of child care and ignore the negative findings. Parents could be informed about the need for a quality child care experience without any recognition that the positive effects are mediated by family relationships. Policymakers could support parents who need to work long hours without any mention of the risk of aggression and negative behaviors. On the other hand, policymakers could side with the negative outcomes and suggest that parents not use child care, or at least very sparingly, for the first five years of life. Policymakers could go so far as to say that children might do better if one parent did not work until children attend kindergarten.

Belsky's (2009) solution to the above policymaking dilemma is consistent with a systems/dialectical perspective. He states that instead of recommending that one parent stay home until kindergarten, or that both parents work without understanding the negative risks, parents should be informed of research on child care and make an individual choice. Policymakers should not make the decision for parents, but should support parents' decision-making process. He believes that coupling information with stipends for families with children would allow families to make choices. Families could use the money to pay for daycare or both parents could work. A systems/dialectical perspective would embrace Belsky's position, because instead to being proscriptive, it is open to new possibilities.

If child care is a lightning rod of emotion for policymakers, the question of whether the child's behavior is more influenced by innate qualities or by external factors has been an ongoing debate dating back many decades. The recurring debate of **nature** versus **nurture** has shifted back and forth due to the advancements in research without either side providing a definitive explanation (Sameroff, 2010). Policymakers have been somewhat chaotic in that no consistent policies tend to be the answer. Waiting for one side to win the debate and then settle on one explanation has not happened and never will. To conclude that it is both nature and nurture provides little explanation for why that might be the case.

Applying a systems/dialectical perspective to this debate is a heuristic tool that might shed light on understanding the shifts in focus. The behavioral models of the 1960s gave way in the 1970s to the belief that genetics account for behavioral differences (Sameroff, 2010). Cognitive theories placed developmental change in the mind of the child. In the 1970s and 1980s, the focus shifted to a belief that the environment was extremely important for the development, particularly as a result of

Moynihan's (1965) report and the provisions of the War on Poverty. Environmental deprivation as the cause and enriched environments as the prevention of child developmental anomalies emerged from many advocates. The ecological theory of Bronfenbrenner (1977, as cited in Sameroff, 2009) depicted the child at the center of a nested environmental system including close family and friends, and more distantly, community and cultural influences. Postmodern influences added another twist in that the meanings of behaviors and events became more important than the actual behavior. The advent of neuroscience with brain-imaging techniques ushered in a new shift to the nature side. Ultimately no explanation has explained enough of the variance to become the dominant theory; shifts in focus between nature and nurture will, no doubt, continue. Is there an explanation for the shifts, or is it merely that neither position can muster enough longer-term clout to be determined the winner?

A systems/dialectical perspective provides a framework for answering the above question. As discussed earlier in this book, the dialectical stance can be understood as the **unity of opposites**. The yin and the yang are bound together and neither can be understood apart from the other (Sameroff, 2010). The **interpenetration of the opposite** means that the black yin dot in the white yang and vice versa means that nature can change nurture and nurture can change nature. Not only are the opposites unified and interpenetrate the other, but neither could exist without the other.

Sameroff (2010) proposed the idea of the **double helix** to explain how opposites cycle from one position to the other. The cycling of the double helix shows how the same issues are rediscovered numerous times as through the ongoing process. The terms differentiation and integration can apply to the double helix in that one helix leads to greater differentiation while the other helix leads to greater integration, which can be simultaneous processes.

According to Sameroff (2010), nature is more dominate in current child development research. Academic fields, such as "molecular biology, endocrinology, and neurology are being rapidly integrated into psychological research" (p. 19). This research is relationship-based; nature, including environmental factors, however, is viewed more holistically. Because research in nature cannot account for all the variability, the pendulum will inevitably swing back toward nurture.

The systems/dialectical perspective would postulate that the future in the debate between nature and nurture will develop much as it did in the past; no one position will answer all the questions and the dynamic interplay of the two will continue to provide the basis for both to develop. The role of each is to explain the other rather than to subsume or be subsumed by the other. Each exists because of the other and neither could continue to exist without the other (Sameroff, 2010). In understanding this coexisting and mutually dependent dynamic, each perspective can provide valuable input that will help deepen knowledge of development. In a broad measure, it is hoped that all of the opposing issues discussed in this book can inform each other and move along the development of ideas to new and creative expressions.

A FINAL NOTE

The systems/dialectical perspective reflects a **deliberative democracy** approach whereby members of society are confronted with a social dilemma to solve and come together to dialogue about possible solutions (Carcasson & Sprain, 2016). The deliberative approach is hailed as superior to an approach that would not allow for the expression of disparate positions. The pros of such an approach include greater possibility for finding a solution that has mutual support (Levin, Fung, & Gastil, 2005). Furthermore, it allows for uncovering issues and giving voice to what is often unspoken or controversial matters. Just making persons aware of opposing views and providing a forum for discussion can lead to uncharted directions. The focus is away from the government and favors representation from a broad base of the community.

While the above pros of deliberation of disparate positions are well noted, it must be acknowledged that there are obstacles to overcome for successful deliberation to take place. One of the most formidable stumbling blocks is that not all constituents are present and able to voice their beliefs (Neblo, 2015; Nunez, McCrea, & Culhane, 2011). While representation from disparate groups would be expected to have a presence, it cannot be assumed that equal participation is the outcome. Oppressed and underrepresented groups may lack equal opportunity to speak and be heard. Minorities and disenfranchised persons, such as the homeless and mentally ill, may lack representation. Some persons simply by the circumstances of status have greater capacity to influence others than those of less status. For example, from jury studies, it has been documented that men speak more in a group than women or minorities and persons who speak the most have the most influence in the decision-making process (Nunez, McCrea, & Culhane, 2011). Consequently, a deliberation on a social issue may reflect a common denominator of likeminded persons and not the whole cadre of interested participants. For deliberation to be socially just, it must provide equal access and involvement by all segments of society.

The problem of representation of underrepresented persons and groups in social deliberation was addressed admirably by Neblo (2015). Not only are marginalized persons more likely to be absent from deliberation, their voices are less influential when they are present. To achieve deliberation that is participatory for all, it must include prerequisites that address social inequality. It cannot be assumed that merely by offering to receive input from all that it will, in fact, happen.

How to effectively include underrepresented persons in policymaking is an ongoing challenge (Neblo, 2015). Some researchers have suggested a number of maneuvers that might increase participation. Coglianese, Kilmartin, and Mendelson (2008) propose a model for exploring policymaking that emphasizes the importance of transparency and participation. Transparency is defined as governmental processes and documents that are open and easily accessible to all members of society. Participation refers to the actual involvement of all stakeholders. According to Coglianese et al. (2008) more effective policies can be established when government and agency regulators operate in an open manner and the spectrum of stakeholders is large. Perhaps the most advantageous aspect of transparency and participation is that they reduce the likelihood that a small elite group could inhibit debate and make backdoor deals that control the outcome. A first step according to Coglianese et al. is to be more proficient at listening to all constituents, which means soliciting input from underrepresented persons.

Coglianese and associates (2008) further criticized the one-way approach that solicits input without debate and dialogue between opposing ideas. Others, such as Sanders (1997), view the deliberation process as unfair to some segments of society, because the concept of deliberation needs to be reexamined. Agreeing with earlier writers in deliberative democracy, such as Cohen and Rogers (1983, as cited in Sanders, 1997) who believed that underrepresented persons will never have the same opportunity to influence policy development because they lack education and schooling,

Sanders goes beyond Cohen and Rogers and believes that bias in establishing social policies is so unconscious that education or skills in debating will not erase the inherent prejudice against underrepresented persons.

Researchers have used the jury as a model for how deliberation should work (Gastil, Deess, Weiser, & Simmons, 2010). The same overall approach that jurors take in a trial is similar to how persons should approach participation in social policy development. While jury selection seems to be an ideal scenario for deliberation about social policies, Gastil et al. acknowledged some caveats. For example, not all jurors have an equal opportunity at being chosen as foreman. Men who talk first, have prior experience on a jury, and are educated tend to be selected more often than others. Verbal loquaciousness adds to the likelihood of being selected as foreman. Although all jurors are considered equal in theory, each juror may not be equally influential. High-status jurors, educated and professional, tend to have more clout in forming the outcome of the jury's decision. The result is that persons of low status on a jury tend to defer to those with more status in making decisions. Moreover, when jurors delay taking a vote on where they stand until after the evidence has been presented, there is greater discussion and more participation, than when an initial vote is made early in the deliberation. Based on these conclusions, the real challenge is not to teach persons debate skills, but to create an atmosphere whereby all participants can be heard, rather than perpetuate a system in which the dominant group continues to dominate. What is needed is a model for decision making on social policies that allows for the oppressed to have equal voice alongside the high status and privileged persons.

The above consideration led Sanders (1997) to promote a model labeled **testimony** in place of deliberation. Testimony does not undermine deliberation, but rather permits a more inclusive meaning or dimension to deliberation. Testimony differs from deliberation in that it attempts to make possible the sharing of different or opposite points of view, rather than the tendency in deliberation to look for commonality. It suggests making possible the expression of a broad range of opinions that may have little in common. It is more akin to storytelling than rational argumentation. Each position should be able to be expressed. According to Sanders, using the concept of testimony can open the door to unique outcomes.

A systems/dialectic perspective reflects the above concerns regarding deliberation that is open to all. The very basis of the systems/dialectical position is that differences are not undesirable, but that sameness or commonality are undesirable. The opposite view, which may also vary in terms of tone and expression, is sought out rather than inhibited. While seeking common ground between opposite points of view is encouraged, it is recognized that commonality is not the goal. The goal and future direction of social policy from a systems/dialectical perspective is the emergence of a new or unique position, not wedded to either position in the deliberation.

Finally, a systems/dialectical perspective assumes ethical behavior on the part of all participants. When deliberation of disparate points of view happens, participants should be guided by truth, honesty, and forthrightness. Polarization is a natural outcome when participants are swayed by ideology rather than a desire to find truth.

KEY TERMS

Ideological beliefs

Polarized

Deliberation

Dialogue

Paradigm

Divergent thinking

Deliberative democracy

Eco-chamber

Cognitive structure

Triangulation

Differentiation

Integration

Synthesis of multiple perspectives

Transformation

Illusion of explanatory depth

Nature

Nurture

Heuristic tool

Unity of opposites

Interpretation of opposites

Double helix

Testimony

REFERENCES

Associated Press. (2013). Another Northern California county votes to secede from the state. Fox News online. Retrieved from http://www.foxnews.com/politics/2013/09/25/another-california-county-votes-to-secede-from-state/#

Basseches, M. (2005). The development of dialectical thinking as an approach to integration. *Integral Review*, 1, 47–63.

Belsky, J. (2009). Effects of child care on children development: Give parents real choices. Institute for the Study of Children and Social Issues, Birkbeck University of London, March, 2009. Retrieved from http://www.mpsv.cz/files/clanky/6640/9_Jay_Belsky_EN.pdf

Belsky, J. (1986). Infant day care: A cause for concern? *Zero to Three*, 6, 1–7.

Campante, F. R., & Hojmanm, D. (2010). Media and polarization. HKS Faculty Research working Paper Series. RWP10-002. John F. Kennedy School of Government, Harvard University.

Carcasson, M., & Sprain, L. (2016). Beyond problem solving: Reconceptualizing the work of public deliberation as deliberative inquiry. *Communication Theory, 26*(1), 41–63.

Coglianese, C., Kilmartin, H., & Mendelson, E. (2008). *Transparence and public participation in the rulemaking process: A nonpartisan residential transition task force report.* Retrieved from https://www.hks.harvard.edu/hepg/Papers/transparencyReport.pdf

Conner, R. L., & Jordan, P. (2010). Attitude, advocacy and polarization: The new triangle of American public policy. Selected works of Roger L. Conner. Retrieved from http//www.worksbepress.com/roger_conner/

Dandekar, P., Goel, A., & Lee, D. (2013). Biased assimilation, homophily, and the dynamics of polarization. *Proceedings of the National Academy of Sciences, 110*(15), 5791–5796.

Delli-Carpini, M. X., Cook, F. L., & Jacobs, L. R. (2004). Public deliberation: Discussion participation and citizen engagement: A review of the empirical literature. *Annual Review of Political Science, 7*, 315–344.

Fowler, A., & Margolis, M. (2013). The political consequences of uninformed voters. *Electoral Studies, 30*, 1–11.

Grossu, A. O. (2014). Gosnell's depravity brings pro-life awaking: Revelations of sordid deaths have triggered restrictions. Washington Post online. Retrieved from http://www.washingtontimes.com/news/2014/feb/17/grossu-gosnells-depravity-and-the-pro-life-awakeni/?page=all

Haidt, J. (2012). *The righteous mind: Why good people are divided by politics and religion.* New York, NY: Vintage.

Haidt, J., & Graham, J. (2009). Planet of the Durkheimians: Where community, authority and sacredness are foundations of morality. In J. Jost, A.C. Kay, and H. Thorisdottir (Eds.), *Social and psychological basis of ideology and system justification* (pp. 371–401). New York, NY: Oxford University Press.

Kessler, G. (2012). Are Obama's policies hurting women? The Fact Checker, *The Washington Post*, April 10, 2012. Retrieved from http://www.washingtonpost.com/blogs/fact-checker/post/are-obamas-job-policies-hurting-women/2012/04/09/gIQAGz3q6S_blog.html

Levine, P., Fung, A., & Gastil, J. (2005) Future directions for public deliberation, *Journal of Public Deliberation, 1*(1), 1–13.

McCarty, N., Poole, K., and Rosenthal, H. (2009). Does gerrymandering cause polarization? *American Journal of Political Science, 53*(3), 666–680.

Moynihan, D. P. (1965). The Negro family: The case for national action. Office of Policy, Planning, and Research. Washington, D.C.: U.S. Department of Labor.

Neblo, M. A. (2015). *Deliberative democracy: Between theory and practice.* New York, NY: Cambridge University Press.

Nunez, N., McCrea, S. M., & Culhane, S. E. (2011). Jury decision making research: Are researchers focusing on the mouse and not the elephant in the room? *Behavioral Sciences and the Law, 29,* 439–435.

Rozenblit, L., & Keil, F. (2002). The misunderstood limits of folk science: An illusion of explanatory depth. *Cognitive Science, 25,* 521–562.

Sameroff, A. (2010). A unified theory of development: A dialectical integration of nature and nurture. *Child Development, 81*(1), 6–22.

Sanders, L. M. (1997). Against deliberation. *Political Theory, 25*(3), 347–364.

Schumpeter, J. (1976). *Capitalism, socialism and democracy.* London, UK: Allen and Unwin.

Sloman, S., & Fernbach, P. (2010). I'm right! (For some reason). *The New York Times,* Saturday Review, the Opinion Pages. Retrieved from http://www.nytimes.com/

Stavins, R. (2011). The credit downgrade and the congress: Why polarized politics paralyze public policy. An economic view of the environment. Harvard Kennedy School, Belfer Center for Science and International Affairs. Retrieved from http//www/robertstavinsblog/2011/08/11/the-credit-downgrade-and-the congress-why-polarized-politics-paralyze-public-policy

Thomson, J. (2010). *Polarization and its effects on RAND.* Santa Monica, CA: Rand Corporation.

CREDITS

INDEX

A

Abcedarian study, 61–63

Achievement gap, 61

Action for Children's Television (ACT), 230

Adoption, 156–159
  nontraditional view of, 158
  traditional view of, 157

Affirmative action, 258

Agency-based approach, 134

Aggravated asthma, 52

Alaska Natives, 255–256

Albumin, 228

Alcohol, 76–78
  and substance use, 57–58
  fetal alcohol syndrome, 77
  pharmacology of, 77–78

American Civil Liberties Union (ACLU), 232

Analytical thinking, 132

Anger management, 198

Anorexia, 180

Anthropomorphic characters, 221

Anti-poverty program, 107–113

Antisocial behavior, 220

Antithesis, 7

Anxiety disorders, 57, 170

Apgar score, 82

Apotheoses, 75

Asian American family, 248–252
  and education, 249–252

Asian cultural imperative, 250

Asylum, 244

Attachment style, 202

Attention deficit hyperactivity disorder (ADHD),
  54–55

Autism spectrum disorder (ASD), 77

Axon, 74

B

Basseches, Michael, 9

Battered child syndrome, 168

Battered wife's syndrome, 206

Behavioral effects, poverty and, 103–104

Bidirectional, 3

Bill of Rights, 232

Birth records, 159

Black American family, 246–248

Blood alcohol concentration (BAC), 77

Blood lead level (BLL), 52

Body mass index (BMI), 217

Boundaries, 5

Bourgeois state, 122

Brain-deprived neurotrophic factor (BDNF), 80

Building Strong Families Project, 51

Bulimia, 180

C

Californian penal laws, 204

California Partnership to End Domestic Violence
  (CPEDV), 203

Catch and release, 245

Catecholaminergic systems, 75

Cell phones, 227–228

Central nervous system, 74

Change, concept, 8

Child abuse, 167–169
  emotional, 177–178
  systems/dialectical perspective of, 186–187

Child Abuse and Prevention and Treatment Act
  (CAPTA), 167

Child care, 58–61
  attachment and, 60
  research on, 59–60

Child characteristics, 59

Childhood schizophrenia, 54

Childhood victimization, 53

Child Protective Services (CPS), 168–169

Children, 47–48
adoption, 156–159
and education. *See* Education
and emotional attachment, 105–106
and sexting, 229
as victims of Crime, 53–54
direct response to media stimuli, 222–223
effects of domestic violence on, 199–201
effects of neglect on, 174–176
effects of poverty on, 101–107
emotional abuse, 177–178
environmental factors, 106–107
family structure and, 48–51
health and safety of, 52–53
impact of television on, 216–223
mental disoders. *See* Mental disoders, children
moral development of, 224
neglected, 173–177
physical abuse. *See* Physical abuse
policy development for, 39–40
resilience in, 202–203
sex trafficking of, 179
sexual abuse of. *See* Sexual abuse of children
social media and. *See* Social media
unborn, rights of, 74, 83–90
Children Online Privacy and Protection ACT (COPPA), 227
Children's Internet Protection Act (CIPA) of 2000, 231
Children's Television Act (CTA) of 1990, 230
Children's Television Act of 1990, 216
Chronic stress, 176
Circular causation, 6
Civil commitment, 89
Civil commitment laws, 185
Civil War, 247
Cliff effects, 114
Cocaine, 79–82
pharmacology, 79–80
Cognitive structure, 272
Cohabitation, 159–161
Colonial education, 122–123
Common Core Standards, 130–133

Community, 256
Community and environmental, 59
Conditional spanking, 170
Conduct disorder, 55
Conflict Tactics Scale (CTS), 194
Conflict theory, 197–198
Conservatives, 10–13, 110–111
Constitutive, 9
Contradiction, 8
Convergent thinking, 15–16
Cooperative game, 31
Corporal punishment, 169–170
Crack babies, 83
Crime, victims of, 53–54
Critical thinking, 14, 131
Cruel and unusual punishment, 88
Cyberbullying, 226
Cycle of poverty, 246

D

DACA (deferred Action for Childhood Arrivals), 245–246
Defense of Marriage Act (DOMA), 146–147
argument against, 147–149
argument for, 147
Deferred Enforced Departure (DED), 244
Deliberation, 272
Deliberative democracy, 277–278
Demand input, 7
Dendrites, 74
Depression, 55–56, 169
Dewey, John, 124
Dialectical theory, 7
Dialectical thinking. *See* systems/dialectical thinking
Dialectics, 7–13
of politics, 9–13
relational, 8
Dialogue, 272
Differentiate, 275
Digital and analog programming, 230
Direct punitive methods, 104
Discriminative parental solicitude, 155

Distant kin, 145

Distributive, social policy, 24

Divergent thinking, 15–16, 272

Diversity Visa Program, 244

Domestic violence, 174, 193–210
    Californian penal laws, 204
    effects on children, 199–201
    effects on victims, 197–203
    ethnicity and, 201–202
    race and, 201–202
    systems/dialectical perspective of, 209–210

Dopamine, 81

Double helix, 277

Drugs
    cocaine, 79–82
    legal, 74–76
    Methamphetamine, 81

Dual-career couples, 174

Due process clause, 86

Duluth Model, 209

E

Earned income tax credit, 99

Easton, David, 6–7

Easy temperament, 202

Eco-chamber, 268

Ecological theory, 200

Ecological theory (Bronfenbrenner), 3–4

Education, 13, 121–122
    Asians and, 249–252
    challenges to, 137
    Colonial, 122–123
    future directions in, 133–134
    history of, 122–126
    in crisis, 126–133
    laws and court cases affecting, 127–128
    parenting, 152
    systems/dialectical perspective of, 134–138

Electromagnetic fields, 228

Elitism, 28–29

Emotional neglect, 174–175

Epinephrine, 79

Epistemology, 4

Equal protection under the law, 87

Equifinality, 6

Equilibrium Theory, 30

Ethnicity, 241–243
    and domestic violence, 201–202
    and immigration, 243–245
    Asian American family, 248–252
    Black American family, 246–248
    defined, 241
    Latinos/Hispanics, 252–255
    Native Americans, 255–258
    social policy and, 258–260

Evaluation phase, policymaking process, 38

Excitation transfer theory, 224

Exosystem, 3

Expedited removal, 245

Exposure to violence, 218

External factors, 202

F

Facebook, 226–227

Failure to protect, 176

Failure to thrive syndrome, 175

Fairness Doctrine of the Federal Communications
    Commission, 231

Families
    and adoption, 156–159
    as diverse institution, 153–154
    Black American, 246–248
    defined, 144–145
    development of, 143–144
    marriage and. *See* Marriage
    parental rights, 149–151
    social media and. *See* Social media
    stepfamilies, 154–156
    structure of, 152–161

Family characteristics, 59

Family preference systems, 244

Family preservation, 158

Family structure, 48–51

Father-absent homes, 247

Federal Communication Commission (FCC), 216
Feedback loops, 5
Female-headed single-parent family, 48
Female sexual perpetrators, 181–182
Fetal Alcohol Syndrome (FAS), 77, 257
Fetal anemia, 81
Feudalism, 122
Fictive kin, 145
Formal operations stage, 9
Forum on Educational Accountability, 126
Fragile families, 51
Freedom of Information Act, 232
Freeman Bureau, 247
Free market, 111
Functional norms, 161
Futures Without Violence (FWV), 204

G

Game Theory, 31
Gay marriage, 145–149
Gender biases, in sexual abuse, 182
Gender identity, 222
Global neglect, 175
Government
   and systems theory application, 6–7
Grooming the victim, 178
Group Theory, 30
Growth restriction, 81

H

Half-life, 82
Harbor hours, 230
Health and safety, of children, 52–53
Hegel, Georg, 7
Hierarchy, systems theory, 5
High-stakes testing, 125
Hippocampus, 78
Hispanics. *See* Latinos/Hispanics
Home environment, 48
Home learning environment, 103
Home observation for measurement of the

environment (HOME), 103
Homeostasis, 5
Homicides, 194
Household, 144
Husband battering, 194–195
Hybrid games, 31
Hydrocephalus, 78
Hypothalalmic-pituitary-adrenal (HPA), 103
Hypothalamic-pituitary-adrenal (HPA) axis, 171
Hypoxia, 75

I

Ideological beliefs, 267
"The illusion of explanatory depth", 272
Illegal immigration, 244–246
Immediate family relatives, 243
Immigration, 243–245
   illegal, 244–246
   legal policy, 243
   permanent, 244
Implementation phase, policymaking process, 38
Incremental Theory, 30–31
Indirect methods, 104
Individualism, 257
Initiation phase, policymaking process, 37
Institutional Model, 32
Integrate, 275
Integrative complexity, 9
Intermarriage, 249
Internal Revenue Service (IRS), 24–25
Internal traits, 202
Interpenetration of the opposite, 277
Intrafamilial sexual abuse (Incest), 181
IPads, 228–229
IPods, 228–229

J

Jessica's Law, 183–184
"Just the Facts" program, 132

L

Latinos/Hispanics, 242–243, 252–255
  acculturation, 254–255
  and divorce, 253–254
  and education, 252–253
  quality of life, 253–254
Learned helplessness, 198–199
Legal drugs, 74–76
Lesbian marriage, 145–149
Liberals, 9–13, 110
Locke, John, 123–124

M

Macrosystem, 3
Male victimization, 194
Mandatory reporting of sexual abuse, 182
Mandatory sentencing, 185
Mandatory warrantless arrest, 206
Market
  free, 111
  welfare state vs., 111–113
Marriage, 144–149
  attitudes on, 161
  defined, 144–145
  same-sex, 145–149
  traditional, 145
Media, and social policy debate, 232–233
Media stimuli, children's direct response to, 222
Media violence, 218
Megan's Law, 183
Mental disoders, children, 54–58
  alcohol and substance use, 57–58
  anxiety disorders, 57
  attention deficit hyperactivity disorder, 54–55
  conduct disorder, 55
  depression, 55–56
  oppositional defiant disorder, 55
  tic disorders, 58
  tourette syndrome, 58
Mesosystem, 3
Metarules, 5
Methamphetamine exposure, 81
Microcephaly, 78

Microsystem, 3
Middle Ages, 122
Minimum wage, raising, 111–113
Model minority, 250
Modus operandi, 135
Monogamous, 145
Mood disorders, 170
Moral development, of children, 224
Morphogenesis, 6
Moynihan's report, 246
"Muddling through", 30
Multigenerational households, 249
Multiple perspectives, 275
Myelination, 171

N

Nash Equilibrium, 31
National assessment of educational progress (NAEP),
  62
National Coalition Against Domestic Violence
  (NCADV), 203, 205
National Defense Education Act of 1958, 124
Native Americans, 255–258
  and alcohol abuse, 257
  and Pacific Island natives, 258
  cultural values, 256–257
  living on reservations, 257–258
Nature vs. nurture, 276
Neglect, 167–169
  effects on children, 174–176
  systems/dialectical perspective of, 186–187
Neglected children, 173–177
  risk factors, 176–177
Neural tube malformation, 74
Neurons, 74
Neurotransmitters, 74
Nicotine Replacement Therapy (NRT), 75
No Child Left Behind (NCLB), 17, 124–126, 134–135
No-drop policy, 207
Noncohabiting unmarried mother, 50
Non-cooperative game, 31
Nonlinear interacting system, 135

Nonlinear systems, 6
Nontraditional view of adoption, 158
Norepinephrine, 75
Nurture, nature vs., 276

O

Office of Management and Budget (OMB), 242
Ontology, 4
Oppositional defiant disorder (ODD), 55
Outputs, 7
Oxytocin, 136

P

Paradigm, to polarization, 272
Parental alienation, 185
Parental authority, 149
Parental rights, 149–151
Parental Rights Amendment, 149–151
Parenting education, 152
Parent(s) reunification, 157
Patriarchy, 205
Permanent immigration, 244
Perpetrators, sexual abuse, 182–183
Personal Responsibility and Work Opportunity
        Reconciliation Act of 1996 (PRWORA), 205
Phenomena, 7
Phenylethylamine (PEA), 228
Physical abuse, 169–173
  and bodily harm, 170–171
  signs of, 171–173
  spanking (corporal punishment), 169–170
  symptoms of, 172
Placenta, 79
Placenta abruption, 81
Polarization, of social issues, 268–271
Policymaking process, 36–41
  evaluation phase, 39
  implementation phase, 38
  initiation phase, 37
  legislative, 39
  systems/dialectical perspective of, 40–41

Political Action Group (PAC), 26
Politics, dialectics of, 9–13
Polyandry, 145
Polygamy, 145
Post-conviction relief, 85
Post-Traumatic Stress Disorder (PTSD), 171,
        179–181
Poverty
  and emotional attachment, 105–106
  and schooling, 102–103
  anti-poverty program, 107–113
  behavioral effects, 103–104
  cycle of, 246
  defined, 97–100
  effects on children, 101–107
  environmental factors, 106–107
  systems/dialectical perspective on, 113–114
Power and control wheel, 197
Praxis, 8
Preference Choice Theory, 27
Prenatal environment, 174
Preschool for all, 62
Prescription medication, 81–83
Primary care practitioners (PCP), 53
"Princess Syndrome", 221
Privileged communication, 182
Procedural, social policy, 24
Process, 59
Process model, 1–2
  systems theory, 4–7
Process Model, 29
Proficiency ceiling, 126
Program-length programming, 230
Progressive, 9
Proposing ideas, 38
Prosocial, 218
Protective factors, 202
Pruning, 171
Public policy, defined, 2
Public utility, 233

Q

Qualitative research, 205
Quality of care, 59
Quality of life, 253
Quantitative research, 205

R

Race, 258–260
  and domestic violence, 201–202
Race to the Top Program, 130
Rating system, 219
Rationalism/Comprehensive Model, 27–28
Redistributive social policy, 24–25
Redundancy principle, 5
Refugees, 244
Regulatory, social policy, 24
Relational dialectics, 8
Reservations, 256
Resilience, in children, 202–203
Restraining orders, 196
Retina hemorrhage, 172
Right to privacy, 87
Risks factors, 202
Rituals, 145
Rousseau, Jean-Jacques, 123–124
Routines, 145
Rules, systems theory, 5

S

Same-sex marriage, 145
Schooling, 122
Secondhand smoke, 52
Self-regulatory social policy, 24–25
Separate but equal law, 124
Separation assault theory of domestic violence, 206
Serotonin, 171
Serotonin reuptake inhibitors, 81
Sexting, 229
Sex trafficking, of children, 179
Sexual abuse of children, 178–186
  effects of, 179–181
  female sexual perpetrators, 181–182

  gender biases in, 182
  intrafamilial sexual abuse, 181
  laws and, 183–185
  mandatory reporting of, 182
  perpetrators, 182–183
  sexual offender recidivism rates, 183
  treatment of, 186
Sexualization, 222
Sexual offender recidivism rates, 183
Sidestream smoke, 52
Sleep disturbance, 222
Social competency, 224
Social dominance orientation (SDO), 10
Social Exchange Theory, 27
Social fathers, 50
Social media, 215, 224–229
  cell phones, 227–228
  Facebook, 226–227
  iPods/iPads, 228–229
  regulation, 231
Social policy, 47–48
  and dialectics of politics, 9–13
  and domestic violence. *See* Domestic violence
  and education. *See* Education
  and ethnicity. *See* Ethnicity
  and technology. *See* Technology
  children. *See* Children
  controversial issues and, 73–74
  debate, media and, 232–233
  defined, 2–3, 23–26
  for families. *See* Families
  policymaking process. *See* Policymaking process
  procedural, 24
  process model for. *See* process model
  substantive, 24
  theoretical models of. *See* theoretical models, of social policy
Social policy for children, 63–66
Social technology, 216
Soma, 74
Spanking (corporal punishment), 169–170
Stability, 49
Stepfamilies, 154–156

Stress-related outcomes, 223

Structure, 49, 59

Student Teacher Achievement Ratio (STAR), 129

Subdural hemorrhage, 172

Substantive, social policy, 24

Sudden infant death syndrome (SIDS), 52

Support input, 7

Survivors shame, 180

Sympathetic nervous system (SNS), 171

Syncytiotrophoblast, 80

Synthesis, 7, 275

Systems/dialectical model, 9, 33

Systems/dialectical thinking, 13–18, 272–277

  and education, 134–138

  and policymaking, 40–41

  convergent vs. divergent, 15–16

  guide for, 16–18

  of child abuse and neglect, 186–187

  of domestic violence, 209–210

  on poverty, 113–114

  on social policy for children, 63–66

  procedure for, 16

Systems Model, 32–33

Systems theory, 4

  application of, 6–7

  components of, 4–7

T

Tabula rasa, 123

Technology, 215–216

  social, 216

  television, 216–223

  video games, 223–224

Television, 216–223

  and early brain development, 220–221

  and sexualization, 222

  public policy and, 230–231

Temporary Assistance for Needy Families (TANF), 17

Temporary Protected Status (TPS), 244

Temporary visa classification, 244

Teratogens, 74

Terminal button, 74

Text-dependent questions (TDQs), 132

Theoretical models, of social policy, 26–36

  application, example of, 33–36

  Elitism, 28–29

  Game Theory, 31

  Group Theory, 30

  Incremental Theory, 30–31

  Institutional Model, 32

  Process Model, 29

  Rationalism/Comprehensive Model, 27–28

  risk and resiliency model, 31–32

  systems/dialectical model, 33

  Systems Model, 32–33

Thesis, 7

Tic disorders, 58

Totality, 8

Tourette syndrome, 58

Traditional marriage, 145

Traditional view of adoption, 157

Transformation, 9, 275

Transition to parenthood, 152

Triangulation, 273

TV watching and aggressive behavior, 221

Type II PTSD, 181

Type I PTSD, 181

U

Umbrella theory, 4

Unborn, rights of, 74, 83–90

United Nations Convention on the Rights of the Child (UNCRC), 149

Unity of opposites, 277

Universal Declaration of Human Rights, 151–152

Unwed biological fathers, 159

Utilitarianism, 27

V

Victimless prosecution, 206

Victim-to-perpetrator paradigm, 182–183

Video games, 223–224

Violence. *See* Domestic violence
Visual/spatial functioning, 224

W

Wage-earning gap, 153
Wages, minimum, 111–113
War on Poverty, 107, 124
Wechsler Individual Achievement Test (WIAT), 53
Welfare state, 109
   market vs., 111–113
   pros and cons of, 114
Wholeness, systems theory, 4–5

Wide Range Achievement Test (WRAT), 53
WISC-R, 53
Woll, Peter, 28

Z

Zero to three, 220

CPSIA information can be obtained
at www.ICGtesting.com
Printed in the USA
LVHW021628141221
706185LV00007B/437